SPECIAL SALES AND FUNDRAISING

Northwest Parent Publishing books are available for fundraising sales in schools, churches and other organizations involved with parents and children. Promotion materials and sales assistance are provided.

In addition, Northwest Parent Publishing books are available at special discounts for bulk purchases for sales promotions or premiums. Special editions, including personalized covers, excerpts and corporate imprints, can be created for special needs.

For more information about fundraising or special rates, write to Northwest Parent Publishing, 2107 Elliott Ave., #303, Seattle, WA 98121 or call 206/441-0191.

ALSO PUBLISHED BY NORTHWEST PARENT PUBLISHING:

Regional monthly newsmagazines for parents
Seattle's Child
Eastside Parent
Pierce County Parent
Portland Parent

SPECIAL SUPPLEMENTS

Education Directory: An annual guide to public and private schools.
Summer Learning: An annual guide to summer classes and camps.
The Activity Guide: An annual guide to enrichment activities.
A New Arrival: A semi-annual guide for new and expectant parents.
A to Z Buying Guide: A holiday season guide to thoughtful gifts for children.

BOOKS

Out and About Seattle with Kids: A 210-page book that provides all the information needed to plan indoor and outdoor active fun, birthday parties, field trips and outings. Also includes family-friendly restaurants. Cost: $12.95.

Call 206/441-0191 for more information.

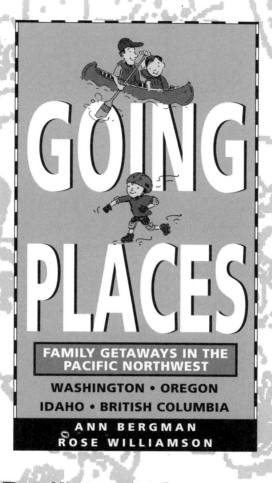

GOING PLACES

FAMILY GETAWAYS IN THE PACIFIC NORTHWEST

WASHINGTON • OREGON
IDAHO • BRITISH COLUMBIA

ANN BERGMAN
ROSE WILLIAMSON

THE ULTIMATE GUIDE FOR TRAVELING IN THE PACIFIC NORTHWEST WITH KIDS

PORTLAND CHAPTER BY ELIZABETH HARTZELL DeSIMONE

THIRD EDITION

Northwest Parent Publishing, Inc.
Seattle Washington

PARENT REVIEWERS:
Shelley Arenas, Allison Arthur, Sally Barnes, Margaret Barney, Lee Evan Belfiglio, Deborah Berger, Amy Berman, Raleigh Bowden, Colleen Carroll, Sonia Cole, Amy Corey, Elizabeth Hartzell DeSimone, Kathy Fletcher, Susan Garrett, Tracey Gilbert, Patti Grant, Ellen Hamblin, Carol Harms, High Heermans, Ellen Hochman, Ilana Hoffman, Sally James, Nancy Johnston, Leslie Loren, Heidi Logar, Breck Longstreth, Meaghan McGavick Dowling, Marcella W. MacKenzie, Barbara Miller, Peter Morgan, Karen Norbeck, Debby Pattin, Anita Rasmussen, Maria Regimbal, Linda Rockey, Michael Rorick, Joe Rutledge, Vicki and Mike Salsbury, Ada Shen-Jaffee, Gerhard Steinke, Peggy Stillman, Alayne Sulkin, Sandy Voit, Harrison Watts, Rose Williamson, Shawn West, Barbara Williams, Hope Zimmerman.

With special thanks to John Bigelow for his encouragement and keen eye.

Printed in the United States of America.

Northwest Parent Publishing, Inc.
2107 Elliott Ave., Suite #303
Seattle, Washington 98121 U.S.A.
206/441-0191

ISBN: 0-9614626-5-5

Art Direction/Design: Simon Sung
Cover Illustration/Maps/Icons: Cary Pillo Lassen
Layout: Melody Comstock
Indexing: Monica Kinney

We all have a different idea of the perfect vacation spot. We wrote this book to give parents reliable information about the whole range of possibilities available to a parent planning a getaway with the kids in the Pacific Northwest.

Places to stay

We selected the places to stay featured in this edition by asking parents about their favorite family vacation spots and sending parent reviewers to check out the facilities. We kept in mind the diverse needs of parents traveling with babies, teens and everything in between.

Accommodation rates were classified as follows:
Inexpensive—Family of four under $70
Moderate—Family of four $70-$110
Expensive—Family of four over $110

Use our price range to get a rough idea of the cost, but if you are interested in a certain place, call and get an exact quote. Rates will vary dramaticaly depending on the time of the year, ages of your children and the type of accommodations you want. Unfortunately, school holidays are typically the busiest and most expensive periods. You can save substantially by going in an off-season.

Many of the places in this book have families that go back year after year. Be sure to make reservations as early as possible and pay close attention to cancellation policies.

Places to Eat

When a grownup is brave or foolish enough to venture into a restaurant with a child, we believe they deserve all the good food and helpful service they can possibly get. To be recommended in this book a restaurant had to have good food, moderate to low prices, genuinely welcome kids and have fast service. Entertainment, such as a box of crayons or a balloon is an added bonus.

THINGS TO SEE AND DO

Figuring out what to do once you arrive at your destination can be more work than any parent wants to do on a vacation. We checked out the popular tourist attractions as well as the lesser-known places of interest recommended by fellow parents. Of course we included cost, hours, addresses and phone numbers so you could spend less time doing the research and more time having fun.

EVERYTHING CHANGES.

Prices, owners, facilities—we expect them to change. Use us as a guide, but check out the details with a phone call or a letter. Describe your family and what you are expecting to confirm that a place will meet your expectations.

SHARE YOUR EXPERIENCE.

If you know of other places that we should include in future editions of Going Places, or if you have comments about one of the places we included, please write to us. We'd like to hear from you.

Northwest Parent Publishing
2107 Elliott Ave., #303
Seattle, WA 98121

TABLE OF CONTENTS

SAN JUAN ISLANDS

This magnificent archipelago is a popular vacation area for families. There are 743 islands at low tide and 428 at high tide; 60 are populated. Four islands — Orcas, San Juan, Lopez and Shaw — share two-thirds of the total population and are served by state ferries.

The ferries are both a highlight and a hindrance. The winding voyage and spectacular scenery provide a fine transition from the world left behind to a slower pace ahead. However the time waiting to board the ferry can be frustrating—except mid-week during the off-season, the ferry lines are long.

Once on the islands, you will find the makings of a well-rounded vacation—plenty of outdoor activity along with the comforts of good food and lodging. As if the natural beauty and abundant recreational opportunities weren't enough, these islands often get more sunshine than the Seattle area. Located in a "rain shadow" created by the Olympic Mountains, they receive about half as much rain as Seattle.

GETTING THERE

The least expensive, most convenient way to get to the islands is by **Washington State Ferry** (206/464-6400), which sails from Anacortes (90 miles northwest of Seattle) through the San Juans to Sidney, British Columbia. To reach the ferry terminal, drive north on I-5 about 70 miles and take Exit 230. Follow Highway 20 west to the Anacortes-Sydney ferry terminal.

The ride to Lopez takes about 45 minutes, to Orcas about $1^1/4$ hours and to San Juan about $1^1/2$ hours. But none of these estimated travel times allows for the long ferry wait you will typically encounter during the summer months and on three-day holiday weekends throughout the year. During these busy periods, you may need to queue up at the dock in Anacortes as long as three hours before sailing time to get on the boat. Also, each island is allotted only a certain number of car slots on the return trip to Anacortes, so we recommend on the morning of your departure you call the local ferry dock on the island where you are staying for advice on when to get in line for your return ferry. Be sure to pack games and books for these waiting times.

If the thought of long lines is already giving you a headache, and you're willing to leave your auto behind, perhaps you'll elect to board the ferry on foot, or with bikes. Or, consider the following travel options (some available during summer months only):

Kenmore Air (206/486-8400) flies seaplanes from Lake Union in Seattle to the islands four times daily. The trip is pricey but thrilling. A roundtrip flight to Orcas costs $99 per adult (midweek) and $130 on weekends; children 18 months and older (accompanied by an adult) fly for $60 round trip. Flying time between Orcas and Seattle is approximately $1^1/_2$ hours.

Harbor Airlines (800/359-3220) flies from the Seattle-Tacoma airport to San Juan Island. From there, you can catch a West Isle Air flight to the other islands or opt for ferry travel. West Isle Air (360/293-4691) has six flights per day departing Anacortes and hopping between the San Juan Islands.

The **Victoria Clipper** hydrofoil boat (206/448-5000) departs Seattle once a day at 7:30 am, makes a stop in Port Townsend and arrives in Friday Harbor around noon. If you depart from Bellingham, you can catch the **Island Shuttle Express** (360/671-1137), which provides passenger-only ferry service throughout the San Juans from May to September.

REFUELING. Aboard the ferries you will find cafeteria-style food service with items such as burgers, sandwiches and yogurt. Or, you can bring your own snacks.

Take binoculars along for the ferry ride!

ROADSIDE ATTRACTIONS. The time spent riding the ferry through the San Juans will likely be a vacation highlight for the kids: They'll have fun just watching the ferry load and unload its assortment of trucks, cars, bicyclists and pedestrians. Cars and trucks traveling between islands often have to back onto the ferry—a sight that amuses the on-lookers (if not the drivers). Between islands, have the kids keep an eye out for deer, bald eagles, seals and other wildlife.

RESOURCES

SAN JUAN ISLANDS VISITOR INFORMATION SERVICE
P.O. Box 65, Lopez, 98261; 360/468-3663

Best Hikes with Children, Vol. 2, by Joan Burton. Published by The Mountaineers, 1992. This second volume of family-friendly hikes includes several on the San Juan Islands.

Let's Discover the San Juans, by Diamond & Mueller. Published by The Mountaineers, 1988. A child's activity book that teaches about area wildlife, history and environmental responsibility. Full of games, puzzles, projects and pictures to color for ages six through 11.

The Curve of Time, by M. Wylie Blanchet. Published by Seal Press, 1993. This delightful, true story is a first-person account of a mother's exploration of the coastal waters of British Columbia with her five children in a 25-foot boat during the 1920s and 1930s. It's intended for adults but makes a captivating read-aloud for school-age kids, especially while you are vacationing in the San Juans.

PLACES TO STAY

ISLAND INSTITUTE

206/463-6722; Write to Island Institute, 4004 58th Place SW, Seattle, WA 98116
Rates: $795/week per person. Family rate is available.
Extras: Charter boat from San Juan Island; meals; lodging; guides and gear.

It is not your usual vacation resort—more like an educational summer camp for the whole family—but if you and your school-age kids would like to learn more about the remarkably unspoiled and wild maritime territory of the San Juan Islands, Island Institute provides a rare opportunity. Started by Jane O. Howard, an environmental and science educator, the Institute is a small entrepreneurial company providing active learning vacations on an uninhabited three-mile long, half-mile wide private island in the San Juans. Some sessions are only for youth ages 9 to 18, others are directed to teachers, college students and other interested adults. But there are day trips, weekend packages, mini-camps and full-week family rates available throughout the summer. Facilities consist of a marina, an attractive and comfortable cedar lodge for dining and group activities, a Jacuzzi and a swimming pool. Visitors sleep on cots in safari-style wood-floored tents.

To get there, you can catch a float plane from Seattle (30-minute ride) or take the ferry boat to San Juan Island where a charter boat will pick you up.

The institute takes visitors on whale watching excursions on its own 43-foot expedition vessel *Navigator*. Kayaking is also very popular. With a minimum of one instructor for every five visitors you'll get in-depth lessons about geology, ecology and marine biology, all in a magnificent setting.

PARENT COMMENTS: *"The island is breathtakingly beautiful and the programs were excellent. My family will never forget spotting a pod of orca whales while out on the* Navigator *one day."*

Lopez Island

Lopez is the first ferry stop—about 45 minutes into the voyage. The moment you drive off the ferry, you'll notice the pastoral calm that envelops the island. With sheep, goats and cows grazing in rolling pastures, a single sleepy village and scant car traffic, a visit to Lopez truly takes you out of the fast lane (and into a world any child older than 10 is likely to describe as "dead"). The few hills (there is one long one as you leave the ferry), light traffic and pleasant scenery have earned Lopez a reputation as the best island for bicycling—many cyclists leave their cars in Anacortes and take their bikes to the island for the day.

Places to Stay

Edenwild Inn B&B
360/468-3238; P.O. Box 271, Lopez, 98261
Rates: Moderate to expensive
Essentials: Credit cards; cribs ($15/night)
Extras: Restaurant; free breakfast; fireplaces (some rooms)

There are several B&Bs on the island, but this is the only one that welcomes children. Designed by owner and architect Susan Aran, it is an elegant Victorian-style inn (built in 1990) that has eight rooms, all with private baths. To avoid disturbing other guests with the sometimes unwelcome "pitter-patter of little feet," it is requested that families stay in the rooms on the lower floor, which, though more spacious, have no view.

The free breakfast typically includes coffee, tea, juice, granola and a fresh-baked bread or roll; it is served in the dining room or on the delightful garden terrace, depending on the season. Lunch and dinner are also served, but the food and atmosphere are too gourmet for family dining.

The Edenwild is located just at the edge of the tiny village of Lopez, which is the largest town on the island and can be investigated on foot in about five minutes. The village consists of a couple of video stores, a grocery store, a few local crafts shops, and a smattering of restaurants (the Bay Cafe is outstanding, see "Places to Eat"). There is also a small historical museum, only open during the summer.

Parent Comments: *"This is a lovely place—beautifully decorated and well run, but like most B&Bs, I wouldn't be comfortable here with a noisy preschooler because it is so peaceful and quiet. It worked great when I brought my 10-year-old for an overnight stay and a day of biking."*

ISLANDER LOPEZ
360/468-2233; P.O. Box 459, Lopez, 98261
Rates: Inexpensive to moderate
Essentials: Credit cards; cribs
Extras: Restaurant; TVs; kitchens (some units); outdoor pool
(summer only), year-round hot tub; volleyball, croquet, horse-
shoes, bicycle rentals; boat rentals, fishing charters, 50-slip marina.

The Islander offers 28 units (two are three-bedroom units). During warmer months, teepees provide the most affordable accomodations. The motel sits right on the main road, so even though traffic is light and noise minimal, it's not a sylvan setting.

Located on Fisherman's Bay, the Islander offers moorage for those traveling by boat. There's also a beach here, where the kids can putter and play.

If you go during the summer, you'll appreciate the pool, which has a nice sundeck and offers a welcome alternative to swimming in chilly Puget Sound.

For those who go to Lopez to bike along the quiet country roads—as so many do—the Islander Lopez is a good place to rest overnight. There is a bicycle rental shop located right next door to the Islander Lopez.

The Islander Lopez Restaurant, located across the street from the motel, serves a continental breakfast and typical American fare. Seafood is fresh and the view is good, but sometimes there's a long wait for dinner.

The beach and the restaurant are across the road from most of the units, so young children will need careful supervision.

PARENT COMMENTS: *"The Islander is a comfortable, pleasant motel. The management was very friendly and helpful, and the rooms are simply furnished and clean."*

VACATION RENTAL PROPERTIES. If you want to look into renting a private cabin on Lopez, contact:

ERA/Island House Realtors, 360/468-3401; P.O. Box 21, Lopez Island, 98261

PLACES TO EAT

BAY CAFE
360/468-3700; Lopez Village
Hours: Dinner, Wed-Sun, 5:30-8:30 pm
Essentials: Credit cards; highchairs

The Bay Cafe is not really a family restaurant, but the atmosphere is laid-back and friendly, and the food is too good for parents to miss. The menu is imaginative and ever-changing— ethnic dishes are popular and there is always at least one outstanding seafood and vegetarian selection. Considering that soup and salad come with every dinner, prices are quite reasonable. Reservations are a must.

FAERIES LANDING
In a trailer next to the ferry landing

On your way home, you'll likely spend some time waiting for the ferry, and this cheerful little snack bar could make your wait a bit more tolerable, especially if the kids are running on empty. You'll be pleasantly surprised by its excellent food and reasonable prices. The burgers and the taco salad are outstanding.

GAIL'S
360/468-2150; Lopez Village
Hours: Year-round breakfast and lunch; dinner seasonal
Essentials: Credit cards; highchairs

Your basic yuppie deli, offering delicious baked desserts, hearty breakfasts, tasty burgers, sandwiches, salads and pasta. Prices are moderate, and the food is reliably good.

HOLLY B'S BAKERY
360/468-2133; Lopez Village
Hours: Seasonal (late Apr-mid-Dec)
Essentials: No credit cards; highchairs

Generous slices of pizza ($4.25), giant, yummy cookies ($1) and other tantalizing goodies for the young snackoholic.

LOPEZ ISLAND PHARMACY
360/468-2644; Lopez Village
Hours: Lunch daily; open 9 am to 5 pm

Sit at the old-fashioned soda fountain and treat the kids to shakes, malts or phosphates to wash down their burgers, sandwiches or soup. Good food, low prices—a fun lunch, 50s style.

WHAT TO SEE AND DO

BICYCLING is a popular sport on Lopez because of the pleasant country scenery and relatively flat roads. There aren't any separate bike trails, but the light traffic poses little danger to young riders, providing they are steady enough on wheels to steer a straight course. You can rent bikes at **Lopez Bicycle Works** (360/

468-2847). Ten-speeds cost $4.50/hour and mountain bikes $5/ hour; the friendly owner will provide helmets and advice on a bike route suitable for your group.

LOPEZ HISTORICAL MUSEUM is tiny but it houses an interesting collection of artifacts, sure to be appreciated by those who want to learn more about the island's history. The exhibits include some nifty ship models and a "please-touch" table for the kids. While you are there, ask for the island map that includes a tour of historical landmarks.

Lopez Village; 360/468-2049. Open summers only; hours vary.

SPENCER SPIT STATE PARK is an outstanding place to camp and a fun area to explore, making it very popular during the summer months. (A sign is posted at the Anacortes ferry if the campground is full so that campers can make other plans.). Next to the parking lot, you'll find a 100-yard trail leading to the park's mile-long sandy beach, which borders an interesting saltwater lagoon. Butter clams, mussels, horse clams and geoducks are abundant here, so bring along a shovel and bucket (always call the Red Tide Hotline at 800/562-5632 to make sure shellfishing is safe).

When the tide rolls in over the long, hot beach, the water temperature is usually warm enough for frolicking and it's sufficiently shallow for young kids. At the tip of the spit is a one-room log cabin—a replica of the Spencer family guest house (from the 1800s) that originally stood there. The new cabin has a picnic table inside, and most children will find it a first-class playhouse.

From the ferry landing, drive 1.1 miles on Ferry Rd to the first junction and turn left on Port Stanley Rd. After 2.5 miles, go left again on Baker View Rd and continue .5 mile until you reach the park.

SHARK'S REEF DAY PARK is a fun destination for a bike ride or car outing. Park your vehicles in the small parking area and take a 1/2-mile hike through the forest to the rock promontory that overlooks a large kelp bed, enormous rocks and the channel to San Juan Island. Chances are good you'll see sea lions and seals snoozing and frolicking near the rocks just off shore, so take binoculars. There are high cliffs here; keep an eye on the youngsters.

To get there, follow Fisherman's Bay Rd about 3 miles past the Islander Lopez Resort (up one very long hill). When you reach Airport Rd, turn right and continue about .5 mile to Shark Reef Rd. Turn left and drive about 2 miles to the park.

RESOURCES

LOPEZ HISTORICAL MUSEUM has maps and brochures (there is no tourist office on the island). You can also get a map of the island at any real estate office.
Lopez Village; 360/468-2049. Open summers only; hours vary.

ORCAS ISLAND

Orcas is the largest of the four islands with ferry service and is often called the most beautiful. This horseshoe-shaped island is topped by the highest point in the San Juans: 2,400-foot Mount Constitution. From the mountain on a clear day, you can see the San Juans, Mt. Baker, Vancouver, B.C., and the Canadian Gulf Islands. Orcas is busier than sleepy Lopez but offers many secluded nooks and crannies for escaping the hustle and bustle.

Orcas Island has only recently been "discovered" as a choice location for vacation property, but ferries have been running there since the 1890s.

PLACES TO STAY

BEACH HAVEN RESORT
360/376-2288; Rte1, P.O. Box 12, Eastsound, 98245
Rates: Moderate (seven-day minimum stay June-Aug, three-night minimum during holidays, otherwise two-night minimum)
Essentials: Credit cards; cribs
Extras: Kitchens (full housekeeping); airtight stoves; boat rentals; mooring buoys

Beach Haven sits on a long, pebbled beach and the cabins are nestled in the woods nearby. Cabins are quite rustic, but clean and comfortable; they all have a nice view of the water and an airtight stove to take off the morning or evening chill. Two of the cabins are large enough to accommodate two small families or one large one. These larger cabins have space to spare and a wonderful view of the water.

As you leave the resort, a sign reads "Leaving Beach Haven. Entering the world." Indeed, this is how the family vacation is likely to feel. Bring your swimsuits and consider renting a rowboat or canoe, or take a hike in the forest. This resort offers no phones, TVs or other distractions, so pack cards, books and games (and lots of popcorn) to pass the evenings. It is some distance to shop or dine out, so you'll probably want to cook most of your meals.

❝❝ **PARENT COMMENTS:** *"This is a place for parents to relax and for kids to run free."*
"The seven-day minimum stay worried us when we first got there, but we really unwound by about the fifth day and wished we could stay another week."

NORTH BEACH INN
360/376-2660; P.O. Box 80, Eastsound, 98245
Rates: Moderate (one-week minimum July-Aug, otherwise, two-night minimum)
Essentials: No credit cards; cribs
Extras: Kitchens; fireplaces; boat rentals; pets OK
If you feel that little changes at the North Beach Inn, you're right. The Gibson family has operated this peaceful resort since 1932. The 11 cottages are in a wooded setting along a 1/3-mile stretch of pebble beach. There are also 90 acres of woods and fields, and lovely views of the Canadian San Juans and sunsets. Cottages are simple and clean. The "Shamrock" cabin has a loft that would be dangerous for toddlers, but older kids love it. In addition to kitchen and fireplace, each cabin has a grill, a great view and comfortable chairs for the beach.

Bring your own entertainment; this is a no-frills vacation spot designed to get the family to beachcomb or play charades.

❝❝ **PARENT COMMENTS:** *"The real fun is in building a fire on the beach at night. But beware—with all the fires over the years, playing in the sand can result in some pretty dirty legs and hands."*
"When we got restless we drove to Moran State Park and climbed to the top of Mount Constitution. Our children, ages seven and 10, did not find the hike too difficult, and the view at the top was spectacular."

YMCA ORKILA FAMILY CAMP
206/382-5009; For reservations: 909 Fourth Ave, Seattle, 98104
Rates: Inexpensive
Essentials: Credit cards
Extras: Meals included; outdoor pool (summer only); craft and pottery shop; archery, riflery, basketball, boating
Five weekends each year, the YMCA of Greater Seattle opens Camp Orkila for use by families. All the traditional camp activities are available, including the exploration of hundreds of acres of beach, forest, meadows and ponds. Orkila Farm offers kids an opportunity to meet pigs, cows, turkeys, llamas and rabbits. For sports activities, enjoy the ball fields, basketball court or swimming pool, or boat to small nearby islands. The strong of

heart will enjoy the challenge of the simulated rock-climbing wall, archery area or BB gun range. For the tamer of heart, the Craft and Pottery Shop usually has several craft projects in progress.

Families stay in the 40 cabins—rustic, open-air buildings located on the beach or nearby in the woods. Sometimes two or more families will share a cabin. Bathroom facilities are located near each cabin. Except the few "winterized" cabins sometimes available upon request, the accommodations are primitive—think of it as camping with a roof over your head. If possible, get one of the three-sided cabins right on the beach, and wake each day to a spectacular view of the water and nearby islands. The kids can scamper out the door to the sand. Meals are served in Norman Lodge (typical camp food—nourishing but not inspired).

Rates are $52.50 per adult and $44 per child for a two-night weekend ($2.50 extra for each participant who is not a YMCA member). Fees include food, lodging, all program activities and transportation from the ferry landing to the camp.

VACATION RENTAL PROPERTIES. If you want to look into renting a private cabin on Orcas, contact any of the numerous local realtors.

PLACES TO EAT

BILBO'S FESTIVO
360/376-4728; North Beach Rd and A St, Eastsound
Hours: Dinner daily; seasonal lunch
Essentials: Credit cards; highchairs
Good Mexican food served in an intimate, charming setting—Mexican tiles and weavings, a large fireplace, mud walls and colorful courtyard flowers in summer. The generous portions are reasonably priced, but the service can be slow. Reservations are strongly advised.

DOTY'S A-1 CAFE AND BAKERY
360/376-2593; North Beach Rd, Eastsound
Hours: Mon-Sat, 6:30 am-8 pm; Sun, 7 am-5 pm
This casual cafe offers cheap, delicious burgers and sandwiches, while the bakery turns out scrumptious baked goods.

LA FAMAGLIA
360/376-2335; A St and Prune Alley, Eastsound
Hours: Lunch Mon-Sat; dinner daily; Sun breakfast

Essentials: Credit cards; highchairs

This spot offers outstanding Italian food, cheerful decor, friendly service and reasonable prices. Its smoke-free environment and outdoor patio make it an especially nice place for families. The menu includes fresh pastas, calzones, pizza and other popular family fare.

ORCAS HOTEL

360/376-4300; Orcas ferry landing
Hours: Breakfast daily beginning May1, otherwise breakfast Sun only; lunch and dinner daily noon to 8:30 pm
Essentials: Credit cards; highchairs

Once you're parked in the ferry waiting line, check out the dining room at the Orcas Hotel for lunch. They serve good burgers, soups and sandwiches.

WHAT TO SEE & DO

BIKE RIDING with children on Orcas is not recommended because most of the roads are hilly, curved and narrow.

KAYAKING is a fine activity in the San Juans with the kids— they usually enjoy the thrill of being so close to the water and having the chance to spot bald and golden eagles, whales and otters. Instruction is provided (no experience necessary) at **Island Kayak Guides,** 360/376-4755.

MADRONA POINT is a lovely, quiet madrona-forested waterside park saved from development by the Lummi Indian Tribe. Pick up food at Island Market in Eastsound and enjoy a picnic here. *Located at the end of the unmarked road just past Christina's Restaurant in Eastsound.*

MORAN STATE PARK is one of the best reasons for visiting Orcas. The fourth largest state park in Washington, it offers miles of trails for hiking, five lakes (the two largest have swimming, fishing and boat rentals), and four campgrounds (reservations required). Topping it all is Mount Constitution—the highest peak in the San Juans and accessible by foot or car. Although the park borders the Strait of Georgia, the saltwater frontage is a rocky cliff with no beach access.

For families, the park has several highlights:

CASCADE FALLS are a spectacular and popular sight in the park. To reach them, either walk ¹/₄ mile from the road, or take the Cascade Falls Trail (2.7 miles) from the south end of Mountain Lake to the falls and on to the South End Campground at Cascade Lake.

CASCADE LAKE has a large day-use area with a pleasant picnic spot, swimming beach, dock and short nature trail (in the trees west of the picnic area). Paddle boats and rowboats are available for rent. Both Cascade and Mountain lakes have a boat launch and provide excellent trout fishing (outboard motors are prohibited on all park lakes). The **Cascade Lake Loop Trail** (2.5 miles) is a mostly level circuit of the lake where you may spot muskrat, otter and great blue heron. The Environmental Learning Center at the south end of Cascade Lake has nine cabins, a fully equipped kitchen and mess hall, infirmary, swimming beach and dock. It is available for rental.

MOUNTAIN LAKE also has rowboat rentals. **Around-the-Lake Trail** (4 miles) is fairly easy and includes a variety of sights and sounds to keep young hikers intrigued, including deserted log cabins, a dam and a foot bridge (south end of the lake). To get to the trail, go to the Mountain Lake Landing and park near the ranger cabins. Take the loop counter-clockwise and stay left on the lake trail. At the north end of the lake there is easy access to the water; have the kids wear bathing suits under their clothes so they are ready for a quick dip.

MOUNT CONSTITUTION offers spectacular views and hikes. Mount Constitution Road is a narrow, steep and winding trip to the top (travelers prone to carsickness, beware). Once you get to the summit, you'll find a magnificent 50-foot stone lookout tower built in 1936 by the Civilian Conservation Corps and modeled after a 12th- century Caucasian mountain fortress. The climb up the tower stairs is fun, even for preschoolers, and the view at the top provides ample reward.

To reach Moran Park from the ferry terminal, follow Horseshoe Hwy north to Eastsound, then continue east and south to the park entrance (13 miles); 360/378-2326.

ORCAS ISLAND HISTORICAL MUSEUM is a fine little museum—well worth a visit. Exhibits of pioneer and Native American artifacts are displayed in four interconnected log cabins. Much of the valuable Indian collection was gathered by Ethan Allen, San Juan Island's school superintendent at the turn of the century. The hand-built boat he used to row between the islands is on display at the museum. The lawn next door has picnic tables—a good spot for a picnic after a journey through history.

Located in Eastsound. Turn north off Main St onto North Beach Rd;

*two blocks to museum. Open Memorial Day through Labor Day;
360/376-4849.*

CALENDAR

MAY: "A" Street Memorial Day Festival, Eastsound
JULY: Historical Day, Eastsound

RESOURCES

CHAMBER OF COMMERCE
P.O. Box 252, Eastsound, 98245
360/376-2273

TRAVEL INFOCENTER
Adjacent to the Historical Museum on North Beach Road in
Eastsound, this unstaffed kiosk has free maps and brochures.

SAN JUAN ISLAND

San Juan Island's historical claim to fame is The Pig War—
aptly named, for its one and only casualty. This 1859 boundary
dispute began when a British pig dug up some potatoes planted
by an American settler. An argument ensued between Britain
and the United States about whose land the pig was on while
committing the offense.

Troops built two separate camps, but the "war" was conducted
cordially—the troops even entertained one another socially. In
1872, the ruler of Germany was asked to decide the boundary
issue, and he decreed the islands belonged to America.

Actually, it is the noble black-and-white orca ("killer whale"),
not the historical pig, that attracts visitors to San Juan Island.
Here are found the first whale museum and the first whale-
watching park in the nation.

Above all, San Juan Island is a place to explore the environment. Let the little ones get wet surveying tide pools. Fly a kite
at American Camp or watch a bald eagle soar overhead. When
you tire of outdoor endeavors—and of emptying the sand from
little tennis shoes—there are other areas to explore.

PLACES TO STAY

INN AT FRIDAY HARBOR/SUITES INN AT FRIDAY HARBOR
360/378-3031; 410 and 680 Spring St, P.O. Box 339, Friday

Harbor, 98250
Rates: Moderate to expensive
Essentials: Credit cards; cribs ($5), rollaways ($7)
*Extras: Restaurant (at Suites Inn); TV; kitchenettes with
microwaves (at Suites Inn); pool, spa, sauna, exercise room (at
Friday Harbor Inn). All guests may use facilities at either inn.*

The Inn at Friday Harbor and Suites Inn at Friday Harbor are
sister establishments, located within two blocks of one another.
The Suites is the newer of the two. Previously a retirement
center, it offers one- and two-bedroom suites, kitchenettes with
microwaves and other amenities.

Though older, the Inn at Friday Harbor was recently remodeled
and features a nice indoor pool, spa, exercise room and sauna. Car
rentals, sightseeing tours and complimentary shuttle service are
available.

 PARENT COMMENTS: *"We had chosen not to take our car to
the islands, so the free shuttle was a real life saver."*

ISLAND LODGE
360/378-2000; 1016 Guard St, Friday Harbor, 98250
Rates: Inexpensive in the winter, moderate in the summer
Essentials: Credit cards; rollaways ($4), cribs ($4)
Extras: Cable TV; in-room coffee machines; Jacuzzi, sauna

This quiet retreat is on the edge of Friday Harbor, next to the
San Juan Island Library. The only phone at the lodge is on the
reception desk (so if it's busy, keep trying). There's a nice outdoor
Jacuzzi and sauna in a well-kept yard.

If your child gets restless watching cable TV, suggest that he go
feed the resident llamas, Jackson and Felon (Felon is so named
because of his black facial mask). It's OK to pet and feed them, so
they are a great source of entertainment.

MARIELLA INN AND COTTAGES
360/378-6868; 630 Turn Point Rd, Friday Harbor, 98250
Rates: Expensive
Essentials: Credit cards; no cribs
Extras: Bikes, kayaks and sailboats for rent; yacht charters

The Mariella is physically close to Friday Harbor but seems far
from the hubbub of downtown activity. Built in 1902, the
waterfront inn was lovingly restored by owners Alison and Art
Lohrey; Alison's artistic talent is evident throughout.

Families with children nine and under are welcome in the
cottages; these range in size and amenities, so be sure to ask for

specifics when making reservations. A breakfast basket with juice, fresh muffins and croissants is delivered each morning. Children older than nine are welcome in the lodge. Dinner at the inn restaurant is suitable for families and offers both indoor and outdoor seating.

There are nine acres to roam or bike, and the waterfront is nice for sunbathing or boating (kayaks and sailboats for rent). A volleyball net is always up in the summer. A 65-foot yacht, the Arequipa, is available for day charters.

PARENT COMMENTS: *"Our family took a picnic out in the sailboat one afternoon. Boating is great, but take care not to fall in the water—it's really chilly!"*

ROCHE HARBOR RESORT

360/378-2155; Roche Harbor Rd, P.O. Box 4001, Roche Harbor, 98250
Rates: Moderate
Essentials: Credit cards; cribs, rollaways ($7), hide-a-beds ($10 for adults, free for kids)
Extras: Refrigerators (condos and cottages); TV (condos only); paddle boats, canoes; tennis courts, playground; grocery store, two snack bars, gift shop; outdoor pool

Located on the northern tip of the island, Roche Harbor Resort manages to be both romantic and family-oriented. For romance, try a dinner reservation at the restaurant overlooking the marina and a saunter in the well-kept gardens. For the family, there's a heated Olympic-sized swimming pool (with a snack bar nearby), boat rentals, tennis courts and a small, old-fashioned playground.

Located near what was once the largest lime mine and kiln west of the Mississippi, Roche Harbor Resort was originally a company town. The Hotel de Haro, at the center of the resort, was built by industrialist John McMillan, who owned the town. (The kids may be interested in the bizarre mausoleum McMillan built on the premises.)

The cottages and new condos are better choices for families than the old hotel. The cottages are comfortable but not fancy, condos slightly nicer but farther from the pool and the beach. The hotel restaurant offers standard fare at moderate prices.

PARENT COMMENTS: *"This is an 'old-time' resort, in good repair, with a young, friendly staff. It feels like a summer camp."*
"The condos are a LONG WALK to the pool!"

BED AND BREAKFASTS

There are 16 B&Bs on the islands, including one on a boat moored at the Port of Friday Harbor. Most accept children on a prearranged basis. For information, call 360/378-3030.

PLACES TO EAT

AMIGO'S

360/378-5908; 40 B Spring St , Friday Harbor
Hours: Lunch daily year-round; dinner seasonal
Essentials: Credit cards; highchairs

Up Spring Street from the ferry dock is a cluster of businesses that includes Amigo's, the "place to go" for delicious Mexican food. The guacamole is especially good. There's a menu for the little amigos, as well as vegetarian fare, and all food is prepared without preservatives, MSG or lard. Prices are moderate to high—$6.95 for a good portion of nachos. If the kids haven't had all they can take of the great outdoors, the family might enjoy dining on the veranda.

THE CANNERY HOUSE RESTAURANT

360/378-2500; 174 No First St , Friday Harbor
Hours: Lunch daily year-round; dinner daily in summer
Essentials: Credit cards; highchairs

This small restaurant with a big view overlooks the Port of Friday Harbor marina; kids will enjoy watching the ferries come and go. A deck with tables and umbrellas is open in the summer, and that's the place to be unless the yellow jackets beat you to it.

The Cannery House is known for its thick, tasty sandwiches, which are named for islands and are usually served hot. There is also a nice selection of Mexican entrees. The children's menu includes a "kid's taco" ($2.50), a grilled cheese sandwich, and the ever-popular peanut butter and jelly. If there's a picnic in your plans, this is also a good spot to order take-out sandwiches.

FRONT STREET CAFE

360/378-2245; 101 Spring St, Friday Harbor
Hours: Breakfast and lunch daily; shorter hours in winter
Essentials: No credit cards; highchairs

If it's scrumptious eggs and breads you seek, try the Front Street Cafe, across from the ferry dock. This spot offers great breakfasts, baked goods (try the beer bread) and espresso. If breakfast time has come and gone, opt for a homemade soup or head straight for the homemade ice cream and Italian ices.

There's a great view of the ferry landing and cars trying to unload. Or if controversy is what you crave, this is also the place where islanders talk politics.

MADELYN'S BAGEL BAKERY

360/378-4545; A Street, Friday Harbor
Hours: Breakfast and lunch
Essentials: No credit cards; highchairs

Owner Jeff Altman is up at three every morning to make homemade bagels, cinnamon rolls, muffins and cookies. This tiny bakery is near the ferry dock, so it's a great destination for restless children while you await the ferry. If the driver needs a pick-me-up, Jeff also makes a decent espresso.

THE SAN JUAN DONUT SHOP

360/378-2271; 225 Spring St, Friday Harbor
Hours: Breakfast and lunch daily; brunch Sun 7 am-3 pm
Essentials: No credit cards; highchairs

Two and a half blocks up Spring Street from the ferry landing you'll find the San Juan Donut Shop, serving homemade soups, doughnuts and pastries in an informal atmosphere. Old photos of Friday Harbor on the walls are interesting; check out the sheep being herded down Spring Street.

The service here is good. But it's a popular spot, so in summer you may have to wait for your chance to "belly up" to the doughnut bar. Kids' fare includes the classic PB&J sandwich or hot dog ($1.25). The hamburgers are great, but fries aren't served (try a helping of potato salad instead). If you're on your way to the park, they'll pack you a nice picnic lunch.

STEWART'S

360/378-6071; 395 Spring St, Friday Harbor
Hours: Breakfast and lunch daily, except Tues
Essentials: Credit cards; highchairs

Owner Glen Stewart has packed this little house with more than 10,000 used books, including children's selections. Lunch is Cajun Creole; all the produce and herbs are grown at the restaurant. A French courtyard, where alcoholic refreshments will be served, is planned. Southern hospitality is Glen's modus operandi, so if you don't see what you're looking for, just ask.

VIC'S DRIVE-IN

360/378-8427; 25 Second Street , Friday Harbor

Hours: Breakfast, lunch and dinner Mon-Fri; breakfast and lunch Sat; closed Sun
Essentials: No credit cards; highchairs

Located across from the county courthouse, Vic's offers a great selection of burgers, fries and shakes, as well as lattes and veggie burgers. If your child doesn't find the books and art supplies behind the back counter, owner Mike Sharkey will likely bring a selection to you.

This place is old-fashioned and child-friendly. But don't be misled by the name; Vic's hasn't been a drive-in for years. In fact, if your child lives for the next stop at McDonald's or Taco Time, the San Juans are a great place to go "cold turkey." There are no franchise restaurants on the islands.

WHAT TO SEE AND DO

STROLL & BROWSE

If you want to stroll the streets of Friday Harbor, that's great, but do some leg stretches first. This charming old fishing village is built on a hillside and the only way to get to the town center is to go up. It can be a real chore with a stroller or a youngster that wants to be carried.

Parking is at a premium. Take the signs seriously; the local authorities don't hesitate to ticket tourists. There's also a shortage of public restrooms, so make use of the facilities on the ferry, at the ferry landing or at the Port of Friday Harbor.

As you walk off the ferry, a good first stop is the **San Juan Chocolate Company** (18 Cannery Landing). This spot offers coffee fresh-roasted daily, a selection of fine chocolates and gourmet ice cream. Strollers need to go behind the building for access. **The Toy Box** (in Cannery Landing) is about the size of a big toy box, but it is packed with a variety of small treasures. **Osito's** (310 Spring St) has uptown clothes and a decent selection of toys. **Peanut Butter 'n Jelly** (260 Spring St) features moderately priced clothes as well as a nice selection of inexpensive consignment items.

Another fun stroll is Nichols St, affectionately referred to by locals as the "Friday Harbor Fringe." Check out the aptly named **Funk & Junk,** (65 Nichols St) or **Sunshine Art Gallery** (85 Nichols St), a co-op for local artists and a great place to pick up jewelry, prints and ceramics. **Mellowoods & Music** (85 West St) has a fine selection of instruments and is a hangout for island musicians; **Windhorse** (155 Nichols St) has crystals, wind chimes and New Age gift items.

PORT OF FRIDAY HARBOR A walk along the docks is a nice way to pass the afternoon. A fun game for older children is to guess why the boats have such unusual names. You can take a net and fish for shrimp (or whatever else happens to be in the water).

There is a nice little park with a tiny pond near port headquarters; whether the pond has water depends on the town's water situation (the town often experiences water shortages in the summer).

For information about the wildlife cruise boats you'll see in the harbor, see Cruises under "Excursions."

PARKS

With some 375 miles of saltwater shoreline—more than any other county in the country—there are plenty of beaches to enjoy in San Juan County.

AMERICAN CAMP. Located at the south end of the island, American Camp boasts the largest public beach in the area. It's a great place to picnic and watch for whales, rabbits and bald eagles. For that after-lunch walk, a variety of trails penetrate the dense forest and meander to the beach.

To escape the afternoon sun, head across the road to the **Fourth of July** picnic grounds. There is a nice long beach here, too, and it's shady in the afternoon.

From Ferry Terminal, drive up Spring St to Mullis. Turn left, drive 6 miles (Mullis will become Cattle Point Rd) and follow the signs.

BRITISH CAMP. The British liked trees and lawn, so this is a lovely place to picnic. There is a small rocky beach for wading, but bring extra tennies; the rocks are hard on little feet. Take the trail up the mountain—note that it crosses a busy road—for an unsurpassed view of the islands.

LIMEKILN STATE PARK. On the west side of the island facing Victoria B.C., is the nation's first, if not only, whale-watching park. There are three resident pods of whales, which are most frequently seen June through August. Even if the whales don't show, enjoy the rocky cliffs and wildflowers.

Park is approximately 7 miles from ferry dock. From Spring St, turn right on San Juan Valley Rd, then left on Douglas Rd. In 1 mile, turn right on Bailer Hill Rd, which becomes West Side Rd. Stay on West Side Rd to park.

SAN JUAN COUNTY PARK. Located on Smallpox Bay (west

side of the island), this park offers 18 camping spaces and fabulous views. Understandably, this is a very popular area, so expect competition for the camping. This is also a good place for beachcombing, picnicking and scuba diving. There are no showers or RV hookups.

380 West Side Rd N; 360/378-2992. $14/night/family of four. Reservations needed two weeks in advance.

FAIRGROUNDS PARK, at the Fairgrounds in Friday Harbor, has a volleyball area, horseshoe pit and a nice toddler playground. Restrooms are in a shed to the west.

JACKSON BEACH is south of Friday Harbor, sandwiched between a gravel pit operation and a fish cannery. Once you've negotiated some driftwood, you'll find a long, sandy beach. This is a great volleyball, kite-flying and picnicking spot.

The inner beach is Argyle Lagoon, a research facility operated by the University of Washington; it is off limits. Also, take care that children do not wander too far up the sandy hill, as there have been cave-ins in this area.

LAKEDALE CAMPGROUND. On a beautiful day, this is a great place to picnic, swim or rent rowboats, canoes or paddle boats. There is no lifeguard, however, and while it's tempting to trust the little ones in the shallow water, better to keep a close eye. There is also a small grocery store here.

2627 Roche Harbor Rd; 800/617-CAMP. Day-use fees: $1.50/ adult, $1/children under 12, children under two free.

EXCURSIONS

CRUISES. Wildlife-watching expeditions set out from the Port of Friday Harbor. If you'd like to get out on the water to view the whales, and everyone in the family is four or older, check out the **Western Prince** (800/757-ORCA). The cost is $43/adult, $31/ children four to 17. **Sea Quest Expeditions** (360/378-5767) also offers kayak trips. Children who enjoy paddling for a few hours in a double kayak are welcome. There's no age limit, but remember, you provide the power!

THE WHALE MUSEUM. If *FreeWilly* was popular in your household, you'll want to visit this spot, reputed to be the first whale museum in the nation. You'll find yourself immersed (sorry) in the world of sea-going leviathans—from the large mural on the building exterior to the whale songs that greet you and the museum store that's replete with whale paraphernalia. Located three blocks northwest of the ferry dock in Friday Harbor, the museum also features complete skeletons of a baby gray whale and an adult killer whale.

62 First St N; 360/378-4710. Memorial Day through Labor Day,10 am-5 pm, off-season, 10 am-4 pm. Cost: $3/adult; $2.50/ students; $1.50/children five to12; children under five free.

CALENDAR

JULY: The Pig War Barbecue, Friday Harbor
AUGUST: San Juan County Fair

RESOURCES

THE NATIONAL PARK SERVICE
125 Spring St, P.O. Box 429, Friday Harbor, 98250
360/378-2240

PLACES TO EAT WITHOUT KIDS
DUCK SOUP INN
360/378-4878; 3090 Roche Harbor Rd
Hours: Dinner, hours seasonal
Essentials: Credit cards

Owner Rick Allison has a child of his own—he likes kids. But as the owner of an elegant restaurant, he appreciates having families come early (5:30 or 6 pm) for dinner, so that adults who are without little ones can enjoy peace and quiet. Wife Gretchen is the chef; she's been named a "Best Chef of the Northwest" by *Pacific Northwest* magazine. Fresh ingredients and inventive seasonings are the common thread on this menu, which features Northwest, French, Cajun and Thai cuisine.

BIRCH BAY/BLAINE

The towns of Blaine and Birch Bay are located near the U.S.-Canada border. Birch Bay, a popular beach community, is on a shallow bay on the Georgia Strait. The water temperature in the bay is uncharacteristically warm for Northwest salt water, so the tidal beach is fine for water play. There's also horseback riding, arcade games, go-carts, putt-putt golf and waterslides. Both towns are well situated for day trips to Bellingham, Mt. Baker or even Vancouver, B.C. (45 minutes north).

GETTING THERE

Birch Bay is about 110 miles north of Seattle. Blaine is a few miles farther north, at the U.S.-Canada border.

REFUELING. Mt. Vernon is a good rest stop on the trip up I-5 from Seattle. There are numerous fast food establishments at Exit 230, on the north edge of town, or if you want a more relaxed break, try the highly-regarded **Pacioni's Pizza** in old downtown (606 S First St; 360/336-3314; no credit cards).

ROADSIDE ATTRACTIONS. If you want to break up the drive with a stop see La Conner or Bellingham.

PLACES TO STAY

DRIFTWOOD INN RESORT MOTEL
360/371-2620; 7394 Birch Bay Dr, Blaine, 98230
Rates: Inexpensive to moderate (three-night minimum in summer)
Essentials: Credit cards; cribs
Extras: TVs; kitchens (some units); fireplaces (some units);
outdoor heated pool; playground; pets OK, except June-Aug

The Driftwood Inn Resort Motel is a collection of cottages, cabins, apartments, motel units and condos. There is nothing fancy about the place, but the location (easy beach access, state park three blocks away) and the accommodations are well suited for families. The cabins in particular work well with children; each has two bedrooms, a fireplace, a veranda overlooking the creek, and a good-sized kitchen.

You have to cross a road to reach the beach, but it is only a 5-minute walk. The small, outdoor heated pool and the playground are nice when the children tire of playing on the beach. There are two small grocery stores within a mile of the inn.

PARENT COMMENTS: *"This place is what you'd expect, or at least hope for, in a beach motel. We wanted to stay near the park and the beach, without stretching our budget. The Driftwood was perfect — family-friendly and accommodating."*

INN AT SEMIAHMOO
360/371-2000 or 360/854-2608; 9596 Semiahmoo Pkwy, Blaine, 98230
Rates: Expensive
Essentials: Credit cards; cribs
Extras: Restaurants; TV, VCR (some units); fireplaces (some

units); indoor/outdoor pool, saunas, steam rooms, spa; weight
room, tanning booths; bike rentals; indoor and outdoor tennis
courts, squash and racquetball courts, indoor track, golf (including
putting area for kids); gift shop and galleries; babysitting by
arrangement

The Inn at Semiahmoo is an elegant resort sitting at the tip of
a spit, across the harbor from Blaine. The main attraction for
families is the deluxe health club with every imaginable convenience. In addition to the first-class indoor athletic facilities,
there are outdoor tennis courts, a pool that is both indoor and
outdoor, and an Arnold Palmer-designed golf course. Tennis,
racquetball and golf lessons are available for adults and kids at
extra cost. There are also cruises to the San Juan Islands (early
May through October) and sportfishing expeditions. The large,
well-maintained sandy areas between hotel and beach are meant
for horseshoes and volleyball, but they wind up being used as
giant sandboxes. Be sure to bring your sand toys.

The rooms are good-sized and beautifully furnished (including
a big wooden chest that works well as a toy chest). The first floor
rooms on the water side may be worth the extra expense for
families; they look out on the beach and sand play area, so you can
supervise children from your room. There's a small sundry and
snack store, as well as laundry facilities, at the marina next to the
resort.

The inn has three restaurants. **Stars**, the gourmet option, has a
good children's menu offering generous servings at low prices,
but the adult fare is pricey and uninspired. **R & R**, with a tasty
grill and pasta menu, a more casual atmosphere and a nice view,
is the best choice for family dining. However, it is only open for
dinner during the summer months — the rest of the year it serves
Sunday brunch only. **Packer's** is a lounge and oyster bar that
serves lunches outside on the deck in nice weather.

The best idea for breakfast is room service (there aren't any
restaurants in the area near the resort). The children's breakfast
menu for room service is very reasonably priced, and kids can stay
in their p.j.s to eat.

For a weekend getaway, or if you happen to have a meeting here
and want to bring the family along, Semiahmoo is a lovely place
to rest and recreate with or without kids.

◀◀ PARENTS COMMENTS: *"We went on a rainy three-day*
weekend. The athletic club was a big treat for us (we got
massages, sat in the steam room) and our school-age kids (they played
indoor tennis and swam swam swam in the indoor-outdoor pool.) One

day we drove to Vancouver, B.C., and loved coming back to the hot tub and pool."

" This spot was expensive (Entertainment coupon book helped), but we came back to Seattle feeling completely refreshed."

"There are no refrigerators in the rooms so bring non-perishable snacks and drinks, unless you want to sell your soul to room service."

JACOBS LANDING RENTALS

360/371-7633; 7824 Birch Bay Dr, Blaine, 98230
Rates: Moderate to expensive (two-night minimum)
Essentials: Credit cards; cribs
Extras: TVs; kitchens; fireplaces; indoor heated pool, Jacuzzi; indoor racquetball courts, outdoor tennis courts (bring your own equipment); babysitting by arrangement

This condo development has a pleasant architectural style and a good location—across the road from the beach and 2 miles from the state park in Birch Bay. Not all units have views, but each has a deck, living room, dining area, fireplace (not always wood-burning), fully equipped kitchen and bath. One-, two- and three-bedroom units are available; two-bedroom units have a queen bed in one room, twins in the other, plus a fold-out couch in the living room. Insulation between the units keeps things quiet.

The beach near the condos is rocky and not particularly inviting. Although the bay is warm enough for swimming in the summer, the indoor pool is a nice alternative.

PARENT COMMENTS: *"Each of our children (ages 10 and 13) brought a friend on the trip. They loved wandering around Birch Bay by themselves, and we had time to do as we pleased."*

PLACES TO EAT

SEA LINKS

360/371-7033; 7878 Birch Bay Dr, Birch Bay
Hours: Lunch and dinner daily
Essentials: Credit cards; highchairs

This is a satisfactory place to feed the family. Food is generally good, prices are moderate, and the service is fast. The lunch menu covers the basics, and some tasty variations, including fajita burritos, stir-fry dishes and gyro sandwiches. Dinner features $6.95 specials—a choice of all-you-can-eat spaghetti, pork roast, swedish meatballs or pot roast. There isn't a children's menu, but the kitchen will happily make "kid-sized" portions from the regular menu.

THE C SHOP SANDWICHES, BAKERY AND PIZZA
360/371-2070; Anderson St and Birch Bay Dr, Birch Bay
Hours: Open daily, May 15-Sept 5
Essentials: Credit cards

Sno-cones, pizza, burgers, a yummy selection of hard ice cream and a full-blown candy shop (candy is made on the premises) — what else could a vacationing child want? After the kids get their goodies, they can go next door to the mini-golf and video games.

WHAT TO SEE AND DO

BIRCH BAY STATE PARK is a popular destination for both Canadians and Americans. With more than 2 miles of outstanding sandy beach, an excellent swimming area and good sites for picnicking, kite flying, volleyball and overnight camping, opportunities for fun abound. Numerous short interpretive trails wind through the marshland and beach grass—home to beavers, muskrats, opossums and great blue herons. The occasional minus tides reveal not only a large section of the gently sloping beach but many intertidal creatures for kids to inspect. If you are visiting during the summer, ask about the park's outstanding Junior Ranger program.

There are a store and cafe nearby. If you plan to camp overnight, be sure to make reservations in advance.

5105 Helwig Rd; 360/371-2800. To get there, take Exit 270 from I-5, head west on Birch Bay/Lynden Rd for 3 miles, then turn south on Blaine Rd. Continue through town, watching for the gate on Birch Bay Dr (about 1 mile).

PEACE ARCH PARK in Blaine has lovely formal gardens and wide, sweeping lawns. The arch that straddles the U.S.-Canada border, engraved with the mottos "Children Of A Common Mother" and "Brethren Dwelling Together In Unity" is a magnificent sight. Peace Arch Park and the companion park on the Canadian side, were developed in 1920 to commemorate 100 years of an undefended border between the two countries, and to acknowledge the countries' shared origins. Displays tell the history of the park.

North of the large parking lot there is a long, tree-bordered lawn with picnic tables and an enclosed kitchen shelter. Above the northbound lanes of the highway, more picnic tables are scattered about a tree-shaded lawn among beautiful flower gardens. The park is a pleasant place to stop for a picnic lunch on your way to or from Vancouver, B.C.

SEMIAHMOO INTERPRETIVE CENTER sits on Semiahmoo Spit, a mile-long sandspit named after the Salish Indians who inhabited this area for 3,000 years. The fish cannery business boomed here from the late 1800s until the 1970s, and now the Interpretive Center and the Inn at Semiahmoo occupy several of the restored cannery buildings.

This well-designed little museum has interesting historical exhibits of the Alaska Packers Association operation and the Native American life in the area. There is a fun display of one of the old fishing boats and an excellent little gift shop.

In Semiahmoo County Park, west of Blaine; 360/371-5513. Open Wed-Sun, 1-5 pm. Free.

SHELLFISH HARVESTING is outstanding in Birch Bay. The bay is quite shallow, and low tides expose miles of tide flats, making this one of the best areas on the Washington coast for digging butter clams and the hefty horseneck clams (good for chowder). To determine the low tide schedule, use the Port Townsend tide table with a correction for Cherry Point. Before you dig, though, make sure the shellfish are safe to eat (Red Tide Hotline: 360/249-4628).

In June, a Celebration of Peace is held at Peace Arch Park and its companion park just across the border.

BIRCH BAY offers a number of resort town activities that make it popular during summer months. If the family tires of the beach, these provide hours of diversion: **Go-Karts** at Birch Bay Kartway (360/371-7700; 4620 Birch Bay/Lynden Rd); **Putt-Putt Golf** at Borderland Mini-Golf (360/371-3330; 4815 Alderson Rd); **Waterslides** at Wild 'N' Wet Waterslides (360/371-7500; 4874 Birch Bay/Lynden Rd).

CALENDAR

JUNE: Peace Arch Celebration, Blaine
JULY: Arts and Crafts Fair, Birch Bay State Park
AUGUST: Kite-Flying Festival, Semiahmoo Park

RESOURCES

BIRCH BAY CHAMBER OF COMMERCE
7806 Birch Bay Dr, Blaine, 98230; 360/371-7675

BLAINE VISITORS INFORMATION CENTER
900 Peace Portal Dr, Blaine, 98230 or P.O. Box 1718, Blaine, 98231; 360/332-8222 or 800/624-3555

BELLINGHAM

Bordered on one side by Bellingham Bay and the San Juan Islands, and on the other side by glorious Mount Baker, Bellingham encompasses an interesting mix of historical architecture, modern commercial districts and urban and semi-rural residential areas.

"Discovered" in 1792 by Capt. George Vancouver, the early settlement was bolstered by the discovery of coal in 1852. Coal mining, lumber milling and connection with the trans-Canada railroad kept the area booming into the late 1800s. Four small settlements originally clustered along the bay were consolidated in 1903 to form the town of Bellingham (the rather jumbled downtown area still shows signs of this consolidation).

Today, Bellingham Bay supports an active waterfront port (the marina here is the second largest in the state). The presence of Western Washington University and the many historic homes and landmarks lend a quiet charm to the town.

GETTING THERE

Bellingham, is the last major town before the Canadian border. From Seattle it's 89 miles north on I-5.

ROADSIDE ATTRACTIONS. Since you're in the area, why not give the kids the thrill of a ride on a train pulled by an old steam engine that dates back to the late 1800s. The **Lake Whatcom Railway** provides a one-hour trip through woods, a tunnel and past a lake. Passengers may work the handcar at the end of the line. The road at the train site is unpaved, so be sure to take boots if the weather is wet.

Train runs Saturday and Tuesday, mid-June through late August, at 11 am and 1 pm. Cost: $10/adult, $5/child 17 & under. Take the Anacortes exit from I-5. Turn north on Hwy 9 at Sedro Woolley and drive ten miles to Wickersham; 360/595-2218.

PLACES TO STAY

BEST WESTERN LAKEWAY INN
360/671-1011 or 800/528-1234; 714 Lakeway Dr, Bellingham, 98226
Rates: Moderate, children stay free with parents
Essentials: Credit cards; cribs
Extras: Restaurants; TV, VCR ($9.95) and movies; indoor pool, children's pool, sauna, jacuzzi, exercise facility, game room; laundry

This is an older hotel, but clean and well maintained. Though also popular with business people, The Lakeway is known for its family atmosphere. With its game room and indoor pools, this spot offers lots of diversion for travel-weary little ones. There are no rooms with kitchens, but the Lobby Cafe serves three casual meals a day. There's a children's menu with mazes and puzzles to work on while waiting.

HOLIDAY INN EXPRESS
360/671-4800 or 1-800-HOLIDAY; 4160 Guide Meridian, Bellingham, 98226
Rates: Moderate, children stay free with parents
Essentials: Credit cards; cribs
Extras: Free breakfast bar; TV, phone, free in-room movies; kitchen (some units); indoor heated pool, spa; babysitting service; free airport shuttle
The locals are proud of this 101-room hotel, the newest of five built in the last two years. It offers several amenities for families—kitchens, indoor pool, free movies—at very reasonable prices.

QUALITY INN BARON SUITES
360/647-8000; 100 E Kellogg Rd, Bellingham, 98226
Rates: Moderate, children stay free with parents
Essentials: Credit cards; cribs
Extras: Free breakfast buffet; TV, VCR (some units); kitchens (some units); outdoor heated pool, spa, some whirlpool suites, exercise room; pets OK; babysitting service; free shuttle service
This is a new hotel, with bright, clean rooms and a lovely outdoor pool that's a big hit with kids. Traveling families might want to check out the rooms with kitchens. The location is convenient to I-5 and restaurants. Visitors who want to explore may use the free shuttle service.

PARENT COMMENTS: *"We took full advantage of the free shuttle service. How refreshing not to hassle driving in a strange town with all the kids in the car."*

SILVER LAKE PARK CABINS
360/599-2776; 9006 Silver Lake Road, Sumas
Rates: Inexpensive
Essentials: Credit cards
Extras: Kitchens; fireplaces in cabin #3, 4 & 7; boats for rent.
Consider it camping with a roof over your head, and you'll be fully satisfied with these rustic but comfortable cabins. Each has

a stove/oven, refrigerator, gas heater, sink, cold water and two or three double beds. There is a central shower building with toilets as well as outhouses are near the cabins. Bring your own cooking utenesils and bedding. Cabins operate year round.

The cabins are close to the pretty little lake, which is fine for swimming, fishing and boating (canoes, rowboats and pedal boats may be rented) and in the 400-acre park there are plenty of hiking trails as well as 100 campsites.

PARENT COMMENTS: *"We like to come in September when the crowds have gone and it is getting a little too chilly at night to camp."*
"Camping made easy!"

SUDDEN VALLEY RESORT
360/734-6430; 2145 Lake Whatcom Blvd, Bellingham, 98226
Rates: Expensive
Essentials: Credit cards
Extras: Restaurant; TV, phone (some units); kitchen, barbecue; two outdoor pools; playbarn, tennis courts, washer and dryer

This former ranch on Lake Whatcom has been converted to a planned resort community. Clusters of condos are spread throughout the 1,800 acres. With the paved streets and mowed lawns, it looks more like a city suburb than a vacation spot, but it offers proximity to great recreational opportunities along with all the conveniences of home.

Children will enjoy the two outdoor pools, both large and well-designed for little ones. Boats can be rented on the small lake at the resort and there is a golf course for mom and dad. If the weather doesn't oblige, there's a large playbarn for "indoor" games. On Friday nights, a family movie is shown at the recreation center.

There are several sandy beaches on Lake Whatcom and swimming is excellent. You'll do a fair amount of walking from condo to pool to woods, so if you have young children pack a stroller or backpack. Bikes will also come in handy. When you reserve your lodging, specify that you want to be close to a pool.

The restaurant at the resort, though very attentive to families, serves mediocre food. The alternatives are to cook in the condo, or make the short drive into Bellingham for meals.

PARENT COMMENTS: *"This was our favorite place when our kids were preschoolers and we couldn't stand the long drive over the Cascades."*

"Don't expect woodsy or you'll be disappointed. We spent every afternoon at a beautiful sandy beach and in the evening our kids liked spotting the deer that came out of the woods to graze."

"Go to Treehouse Park! We took our books and read while the kids were content to play in the fabulous treehouse for hours. It's hard to find—get directions at the front desk."

PLACES TO EAT

RED ROBIN
360/7349991; 100 W Telegraph
Hours: Lunch and dinner daily
Essentials: Credit cards; highchairs

This is a fun place for kids of all ages and the food is reliably good, if not inspired. Offering gourmet burgers, chicken, salads and assorted entrees, Red Robin has something to suit everyone's tastes (all children's items $2.99). It definitely caters to the younger set, with crayons, coloring placemats and balloons.

STANELLO'S
360/676-1304; 1304 Twelfth St, Fairhaven
Hours: (Carry-out service), Mon-Thu from 4 pm, Friday from 2 pm, Sat & Sun from 11:30 am; (Dining room) Mon-Thu from 4 pm, Sun from 1 pm
Essentials: Credit cards; highchairs

This casual, family-oriented Italian restaurant, located in the Fairhaven historical district, has been the place to go for pizza since the mid-70s. They've developed a gourmet pizza that works well for families with picky eaters. Diners choose a combination of toppings from an incredible list of possibilities.

But don't pass this one just because you're not in a pizza mood; the menu features a wide range of tasty Italian entrees, steak dinners and soup/salad combinations. Though there's no kids' menu, the staff is happy to accommodate families with half-orders for smaller appetites and free spaghetti and sauce for those under five.

WHAT TO SEE AND DO

STROLL & BROWSE
HISTORIC FAIRHAVEN DISTRICT. When Fairhaven, one of the original towns incorporated into Bellingham, was believed the natural terminus for a transcontinental railroad, speculators

made big bucks on land sales and development. That boom ended when Great Northern chose to terminate the tracks in Seattle, but many of the interesting old buildings and homes remain. It's a lively place to stroll, with businesses, restaurants and galleries, some still clinging to a historic theme. Ask for a Walking Tour guide to public buildings and nearby Victorian homes.

SQUALICUM HARBOR. Once host to sailing ships carrying timber and coal, today Squalicum Harbor bustles with industry, shipping, pleasure boats and commercial fishing vessels. A two-mile promenade along the inner basin affords sweeping views of the city and close observation of water activities. Be sure to take a kite; this is a favorite kite-flying spot.

PARKS

Thanks perhaps to founding mothers and fathers with foresight, Bellingham is an absolute paradise of parks. For a complete list, contact Bellingham Parks & Recreation, 360/676-6985.

BOULEVARD PARK. With one-half mile of saltwater shoreline on Bellingham Bay, Boulevard Park is a popular spot for fishing, crabbing and windsurfing. There is a fun play structure and a large, grassy area for flying frisbees and kites.
At S State & Bayview Dr; 360/676-6985.

FAIRHAVEN PARK. Developed early this century, Fairhaven Park features a test garden for the American Rose Society. Families enjoy hiking trails, picnic shelters, barbecues, playground and wading (toddler pool in the summer, or anytime of the year in Whatcom Creek).
107 Chuckanut Dr; 360/676-6985.

LAKE PADDEN PARK. The 2.6-mile gravel trail around scenic Lake Padden is just about right for most families—long enough to provide exercise and entertainment, short enough to avoid complaints and "pick me up" pleas. The trail is partially wooded, and there are bridle trails through the woods as well. Or if hiking's not your pleasure: take a swim, enjoy the playground, rent a paddleboat.
4882 Samish Way; 360/676-6989.

SAMISH PARK. Located on Lake Samish, this 39-acre park was formerly a log rafting site and fishing resort. During the summer

there is a lifeguarded swimming area, boat rentals, fishing dock and children's play area. Terraced picnic sites provide an opportunity for the family to refuel.
673 N Lake Samish Dr; 360/733-2362.

WHATCOM FALLS PARK. Occupying 241 acres on Whatcom Creek, this park offers hiking trails, lovely waterfalls, picnic shelters, tennis courts and a basketball hoop. Especially popular with kids are the juvenile fishing pond and fish hatchery.
1401 Electric Ave; 360/676-2138.

THE GREAT OUTDOORS

BOATING. With saltwater coastline and several beautiful lakes in the vicinity, you'll find plenty of boating opportunities in Bellingham. **Washington Wind Sports** (360/676-1146), located near the ferry terminal in Fairhaven, offers summer rentals on Lake Padden (kayaks, paddleboats, windsurfers) and two-hour windsurfing lessons. At the same location is **Fairhaven Boatworks** (360/647-2469), which rents sailboats and rowboats. Kayaks also available at **The Great Adventure** (360/671-4615).

HIKING. Short, easy hikes abound in area parks and neighborhoods. Two are noteworthy: *Lake Padden Park Trail* (see Lake Padden Park, under "Parks") and the *Interurban Trail, a* 5.6-mile hike from Old Fairhaven Parkway through Arroyo Park to Larrabee State Park. This flat trail follows a former railroad bed, and offers some scenic views. It's probably most appropriate for frequent hikers or older kids; the trail becomes a bit steep as it traverses Arroyo Park Canyon.

See also **Mt. Baker.**

ANIMALS, ANIMALS

MARINE LIFE TANK. Located at Harbor Center Mall, a small marine mall with a view of the harbor, this is a cost-free opportunity for families to observe sea life in semi-natural habitats—a small marine life tank and various aquariums. There's even a touch tank for those kids (OK, you big kids, too) who can't resist the urge to feel some of those slimy, squishy creatures.
Squalicum Harbor.

MARITIME HERITAGE CENTER. Here you'll learn as much as you ever wanted to know about the spawning, hatching and rearing of *Salmo salar* (salmon). For families, this interpretive center has informative displays and a self-guided tour (pick up a brochure). Personnel are available to answer all the "why?" questions. By the way, the time to see the hatchling salmon released is in the spring; in fall, the adults return to spawn.

1600 C St; 360/676-6806. Hours: 10 am-3 pm weekdays. Free.

MUSEUMS

WHATCOM CHILDREN'S MUSEUM features hands-on exhibits to touch, climb and explore. Now affiliated with the Whatcom Museum. Recently remodelled and well worth a visit.

227 Prospect St; 360/733-8769. Hours: Sun, Tues, Weds noon-5 pm; Thurs, Fri, Sat 10 am-5 pm. Closed Mon. Cost: $2/person.

WHATCOM MUSEUM AND SYRE EDUCATION CENTER. One of the largest museums in the state, the Whatcom's three-building complex offers exhibits of historical significance, including Eskimo and Indian artifacts, indigenous birds and logging memorabilia. For budding young artists, there is a changing collection of contemporary art.

121 Prospect St; 360/676-6981. Open Tues-Sun, noon-5 pm. Free.

SHOPPING

BELLINGHAM BAY CHILDREN'S BOOKS AND BINDERY features a large selection of quality books for parents and children of all ages.

Located downtown at 1324 Cornwall Ave; 360/647-9562.

BELLIS FAIR MALL. This is the newest and largest shopping mall in the Bellingham area. In addition to Toys R Us, you'll find a fun nature store, Natural Wonders, featuring nature and science education products. The mall has five department stores and more than 150 specialty shops.

Intersection of I-5 and Meridian. Mon-Sat, 9:30 am-9 pm; Sunday, 11 am-6 pm.

EXCURSIONS

HOVANDER HOMESTEAD PARK/TENANT LAKE NATURAL HISTORY INTERPRETIVE CENTER. An old farmhouse, a big red barn and a mile of river bank—what else does any kid need to spend an afternoon exploring? As a National Historic Home, Hovander has been restored to its turn-of-the-century elegance, surrounded by gardens and orchards. Near the barn are animals and displays of antique farm implements. Families who explore these 200 acres will find walking trails, fishing facilities, a treehouse, picnic tables and a water tower with a look-out.

At Tenant Lake, the old Neilsen Homestead has been transformed into an interpretive center for the environment. A one-half mile system of trails and a birdwatching tower tie interpretive displays to the 500 acres of marshy habitat. Be sure to bring the boots.

5236 & 5299 Nielsen Rd, Ferndale; 360/384-3444. To get there, take the Ferndale turnoff (Exit 262) off I-5 and drive west to the railroad underpass. Turn left to park. Free.

ISLANDER MARINER CRUISES. These whale-watching cruises have a great success record, with Minke whales and/or Orcas ("killer whales") spotted on 19 of every 20 trips out. The 110-foot boat has two viewing decks, a snack bar and adequate indoor seating for rainy days. A special feature is the hydraphone, which allows cruisers to listen to the underwater "songs" of the whales. The cruise is seven and one-half hours long, probably too tiresome for most younger children.

360/734-8866; Squalicum Harbor, #5 Harbor Esplanade. Cruises operate Saturdays, late-May to early-Sept; Mondays and Wednesdays July and August. Cost: $45/adults, $40/seniors, $35 children.

THE MOUNT BAKER THEATRE. This historic, 1,500-seat theater has served the Bellingham community since 1927. Its Spanish-Moorish architecture is an example of the opulent Movie Palace Era. Programs are offered year-round—most are musical and many are suitable for family viewing. Four times a year, the American Family Theatre offers productions specifically for children.

360/734-6080; 106 N Commercial.

CALENDAR

MAY: Ski to Sea, an 85-mile, one-day race from Mt. Baker to Bellingham Bay
JULY: Sudden Valley Summer Festival
AUGUST: Northwest Washington Fair, Lynden
SEPTEMBER: Fairhaven Festival of Dixieland Jazz

RESOURCES

CONVENTION AND VISITORS BUREAU
904 Potter St, Bellingham 98226
360/671-3990 or 800/487-2032

WHATCOM TRANSPORTATION AUTHORITY
360/676-RIDE

MT. BAKER

Mount Baker, one-hour's travel from Bellingham, has the state's longest ski season (November through May) and is especially popular with snowboarders. Almost half the visitors to the area are from Canada. It is a laid-back, family-style ski area where lift lines are usually short and lift tickets cost less than other ski areas in the state ($16 midweek: $24 weekends.)

In the summer, the area boasts an abundance of hiking trails and spectacular views of nearby mountain peaks. But expect "Northwest funky" or you'll be disappointed; the places to sleep and eat are down the road from the ski area near the tiny town of Glacier and there is nothing fancy about them.

GETTING THERE

Mt Baker is located 56 miles east of Bellingham on State Route 542-A.

THE LOGS

360/599-2711; 9002 Mt. Baker Highway, Deming, 98244
Rates: Inexpensive to Moderate
Essentials: Credit cards; playpen
Extras: Kitchens; fireplaces, free firewood; outdoor, solar-heated pool; pets OK by permission

Situated where Canyon Creek runs into the Nooksack River, these five rustic log cabins are well suited to the needs of families. Each features a natural rock fireplace, two bedrooms, full kitchen and bath (there is a double hide-a-bed in the living room). Depending on the season, families may enjoy swimming in the solar-heated pool, hiking, fishing, badminton and horseshoes or downhill and cross-country skiing at nearby Mt. Baker. There is a two-night minimum on weekends and this place has loyal, repeat customers so book early.

PARENT COMMENTS: *"Rustic but comfy."*
"While relaxing at the pool, we spied an eagle and were 'visited' by two deer. We were as excited as our daughter!"

PRIVATE CABINS

Several agencies handle rental of private cabins and condos in and near Glacier. These are often a good choice for a family that wants more space and conveniences. See Resources below for places to call.

What to See and Do

Downhill Skiing and Snowboarding are very popular on the 1,000 acres covering the two mountain faces. With the only natural halfpipe in the region, the area is especially popular with the snowboarding crowd. With two new quad chairs and expanded intermediate terrain, Mount Baker boasts no lift line wait longer than five minutes. If you have a pre-skier in the group, child care is available.

Cross-Country is also popular on Baker. At the downhill ski area there's a 4-kilometer groomed loop trail; trailhead is near the southeast corner of the upper parking lot and trail fee is $3.

There are several spots in Glacier to help families prepare to hit the slopes. **The Great Adventure** (201 E Chestnut; 360/671-4615) rents downhill equipment in child and adult sizes. Nordic skiers will find assistance at **Base Camp** (901 Holly; 360/733-5461). For snowboarding, rental equipment is available at **Carter's Carving Edge** (3360 New Orleans; 360/671-9738). However all these stores are small with limited selection so be sure to call in advance to make sure they have the equipment you need before leaving your home town.

Places to Eat

Milano's
360/599-2863; 9990 Mt. Baker Hwy, Glacier
Hours: Breakfast, lunch and dinner daily
Essentials: Credit cards; highchair
  A casual, cafe-style spot serving tasty soups, pastas, salads, espresso. They have no kids' menu, but families may order half-servings or sauceless pasta. There are specials each evening; the pasta is homemade and delicious. One highchair is available.

Innisfree
360/599-2373; 9393 Mt. Baker Hwy, Deming
Hours: Dinner
Essentials: Credit cards; highchairs
  At Innisfree you'll enjoy local fresh organic foods in a cozy, wooded setting about 10 minutes west of Glacier. The excellent, though somewhat pricey, dinner menu changes weekly. Al-

though there is no children's menu, some kid fare is available upon request: pizza, sauceless pasta, bratwurst "hot dog." Reservations advised.

RESOURCES

MOUNT BAKER CABIN RENTALS
360/599-2453
Offer private cabins and condos for rent in the Mt. Baker area.

MOUNT BAKER RANGER DISTRICT
360/856-5700 weekdays
Information about hiking and cross-country skiing.

MOUNT BAKER RECREATION COMPANY
360/734-6771
Information about downhill ski conditions, rentals, child care or family lift passes.

MOUNT BAKER SNOW PHONE
360/671-0211
Snow conditions.

GLACIER PUBLIC SERVICE CENTER,
360/599-2714
Provides information about cross-country ski routes.

Best Hikes with Children in Western Washington, Vol.1, (Mountaineers, 1988). Includes several good mountain hikes near the town of Glacier.

Cross Country Ski Tours 1: The North Cascades. (Mountainers, $10.95). A very useful book for finding out about logging roads in the area that make good cross-country routes.

LA CONNER

La Conner is a quaint, little waterside town about 60 miles north of Seattle on the Swinomish Channel in the Skagit Valley. With La Conner's reputation for good restaurants, its wide assortment of B&Bs and an abundance of antique and gift shops, it would seem the ideal getaway for parents traveling *without* kids.

But don't scratch it off the list: Many features of this area will appeal to school-age children, including the opportunity to explore—by foot, bike, horse or boat—the fields, forests, waterways and rare saltwater estuary, all within a 20-minute drive from town.

GETTING THERE

Located approximately 60 miles north of Seattle, and west of Mt. Vernon.

REFUELING. If you are coming from Seattle and want to feed the group en route (there are no fast-food outlets in La Conner), you will find a good assortment of quick and reasonably priced restaurant options in both **Marysville,** just outside Everett, and **Mt. Vernon.** Coming from Canada, **Bellingham** is the best stop for refreshments.

ROADSIDE ATTRACTIONS. Once you exit I-5, you'll be driving through the Skagit Valley. One of the most fertile farming areas in the country, the valley is famous for its flower industry. In the spring, you'll be treated to a visual feast of color in the **tulip** and **daffodil fields.** There are at least a dozen greenhouses on the way to La Conner, and most of them are open for visitors—and business.

During the winter, keep your eyes peeled for huge flocks of **trumpeter swans** and **snow geese** in the fields.

The **Pacific Edge Outlet Center** (360/757-3549), a clothing discount mall, is located right off I-5 at the George Hopper Road Exit (229) near Burlington.

PLACES TO STAY

ART'S PLACE
360/466-3033; 511 Talbot (P.O. Box 557), La Conner, 98257
Rates: Inexpensive
Essentials: Credit cards
Extras: TV; stereos; microwaves, small refrigerators

In an area blooming with B&Bs, there are precious few places that actively welcome families. This lovely guest house, conveniently located in town, is a wonderful place to stay with school-age children.

Adults can sleep in the loft (the spiral staircase and loft bedroom are not safe for younger visitors), while the kids share the sofa hideaway in the living room (a foam pad is also available). The mini-kitchen comes in handy for snacks.

PARENT COMMENTS: *"The owners of this B&B, Art and Rita Shupy, are very gracious about accommodating families and generous about sharing their extensive knowledge of the area. We learned that they opened the first art gallery in La Conner in 1977— Art now runs the art museum in town."*

LA CONNER COUNTRY INN
360/466-3101; 2nd & Morris (P.O. Box 573), La Conner, 98257
Rates: Moderate
Essentials: Credit cards; cribs
Extras: Free breakfast; TV; fireplaces; babysitting by arrangement
This is an older, rather nondescript hotel located in downtown La Conner within easy walking distance of the shops, restaurants and channel. Not as elegant or expensive as its companion hotel, the La Conner Channel Inn, it is nevertheless a very convenient and comfortable place for families.

Adjacent to the front deck is a pleasant sitting area with a rock fireplace and plenty of comfortable chairs and tables—nice for those who need some space for reading or games. A breakfast of tasty baked goods, granola and beverages is served in this room.

Special events weekends in La Conner mean long lines and crowds—not good for the family scene.

PARENT COMMENTS: *"We liked the fact that our room at La Conner Country Inn came with a gas-powered fireplace and a table and chairs—it was more homey and functional than your standard hotel room."*

SCIMITAR RIDGE RANCH
360/293-5355 or 800/798-5355; 527 Miller Rd,
Anacortes, 98221
Rates: Inexpensive to moderate
Essentials: Credit cards
Extras: Horseback riding (lessons available), hay rides; hot tub; sport courts, golf; playground. Cabin has TV, kitchen, fireplace.
Scimitar is a first-class ranch and resort that opened in 1989. Built in part from logs salvaged from Yellowstone Park after the 1988 fire, the ranch and the cabins blend gracefully into the scenery just outside Anacortes.

The ranch was designed primarily for RV campers, but there are two other types of accommodations available: one cabin and 24 covered wagons.

The only cabin has one bedroom and a hide-a-bed in the living room (maximum occupancy four). There is a fireplace, a big screen cable TV and a fully stocked kitchen.

The covered wagons, built by the ranch's own craftsmen, offer an adventurous opportunity for brave parents and an unforgettable thrill for young pioneer-wannabes. The large wagons accommodate four people in sleeping bags, and each wagon comes with its own picnic table and grill, as well as full access to all the amenities of the ranch, including the large, outdoor hot tub. Cost for one night in a wagon is $30.

PARENT COMMENTS: *"This is a beautiful resort with a very friendly staff. Our horse-loving kids were in heaven; we also enjoyed hiking in the nearby forest. The covered wagons were our six-year-old's idea of ideal accommodations, and we appreciated not having to set up a tent."*

PLACES TO EAT

AT'S A PIZZA
360/466-4406; 201 E Morris St
Hours: Sun-Thurs, 11 am-9 pm; Fri-Sat, 11 am-10:30 pm
Essentials: Credit cards

A local family favorite, At's A Pizza serves spaghetti and other standard pasta dishes, plus—you guessed it—pizza. They will deliver within a 5-mile radius for an extra $2.

If your kids are old enough to be left alone in the hotel, consider ordering them a pizza and treating yourselves to a night on the town. See "Places to Eat Without Kids."

CALICO CUPBOARD
360/466-4451; 1720 S First St
Hours: Breakfast, lunch and tea daily
Essentials: No credit cards; highchairs available

Calico Cupboard is a bakery and cafe offering delicious food and a good basic child's menu. The bakery goods, soups, sandwiches and hearty breakfasts are exceptional and the prices reasonable, so expect long lines on busy weekends. Put your name on the waiting list (they don't take reservations), and stroll the town to pass the time—and to distract the kids from their rumbling bellies. Once seated, service is speedy.

HUNGRY MOON DELICATESSEN
360/466-1602; 110 N First St
Hours: Light breakfast and lunch (until 5:30 p.m.) daily; extended

hours in the summer
Essentials: No credit cards
The Hungry Moon Channel serves good deli fare that can be eaten inside or outside in the garden courtyard (or taken out for a picnic at Bay View State Park or Deception Pass).

LA CONNER SEAFOOD & PRIME RIB HOUSE
360/466-4014; 614 S First St
Hours: Lunch and dinner daily
Essentials: Credit cards; highchairs
Located on the Swinomish in the middle of town, this restaurant boasts a great view of channel activity. It is the place to go if you want a nice atmosphere and good food—steak, seafood, pasta and sandwiches—without spending the kind of money you'd have to at some of the more gourmet spots in town. Though there is no child's menu per se, most kids will be happy with the chicken strips off the appetizer menu or the fish and chips. Outdoor dining is available in the summer.

LEGENDS
360/466-5240; 708 First St (on the waterfront)
Hours vary
Essentials: Credit cards
This take-out eatery sits on the public deck at the Swinomish Waterfront Park on First Street. Hours are sporadic—especially during the winter months—but you'll know they're open when you catch a whiff of salmon barbecuing on their outdoor fire. They also have tasty hot dogs and an Indian fry bread that shouldn't be missed. Take your meal to one of the public picnic tables nearby, where you'll find a lovely view of the channel.

THE TERIYAKI BAR
360/466-5560; 128 S First St, Pier 7
Hours: Lunch and dinner daily
Essentials: Credit cards; highchairs
Here's another good choice for parents with hungry kids. Service is fast and prices are reasonable. Dine inside or on the deck, or take out.

WHERE TO EAT WITHOUT KIDS
PALMERS RESTAURANT AND PUB
360/466-4261; 205 E Washington
Hours: Lunch and dinner daily
Essentials: Credit cards

Located inside the La Conner Country Inn, this is where La Conner natives go for a first-class meal without the kids.

WHAT TO SEE AND DO

STROLL & BROWSE

The town of La Conner is rich in history and culture. Note the turn-of-the-century architecture, especially **City Hall**, just off Second, a triangular-shaped building built in 1886. The nearby **Magnus Anderson Cabin** is a pioneer home that was constructed in 1869. The **Gaches Mansion**, at Second and Calhoun, was built in 1890 by a merchant who wanted the "finest house in La Conner." It has recently been restored and houses the **Valley Museum of Northwest Art**.

A stroll along First Street reveals La Conner's charm. If you have trouble finding street parking, there are parking lots at both ends of this waterfront stretch.

Most of the gift and specialty shops here abound with fragile and precious items, the kind you don't even want your child to look at, let alone touch. But if shopping is on the agenda, you may want to check out **Dinghy Baby** (360/466-4727; 707 S First St), a spunky children's clothing store with a few toys, and **Casey Jones Toys** (360/466-2116; 610 S First St), which specializes in traditional handcrafted wooden toys.

One other shop, **Bunnies by the Bay** (360/466-5040; 617 E Morris St), next to the Tillinghast Seed Co. (the oldest seed company in the Northwest), is worth visiting on your way in or out of town. This Bloomsbury-inspired shop is overflowing with exquisite handmade bunnies. These creations are often fragile, however, so you may be better off window shopping if you have a rambunctious preschooler in tow.

Any parent who has frantically searched for a restroom for a desperate child will appreciate the efforts of former mayor Bud Moore to get a restroom built smack in the middle of downtown La Conner. **One Moore Outhouse** sits next to the **Volunteer Firemen's Museum**. Look for "The Outhouse Poem," written by *Seattle Post-Intelligencer* columnist Jon Hahn, which is posted on the restroom wall.

When the kids show signs of restlessness, walk to the beach at the north end of town—a spot locals favor for jogging, playing in the dunes or just puttering near the water. Other good places for outdoor respite include **Pioneer Park** at the La Conner side of

Rainbow Bridge, which has barbecue facilities, picnic tables and restrooms; and **Totem Pole Park** at the corner of First and Commercial streets on the south end of First, a small park where younger kids can watch the vessels ply the Swinomish Channel.

SKAGIT COUNTY HISTORICAL MUSEUM, which sits on a hill a couple of blocks from downtown La Conner, offers a good view of the Skagit Flats. In the north wing, kids can get a sense of what domestic life was like in early Skagit County—what kinds of toys were popular and what furniture would have been found in a typical farmhouse kitchen. In the south wing, they will learn about the Swinomish Indian tribe and find out how early settlers made a living. The museum occasionally offers family programs, which are excellent; consult the schedule when you get to town. *501 S Fourth St; 360/466-3365. Open Wed-Sun, 12-5 pm (every day during the Tulip Festival). Cost: $1/adult, $.50/child 12 and under, children under 5 are free.*

EXCURSIONS

BAY VIEW STATE PARK, situated just south of the Padilla Bay Interpretive Center, is a fine place to go bird watching and beachcombing—especially when a minus tide almost empties the bay. There are picnic tables and 99 campsites. *1093 Bayview-Edison Rd, Mt. Vernon; 360/757-0227.*

BIKING is popular in the Skagit Valley because the terrain is flat and the scenery picturesque. But if you want to two-wheel it with the family, come prepared: Few paths are designated solely for cyclists, and there are no bike-rental shops. Most riding is done on wide, well-marked shoulders off the main roads, though you may want to stick to the side roads if you have a wobbly rider.

One fun bike ride takes you on the La Conner-Whitney Road out of La Conner (riding on the wide shoulder of a fairly busy road) to SR 20. About 1/4 mile after crossing SR 20 (road name changes to Bayview-Edison Road), you'll come to the Padilla Bay Shore Trail, a delightful 2.2-mile ride. If the group has the energy, you can continue another 4.4 miles to the Interpretive Center. (The ride from La Conner to the Interpretive Center is 8.2 miles one way.) See "Padilla Bay Shore Trail" and "Breazeale-Padilla Bay Interpretive Center."

BIRD WATCHING is a popular activity in the Skagit Valley, so bring binoculars. Even the child who never wants to feed the ducks may show some interest in the magnificent creatures that grace this area; the kid who hyperventilates every time he sees a mere pigeon will probably need an oxygen tank.

Snow geese begin arriving in early October, but peak viewing is after hunting season has ended—mid-January through mid-April. It is not unusual to spot a flock of 5,000 geese, as well as the large, graceful trumpeter swans. Fir Island offers the best viewing opportunities—get on Fir Island Road (just west of Conway) and take any one of the side roads. Maupin Road has a particularly good view of the flats.

Bald eagles are flocking in increasing numbers to the Upper Skagit River Valley, which is great news for bird watchers. The stretch of river on the east side of I-5 is a popular area for spotting them, and it's an easy drive from La Conner. Favorite viewing time is late January through mid-February when the eagles feast on the chum salmon run. With over 400 eagles in the area during these weeks, it is not uncommon to spot 25 or 30 at a time.

Every year, on the first weekend in February, the towns along the Upper Skagit sponsor the Upper Skagit Bald Eagle Festival, with Native American storytelling, volunteers situated at the best viewing spots, and numerous displays and programs. For information about eagle watching and other festival activities, call 360/853-7009.

BREAZEALE-PADILLA BAY INTERPRETIVE CENTER is approximately 8 miles northeast of La Conner on the Bayview-Edison Road. It is the headquarters for the Padilla Estuarine Research Reserve, housing an outstanding interpretive museum with exhibits, saltwater aquariums and an excellent hands-on room for children. Every Saturday morning at 10:30 staff members feed the fish and tell tales about saltwater creatures.

There's also access to outdoor observation decks and the beach (except in the winter months to protect wildlife). From 1-2:30 pm on Saturdays, kids can participate in a Junior Ecologists program. When planning a visit to the Center, be sure to inquire about bird-watching classes, storytelling, Sunday movies and other activities that may be occurring during your stay. Write for a calendar of Padilla Bay Events.

1043 Bayview-Edison Rd, Mount Vernon, 98273; 360/428-1558. Open Wed-Sun, 10 am-5 pm. Free.

CHANNEL BOAT TOURS are narrated tours offered by Viking Cruises. Your family will glean a quick history of La Conner, while taking in the action of the tugs, fishing vessels and wildlife along the channel. Tours depart at 12:30 pm every Saturday and

Sunday between October 15 and May 31; boats run daily during summer months.

109 N First St; 360/466-2639. Cost: $10/person.

DECEPTION PASS is the beautiful and tumultuous waterway between Whidbey and Fidalgo islands. From the lofty bridge above, your family will enjoy a breathtaking view of this deep gorge and of the smaller neighboring passage, Canoe Pass.

Deception Pass State Park, which blankets both sides of the pass with 2,300 acres of forest and beach, is the most popular state park in Washington, featuring lake and saltwater fishing and an abundance of campsites, swimming beaches and hiking trails.

Two short (2-mile) hikes that are especially good for kids, Cranberry Lake and West Point, begin at the large parking lot at West Beach (on the west side of the pass), near Deception Pass Park headquarters.

Follow SR 20 west to Fidalgo Island, then follow signs to Deception Pass; 360/675-2417.

HORSEBACK RIDING is offered on Fidalgo Island at Scimitar Ridge Ranch, a fancy new 350-acre facility adjacent to Mount Erie (about a 10-minute drive from La Conner). For $20 ($15 off-season), riders ages seven and up can take an hour ride up the fir-clad slopes of Scimitar Ridge. During the summer, half-hour rides are available for younger kids for $10. The ranch also offers camp and RV sites, overnight accommodations in covered wagons (see "Places to Stay"), a spa and all kinds of other recreational activities—all done in first-class fashion.

Bring binoculars! The Skagit Valley is a wildlife paradise.

527 Miller Rd, Anacortes; 360/293-5355 or 800/798-5355.

KAYAKING in the Swinomish Channel and Padilla Bay is outstanding. Winter is a good (maybe the best) time to take a guided day trip because of the thousands of birds that migrate to this area from mid-October to January. Be sure to dress warmly (rubber boots, gloves and hat are essential), and take along binoculars and a camera. Children 12 and under must ride with an adult.

Call Northwest Sea Ventures (Anacortes, 360/293-3692) for information. They provide training, safety reviews, life vests and single- or double-seat kayaks.

PADILLA BAY SHORE TRAIL is a level, 2.2-mile trail along the shoreline of Padilla Bay. If the boat traffic doesn't keep your young walker entertained, the ducks and gulls will. And, although we can't guarantee it, you just might spot raccoons, harbor seals, muskrats, otters, blue herons and eagles. Visit the Interpretive Center first to gain a better understanding of the plant and animal life that flourishes when the fresh water from the Skagit River meets the salt water of the bay. Advance arrangements can be made at the Interpretive Center for stroller/ handicapped access.

Located about 1/4 mile off SR 20 on Bayview-Edison Rd.

The **Skagit Valley Tulip Festival** (800/4-TULIPS) is an annual celebration of the explosion of color that fills the Skagit Valley every April. In addition to the flowers, events of interest to families include the Great Skagit Duck Race, a race of approximately 6,000 rubber ducks on the Skagit River; pony rides and pony-drawn wagon rides through the tulips from the Carriage House Pony Farm (at the corner of Young and Best roads); a street fair in Mt. Vernon; numerous concerts; and the "tulip pedal," a noncompetitive bike tour starting in Mt. Vernon.

To avoid the hassle of trying to negotiate the crowded roads, you might take advantage of the numerous Tulip Transit Park and Ride stations operating daily throughout the festival. Or avoid the road altogether by cruising to La Conner on the Victoria Clipper III (206/448-5000). The cruise, which departs from Pier 69 on the Seattle waterfront, is 2 1/4 hours each way and includes a 2 1/2-hour guided bus tour of the fields.

> Don't plan to stay more than one weekend in La Conner— there's just not enough to keep kids entertained longer.

CALENDAR

JANUARY: Peak time for viewing snow geese, trumpeter swans, eagles
FEBRUARY: Smelt Derby in La Conner (first Saturday)
APRIL: Skagit Valley Tulip Festival
NOVEMBER: Art's Alive Celebration
DECEMBER: Christmas Boat Parade in La Conner (first Saturday)

RESOURCES

LA CONNER CHAMBER OF COMMERCE
P.O. Box 1610, La Conner, 98257
360/466-4778

WASHINGTON DEPARTMENT OF WILDLIFE provides information about the snow geese and other wildlife in the Skagit

wildlife area.
16018 Mill Creek Blvd, Mill Creek, 98012
360/775-1311

From the Mountains to the Sea: A Guide to the Skagit River Watershed is a booklet that contains information about the Skagit River Watershed, including its cultural and geological history. It is available from the North Cascades Institute, 2105 Hwy 20, Sedro Woolley, 98284; 360/856-5700.

WHIDBEY ISLAND

The longest of all the islands in the continental United States, Whidbey is one of the easiest getaways for Western Washington families. While not far from the Seattle metropolitan area, it has a distinctive island atmosphere, far removed from the faster pace of the mainland.

Exploring Whidbey is a varied experience. It is a long, narrow island, with miles and miles of beaches stretching from the densely populated Oak Harbor area at the north end, through the quieter southern half to Clinton. Young explorers will not be disappointed with the forests, beaches, wildlife and history the island's six state parks have to offer, and even the most sophisticated pint-sized urbanite will be enticed by the great shops and tasty eateries found in the charming towns of Langley and Coupeville.

GETTING THERE

From Seattle, head north on I-5 to the Mukilteo-Whidbey Island Ferry Exit (182). Drive west on Highway 525 to the ferry terminal. Travel time to the ferry is about 35 minutes (much longer during the 4 to 6 pm weekday commute out of Seattle). Take the 20-minute ferry ride to Clinton, the southernmost community on the island. Ferries run on the hour and the half-hour. For ferry information, call 360/464-6400 or 800/843-3779.

During summer months, it is not unusual to encounter a 1 to 1-1/2-hour wait on Friday after 2 pm and anytime on Sunday (or Monday, if it's a holiday weekend). If you must travel during these times, be sure to bring games and books for the kids, or plan to explore the area near the ferry dock (fishing is very popular off the pier next to the Mukilteo ferry—lots of fun to watch while you're passing time). Ivar's has opened a restaurant and take-out counter at the ferry dock on the Mukilteo side—the take-out option is ideal for hungry travelers.

A pleasant alternative to the ferry wait is to drive to Whidbey via Deception Pass, across the bridge that connects the mainland and Fidalgo Island to the northern tip of Whidbey. If you opt for this route, take I-5 north to the Anacortes-Whidbey Exit (230). Head west on Highway 20 and follow the signs to Whidbey. The Deception Pass route takes about 1 1/2 to 2 hours from Seattle, depending on where you are going on the island (it is the better route if you are staying in the Coupeville area or further north on the island). You'll want to allow a little more time so that you can stop at Deception Pass State Park, where you'll find incredible scenery, hiking, fishing and beach access.

ROADSIDE ATTRACTIONS. The **Boeing Everett Plant** (Exit 189 from I-5; 360/342-4801) sits on either side of Highway 525 as you approach the Mukilteo ferry terminal. Just a glimpse of the awesome metal birds under construction here will thrill the kids. Public tours for ages 10 and up are offered weekdays on a first-come, first-served basis. During the summer, the tours are very popular, so expect a wait. If you'd rather make just a quick visit you can browse in the lobby and gift shop, open weekdays 8:30 am-4:30 pm.

For information about interesting stops on the **Deception Pass** route, see "La Conner: What to See and Do."

PLACES TO STAY

Over the last few years, there has been an explosion of B&Bs and inns around Coupeville and Langley. However, many are self-described "quiet, romantic" places (i.e. children not allowed), so when travelling with the progeny, your choices are limited.

Also, when you choose your accomodations, take into consideration that Whidbey Island is the longest of all the islands in the United States. Both Langley and Coupeville are interesting towns with good restaurants but if you are only on the island for the weekend you probably won't want to spend your time driving up and down the island betwen the two towns (it is a fifteen-minute drive from the ferry to Langley and forty minutes to Coupeville). Your best bet is to pick accomodations near either Langley or Coupeville and plan to explore the other part of the island on your next trip.

You may want to consider renting a house on Whidbey. **Tara Vacation Rentals** (360/221-1700; P.O. Box 205, Langley, 98260)

Make your trip to Whidbey Island a circular tour by driving over Deception Pass on the way and returning on the Mukilteo ferry.

arranges daily, weekly and monthly rentals of private waterfront and view homes, as well as condos and cabins—completely furnished. There are several businesses that specialize in renting vacation properties on Whidbey, but Tara places emphasis on finding rentals where "children are welcome." If renting a private home doesn't appeal to you, check out the following.

BOATYARD INN
360/221-5120; 200 Wharf Street, Langley, 98260
Rates: Moderate to expensive
Essentials: Credit cards; crib, futons
Extras: Kitchens; fireplace; TV; dock

Hurrah! As this book went to press, we heard that at last there is a place to stay on the waterfront in the charming town of Langley that is right for kids. The location of this attractive new inn (opened ?) is ideal—tucked on the beach, next to a fishing pier and a five-minute walk from the center of town. Galley kitchens have a cook-top stove, microwave, dishwasher and refrigerator. Each room has a private balcony overlooking Puget Sound and the beds sit up extra high so you can soak up the view while you lie in bed.

The only downside for parents is that there are no units with separate bedrooms—even when you get the larger accommodations with a loft you won't be separated from the kids by a wall.

We didn't have time to send a parent reviewer, but given the looks of the place, the great location and the warm response of the owner when asked if she welcomed kids, the Boatyard Inn looks like an excellent choice for families visiting Whidbey.

CAPTAIN WHIDBEY INN
360/678-4097, 800/366-4097; 2072 W Captain Whidbey Inn Rd, Coupeville, 98239
Rates: Expensive
Essentials: Credit cards; cribs and highchairs (request in advance)
Extras: Restaurant; lodge; babysitting by arrangement

This charming madrona log inn, situated on the wooded shores of Penn Cove, has a variety of accommodations. The rooms in the lodge itself are not practical for families, as they are furnished with antiques and share a bathroom down the hall. There are, however, one- and two-bedroom waterfront cottages that are suitable for those visiting with kids, as well as reasonable accommodations in the multi-unit Lagoon lodge.

All the cottages have fireplaces or woodstoves, complete kitchens and beautiful views. "Rachel's House" is $255/night for two

If you were leaving the kids with Grandma, we could easily recommend a handful of the self-described "quiet, romantic" B & B's that have sprung up on Whidbey over the last few years but since you're traveling with the progeny, your options are narrowed adults and two kids. A more economic possibility is to take room #15 or #18 in the Lagoon (two double beds; $125/two adults, $15/ each additional occupant), each of which has a private bath but no kitchen. One parent traveling with a child over the age of 10 could stay in the main lodge ($85-$145) if they don't mind the shared bath. All accommodations have feather beds and down comforters.

There is a common room in the main lodge, which has a grand river-rock fireplace, a few board games and the inn's only TV but we recommend this area only for kids sensible enough to treat the antiques with care.

The restaurant in the lodge has had a high turnover of chefs, and reviews on the food are mixed. With kids, you are definitely better off eating at one of the many good restaurants in Coupeville or Langley.

PARENT COMMENTS: *"If you can afford it, the cottages are charming places to stay with out-of-town guests, to give them a good dose of Northwest history and the beauty of the land."*

FORT CASEY INN
360/678-8792; 1124 S Engle Rd, Coupeville, 98239
Rates: Expensive
Essentials: Credit cards; no crib
Extras: Free breakfast; woodstoves, free wood

Originally built in 1909 for the then-active defensive installation at Fort Casey, this inn is located next door to Fort Casey State Park. The inn has several houses, each with two bedrooms and a good-sized bath upstairs, and a living room and large kitchen downstairs. They are beautifully decorated with comfortable furnishings from the World War I era (romantically patriotic). Although relatively expensive, this inn seems like a good value in that families have an entire "home" to themselves, with plenty of space. It would be a good spot for a family reunion or for vacationing with another family. Groups could stay in houses adjacent to one another.

There are no cribs or highchairs available; families traveling with infants or young toddlers should pack a travel crib and a safety gate (the stairs in the houses are steep and long). Also, during winter visits, parents with crawlers and toddlers will need to be concerned about the woodstoves, which, though not the only source of heat, keep things cozy.

The inn is located amid pastures in a sparsely populated area and is fairly isolated. The kids will probably think they've reached the end of the earth when they learn there are no television sets here, but they'll soon discover that the outside world has much to offer. Tell them to look for the pretty little hiking trail that begins behind the houses and goes through the woods to the beach, or take them to Fort Casey State Park (less than a mile away), where they'll find bunkers, a lighthouse, beaches and trails to explore.

If you want a change of scenery and more activity, hop in the car and visit one of the nearby towns. It's only 4.5 miles (a pretty drive) to Coupeville and a 27-mile trip to Langley. Less than a mile from the inn, you can catch the Port Townsend/Keystone ferry for a fun day trip to Port Townsend.

PARENT COMMENTS: *"Our 'city' girls (ages 3 & 6) loved the 'country' feel of this charming spot. Each night we went to sleep hearing owls in the woods and awoke to deer grazing on our lawn."*

THE VICTORIAN BED AND BREAKFAST
360/678-5305; 602 N Main (P.O. Box 761), Coupeville, 98239
Rates: Moderate
Essentials: Credit cards; small crib, highchair and booster seat
Extras: Free breakfast; TV, VCR (in cottage and common area only); pets OK (with certain restrictions)

Guests at this 100-year-old home in the charming town of Coupeville may choose one of the upstairs bedrooms (each with private bath) or the Cottage Hideaway. The latter is clearly the best choice for families. It is a small cabin behind and across a courtyard from the house, featuring four nicely appointed rooms: a master bedroom with TV and VCR, a day room with a trundle bed (can sleep two children), a full kitchen and a bath.

This is a space for families who can coexist peacefully in close proximity—spacious it is not. The bathroom is small and not suited for diaper changing. But there is a courtyard to spill into, weather permitting, as well as common areas in the main house. Overall, the Victorian's cottage is a nice compromise for parents who want the B&B ambiance without having to worry about their kids disturbing other guests.

PLACES TO EAT

THE DOG HOUSE
360/321-9996; 230 First St, Langley
Hours: Lunch and dinner daily
Essentials: No credit cards; highchairs

The Dog House is a local institution with a long and colorful history. It is a funky, comfortable sort of place where generations of locals have gone for good talk, good service and good food. This is also a wonderful place to take kids—they are more than welcome, as is evidenced by the sign outside stating "Family entrance—kids welcome" and the crayons and paper that arrive once you get seated.

Though the kitchen doesn't offer a kid's menu, there are plenty of choices to please young palettes—mini-burgers, fish and chips, grilled cheese sandwiches, tacos—at very reasonable prices. The menu is also good for adults (try the Ghivetch, a hearty veggie stew), and the selection of beers and ales is top-notch.

The Dog House provides excellent complimentary maps of Whidbey Island.

GREAT TIMES ESPRESSO
360/678-5358; 12 Front St, Coupeville (on the waterfront)
Hours: Mon-Sat, 8 am-5:30 pm; Sun, 12-5:30 pm

Guests are encouraged to sit down and stay awhile at this funky wake-up stop. (Indeed, the comfortable, overstuffed furniture and random selection of reading material make it a slacker's paradise.) A good assortment of drinks and tasty pastries will keep the kids' taste buds happy while you down a hot cup of whatever. The outdoor seating area is delightful on a sunny morning.

ISLAND BAKERY
360/331-6282; 1675 E Main St, Freeland
Hours: Mon-Sat, 7:30 am-5 pm; lunch served 11:30 am-3:30 pm
Essentials: No credit cards; highchairs available

Healthy and delightful soups, sandwiches, salads and quiches, plus magnificent baked goodies. Located just off the highway in the tiny town of Freeland, this bakery/deli is well worth a stop on your way to or from Coupeville.

JAMPSA'S PENN COVE RESTAURANT
360/678-5474; 11 NW Coveland, Coupeville
Hours: Breakfast, lunch and dinner daily
Essentials: Credit cards; highchairs

This restaurant bills itself as a "fine family restaurant" and meets our criteria as such. The food (steaks, seafood, Penn Cove mussels, chowder) is good and moderately priced; the service is fast. Kid benefits include a child's menu, highchairs, crayons and coloring books. Adults will appreciate the family-sized booths.

KNEAD AND FEED
360/678-5431; 4 Front St, Coupeville (under Front St)
Hours: Mon-Fri, 10:30 am-3 pm; Sat-Sun, 10 am-4 pm
Essentials: Credit cards
This small, informal spot on the water has a great view and scrumptious baked goods, sandwiches, soups and salads. The people here go out of their way to accommodate families and make kids feel welcome, though children's menus and highchairs aren't offered (booster seats are available). The only real drawback of this place is that the seating is rather tight—not good for a fussy infant or super-active toddler.

LANGLEY VILLAGE BAKERY
360/221-3525; 221 Second St, Langley (at Langley Village)
Hours: Mon-Sat, 7:30 am-5 pm; Sun, 8:30 am-4 pm
Essentials: No credit cards
This is a good place to grab take-out food for a picnic. They offer a good deli selection, outstanding pesto pizza, hearty soups and delicious baked goods. The bakery itself is small, but if you can't wait to sample your treats, you'll find tables in the adjacent courtyard.

STAR BISTRO CAFE AND BAR
360/221-2627; 201 1/2 First St, Langley
Hours: Lunch Mon-Sun; dinner Tues-Sun; breakfast items
available on lunch menu, beginning at 11 am
Essentials: Credit cards; highchairs
Sitting on top of the Star Store, this cafe has it all: outstanding food, good atmosphere and reasonable prices. Don't be put off by the trendy appearance, kids are graciously welcomed. The kid's menu shows an appreciation for kids' preferences and includes word games and puzzles to distract hungry young diners. Highchairs and booster seats are available, and service is prompt. Our parent reviewers enjoyed the spinach salad, onion soup and pasta. On a nice summer evening, take advantage of the lovely outdoor dining area.

PLACES TO EAT WITHOUT KIDS
You're on vacation, too, right? If you can find a sitter, here are two places where you'll enjoy fine dining *sans enfants*.

CAFE LANGLEY
360/221-3090; 113 First St, Langley
Hours: Lunch and dinner daily (closed Tues during winter)

Essentials: Credit cards

This small, intimate restaurant is probably best visited without the children, unless yours are older and very civilized. Owners Shant and Ashavir Garibyan and the friendly staff prepare and serve an exquisite Middle Eastern meal, with daily specials such as fresh tuna and Copper River salmon. Your dining experience is likely to be well worth the price of a babysitter. Be sure to make reservations.

FRANCISCO'S

360/221-2728; 510 Cascade Ave, Langley
Hours: Dinner only, Wed-Sun; hours are inconsistent so call for current information
Essentials: Credit cards; highchairs

This is where the locals go for a fancy night out. Francisco's has the best view in town, so be sure to request a window seat. The food reviews have been a bit uneven in the past but, under the direction of a new chef, are becoming more and more favorable. Especially recommended are the pasta and seafood dishes. Expensive and leisurely dining—i.e., not for kids.

WHAT TO SEE AND DO

STROLL & BROWSE

Located in the middle of Whidbey Island, the charming seaside town of **Coupeville** is a delightful place to browse and learn about the region's history. Don't bother with an umbrella here—smack in the rain shadow of the Olympic Peninsula, this area has only 18.64 inches of precipitation annually, compared with 25 inches at the south end of Whidbey and 36 inches in Seattle.

Stop at Langley's tiny park in the middle of Main Street to show the kids the charming Georgia Gerber sculpture of a boy and his dog gazing out to sea.

Coupeville's architecture consists of many buildings that date back to the last half of the nineteenth century, and, for 10 cents, you can pick up a walking tour map to help you identify the most interesting historic landmarks (maps available at most stores on Front Street). A visit to the Island County Historical Society Museum (see "Museums") is a fun way to get a quick overview of the history of the town. (Ask about their historic walking tours offered during the summer). For a self-guided historical tour of the region, go to the National Park Service Office in Mariner's Court on Front Street and pick up a free brochure on the Ebey's Landing National Historical Reserve.

LANGLEY is a 6-mile drive from the Mukilteo-Clinton ferry, on Langley Road off Highway 525. Sitting on a bluff overlooking

Saratoga Passage, it is a pretty little town that is great fun to stroll with an espresso or ice cream cone in hand.

Over the last 20 years, Langley has evolved from a sleepy haven for big-city drop-outs seeking healthy living to a popular tourist destination, replete with art galleries, clothing and book stores, and a good assortment of restaurants. The Choochokum Festival in July is a delightful hodge-podge of street entertainment, good food, and arts and crafts booths; the Island County Fair in August is old-fashioned fun. Note: Expect a longer ferry wait if you visit Whidbey on the weekend these events take place—they are both very popular.

PARKS

COUPEVILLE TOWN PARK has a nice playground, a covered community kitchen area, tennis courts and a lovely walking trail along the bluff overlooking the cove. Kids (and adults) will be impressed by the cross-section of a gigantic old tree that dates back to Columbus' time.

Located one block west of the wharf on Coveland St in Coupeville.

FORT CASEY STATE PARK is located on the site of Fort Casey, one of the coast artillery posts established during the late 1890s for the defense of Puget Sound. Today, it is an expansive park, with playing fields, picnic areas, camping sites and many acres of fields and beaches to explore. The emplacements, fortifications and underground bunkers are still in place, offering bold school-age kids endless possibilities for hide-and-go-seek (flashlights will make it safer and more fun). The cannons now on display at the park are not the originals—they were brought by the navy as surplus from the Philippines in 1968.

There are surprisingly few fences and "Do Not Climb" signs, considering the number of places where a serious fall could occur, so supervise the kids closely. The parade grounds behind the bunkers are ideal for kite flyers, and the numerous short, easy hiking trails in the area are perfect for young adventurers. The 1860 lighthouse now houses a small museum describing the fort.

Located 3 miles south of Coupeville on Hwy 20, next to the Port Townsend/Keystone ferry landing; 360/678-4519.

FORT EBEY STATE PARK. Colonel Isaac Ebey, the first white settler on Whidbey Island, homesteaded the fertile land on the bluff above what has become Fort Ebey State Park. He held several government positions in the newly formed territory but suffered an untimely death at the hands of Tlingit Indians, who were seeking to avenge the murder of an Indian chief. The beach section of Ebey's property later became the state park, with campsites, picnic areas and a fishing lake (Lake Pondilla).

Fort Ebey was established in 1942 as part of the World War II armament buildup and was provided with two 6-foot guns for use against any enemy ships that entered Puget Sound. Kids will enjoy exploring the fortifications and gun battery, and will likely pick up a little history in the process. If that's not enough to keep them entertained, the 3 miles of hiking trails and 3 miles of beach will. Try the easy 1-mile hike from the parking area to Lake Pondilla. The tiny lake, less than 1/4 mile around, is stocked with bass and teeming with wildlife activity. Look for bald eagles nesting in nearby snags, as well as visiting deer, coyotes, raccoons, pheasants and foxes.

The views from this area are spectacular: On a clear day, hike out on the bluff and take in the panorama of the San Juan Islands, the Strait of Juan de Fuca and the Olympic Mountains.

Near the south entrance to the park, notice the Coupeville Outlying Landing Field, which was built during WWII to train Navy pilots and is still in use today. You may get lucky and see a jet landing or taking off.

Three miles west of Coupeville on Ebey Landing Rd; 360/678-4636.

EBEY'S NATIONAL LANDING HISTORICAL RESERVE (360/ 678-6084) adjoins Fort Ebey State Park. It's a preserved and protected 17,000-acre area of central Whidbey that provides an unbroken historic record of this rural community, from nineteenth-century exploration and settlement to the present. The 22 square miles of historic and scenic farmland, beaches, prairies and parks include 91 nationally registered historic structures and the cemetery containing Ebey's grave. Though 90 percent of the territory is privately owned, there is public access.

One of the nicest hikes on Whidbey Island can be found on the ridge trail that crosses Ebey's Prairie. To reach the trailhead, turn south on Shurman Road, and bear right to the parking pullout across from the cemetery. The trail takes walkers along the fence line between the original land owned by Isaac Ebey and the property his brother owned. If you decide to stroll through the cemetery as well, you'll not only see Isaac's grave, but an old blockhouse—one of the few remaining log forts from the time of the Puget Sound Indian wars.

KEYSTONE STATE PARK is home to one of the two scuba diving sites in Washington and is an excellent place to beachcomb and observe marine animals in their natural habitats.

Located 3 miles south of Coupeville near the Keystone Ferry Landing.

MEERKERK RHODODENDRON GARDEN is a 53-acre, beautifully maintained garden with many well-groomed paths for easy strolling.

To get there, take Hwy 525 to Honeymoon Bay Rd. Drive 7 miles to Meerkerk Lane, turn right, then left into the drive marked "Rhododendron Garden." Open daily during the summer. Cost: $2.

SOUTH WHIDBEY STATE PARK comprises 85 acres, including 2.5 miles of hiking trails and 2 miles of shoreline. The forest contains some of the last old-growth trees on the island.

A network of short, easy trails ($^3/_4$-1$^1/_2$ miles) allows you to walk among ancient Douglas fir, grand fir, moss-covered elders and large maples. The Forest Discovery Trail offers the most variety of trees; pick up a Forest Discovery Trail brochure at the parking lot for an educational, self-guided tour. On the Harry Wilbert Trail, across Smuggler's Cove Road, hikers pass the most ancient trees on the island. One cedar is 40 feet in circumference and estimated to be 500 years old. The Beach Trail and the Hobbit Trail wind through beautiful forest down to the pebbled beach.

Located 4 miles northwest of Freeland on Smuggler's Cover Rd. Open dawn to dusk daily, except between mid-November and mid-February, when it is open sporadically on weekends.

MUSEUMS

ISLAND COUNTY HISTORICAL SOCIETY MUSEUM has recently moved to a new building near the Coupeville Wharf. It houses Native American artifacts, various items from the homes of local pioneer families, personal histories of some of Whidbey's earliest settlers, and a doll collection. Next door, you'll find the Alexander blockhouse (built in 1855) and an exhibit of Indian dugout canoes.

Alexander & Front streets; 360/678-3310. Open Fri-Mon, 11 am-4 pm, during winter; Mon-Fri, 11 am-5 pm, and Sat-Sun, 10 am-5 pm, during summer. Free.

SOUTH WHIDBEY HISTORICAL MUSEUM is another fun place to learn about early Whidbey. It features an old-time kitchen, early photographs, antique tools, vintage clothing, Native American artifacts, prehistoric woolly mammoth bones (a big hit with kids), and a variety of memorabilia from pioneer families who settled on the island. The gift shop carries books and local crafts. *312 Second St, Langley; 360/321-4696. Open Sat-Sun, 1-4 pm. No charge.*

ASSORTED FUN

BLUE FOX DRI-VIN MOVIE THEATER. Remember how thrilled you were when your parents took you to drive-in movies? Put the kids in their jammies, grab some blankets and pillows, and seize this endangered opportunity!

On the corner of Hwy 20 & Monroe Landing Rd, 2 miles south of Oak Harbor; 360/675-5667. Cost: $4/adult; free 11 and under.

BRATTLAND GO-KARTS. Just a spin around the track in one of these high-powered, low-ridin' machines may be your youngster's rite of passage from big-wheels and bumper cars to driver's ed.

On the corner of Hwy 20 & Monroe Landing Rd, 2 miles south of Oak Harbor; 360/675-5667. Open Sat & Sun.

GREENBANK LOGANBERRY FARM is a fun outing, regardless of the weather. This farm is the largest single producer of loganberries in the country and the maker of the popular loganberry liqueur, "Whidbey's." You may want to take a short, self-guided tour, which includes information about the harvesting and processing of the berries, or you may choose to simply stroll or picnic (tables are abundant) on the beautiful grounds. There's a complimentary tasting bar where adults can sample "Whidbey's," and a small shop that sells delicious loganberry preserves and syrups. In the summer, visitors can pick and purchase berries.

Located 1/4 mile from the town of Greenbank at the intersection of Hwy 525 & Wonn Rd. Open daily 10 am-4:30 pm. Free.

JOHN VANDERZICHT MEMORIAL POOL is a first-class facility in Oak Harbor that you might consider visiting if the rain is soaking your beach fun.

2299 20th NW, Oak Harbor; 360/675-7665. Open daily. Cost: $2/adults, $1.75/youth, free for children 3 & under.

SHELLFISHING is a popular activity on the beaches and in the shallow waters of Whidbey Island—soft and hard-shelled crabs, Pacific oysters and mussels are abundant. Mussels are especially easy to harvest, if you can get locals to direct you to the right beach. As of January 1, 1994, it is necessary to obtain a license to gather shellfish on any Washington beach. Licenses are readily available at local stores. For up-to-date information regarding shellfishing, phone the Washington State Department of Fisheries at 206/902-2200.

There is a danger of shellfish poisoning from a microscopic organism that can turn the water red (called "red tide"). It is a highly toxic organism for humans that even cooking doesn't eliminate, so be sure to call the Red Tide Hotline (800/562-5632) before venturing forth with buckets and shovels.

CALENDAR

JULY: Choochokum Arts and Crafts Fair, Langley
Greenbank Farm Loganberry Festival
AUGUST: Dixieland Jazz Festival, Oak Harbor
Arts and Crafts Festival, Coupeville
Island County Fair, Langley

RESOURCES

ISLAND TRANSIT (360/678-7771 or 360/321-6688), the bus system on Whidbey, is extensive and free. A bus ride with your child is an easy way to sit back and enjoy the countryside together. Buses run Monday through Saturday between the Clinton ferry dock, Langley, Freeland, Greenback, the Keystone ferry dock, Coupeville and Oak Harbor. Schedules are available throughout the island.

CENTRAL WHIDBEY CHAMBER OF COMMERCE
P.O. Box 152, Coupeville, 98239
360/678-5434

LANGLEY CHAMBER OF COMMERCE
P.O. Box 403, Langley, 98260
360/321-6765

OLYMPIC PENINSULA

The Olympic Peninsula is a 7215 square-mile area between the Pacific Ocean and Hood Canal encompassing about every kind of geography, wildlife and climate to be found in the state. Rainfall varies from 15 inches annually in the sun belt at Sequim on the north side to a perpetually moist 200 inches in the rain forests of the Olympic National Park. It is a richly endowed chunk of nature, too much to be digested at one time. Fortunately, the Peninsula is reasonably close to the Seattle metropolitan area. In two hours driving time from Seattle, you can be nibbling away at it.

GETTING THERE

There are many ways to get to the Peninsula. The most direct routes from Seattle are the Seattle-Winslow ferry from downtown Seattle and the Edmonds-Kingston ferry from Edmonds, twenty minutes north of Seattle. There is also a two-ferry route: the Mukilto-Whidbey Island ferry and then from Whidbey Island the Keystone-Port Townsend ferry.

If you want to avoid a ferry ride, you can exit I-5 south at Olympia and follow the U.S. 101 turn off to connect to Highway 8 to Aberdeen. This becomes Highway 12.

From Portland, take U.S. 30 north along the Columbia River to Astoria. Take the toll bridge across the Columbia from Astoria to Megler. Follow U.S. 101 to Aberdeen-Hoquiam. Continue north on U.S. 101 to circle the Olympic Peninsula.

ROADSIDE ATTRACTIONS. Depending on your destination, the town of **Gardiner** is worth a detour. On Hwy 101 on the way to Sequim, look for signs to the boat launch at Gardiner. Turn onto the Old Gardiner Highway. Follow the road to the boat launch and then turn left at the boat launch and go up the hill. Soon you'll notice carved fence posts and then trolls, castle-like houses, dragons, goblins and other creatures. These homes are private but you can walk up the road to give the kids a good view of this amazing place. The detour will take about 10 minutes.

See also **Kitsap Peninsula:** What to See and Do.

PLACES TO STAY

MANRESA CASTLE

360/385-5750 or 800/732-1281; 7th & Sheridan, P.O. Box 564, Port Townsend, 98368
Rates: Moderate to expensive
Essentials: Credit cards
Extras: Buffet breakfast; private bath, TV

Built by a Prussian baker who amassed a fortune by supplying bread and crackers to ships that put into harbor in Port Townsend and designed to resemble a medieval castle of Europe, Manresa Castle sits on a cliff overlooking the town of Port Townsend. Because it looks like a castle, turret and all, it is a grand place to bring a child. (A door marked 'Dungeon' near the end of a dimly lit hall adds to the illusion.) Parents will appreciate the fine antique furnishings and the majestic view.

PARENT COMMENTS: *"If you have a child who prefers castles to camping, this is your place. I spent one night here with my five-year-old daughter and it was the perfect 'fru-fru' weekend."*

BISHOP VICTORIAN
360/385-6122; 714 Washington Street, Port Townsend, 98368
Rates: Moderate
Essentials: Credit cards, crib
Extras: Kitchens; free continental breakfast; pets ($10/night with prior approval)

In a town awash with Victorian charm, Bishop Victorian is a rare and wonderful treat—a hotel that truly welcomes kids. Games and playpens are available and each room has its own stuffed animal. There are kitchens in each room, so you don't have to go out for every meal. The two suites have ample room— two bedrooms with double or queen beds plus sofa beds. Every morning fruit and pastries are served on the second floor landing. The three-story brick building is well-situated just a block from the waterfront.

PARENT COMMENTS: *"Both the kids and the parents were well-taken care of. They gave our girls crayons and games and were very helpful about suggesting good restaurants and places of interest to visit. If only every town had a hotel for families like the Bishop Victorian!"*

BAY COTTAGE
360/385-2035; 4346 S Discovery Rd, Port Townsend, 98368
Rates: Moderate
Essentials: No credit cards
Extras: Kitchens; feather beds

The well-kept cottages sit on the edge of Discovery Bay, just six miles from Port Townsend. The beach is fine for swimming, gathering sand dollars, digging for clams and bonfires. Furnishings are in the antiques and feather beds category, so a rambunctious preschooler might not be a good idea.

Fully-equipped kitchens come stocked with the basics, including pancake mix and cereal, and often fresh fruit and homemade cookies. Each cottage has its own picnic basket, binoculars and library.

◄◄ **PARENT COMMENTS:** *"Owner Susan Atkins goes out of her way to make families feel welcome. Pure relaxation. The feather bed was a real treat!"*

SALMONBERRY FARM
360/385-1517; 2404 35th St, Port Townsend 98368
Rates: Moderate
Essentials: Credit cards
Extras: Washer/Dryer; woodstove; breakfast items supplied; pets OK, horses may be boarded.

The setting is peacefully rural with the historic district of Port Townsend just minutes away. Best of all, unlike many B & B's, this one genuinely welcomes children. Adjacent to the farm there are wooded trails for exploring and owners Meg and Doug Mason suggest you bring your bikes to enjoy North Beach and Fort Worden State Park.

The three-room fully furnished suite sits above the carriage house/stable (your horse is welcome also). There is a queen-size bed in the bedroom, a hide-a-bed in the living room and a full bath with a washer/dryer. The suite can accommodate four-six guests. They don't serve you breakfast, but the fully-equipped kitchen includes farm-fresh eggs and hot bread or muffins delivered daily.

◄◄ **PARENT COMMENTS:** *"Not really a B&B—you have the place to yourself. The location was idyllic and our hosts very cordial."*

THE ECOLOGIC PLACE
360/385-3077; 10 Beach Drive, Nordland, 98358
Rates: Moderate
Essentials: Credit cards
Extras: Kitchens; wood stoves

The eight rustic cedar cabins, situated around a lodge in a meadow above the beach, vary in size and accommodate from two to six guests each. They have relatively new bathrooms, kitchens and wood stoves and are equipped with linens, towels, dishes and basic utensils. Cabins have views of Oak Bay and the Olympic mountains to the west and Mt. Rainier to the southeast.

The Ecologic Place is a good place to relax and ride bikes, walk or play on the three miles of driftwood-strewn beach, explore the salt marsh. As a wildlife refuge with special attention to ground-nesting birds, pets are not allowed. Bird books, binoculars and a telescope are available to guests. Indoors, the lodge has a supply of books, board games and a piano. For information about nearby Port Townsend, see "What to See and Do" below.

PARENT COMMENTS *"The Ecologic Place is very quiet and blends well in the beautiful natural surrounds. The idea is to make your own fun—teenagers might get restless. We liked going into Port Townsend to browse and eat. An easy way to get the kids to a beautiful beach without the long drive to the coast."*

FORT WORDEN STATE PARK OFFICERS' QUARTERS

360/385-4730; 200 Battery Way, Port Townsend, 98368
Rates: Inexpensive to moderate
Essentials: No credit cards
Extras: Kitchens; cafeteria; tennis courts; fishing rentals

Fort Worden State Park is a 448-acre park located one mile north of Port Townsend on wooded hillsides overlooking the Strait of Juan de Fuca. Eighteen stately two-story houses, once officers' quarters at the turn of the century, house visitors. Most of the houses are completely refurbished, with carpeting and reproductions of Victorian furniture. The unrefurbished units have wood and linoleum floors with furnishings that aren't quite so nice but fully adequate. All accommodations are comfortable with good beds and most have fireplaces. Bed linens and towels are provided and the houses are heated to be comfortable all year. Most of the houses are large enough for two families (or even three) to share, which brings the cost well into the "inexpensive" range.

The kitchens are large and fully equipped. If you don't feel like cooking every meal, you can eat at the cafeteria with advance notice. Or, a short trip into Port Townsend offers several good dining possibilities (see "Places to Eat" below).

Fort Worden is a fine place for a family to bring their bikes. The beach is good for romping, but the water is too cold for all but the hardiest swimmers. The highlight is the old fort itself, complete with gunmounts, bunkers and cliffs to explore.

These facilities fill fast: plan to make reservations one year in advance. Cancellations must be three weeks prior to scheduled date of arrival or deposit will be forfeited unless the unit is re-rented. There is a $10 fee for cancelling.

PARENT COMMENTS: *"We loved the spacious rooms. Two families with a total of five young children shared a refurbished six-bedroom house for four days in July and had a ball. Remember to bring flashlights for the kids—they are essential for hide-and-go-seek in* *the maze of corridors in the bunkers at the park. And bring kites to fly on the parade grounds."*

OLYMPIC PARK INSTITUTE
360/928-3720; HC 62, Box 9T, Port Angeles, 98362
Rates: Moderate
Essentials: Credit cards
Extras: All meals; full educational program

The award-winning Olympic Park Institute offers educational vacations for families to learn about the park's inter-tidal life, rainforest, marine mammals, Native American culture and history. A non-profit organization based at historic Rosemary Inn at Lake Crescent, under a cooperative agreement with the National Park Service, the programs teach 4000 people a year, including many school groups during the school year.

During the summer some sessions are two days mid-week, some are one day and several are weekend sessions intended for all ages. Topics include Nature Photography, Birds and Bugs, Art in the Wilds, Seashore Safari, Critters and Creatures and Things that Go Bump in the Night. The season runs from May to October.

The Institute recommends the family sessions for ages four and up, although they will allow younger ages if proper supervision is provided. The cost for a typical weekend program, including room, board and most materials, runs about $175 per adult and $85 per child.

PARENT COMMENTS: *"It was great fun to be learning alongside our kids and to meet other families with similar interests. The instructors were first-rate and the facilities excellent. A wonderful program in a breathtakingly beautiful setting."*

LAKE CRESCENT LODGE
360/928-3211; 416 Lake Crescent Rd, HC 62, Box 11, Port Angeles, 98362
Rates: Moderate
Essentials: Credit cards; cribs
Extras: Restaurant; row boat rentals; fireplaces in four cottages; pets OK in cottages

This national park concession is open only from late April through October. Located 25 miles west of Port Angeles on U.S. 101, the lodge was built in 1915. With majestic peaks rising from the shores, and the color of the water in the 642-feet-deep lake varying from turquoise to green, Lake Crescent is breathtakingly beautiful in the summer.

Children are not allowed to stay in the rooms in the historic lodge but that's okay, you wouldn't want to stay in there with kids—too cramped and quaint. The cabins and the motel units are the best accommodations for families and they are clean and comfortable, but not fancy. There are no kitchens or refrigerators but you'll have a fireplace. (Cabin 34 is rumored to be the place President Franklin D. Roosevelt stayed in 1937 when he was debating whether or not to create Olympic National Park).

On very warm days, swimming in the cold water can be fun for the hardy and there is a nice beach at the lodge. For warmer swimming, it is not far to drive to the hot springs at Sol Duc. In addition to swimming, guests can boat, fish from the dock, go on short hikes, attend evening nature programs, or just use the facility as a base for excursions into the Olympic National Park.

PARENT COMMENTS: *"After camping in the rain, Lake Crescent Lodge looked very nice for a couple of nights."*
"We like to go here for a weekend in late September. We don't swim at that time of the year, but the weather is usually good and we do lots of hiking."
" No TVs or telephones! Hurrah!"

LOG CABIN RESORT
360/928-3325; 3183 E. Beach Rd., Port Angeles, 98363
Rates: Inexpensive to moderate
Essentials: Credit cards
Extras: Restaurant; small store; kitchens in some cabins; boat rentals; hiking trails; pets OK in some units

This is an old-fashioned family resort where the chief attraction is the natural beauty and slow pace. The resort consists of a collection of cabins, motel rooms adjacent to the lodge, A-frame chalets, trailer sites and walk-in camping sites. It sits on 17 acres on the north (sunny) shore of Lake Crescent inside the Olympic National Park. The resort is open from late April to October 1.

Individual rustic cabins (built in 1928) are the best accommodations for a family. They have a lake view, double and single beds and a front porch with chairs where you can read away the hours. Most have kitchens; bring your own cooking utensils.

There is a good swimming area that gets plenty of sun and a small play area. The restaurant in the lodge is very good but moderately expensive; you will want a kitchen in your cabin. The Sol Duc Hot Springs are only 12 miles away if you want to swim/soak in warmer waters. See Sol Duc Resort below for more details.

PARENT COMMENTS: *"Emphasize the word "rustic" when you describe this place."*
"My husband and I thought the water was cold for swimming, but our two preschoolers spent all afternoon puttering in the lake."
"Service was warm and friendly, the setting beautiful. The kids fished, mom and dad read, we all relaxed."

JUAN DE FUCA COTTAGES
360/683-4433; 182 Marine Drive, Sequim, 98382
Rates: Moderate to expensive
Essentials: Credit cards
Extras: Kitchens; TV, VCR, free movies; whirlpool baths; fireplace in the two-room cottage; pets OK with prior approval

Located seven miles north of Sequim on Dungeness Bay and the Strait of Juan de Fuca, these six well-kept cabins are comfortable and tastefully done. Each cottage has a fully-equipped kitchen, a whirlpool bath and a bay or mountain view. The two-room cottage also has a lovely fireplace. There's a nice big yard in front for playing and reading and nearby Dungness Spit beckons to explorers.

PARENT COMMENTS: *" First-class accomodations in a lovely setting. We brought bikes to explore the area."*
"Our ten-year-old loved the Jacuzzi in our cottage!"

SOL DUC HOT SPRINGS
360/327-3583; PO Box 2169, Port Angeles, 98362
Rates: Moderate
Essentials: Credit cards; crib
Extras: Kitchens in some cabins; swimming (three hot sulphur pools and one freshwater pool); pets OK

Located 12 miles off Highway 101, between Port Angeles and Forks, this was a famous resort in the days when it was popular to visit such spots for the waters. It lost its charm over the years and became downright dismal, so we were pleased when new owners set out to restore it. Unfortunately, the restoration was done with little imagination or charm. If you expect natural springs in a sylvan, pristine setting, you will be disappointed. The 32 cabins are minimal and we do not mean charmingly rustic. They have thin walls and sit close together near the parking lot.

On the plus side, the hot pools are a novel experience. The hot springs consist of three tiled sulphur pools (98 to 104 degrees). There is also a freshwater pool. The resort is located at the trailhead for several beautiful hikes. (Dogs not allowed on trails in the National Park.)

The outdoor burger stand makes an easy meal and the dining room is quite good, with a fairly-priced children's menu. Keep in mind, though, there are several other more appealing places to stay that are within an easy drive of the springs and you do not have to be a guest to use the springs. Open weekends for day use beginning in April, for lodging from mid-May to the end of September.

> **PARENT COMMENTS:** *"We have been coming here since I was a child and it is great to see the place repainted and generally spruced up. We like to visit in early summer when it is less crowded. Our eight-year-old son didn't like the hot springs, so he stayed in the cooler freshwater pool."*
>
> *" We were shocked at the ugliness of the lodgings — a shame in such a spectacular setting. Prefab cabins are deposited military-fashion in a compound that is barren of trees. We were particularly offended that we had to pay just to get in the pool area to watch our children swim."*

LAKE QUINAULT LODGE

#94396

800/562-6672 or 360/288-2571; South Shore Rd, PO Box 7, Quinault, 98575

Rates: Moderate

Essentials: Credit cards; crib

one nite

2 3/4 2 5

Extras: Restaurant; indoor pool, hot tub, sauna; bikes; game room; nature programs (spring and summer); playground, hiking trails, 9-hole golf course; babysitting (by pre-arrangement); pets OK ($10 per night in Annex only)

The setting of this lodge, on a beautiful lake in the middle of the rain forest, is one of the best on the Olympic Peninsula. The lobby of the main lodge, with its huge fireplace, rustic decor and Indian art, is charming. The least expensive rooms, located in the main lodge, either share a bathroom between two rooms or have no bath, with facilities down the hall. Some of these rooms have views of the parking lot rather than the lake. Lakeside Inn rooms, built in 1923 and recently remodelled, have private baths. Newer yet are the "gas fireplace units," which offer a queen size bed and a queen hide-a-bed. The lodge offers lots of special deals — mid-week, or off-season—but there is a two-night minimum on weekends and a three-night minimum on holiday weekends and school vacations.

Lake Quinault Lodge is obviously geared to families. Adjacent to the pool there is a game room with equipment for horseshoes, volleyball, frisbee and badminton, as well as pinball, ping pong and video games, pop and candy machines. Hiking trails through the rain forest of $^1/_2$, $1^1/_2$ and 3 miles start at the lodge; maps are at the front desk. Also at the front desk are lobby games, puzzles and arrangements for sitters. Nature programs and canoe and rowboat rentals are available in the summer. The playground has swings, a slide, see-saw and rings.

The dining room, located in the main lodge, has fair to good food, nice personnel, and slow service. Window seats are the best because you can watch the hummingbirds feed. A good alternative to using the restaurant is the bar, which offers carry-out sandwiches and drinks.

Nearby alternatives to eating at Quinault are very limited.

PARENT COMMENTS: *"The service in the restaurant was incredibly pleasant and incredibly slow. Waiters and waitresses are very nice to kids, but the setting is difficult. The gift shop is located right with the restaurant: millions of breakables are begging to be broken by curious little hands."*

"A nice place for kids — plenty to keep them busy, although we were sorry to see video games in such a tranquil setting."

LOCHAERIE RESORT
360/288-2215; 638 North Shore Rd, Amanda Park, 98526
Rates: Inexpensive
Essentials: No credit cards
Extras: Kitchens; fireplaces, pets $10/night

Established in 1926 on the sloping north shore of Lake Quinault, the five charming cabins are named after peaks in the Olympic range and each is unique. Christie (sleeps three) is closest to the lake and is in the highest demand, but it is down some steps and probably not suitable for a family with a toddler. Storm King, a large two-bedroom cottage built in 1936, has a river rock fireplace, a bedroom loft that hangs right over the lake, a large porch and sleeps five comfortably. Colonel Bob (sleeps six) is the most recently built (and most expensive at $65/night). It sits near the beach and works well for families with school-age kids. The owners are very helpful about recommending the best cabin to suit the ages of your children. Note that the first night deposit is refunded only with cancellation seven days in advance and Storm King and Colonel Bob have a two-night minimum. Open year round.

PARENT COMMENTS: *"A real find and the right price. The well-preserved cabins sit unobtrusively amid gorgeous natural* *beauty. We stayed three days and had a grand time exploring Olympic National Park."*

THE RESORT AT PORT LUDLOW

800/732-1239 or 360/437-2222; 9483 Oak Bay Rd.,
Port Ludlow, 98365
Rates: Expensive
Essentials: Credit cards; crib
Extras: Restaurant; TV; kitchens; indoor and outdoor pools,
sauna, hot tub; boat and fishing rentals; playground; bicycle
rentals; golf, squash, tennis; sailing charters in summer; organized
activities for kids

The Resort at Port Ludlow has an indoor and outdoor swimming pool and jacuzzi, golf course, seven tennis courts, supervised outdoor program for kids. Rooms at the resort have twin or queen beds and private baths. Apartments have living room, fully-equipped kitchen, dining room, fireplace, private deck and view. The units are individually-owned and therefore decor varies but is uniformly comfortable. Several families could share one of the larger units with ease — a good way to cut down the cost.

Grounds are large and well-maintained and there are lots of room for children to explore and roam. There are paved bicycle paths, nature hikes, and lots of water sports: boating, fishing, clamming and crabbing. During the summer, a recreation director arranges field games, water games on the lagoon and trips to nearby places like the Olympic Game Farm, Port Townsend, and Olympic National Park.

The Harbormaster is the name of the resort's restaurant. It is moderately expensive standard steak fare. A better alternative at the resort is the deli at the golf course, which serves hamburgers, hot dogs, and sandwiches. Port Townsend, 20 miles away, offers ample opportunities for diversion and meals (See "Places to Eat" and "What to See and Do" below).

PARENT COMMENTS: *"We left spouses at home and spent two nights here with four kids. The atmosphere was a little too golfy-condo for the grown-ups but the pool and beach were great for the kids and the accommodations very comfortable."*
"Don't expect woods."
"We visited in the fall with our kids ages five and nine. The indoor pool was nice and we enjoyed exploring Port Townsend."

KALALOCH LODGE
(see Washington Coast-Places to Stay)

PLACES TO EAT

FERINO'S PIZZERIA
360/385-0840; Kivley Center, Port Hadlock
Hours: Lunch, dinner Wed-Mon
Essentials: Credit cards; highchairs
    If you are staying around Port Townsend or Port Ludlow, it is worth driving to Port Hadlock for this scrumptious pizza—crisp, tasty crust, piled with fresh toppings.

KHU LARB THAI
360/385-5023; 225 Adams St, Port Townsend
Hours: Lunch, dinner daily
Essentials: Credit cards; highchairs
    Well-prepared Thai food is served in a relaxed setting well-suited to family dining at Khu Larb Thai. Noodle dishes are especially popular with kids (be careful to order dishes for kids with "no stars" to avoid hot spices). Chicken Satay (marinated chicken pieces grilled on a stick) is also usually well-liked by tykes. Grown-ups will appreciate the interesting soups.

ELEVATED ICE CREAM CO.
627 Water St., Port Townsend
    The place to go for a holiday treat—yummy homemade ice cream, chocolates, Italian ices, espresso.

THE PUBLIC HOUSE
360/385-6532;1038 Water St, Port Townsend
Hours: Lunch, dinner daily
Essentials: Credit cards; highchairs
    The spacious room works well with kids and the food—seafood grill, steaks, fresh pasta—is exceptionally well prepared. Moderate prices, plus a kids' menu with the usual burger, fish and chips, PB&J. Nice bar for the grown-ups, too.

THE LANDFALL
360/385-5814; 412 Water St, Port Townsend
Hours: Breakfast, lunch daily, dinner Wed-Sun
Essentials: No credit cards; highchairs available
    Overlooks the marina. Funky and cozy—good burgers, fish and chips, some Mexican fare and seafood.

SALAL CAFE
360/385-6532; 634 Water St, Port Townsend

Hours: Breakfast, lunch Weds-Sun
Essentials: No credit cards, checks ok; highchairs
   A light, cheerful deli—great place for vegetarians. Breakfasts
are best. A typical kids' plate includes a grilled cheese sandwich
in the shape of a heart, yogurt for dessert, fresh fruit ($2.95).

BURRITO DEPOT
609 Washington, Port Townsend
Essentials: No credit cards; highchairs available
   Eat in or take out. Very reasonable. Good kid food.

HIWAY 101 DINER
360/683-3388; 392 W Washington, Sequim
Hours: Breakfast, lunch dinner every day
Essentials: No credit cards; highchairs available
   The 50's theme (neon and the back end of a '56 T-bird that is
the CD player) and the hefty, juicy burgers and outstanding pizza
will make everybody happy. Watch out, service is sometimes slow.

OAK TABLE CAFE
360/683-2179; 292 W Bell St, Sequim
Hours: Breakfast and lunch daily, early dinner Fri and Sat
Essentials: No credit cards, checks ok; highchairs
   Go before 8 pm on Friday and Saturday nights and you'll find
a homestyle, delicious meal—seafood, mashed potatoes, roast
beef, etc. Breakfast and lunch are also well worth a visit—giant
puffy apple pancakes, huge omelettes, quiches, soups, sandwiches, salads.
   Moderate prices, generous servings, fast, friendly service.

JEAN'S MINI MART AND DELI
360/683-6727; 20 Carlsborg Rd, Sequim
Hours: Breakfast, lunch, Mon-Fri
Essentials: No credit cards
   Stop by for the marvelous homemade soups, delectible desserts,
generous sandwiches. In the morning there's fresh-out-of-the-
oven muffins, cinnamon rolls, pecan sticky buns. Yum.

FIRST STREET HAVEN
360/457-0352; 107 E 1st St, Port Angeles
Hours: Breakfast, lunch Mon-Sat, brunch Sun
Essentials: No credit cards; highchairs available
   Fresh, generous salads and pasta dishes are the main attraction:
the fajitas are good too. Reasonable prices, good service.

WHAT TO SEE AND DO

PORT TOWNSEND

Port Townsend is called the Victorian seaport. It is a National Historical Landmark on the northeastern tip of the Olympic Peninsula. It is about a one-hour drive from the Seattle-Winslow Ferry and the Port Angeles-Victoria Ferry and just 45 minutes from the Edmonds-Kingston Ferry.

The more than 70 Victorian residences, old forts, parks and monuments scattered throughout the town are the main attraction. Many commercial buildings have been restored and contain shops offering the work of local artists. Pick up a map at the Visitor's Information Center for a self-guided walking tour.

At the end of Front Street there are several attractions of interest to children. The **John Pope Marine Park**, with carved dolphins, a swing set and picnic tables sits right on the beach. Nearby at the **Jefferson County Historical Society Museum** kids will enjoy seeing the original jail cell on display and reading stories about how prisoners tried to excape. The museum is located across from City Hall.

Across the street from City Hall you can't miss the **Carousel of the Olympic Sea**, a fantastic, magical creation built by William H. Dentzel, a fifth generation carousel maker. Dentzel's work is characterized by simple wooden animals with a hand or foot-powered mechanism rather than an electrical motor. Installed in the summer of 1994, the figures on this carousel include an orca whale leaping, a grizzly bear, a salmon and a sea cucumber. Students at Port Townsend high school helped in the construction and painting of the carousel.

Port Townsend is a charming place for a romantic getaway but if you bring the kids along, you'll probably want to soon head out of town to the many parks and beaches in the area.

FORT WORDEN STATE PARK, just outside Port Townsend, has endless parade grounds for kite flying, picnicking and playing, as well as overnight accommodations in the Officers' Quarters (see Places to Stay). A pleasant mile-long beach walk beckons between Fort Warden and Point Hudson. The **Centrum Center for Arts and Creative Education** has educational programs and workshops for writers and musicians and a series of festivals and concerts throughout the year (Centrum Festival information: 360/385-3102). Visitors can often watch artists-in-residence at work. The **Cable House Canteen**, located across from the park and open only during the summer, is a good spot to grab a burger or fish and chips.

FORT FLAGLER STATE PARK, a few miles out of Port Townsend, has over 100 campsites, along with many hiking trails and picnic sites on over 783 acres. Boats are also available for rent. Between Flagler and Port Townsend, **Old Fort Townsend State Park** has a pretty, secluded picnic area, a small campground and a lovely outlook.

SEQUIM

Between Port Townsend and Port Angeles on Hwy 101, lies the driest coastal area north of Southern California. This oasis of sun has grown rapidly in the last few years as a retirement center, but has much to offer younger visitors.

THE MANI MASTODON SITE, where a team of archaeologists from Washington State University is collecting evidence that early man hunted mastodons, is closed now, but the massive bones can be seen at the **Sequim-Dungeness Museum**. This fine museum has exhibits spanning 12,000 years of local history from Ice Age Man to the early Klallam Indians.

360/683-8110; Sequim. Open noon-4 pm, Wed -Sun, May 1 to October 1, winter hours vary.

THE OLYMPIC GAME FARM near Sequim, a 90-acre preserve for animals used in wildlife films and television shows, is worth a visit. Two loop drives allow viewing of 56 species of animals including wolves, bison, bears, and even Siberian tigers. Our parent reviewers reported an enthusiastic response from the kids and a so-so vote from the adults. You'll have the opportunity to purchase loaves of bread at the front gate, where you'll also be told to remain in your car. Kids will thrill at the sight of free-ranging llamas, zebras and buffalo coming right up to slobber on the car windows.

360/683-4293; 383 Ward Rd, Sequim. Open daily in summer 9 a.m.-dusk; winter 9 a.m.-4 p.m. $6/ adult, $4/ages 5 to 12. Winter admission is $4/adult, $3/youth.

Bring along binoculars to spot the abundant wildlife on the Peninsula.

DUNGENESS SPIT, formed by eroding soil, wind, and water currents, stretches for 5-^{1}/2 miles out into the Strait of Juan de Fuca. It breaks the rough sea waves to form a quiet bay, sand and pebble beaches, and tide-flats. The area is rich with wildlife so bring binoculars! An easy ^{1}/2 mile trail takes visitors through upland forest to an overlook on the bluff. Beyond the bluff the trail becomes a 5 1/2 mile beach walk to the end of Dungeness Spit. Visitors are welcome to dig clams but oysters are privately owned. The best time to see shorebirds and waterfowl is during the fall and spring migration. Harbor seals are there year round. Pets, bikes, fires, camping not permitted, okay at the adjacent Dungeness Recreaton Area.

360/457-8451. Open to the public during daylight hours throughout the year. Cost is $2 /family.

PORT ANGELES

While Port Townsend capitalizes on the past, most visitors come to Port Angeles because it is a gateway to Victoria and the vast and beautiful Olympic National Park.

While in town consider a stop at the **Arthur D. Feiro Marine Laboratory** on the Municipal Pier, where curious kids can hold sea stars, anemones and sea cucumbers. It has a good collection of marine life, including touch tanks and a giant octopus.

Open daily 10 am - 8 pm mid-June to Labor Day; Other months noon-4pm Sat & Sun. Cost: $1/adult, $.50/child 6-12.

FORT HAYDEN, in nearby Salt Creek County Park, has gun emplacements, bunkers, playgrounds and rich tidal pools at Tongue Point Marine Sanctuary.

If you want to spend a day in **Victoria** (a 1 1/2 hour ferry ride), walk on the Coho ferry (cars are a nuisance on a day trip to this compact city). For ferry schedules call Black Ball Transport at either 360/457-4991 or 206/622-2222. (They do not take reservations). Another alternative in the summer only is the faster (and more expensive) Victoria Express, 800/633-1589, reservations advised.

AT OLYMPIC NATIONAL PARK VISITOR CENTER in Port Angeles pick up a list of suggested family hikes and visit the **Pioneer Memorial Museum** and its Discovery Room, just for kids. Several books of interest to children visiting the area are on sale at the museum.

Open daily 8 am- 8 pm, July to September; other months 8am-4pm.

NEAH BAY

On the northwestern tip of the Olympic Peninsula, Neah Bay is home to the Makah Indians, a tribe that traces its ancestry as far back as 1000 B.C. More than 500 years ago a mud slide buried five Makah houses at the village of Ozette, 12 miles south of Cape Flattery. By 1970, tides had washed away enough soil to expose the Makah artifacts. That year a team of archeologists from Washington State University began a dig that lasted 11 years and produced more than 97 percent of all Northwest Coast Indian artifacts to date. The best are on display at the outstanding **Makah Cultural and Research Center**, which includes artifacts from the Ozette dig as well as other sites, full-scale reproductions of canoes and a longhouse. Highly recommended. *360/645-2711; Neah Bay. Open daily 10 am-5 pm, September 15 through May 31, closed Mon & Tues.*

THE GREAT OUTDOORS

A fitting introduction to the majestic beauty of the area is a drive to **Hurricane Ridge**, 17 miles from Port Angeles. You go from sea level to the top of the world in only a half-hour drive, and one-mile gain in elevation. At the road end there is an easy 1 1/4 mile hike on an asphalt path that takes you to the top of the hill and a spectacular 360-degree view. The best time to visit the top of the ridge is late July through October, unless you are looking for snow.

In the winter the Ridge has the only downhill skiing in the area—two rope tows and one poma. The visitor center provides maps of cross-country ski trails. On weekends you can catch a bus from downtown Port Angeles to Hurricane Ridge for $8 roundtrip (360/452-4511).

At scenic **Lake Crescent**, 22 miles west of Port Angeles, there is a short, easy (2 1/2 miles round trip) trail through old-growth forest to the 98-foot **Marymere Falls**. To get to the trail head, take Highway 101 to Lake Crescent. Turn right on the road into a large parking lot that marks the start of the trail.

At Lake Crescent you can also take a 90-minute interpretive cruise on the **M/V Storm King**, a 64-foot simulated paddle wheeler, with narration provided by an Olympic Park naturalist. Cruises depart at 10am, noon, 2pm, and 4pm on weekends in May and October and at the same times daily during the summer. Tickets are sold at the Shadow Mountain Store, near milepost 233 on Highway 101. Cost is $15 for adults and $10 for children ages 6 through 17. Families get a special deal—one child is allowed to board free, regardless of age, for each paying adult. You can just pick up tickets at the Shadow Mountain Store at least a half-hour before departure but reservations are advised a week ahead. Call 360/452-4520.

SOL DUC HOTSPRINGS, is up a 12-mile road from Highway

101 just west of Lake Crescent. There are overnight facilities or you can go just to soak and swim. See Places to Stay below for more details.

CAPE FLATTERY, just beyond Neah Bay, is the northwestern most point of land in the mainland United States and 66 miles from Port Angeles on Highway 112. There's a half-mile trail through the forest to a view of the ocean, Tatoosh Island and the lighthouse that sits on the island. Don't miss a visit to the outstanding Makah Museum (see Neah Bay above).

One of the most interesting and scenic hikes on the Peninsula departs from the **Lake Ozette** Campground. There are two trails, Sand Point and Cape Alava. For kids the preferable trail is Sand Point because it is shorter (6 miles roundtrip), all on boardwalk and there is a sandy beach at the end. Once on the beach you can hike an extra 1 1/2 miles north to see Indian petroglyphs located at the high-tide mark on the only rock outcropping. It is possible to hike farther north to Cape Alava and then return on the Cape Alava Trail but that is an ambitious hike with kids. You need to be careful not to get caught on the beach by the tide. Camping is also popular along this stretch of the beach.

To get there, drive west from Port Angeles on Hwy 101; at 4.6 miles, turn right on Road No. 112, which takes you along the Strait of Juan de Fuca past Sekiu. Turn left on the Ozette Lake Road and drive 21 miles to the ranger station, campground, and parking lot.

A trip to this part of the state without venturing into the **rain forest** would be unthinkable. Easy to reach is the **Hoh Rain Forest,** 18 miles up the Hoh River from Highway 101. There is a Visitor Center with information about the trail through the Hall of Mosses and other remarkable sights. One of the largest Sitka spruces in the park is about two miles west of the Hoh River campground. It is 230 feet tall and 11 feet, 8 inches in diameter.

OYSTERS are bountiful on the Peninsula; good beaches for digging include Twanoh State Park, Bywater Bay and Potlatch State Park. Be sure to check the redtide hotline before digging in: 800/562-5632.

CALENDAR

MAY: Rhododendron Festival, Port Townsend
JUNE: Olympic Music Festival, Port Townsend. Thru August.

JULY: Jazz Festival, Port Townsend.
SEPTEMBER: Wooden Boat Festival, Port Townsend.

RESOURCES

PORT ANGELES VISITOR INFORMATION CENTER
121 E Railroad St, Port Angeles
360/452-2363

PORT TOWNSEND VISITOR INFORMATION CENTER
2437 Sims Way E, Port Townsend
360/385-2722

SEQUIM VISITOR INFORMATION CENTER
1192 E Washington, Sequim
360/683-6197

OLYMPIC NATIONAL PARK HEADQUARTERS
600 East Park Ave, Port Angeles, 98362
360/452-4501

KITSAP PENINSULA

The Kitsap Peninsula is a crooked finger of the mainland that rests in the middle of Puget Sound between the Tacoma-Seattle-Everett area to the east and Hood Canal to the west. Urban sprawl is creeping into the region, but you can still find abundant local history and natural beauty to explore with the kids.

GETTING THERE

There are several ways to get to the Kitsap Peninsula. Our first two getaways, Alderbrook Inn and the Seabreeze Cottage, are on Hood Canal at the south end of the peninsula. The third getaway, Silverdale Resort and Hotel, is close to the middle of the peninsula. A loop route to any of these places, using the Bremerton ferry on the way and the Winslow ferry on the return journey (or vice versa) is a good way to really see the land. Both ferries leave from downtown Seattle—the Bremerton ride is about one hour, the ride to Winslow on Bainbridge Island about thirty-five minutes. (Ferry info: 1-800-843-3779)

If you prefer to skip the ferry rides, you can take the Narrows Bridge from Tacoma or if you are coming from Portland, connect with Highway 101 just south of Olympia and head north.

REFUELING. If hunger should strike while on the ferry, you'll find an assortment of kid-friendly food at reasonable prices. For food ideas once you are on the Peninsula, see Places to Eat below.

PLACES TO STAY

ALDERBROOK INN

800/622-9370; E701 Hwy 106, Union, 98592
Rates: Moderate to expensive
Essentials: Credit cards; crib
Extras: Restaurant; TV; kitchens (cottages only); indoor pool, Jacuzzi; tennis courts; golf; boats, waterski and fishing rentals; game room; babysitting by arrangement

Alderbrook sits on 525 wooded acres on the shore of Hood Canal. Accommodations consist of 79 guest rooms and 17 cottages. The guest rooms are small and — depending on your neighbors — sometimes noisy, so most families will want to be in the cottages. These have good-sized kitchens and a fireplace and are arranged in a horseshoe shape around a pleasant grassy area with a small playground.

The indoor pool is one of the chief attractions of the resort— it is warm, large and usually uncrowded. The hot tub is also exceptionally nice. The beach and a little creek are just a "stone's throw" from the cottages. The water in Hood Canal gets surprisingly warm in the summertime so swimming in the salt water is an option. Kids will also enjoy the paddleboats that are available for rent.

No gathering of shellfish is allowed at the resort beach but you can go crabbing: crab pots are available for $4.50 an hour from the resort and they also sell bait. You can dangle your pot off the resort dock and if you are lucky you'll get a good-sized crab to steam on the barbecue.

The restaurant at the resort graciously accommodates children with a children's menu and highchairs but the food is prepared without flair and overpriced. Families are better off cooking in their cottages or going to other restaurants in the area (see Places to Eat).

Given all that Alderbrook has to offer and its close proximity to Seattle, you'd expect this resort to be a first-class getaway for families. However, while the setting and the pool are lovely, our parent reviewers were disappointed that the cottages were a bit "down at the mouth." This is less troublesome during the summer months, when most of the time is spent outdoors. We still recommend Alderbrook as a good place to take a short break with the kids, while warning parents not to expect first-class accommodations.

PARENT COMMENTS: *"My husband and I had mixed reactions. It was wonderful getting on the ferry on a dreary February weekend and after a short, scenic drive arriving at a place where our two kids (ages 6 and 3) could explore the beach and frolic in a lovely pool (which we had all to ourselves). If the rates had been lower we probably would have been completely satisfied. However the rates were quite high ($139 for a 2-bedroom cottage in February) so we were disappointed that the cabins were not in top-notch shape (faded paint, a slow drain in the shower, etc.) We had a great time, but the cottage could have been cheerier and better maintained."*

SEABREEZE COTTAGE
360/692-4648; 16609 Olympic View Rd. NW, Silverdale, 98383
Rates: Moderate
Essentials: Credit cards
Extras: Continental breakfast; TV, VCR; kitchen; hot tub; washer/dryer; stereo; Franklin stove

Located 20 minutes from the Winslow ferry, with a 180-degree view of the mountains and water, this private beach house offers a quick escape to peace and tranquillity. With two loft bedrooms and a sleeper sofa, it sleeps four comfortably and the kitchen is fully equipped. If you care to bring your own boat, launch facilities are available at nearby Seabeck marina and a mooring buoy is available in front of the cottage. Restaurants and shops are five minutes away in Poulsbo and Silverdale. Two-night minimum on weekends.

PARENT COMMENTS: *"It was wonderful to be able to get to the beach with so little driving. Our kids loved the hot tub at the water's edge!"*

SILVERDALE HOTEL AND RESORT
360/698-1000, 800/528-1234; 3073 Bucklin Hill Road, Silverdale, 98383
Rates: Moderate to expensive
Essentials: Credit cards; crib
Extras: Restaurant; TV; indoor pool, Jacuzzi, exercise room, taning booth; pool table, ping-pong, video game room, basketball hoop, tennis courts, horseshoe pit, shuffle board (indoor and outdoor); babysitting by arrangement

This isn't the sort of place you go for a week's vacation but it is well-suited for a family weekend of R & R any time of the year. Rooms are spacious and comfortable (most have a majestic view of Dyles Inlet) and there is plenty to keep children busy.

The rooms on the ground level on the water side have sliding glass doors that lead out to the grass and down to the beach— very nice for parents who want to sit on the patio and keep an eye on the kids.

The Mariner restaurant at the resort is quite good and welcomes children with a friendly staff and a good children's menu. Fish tanks next to the restaurant keep kids entertained while waiting for the food to arrive and at-the-table preparation of the many flambe items on the menu will impress the youngsters.

PARENT COMMENTS: *"We stayed in the "mini-suite" (two doubles and one Murphy bed , cost $145) and it was ideal for our family of five. The Sunday brunch at the restaurant at the hotel looked wonderful but we skipped it because it seemed like too big a splurge with our three kids (adults $11.95, kids $5.95)."*

" I love to escape to this place on a dreary winter weekend. Just a pleasant ferry ride from the city, there's minimal travel hassle for a nice getaway. My kids spend most of their time in the pool, and I bring several books and kick back."

PLACES TO EAT

THE BOAT SHED
360/377-2600; 101 Shore Drive, Bremerton
Hours: Lunch and dinner daily, Sunday brunch
Essentials: Credit cards; highchairs

Sitting only one mile from the ferry terminal, just across Manette Bridge, the delicious food, cheerful nautical decor (including a big aquarium) and reasonable prices make the Boat Shed an ideal family restaurant. All the food is fresh and tasty and there is a good kid's menu (kids under 11 eat free off the kid's menu on Mondays and Tuesdays).

HADI'S RESTAURANT
360/895-0347; 818 Bay St, Port Orchard
Hours: lunch, dinner every day
Essentials: No credit cards, checks ok; highchairs

If you are staying at the Alderbrook Inn, you'll have to travel too far to eat at this scrumptious little spot, but if you visit Port Orchard during your stay on the Kitsap Peninsula and you like Middle Eastern food by all means come to Hadi's. You'll find reasonable prices, generous portions, relaxed attentive service and fabulous kabobs, humus and baba ganooj.

STREAMLINER DINER
360/842-8595; 397 Winslow Way, Winslow
Hours: Breakfast daily, lunch Mon-Sat
Essentials: No credit cards; highchairs available

This Bainbridge Island institution hums with contented diners enjoying delicious comfort food at reasonable prices. It is a nice place to stop at the start of your trip or well worth a special trip from Seattle—just walk on the ferry some morning and enjoy a leisurely breakfast and browsing in the charming town of Winslow before catching the ferry back to the city.

VICTORIA'S
360/898-4400; Hwy. 106 in Union
Breakfast, lunch and dinner
Essentials: Credit cards; highchairs

The food is excellent, prices moderate and the setting charming in this "Old English" style restaurant in the tiny town of Union (approximately 1/4 mile west of Alderbrook Inn). The grounds are lovely—including a mini-croquet course, a small brook and towering firs. Outdoor dining is quite pleasant in the summer.

Pasta and seafood dishes are especially recommended. The staff is very accommodating about special orders for both adults and kids, and glad to split the generous portions. Sunday brunch is popular so arrive before 9:30am.

WHAT TO SEE AND DO

The southern end of the Kitsap Peninsula is dominated by Hood Canal. Unlike other Pacific Northwest salt waters, the temperature of the canal reaches into the 70s in the summer, a boon for swimmers. It's shoreline is rich with shrimp, clams, oysters and crabs. In season, seafood stands skirt the roads. Many public beaches near the northern end of the canal are good for clam and oyster gathering, a beach activity most children love.

Farther north, there are several picturesque towns rich in Northwest history.

For more ideas about what to see and do in this region, see **Olympic Peninsula**: What to See and Do.

THE BREMERTON NAVAL MUSEUM is located just a half-block

from the Bremerton ferry terminal, near the Puget Sound Naval Shipyard. Although you might expect it to be dull for anyone without a passion for naval history, in fact all ages seem to find something of interest in the small but fascinating collection of ships models. And don't miss the world's oldest surviving cannon (dated 1377).

On the other hand, a self-guided tour of the destroyer **USS Turner Joy** anchored at the nearby Puget Sound Naval Shipyard, was described as "disappointing" by our parent researchers. There is usually one of the big aircraft carriers moored at the docks which you can view from several side streets close to the ship yard or by taking the passenger-only ferry to Port Orchard from the Bremerton ferry dock.

Museum located on Washington Ave; 360-479-7447. Open Tues-Sat, 10 am-4 pm, Sun 1-4 pm. Free.

PORT ORCHARD is a scenic little town that is a 15- minute drive from Bremerton and also accessible via passenger-only ferry from Bremerton across Sinclair Inlet. The ferry ride offers a good view of the big ships in the shipyard as you leave Bremerton. There is excellent clamming in the inlet of Port Orchard, and in season, **squid fishing**. The Port Orchard pier extends 150 yards into the water, with a floating dock winding around the marina. Fall is squid season, and the pier gets crowded with excited kids catching their limits in less than 30 minutes. This is a hit with even the very young, for patience and a long attention span are not needed. When squid run, they run by the thousands, and can be caught with a bare hook.

PORT GAMBLE, 23 miles north of Bremerton via State 3, is the oldest continually operating company town in the US. Situated on a bluff at the intersection of Admiralty Inlet and Gamble Bay, it was founded by New Englanders in the middle of the nineteenth century and is still owned by the Pope and Talbot lumber firm. The town has been lovingly restored to its turn-of-the-century appearance and is designated a historical landmark. A walking-tour map can be obtained at the **Port Gamble Country Store**, where you'll also find a good deli. The tiny **Sea and Shore Museum**, located on the second floor of the store, houses aquariums and allegedly the largest collection of shells in the United States. This is usually a hit with the kids—for pennies they can take home a pocketful of shells.

THE PORT GAMBLE HISTORICAL MUSEUM, located behind the store, is one of the finest museums of its kind in the Northwest and worth coming all the way from Seattle to visit. Designed by Alec James, who designed the displays for the Royal Provincial Museum in Victoria, B.C., the life-size dioramas will hold the interest of all ages, while teaching the rich history of the region. *360/297-3341. Open daily Memorial Day thru Labor Day, 10 am - 4 pm. Cost: $1/ adult, $0.50 /child.*

SUQUAMISH MUSEUM AND TRIBAL CENTER is located just off Route 305 on the Port Madison Indian Reservation. It is a good stop on your way to or from the Winslow ferry on Bainbridge. The excellent exhibits give a vivid account of life on Puget Sound for the thousands of years before white settlers arrived. There are also two short films about the tribe narrated by tribal elders. Near the museum, on Suquamish Way off Route 305, you can visit the grave of the famous Salish leader Chief Seattle (or Sealth). During Chief Seattle Days in August, the tribal center comes alive with traditional Indian dancing, games, canoe races, storytelling and salmon bake.

Route 305, Suquamish; 360/598-3311. Winter Hours; Fri , Sat & Sun, 11 am -4 pm. Summer hours, daily 10 am-5 pm. Cost: $2.50 /adult, $1/child under 12. Group tours $15/hour.

POULSBO, known locally as " Little Norway," has had some of its Scandinavian charm obscured by rapid growth and develop-ment over the last ten years but once you get past the strip malls you'll find a charming little town with a fine view of Liberty Bay and the Olympic Mountains. If you are making this your lunch stop, grab a sandwich at one of the many delis along the boardwalk that runs between the bluff and the water and take your picnic to **Liberty Bay Park** where you can enjoy watching boats come and go. The Chamber of Commerce will provide a walking map if you 'd like to enjoy the historic architecture.

The **Marine Science Center** has aquariums, touch-tanks of marine life and other well-presented exhibits that will educate all ages about the biology and geology of Puget Sound.

360/779-5549; 18743 Front St Northeast, Poulsbo. Open Tues-Sat, 10 am-4 pm. Cost: $2/adult; $1/child ages 2-12, $5/family.

CALENDAR

MAY: Viking Fest, Poulsbo
JUNE: Skandia Midsommarfest, Poulsbo
AUGUST: Chief Seattle Days, Suquamish
DECEMBER: Yule Fest, Poulsbo.

RESOURCES

WASHINGSTON STATE FERRIES
1-800-843-3779
BREMERTON VISITORS BUREAU
360/479-3588

OLYMPIA/SOUTH PUGET SOUND

Many people regard Olympia as a stop-off on Interstate 5 on the way to someplace else, but this capital city deserves consideration as a final destination. Nestled at the southern tip of Puget Sound, Olympia has plenty for families to see and do throughout the year.

To see democracy in action, visit Olympia when the legislature is in session, usually January through April. Your children may study civics, but the classroom can't match the experience of seeing the legislative system first-hand.

GETTING THERE
Olympia is right on I-5, 66 miles south of Seattle.

PLACES TO STAY

DEEP LAKE RESORT
360/352-7388; 12405 Tilley Road S, Olympia, 98512
Rates: Inexpensive
Essentials: Credit cards
Extras: Kitchens; swimming beach with slide; volleyball,
horsehoes, basketball, miniature golf; boats; bikes; pets OK

Deep Lake Resort is the type of resort that it is getting harder and harder to find—a comfy place, set-up for families to have fun at a reasonable cost (two-bedroom cabin for seven nights with no shower is $333). Located on a small lake just outside Olympia, next to Millersylvania State Park, it is the kind of place where your kids will find friends and you can settle into your long vacation novel/nap. Six tidy cabins sit along the lakefront, each with a fire pit, a picnic table and a rowboat. All the cabins have kitchens—bring your own linens, dishes and cooking utensils. Four cabins have showers—for the rest, public showers are nearby, along with laundry facilities, camping and RV sites. The resort is open late April through September. In July and August cabins are only available by the week. Book early!

PARENT COMMENTS: *"Staying on the west side of the Cascades can be risky as far as the weather is concerned, but we couldn't stand to drive more than an hour from Seattle with our preschoolers so we went to Deep Lake Resort. The weather was great, there were kids all over the place and we had a super laid-back, pleasant stay—without blowing our budget."*

COMFORT INN OF LACEY
360/456-6300; 4700 Park Center Ave NE, Lacey, 98503
Rates: Inexpensive
Essentials: Credit cards; crib and rollaways
Extras: Continental breakfast; TV; indoor pool, hot tub
The Comfort Inn is located near I-5, shopping, parks, theaters and St. Martin's College. It is new, nicely decorated and, despite its proximity to the freeway, enjoys a wooded setting. Most of the rooms are designated non-smoking, and eight suites have microwaves and refrigerators.

PARENT COMMENTS: *"My preschooler and I stayed here while looking for a house to buy. The staff was friendly and the pool was great. For convenience, you can't beat the location."*

PUGET VIEW GUESTHOUSE B&B
360/459-1676; 6924 61st NE, 98516
Rates: Inexpensive to moderate
Essentials: Credit cards; no crib
Extras: Continental breakfast; microwaves, refrigerators; barbecue
Though known as a romantic get-away, this B&B works well for families. The private, wooded grounds are adjacent to Tolmie State Park and provide views of the Olympic Mountains and Puget Sound.

The guest house has a bedroom with a queen bed, as well as a living room with a sofa sleeper, so it can comfortably accommodate a family of four. The refrigerator comes in handy for snacks or restaurant leftovers, and there's a microwave and a barbecue. A continental breakfast is served.

With a treehouse on the grounds and a private trail to the beach, the kids won't have to look far for entertainment (be sure to pack binoculars, beach shoes and rainwear). But if the little ones burn out on beachcombing, Olympia is a short drive away.

PARENT COMMENTS: *"The owners are exceptionally nice. Our kids loved the beaches, opportunities to explore tidepools and other marine life. The only drawback was the lack of a full kitchen."*

WESTWATER/HOLIDAY INN
360/943-4000 or 800/551-8500; 2300 Evergreen Park Dr, Olympia, 98802
Rates: Moderate
Essentials: Credit cards; crib
Extras: Restaurant with kids' menu; refrigerators (suites); outdoor pool (seasonal) and hot tub; babysitting with advance notice; TV; shuttle service to capital buildlings; coin laundry

This is a large motel (191 units) in an attractive setting overlooking Capital Lake. The building was recently remodelled, with nicely-appointed rooms. In warm weather, the pool is great for kids (and a godsend for parents).

PARENT COMMENTS: *"Definitely request a remodelled room, preferably with a view. Our five-year-old enjoyed the pool and the grounds."*

RAMADA INN GOVERNOR HOUSE
360/352-7700; 621 S Capitol Way, Olympia, 98501
Rates: Inexpensive to moderate (seasonal)
Essentials: Credit cards; rollaways; crib
Extras: Restaurant with kids' menu; outdoor pool (seasonal), hot tub and sauna; exercise room; TV; laundry; shuttle service

Located downtown, this hotel offers easy access to shopping and the capital. There are view rooms on both sides of the motel; request one that's newly remodelled. Families looking to save money on meals may prefer one of the five mini-suites with kitchenettes. In-season, the pool is great for kids; also, children may use the exercise center, with adult supervision.

The adjoining restaurant has a children's menu and highchairs, but can be a bit smoky. If you choose to avoid the fumes, there are many restaurants within easy walking distance.

PARENT COMMENTS: *"The motel is located across the street from Sylvester Park and easy walking distance from Capital Lake — we found both helpful for burning off excess energy."*

TYEE HOTEL
360/352-0511; 500 Tyee Dr, Tumwater, 98502
Rates: Inexpensive
Essentials: Credit cards (no checks taken in restaurant); crib
Extras: Refrigerators (some units); tennis, basketball, access to nearby athletic club ($6); TV; public shuttle to airport

Situated on 20 wooded acres, the Tyee has 146 guest rooms and suites. Energetic guests will enjoy the large outdoor pool and tennis and basketball courts.

The adjoining restaurant offers a kids' menu with traditional favorites at reasonable prices.

PARENT COMMENTS: *"This is a nice, family-oriented motel; the staff seemed to genuinely enjoy having kids around. The rooms are large and clean, and there's plenty of parking!"*

PLACES TO EAT

BAYVIEW MARKET DELI
360/352-4901; 516 W 4th Ave
Hours: 7 am-8 pm daily
Essentials: Credit cards; highchairs (indoors only)
Located in Bayview Thriftway at the north end of the waterfront area, this spot offers a wide variety of hot and cold deli salads and sandwiches, and great ice cream. There is no specific kids' menu, but there are so many choices that most kids will find something they like. The upstairs eating area has a view of the water, or enjoy the outside tables in nice weather.

FALLS TERRACE
360/943-7830; 106 S Deschutes Way, Tumwater
Hours: Lunch and dinner daily
Essentials: Credit cards; highchairs
This Tumwater restaurant has become an institution. Not only does it have a gorgeous setting overlooking the Tumwater Falls of the Deschutes River, it also serves a fine American/Northwest cuisine at reasonable prices. The limited children's menu (grilled cheese, burgers, steak, fish and chips) is moderately priced.

Because a recent remodelling has made The Falls even more popular; reservations are advised. By dining early, you can avoid the crowd and take advantage of the "early bird" specials. Request a window seat so children can watch the tumbling waterfalls.

JOMAMAS
360/943-9849; 120 N Pear
Hours: Lunch and dinner Mon-Sat, dinner only on Sun
Essentials: Credit cards; highchairs
This is a non-traditional pizza place with incredible custom pizzas. At first glance the pizzas may seem expensive, but they're so loaded with goodies that a little goes a long way. For non-pizza

eaters (are there any?), JoMamas serves sandwiches, soups and salads at lunch and a few pasta dishes at dinner.

Located in an old house with spacious wooden booths and an upstairs area, this is an informal, kid-friendly restaurant. The service is attentive, but not necessarily fast, so you will be grateful that crayons are supplied.

SAKURA JAPANESE STEAK HOUSE
360/943-1200; 1200 Cooper Pt Rd
Hours: Dinner daily Mon-Sat
Essentials: Credit cards; highchairs

Looking for a different kind of eating experience? This is a "Benihana"-style restaurant that's entertaining for children and parents. The service is good and the food is delicious. While steak is the specialty, the chicken and seafood are also tasty.

URBAN ONION
360/943-9242; 116 Legion Way SE
Hours: Breakfast, lunch and dinner daily

Located downtown in the old Olympian Hotel, the Urban Onion serves healthy Northwest food and pasta dishes. There is a low-priced kids' menu.

This is a popular spot and service sometimes is slow; request some crayons and drawing paper to help youngsters pass the time.

WAGNER'S EUROPEAN BAKERY AND CAFE
(360) 357-7268; 1013 Capitol Way S
Hours: Breakfast and lunch
Essentials: No credit cards; highchairs available

This full-scale bakery and cafe, walking distance from the capital, is an Olympia landmark. Wagner's serves up pastries, sandwiches and salads or box lunches (one will feed two children).

THE WHALE'S TAIL
360/956-1928; 501 Columbia
Hours: Breakfast and lunch
Essentials: Credit cards; highchairs

This is a good place for breakfast, lunch or snacks while exploring the Olympia waterfront (walk-up or bike-up service available). The proximity to the water, marvelous whale decor and outdoor tables make it a fun, relaxed place for kids.

WHAT TO SEE AND DO

STROLL & BROWSE

DOWNTOWN. Olympia's town square, **Sylvester Park** (Seventh between Washington and Capitol), is named for founding father Edmund Sylvester. Landscaped in 1893, its huge trees provide a park-like feeling. Nearby you will find renovated turn-of-the-century buildings, most notably the Old Capitol (Seventh and Washington), a magnificent, turreted structure built in 1892. It had a clock tower, which had to be removed after a 1949 earthquake left it unstable.

If modern-day shopping is more to your liking than historical architecture, visit **Wind up Here** toy shop (406 Washington St) or **Archibald Sisters** (406 Capitol Way S), an eclectic gift/toy/card/fragrance shop. There are two great nature stores in this area: **Wild Side Nature Store** (507 Washington SE), featuring great nature books, bird houses and nature-related toys, and **Earth Magic** (205 E Fourth), with wonderful rocks and crystals.

For quality kids' clothes for ages newborn through five, stop by **Capitol City Kids** (408 Washington SE). A must-visit if you're in the area is **Four Seasons Books at Carnegies** (302 E. Seventh), located in an original Carnegie library building. The entire lower level is devoted to children's books, and families are encouraged to browse. Upstairs, grab an espresso for mom and dad, or a light lunch for the family.

WATERFRONT. The waterfront park at **Percival Landing** is fast becoming a focal point for community activity in Olympia. The waterfront area features 1 $\frac{1}{2}$ miles of boardwalk, with moorage facilities and views of the Capitol, Port of Olympia, Budd Inlet, Mount Rainier and the Olympics. The **Olympia Farmers Market**, second largest in the state, displays local produce, flowers and crafts April through October, and is open for holiday buying of crafts only through December.

CAPITOL GROUNDS. The capitol campus is a lovely place to stroll. The greenhouse and conservatory are open Monday through Friday. Also worth a visit are the rose garden, Tivoli Fountain, Vietnam and Korean War Memorials. This is a great place to eat your picnic lunch, fly a kite or just let the troops run loose. In spring, enjoy the abundant pink cherry blossoms; in fall, walk in the autumn foliage.

PARKS

TUMWATER FALLS PARK, near the Olympia Brewery, is a pleasant stop for families. A paved trail along the Deschutes

River crosses the lower falls to form an easy, one-mile loop. (Be sure to hold young and/or impulsive children by the hand.) In the fall, children will learn a lesson in nature as they watch salmon swim up the fish ladders to their hatchery. The park has picnic areas and restrooms.

Off Deschutes Parkway, adjacent to the brewery.

CAPITOL LAKE PARK offers 10 acres of waterfront along a man-made saltwater lake. Play equipment, a picnic area, ducks to feed, boat rentals and restrooms.

Fifth and Water St, at the edge of downtown Olympia.

PRIEST POINT PARK has 265 wooded acres, six miles of trails, sheltered picnic areas, wading pool and restrooms. Or walk the four-mile Ellis Cove Trail to the beach. The trail is hilly, but there are benches for resting along the way.

On East Bay Drive between Mission and Flora Vista Avenues.

TOLMIE STATE PARK. The big attraction of this park is a man-made reef which attracts fish and other sea life—a great place to be during low tide! Families will also enjoy 180 feet of Puget Sound waterfront and 105 acres with trails, picnic facilities and restrooms.

Take Exit 111 from I-5 and follow signs west (approx. 5 miles).

WOODARD BAY CONSERVATION AREA. A State Department of Natural Resources conservancy area located on Henderson Inlet, Woodard Bay has four miles of marine shoreline and 450 acres of upland and tideland. This is a great place to observe marine animals and their habitats, especially seals. A six-mile walking and biking trail offers exercise for energetic families.

Take Libby Road north, turn right on Woodard Bay Road and continue to the bay.

ANIMALS, ANIMALS

LUNCH WITH LLAMAS. The Llama Tree Ranch offers five-hour hiking trips using llamas as pack animals—you hike, the llamas carry the goodies. Lunch is catered by the Wild Berry Restaurant, located near Paradise (Mount Rainier). The llama trips depart from the restaurant daily at 11 am and return between 3:30-4 pm.

4235-36th NE, 360/491-LAMA. Cost: $35/person (infants free), special rates for 20 or more.

NISQUALLY NATIONAL WILDLIFE REFUGE, located in the

Nisqually River delta, is home to nearly 400 wildlife species. The refuge offers more than 3,700 acres of grasslands, marshes and meandering streams. Families will enjoy the level, five-mile hiking trail that follows an old dike around the wetlands (bring binoculars). There is a rookery of great herons will that is an amusing sight—a bird condo. If you visit on a weekend, plan to arrive early; the refuge often reaches capacity by 10 am, and reopens as space becomes available.

Take Exit 114 off I-5 and follow signs; 360/753-9467. Cost: $2/ family.

WOLF HAVEN INTERNATIONAL, a sanctuary for captive wolves from all over the country, is home to more than 35 wolves. "Howl-ins" and tours are available year around. "Howl-ins" include a tour, storytelling, sing-along, campfire and howling with the wolves.

Offut Lake Rd, Tenino; 360/264-4695 or 800/448-WOLF. Cost: tours are $5/adult, $2.50/child, "howl-ins" are $6/adult, $3/child ages 6-12.

EXCURSIONS

HANDS-ON CHILDREN'S MUSEUM Dedicated parents spent several years planning and raising funds to open this museum. Fun times abound for the kids: dress up as sea creatures and play on a fishing pier, explore a ship-building center or splash in a water play area.

Downtown at 108 Franklin St NE; 360/956-0818. Open Tues-Sat, 10 am-5 pm; Sun, noon-4 pm. Cost: $2.50/person (ages one and over).

MIMA MOUNDS A bizarre phenomenon, the Mima Mounds are six-foot-high, 30-foot-wide earth mounds that have baffled scientists for years. Prevalent theories about the origin of the mounds range from Indian buffalo decoys to giant, prehistoric gophers. Whatever they are, they are intriguing any time of year. They're especially beautiful in the early summer, when they blossom with bluebells, oxeye daisies and camas. Self-guided tour instructions are available at the interpretive center.

Take exit 95 from I-5 and drive 4 1/2 miles on State 121. Open daily, 8 am-dusk. Free.

MOUNT ST. HELENS VISITOR CENTER AND OBSERVATORY. The Mount St. Helens Volcanic Monument was created two years after the 1980 eruption to protect 110,000 acres of land as a resource for scientists and the public. The interpretive center, opened in 1986, introduces visitors to the history of the mountain. The center offers interpretive exhibits, theater presentations, a ten-minute slide show, a short interpretive trail and an information desk.

Located five miles east of Castle Rock on SR 504; 360/274-2100 (274-2103 for a 24-hour taped message). Open daily, 9 am-5 pm in winter, 9 am-6 pm in summer). Free.

PABST BREWERY TOUR. "Take children to a brewery?," you ask. In this case, sure. The Olympia Brewery has been a local institution since 1896, and the tour is fun for young and old alike. Following the brewing process from grain to bottles, visitors get a close look at huge vats of brew and high-speed bottling machines (children are fascinated by how fast the tops pop on). Children under 16 must be accompanied by an adult. After the tour, kids are served soft drinks and adults may sample the beer.

At Exit 103 from I-5; 360/754-5000. Tours leave hourly on the half-hour, 8:30 am-3:30 pm. Free.

STATE CAPITOL AND MUSEUM. The lavish dome of the Washington State **Legislative Building**, the capitol's centerpiece, was spiffed up for the state centennial in 1987-88. With its ornate five-ton Tiffany bronze chandelier, it is truly a sight to see. Just opposite is the **Temple of Justice**, seat of the Washington State Supreme Court. The governor's mansion next door is open to visitors Wednesdays, 1-2:45 pm, by reservation (360/586-TOUR).

Also of interest to older children are the **State Library**, which holds artifacts of the state's early history, and the newly-remodelled **State Capitol Museum** (360/753-2580). The museum houses a permanent collection of Native American and early pioneer artifacts and Northwest art exhibits.

Take State Capitol Exit from I-5 and follow signs. Activities are free; museum suggests a donation.

CALENDAR

MARCH: Art Burst
MAY: Zabel's Rhododendron Garden
JUNE: Super Saturday
JULY: Capitol Lakefair
AUGUST: Renaissance Faire
SEPTEMBER: Harbor Days
NOVEMBER: Art Walk

RESOURCES

LACEY AREA CHAMBER OF COMMERCE
7 South Sound Center, Lacey
360/491-4141

OLYMPIA THURSTON CHAMBER OF COMMERCE
1000 Plum St SE (adjacent to City Hall)
360/357-3362

TUMWATER AREA CHAMBER OF COMMERCE
488 Tyee Dr SE, Tumwater (adjacent to Tyee Hotel)
360/357-5153

South Puget Sound Afoot and Afloat, by Marge Mueller,
Mountaineers Publishing.

South Sound Places: A Guide to Olympia, Lacey,
Tumwater and Thurston County, by Nancy Patterson, Four
Seasons Publishing.

WASHINGTON COAST

Many familiar images of the Pacific Northwest are found on the coast of Washington: soaring mountains and rain forest, mile-long stretches of wide sandy beaches, and windblown little towns that cling to the dunes.

The Washington coast stretches from Neah Bay, at the entrance to the Strait of Juan de Fuca (the passage to Puget Sound), south to Ilwaco, where the Columbia River empties into the Pacific. If you want to take in rugged coastline, mountains and rain forest, your best destination is Kalaloch to the north. If wide-open beaches and the ocean "out of the cradle endlessly rocking" are your desire, the resorts near Copalis, Moclips and Ocean Shores are a good choice. To witness the pure, brute force of nature, head to the Long Beach Peninsula at the southwestern tip of the state, where the mighty Columbia River meets the world's largest ocean.

GETTING THERE

To get to the Washington coast from Seattle, head south on I-5. Just past Olympia, take Highway 101 west, then continue on Highway 8 toward the coast. It will turn into Highway 12.

If you are going to **Kalaloch,** at the northern end of the Olympic Peninsula, drive Highway 12 to Aberdeen/Hoquiam and then take Highway 101 north. An alternative (and shorter) route to Kalaloch is to take either the Winslow ferry from Seattle or the Kingston ferry from Edmonds and follow signs to Port Gamble and the Hood Canal Floating Bridge on Highway 104. Follow Highway 104 as it joins Highway 101 to Port Angeles and keep going until you reach Kalaloch.

To go to **Ocean Shores,** take State Route 109 west from Hoquiam, then follow State Route 115 south.

To reach the **Pacific Beach/Moclips** area from Hoquiam, take Highway 109 west to the ocean beaches and turn north on State Route 115.

If your destination is the **Long Beach Peninsula,** head toward Aberdeen/Hoquiam, and take Highway 107 south at Montesano. It connects with Highway 101 south to the Long Beach area.

REFUELING. There are several fast-food options along the I-5 corridor between Seattle and Olympia, then mostly farms, forest and fields once you leave the freeway and head to the ocean. The Aberdeen/Hoquiam area has numerous restaurants. On the north side of Hoquiam, just across the road from the high school, you'll find the **Grizzlie's Den,** a dandy local drive-in with a wide variety of menu items. It's an ideal spot for a quick lunch, with seating both inside and out.

ROADSIDE ATTRACTIONS. The major point of interest on the way to the ocean is the state capitol in Olympia. If you want to include a tour of the capitol grounds in your trip, see "Olympia: What to See and Do."

If you are traveling between Olympia and Aberdeen, watch for the controversial, mothballed WPPSS nuclear power plants between Elma and Satsop. The cooling towers are gigantic.

Cold water and strong undertows make ocean swimming unappealing on the Washington coast, but count on the kids wanting to romp at the water's edge no matter what the weather is like and pack accordingly.

OCEAN SHORES

Sitting on a 6,000-acre peninsula between Grays Harbor and the ocean, Ocean Shores is the closest destination for Seattleites in search of an ocean beach. The area, which was a ranch prior to the 1960s, tries hard to be a picturesque seaside resort town, but the modern high-rise condos that line the dunes are anything but quaint, and the six miles of beach and vast prairies of beach grass are not especially scenic.

Although the topography is more wild and beautiful as you

head north or south along the coast, the video game parlors, horseback riding, bumper cars and other such diversions make Ocean Shores a kids' paradise—and some parents don't mind sacrificing a bit of beauty and a couple rolls of quarters to have a few days of not hearing "I'm bored."

Ocean Shores has 2,500 residents, but in the summer it hosts as many as 25,000 visitors daily. Therefore, a winter visit will be much different than a visit in August, in terms of crowds, prices and the availability of services and recreational activities.

PLACES TO STAY

GREY GULL
360/289-3381; P.O. Box 1417, Ocean Shores, 98569
Rates: Expensive
Essentials: Credit cards; crib
*Extras: TV, VCR; microwaves, dishwashers; fireplaces; pool
(outdoor, heated, open year-round), sauna, hot tub; coin-operated
laundry; pets (under 20 lbs) OK in some units*

The Grey Gull sits on the condo strip, among the dunes, within walking distance of "downtown" Ocean Shores—which may be an advantage if you have older kids. It is modern and a bit expensive, and doesn't have the family-friendly atmosphere parents of younger kids may seek. The views are nice, however, and the fact they allow dogs (up to 20 pounds) in some rooms is a real plus for those who can't imagine embarking on a true family vacation without Spot.

POLYNESIAN CONDOMINIUM RESORT
360/289-3361; 615 Ocean Shores Blvd, Ocean Shores, 98569
Rates: Moderate to expensive
Essentials: Credit cards; crib and highchairs
*Extras: Restaurant; TV, VCR; kitchens (most units); fireplaces;
indoor pool, sauna, Jacuzzi (adults only)*

At the end of the condo strip sits the Polynesian—a three-story condominium (with a penthouse) that provides direct access to the beach. It's a pleasant place to stay during the quiet off-season, though the summer months are optimum. Rooms are nicely furnished with modern decor, and each unit is equipped with a microwave, dishwasher, refrigerator, stove, oven and coffee maker (you'll find groceries a half mile away at Thriftway). Maid service makes the beds, changes towels and empties the garbage each day.

The Polynesian owns a private park just south of the condo, where kids can play basketball (on a half-sized court), volleyball,

Given the overall mediocre quality of the food in the area's restaurants, we recommend that you choose lodging that has a kitchen unit. It will be handy for snacks, breakfasts and the special needs of kids, and will no doubt save you money.

tetherball or horseshoes, and families can picnic and barbecue. Frisbees are available at the front desk. Young children will enjoy the play structure and sandbox in the park; older kids will appreciate the indoor game room, with its video games, pool and ping-pong.

Moriah's, the restaurant at the resort, has an extensive menu and kid-friendly service, but the food is mediocre. Our family reviewers reported they probably would eat elsewhere next time.

PARENT COMMENTS: *"The staff was very helpful. They provided a list of six babysitters, with ages, and made specific recommendations for us. Our kids went to the front desk to ask for paper for an art project and came back with tape and ribbon as well."*

PLACES TO EAT

DUGAN'S PIZZA
360/289-2330; 690 Ocean Shores Blvd
Hours: Lunch and dinner; hours vary
Essentials: Credit cards; highchairs
This is the only place to buy pizza in town. The food is adequate but not memorable. Dugan's supposedly delivers, but on the winter day our testers requested this service, it wasn't available.

HOMEPORT
360/289-2600; 857 Point Brown Ave
Hours: Breakfast, lunch and dinner daily
Essentials: Credit cards; highchairs
Our reviewers sampled only breakfast (which cost just over $20 for four people). The waffles and French toast were great; service was excellent. According to the locals, lunch and dinner are also first-rate.

WHAT TO SEE AND DO

DUCK LAKE AND LAKE MINARD and the 23 miles of interconnecting freshwater canals provide plenty of opportunities for canoeing, water-skiing, fishing and exploring.

HORSEBACK RIDING has always been a popular way to explore the trails and beaches of Ocean Shores. **Nan-Sea Stables** (360/289-0194; Hwy 115 north of Ocean Shores) arranges such excursions. **Seahorse Ranch** (360/532-6791; Milepost 9, Rte 109, east of Hoquiam) has numerous trails traversing its 400 acres and an indoor arena for rainy days.

If you would like to see some of the other terrain the Washington coast has to offer, buckle the kids in their car seats and take a **drive north on Highway 109**. Count on a few stops—the rocky bluffs, timbered hills and many vistas are spectacular. The road ends at Taholah, a tiny town on the Quinault Indian reservation. (There's no tourist office or public beach access here.)

Displays at the **Ocean Shores Environmental Interpretive Center** trace the natural and human history of the area. Visitors learn about native wildlife and formation of the peninsula.
1013 Catala Ave SE; 360/289-4617. Open summers only; Wed-Sun, 11 am-6 pm. Free.

THE WESTPORT/OCEAN SHORES PASSENGER FERRY operates between Ocean Shores and Westport on weekends in May and daily from June 1 through Labor Day. The ferry departs the Ocean Shores dock every 1 ¹/₂ hours, 9:30 am-6:30 pm.
Marina Store Main Float; 360/268-0047.

WHALE WATCHING is popular off Westport from early March to late May, when gray whales migrate toward Arctic feeding waters and in the fall head back down to winter in Baja. Seeing these magnificent creatures in the sea should be experienced at least once in a lifetime. Boats usually go out twice a day: Call for reservations on the day you plan to go to see if the whales are in the area and try for calm weather to avoid seasickness. Most of the charter boats will take children as young as four, although six-year-olds and up are better suited. Good companies include **Deep Sea**, 800/562-0151 and **Cachalot**, 360/268-0323.

The Ocean Shores phone book contains tide tables, service listings, maps and other good information, as well as a history of the area.

CALENDAR

FEBRUARY: Beachcomber/Fun Fair
JULY: Olympic Art Show
OCTOBER: Kite Festival
NOVEMBER: Dixieland Jazz Festival

RESOURCES

OCEAN SHORES CHAMBER OF COMMERCE
P.O. Box 382, Ocean Shores, 98569
800/762-3224

PACIFIC BEACH, NORTH

Washington's most accessible, broad and sandy beaches
extend north from Ocean Shores for a stretch of about 29
miles to the end of the road at Tahoulah.

PLACES TO STAY

THE BEACHWOOD RESORT

360/289-2177; PO Box 116, Copalis Beach, 98535
Rates: Inexpensive to moderate
Essentials: Credit cards; crib and highchairs
Extras: TVs; fireplaces, free firewood; outdoor pool (seasonal),
sauna (adults only), hot tub (14 and older); indoor recreation
room with ping-pong; playground, lawn games, mini-golf for kids,
barbecue; pets OK

Beachwood is located between the tiny towns of Ocean City
and Copalis on Highway 109. The 21 slightly rundown, one-
story units border a large grassy play area just steps away from the
long, wide beach, making it an ideal setting for kids. Each cabin
has a kitchen, a separate bedroom with two double beds, and a
living room with a hide-a-bed and fireplace. Plan to cook your
own meals—there are few restaurants in the area.

The playground is nothing special—just a slide and swings—
but it is fenced. There is also a comfortable reading/game room
that has a sweeping view of the ocean and provides an escape if
you get cabin fever. The heated pool is open from Memorial Day
through Labor Day.

Beachwood is at its best in the summer, when you can take full
advantage of the beach. If you are enticed by the sound of its
simple, well-worn charm, you'll probably find it to be the ideal
place for a visit with the kids (and the dog). Make reservations
early for a summer visit—many families have been coming back
to this place for years.

PARENT COMMENTS: *"It's a good idea to bring along your
favorite utensils because the kitchen furnishings are pretty hit
and miss. For a treat, we go up to the restaurant at Ocean Crest for
dinner or a Sunday brunch. This place is borderline funky, but the
beach access—right out the door—can't be beat."*

THE SANDPIPER BEACH RESORT

360/276-4580; PO Box A, Pacific Beach, 98571
Rates: Inexpensive to expensive
Essentials: Credit cards; cribs and highchairs

Extras: Kitchens; playground; barbecues (some units);pets OK

With no TVs, video games or in-room telephones, this is a good spot to get away from it all (your adolescent may disagree). Located 6 miles north of Copalis on Highway 109, the resort includes 29 units of various configurations—studios, suites and separate cabins—all of which have complete housekeeping services, as well as puzzles, magazines and rocking chairs. All but one of the units have a full ocean view, and all but three have fireplaces. The older units in the northern complex are slightly bigger, and any units above ground level have lanais with space for barbecuing, hanging out wet clothes and displaying treasures. The grounds are beautifully landscaped and maintained.

You'll find a playground on the beach, as well as a fire pit, which is convenient for barbecues or fireworks. There is also a well-stocked gift shop that sells books, toys and kites. Grocery shopping is available at nearby Copalis, but if you prefer dining out, the restaurant at the Ocean Crest is the best in the area. (See "Ocean Crest Lodge" for more details.)

PARENT COMMENTS: *"The Sandpiper is very well-managed by the resident owners, and they make a big effort to help families feel welcome."*

Due to recent changes in the law, driving on beaches is allowed only from October 15 to April 15.

OCEAN CREST LODGE
360/276-4465; Sunset Beach, Moclips, 98562
Rates: Inexpensive to expensive
Essentials: Credit cards; one-time charge of $3 for cribs
Extras: Restaurant; TVs; kitchens (some units); fireplaces; health club with indoor pool, sauna, hot tub, exercise room, masseuse; playground; coin-operated laundry; gift shop

This attractive resort sits on a bluff above the ocean and takes full advantage of the magnificent views. Accommodation options include studio and two-bedroom units on the ocean side with full views, a multi-unit A-frame on the opposite side of the road, and a two-unit annex 1/4 mile down the road.

The rooms on the ocean side have the best views, but the A-frame units, though they sit across the road and have no views, are more convenient for parents who don't want to worry about their kids crossing the road to use the playground and health club. The playground is small, but safe and well designed; the health club is an especially nice facility that houses a large pool, hot tub and sauna, as well as massage and exercise rooms.

If you are traveling with another family, the annex may be your best option because it has two completely separate units—each with two bedrooms, a deck and a view of the sea—connected by an inside door. The disadvantage of the annex is that you have to walk or drive ¹/₄ mile on a fairly busy road to access the pool, restaurant and beach.

The path to the beach from the resort is steep with many steps, but well maintained. Carrying a young child back and forth would get tiresome—bring a backpack, but don't let your four-year-old convince you she can't walk it herself.

The restaurant is one of the main attractions at Ocean Crest. It has a lovely view of the wooded bluff overlooking the ocean, illuminated by floodlights at night. Tell the kids to keep an eye out for raccoons—these little masked bandits frequently appear outside the restaurant's windows in the evening.

Dining here with the family is easy—children's menus and highchairs are available, and the service is friendly. Menu choices for adults emphasize seafood, and the food is consistently good. Breakfasts are also excellent. Be sure to make reservations when you first arrive at the resort, or you can expect a long wait. (If you prefer to eat in your room, you may place an order to go.)

Prices at the restaurant are moderately expensive; families will want to cook most of their own meals. There is a small but well-stocked grocery store (fresh meat and vegetables) in the nearby town of Moclips, just a 5-minute drive away.

PARENT COMMENTS: *"Ocean Crest has been a favorite getaway for our family for the last five years. We prefer to go in the winter—we love walking the beach on a stormy day, and then enjoying the pool and hot tub."*

"The resort rents video machines and tapes, so we rented a movie for the kids and went to dinner by ourselves."

WHAT TO SEE AND DO

This stretch of the coast is especially good for **clam digging**—a fun family activity that typically yields tasty results. Most kids love the chance to get elbow-deep in the sand and dig for these bivalve mollusks. The open season for clamming varies from year to year. There are occasional alerts for red tide when the clams are highly toxic to eat. Call the State Fisheries Information Line at 360/249-4628 for up-to-date information. Licenses cost $3.50 (not necessary for kids under 15 years of age) and are good for one year. The daily limit for each person is your first 15 clams—enough for a steaming kettle of clam chowder. You are forbidden to discard small clams.

KITE FLYING is outstanding on this beach. It's always breezy, and there are no trees or overhead wires in the flight path. Be sure your kite (and string) are very sturdy.

SWIMMING is not recommended here, or anywhere else on the Washington coast, because of undertow and rip tide. If you don't have access to a pool, consider swimming at the health club at Ocean Crest Lodge. It has a beautiful indoor pool and hot tub and is open to non-guests. Cost is $6.50 per day for adults and $3.50 for children.

CALENDAR

MARCH: Beachcomber/Fun Fair, Ocean Shores
JULY: Annual Sand Sculpture Contest, Copalis Beach
Annual Kite Flying Contest, Pacific Beach

Beach Packing List: Kites, rubber boots, plenty of grubby clothes (including extra shoes and socks), buckets, shovels.

KALALOCH

From Cape Flattery (Neah Bay)—the northwestern-most point of the continental U.S.—south to Kalaloch, the ocean beach is either Native American reservation or national park. Right at Kalaloch you'll find some of the wildest surf and best beachcombing on the entire Washington coast.

PLACES TO STAY

KALALOCH LODGE
360/962-2271; HC 80, PO Box 1100, Kalaloch, 98331
Rates: Moderate to expensive
Essentials: Credit cards; cribs
Extras: Kitchens in cabins; pets OK in cabins
Kalaloch offers lodge, motel, duplex and cabin accommodations. The lodge rooms are a bit noisy and too cramped for a family. The duplexes are perched on a bluff overlooking the ocean and have lovely views. The newer log cabins are more expensive and nicer than the funky, older cabins, but bring your own utensils, pots and pans—the kitchenettes are poorly equipped. There's a small grocery on the site, but it is best to shop ahead.
Although the resort is perched above the beach, there is a short, easy trail between the two. The beach is beautiful—filled with craggy driftwood, rocks, sand and seashells—but the water is too cold and too dangerous for swimming. There is a small, calm lagoon for paddling about in the summer, right in front of the lodge. Kalaloch is a popular place: plan to make reservations

several months in advance for holidays and the summer season.

The lodge has a dining room and a coffee shop, both of which have the same menu, same (pricey) prices and same so-so food (best bets are fish and oysters). If you want to take the kids to the dining room, go early. The coffee shop has faster service.

PARENT COMMENTS: *"We like to go to Kalaloch in the winter, when it is stormy. We bring plenty of books and games as well as raincoats and boots so we can take beach walks in the wind and rain."*

WHAT TO SEE AND DO

Kalaloch is a good home base for day trips, either to explore the rain forest, follow a tree-lined boardwalk from Lake Ozette to remote beaches, or visit the Makah Indian Village at Neah Bay. (See Olympic Peninsula: What to See and Do for details.)

GUIDED WALKS AND TALKS are offered by the Kalaloch Ranger Station (360/962-2283).

LONG BEACH

The Long Beach Peninsula, about a 3-hour drive from Seattle, stretches 28 miles from Cape Disappointment at the mouth of the Columbia River to Leadbetter Point, dividing Willapa Bay from the Pacific. The point at which a mighty river meets the sea is inevitably rich in natural beauty and history, so visiting families will find much to explore here.

The peninsula's environment has also made it attractive to industry. The marshes are ideal for growing cranberries; there are over 475 acres in production. In the Willapa Bay area, oysters are a big commercial crop. They are not available for public harvesting.

PLACES TO STAY

KLIPSAN BEACH COTTAGES
360/665-4888; 22617 Pacific Hwy, Ocean Park, 98640
Rates: Inexpensive to moderate
Essentials: Credit cards; cribs
Extras: TV; kitchens; fireplaces/woodstoves, free firewood

There are nine Klipsan Beach Cottages—comfortable cedar-shingle cabins with fireplaces (or woodstoves) and west-facing decks. The expanse of dunes and sea visible from the cabins makes up for their close proximity to one another. Cabins have either one, two or three bedrooms, a hide-a-bed in the living room and fully equipped kitchens.

This is a popular place for families, so there are usually many children around. Hide-and-seek enthusiasts will find plenty of hiding places in the small rhododendron forest and along the safe stretch of dunes between the cabins and the beach.

 PARENT COMMENTS: *"The style is not elegant, but it's inoffensive, and there's nothing your kids can destroy."*

THE SOU'WESTER LODGE

360/642-2542; 38th & "J" Pl (PO Box 102), Seaview, 98644
Rates: Inexpensive to moderate
Essentials: Credit cards; cribs
Extras: TV (require reservation); kitchens; pets OK; babysitting by arrangement

The Sou'Wester, built in 1982 by a U.S. senator from Oregon (who originally called it "Westborough House") is now in the competent hands of Len and Miriam Atkins.

The decor at the Sou'Wester is described by the owners as "early Salvation Army." The Atkins want to attract the kind of people who will come "in spite of the fact the lodge is not painted or furnished like the Hilton—people who are looking for a place where the setting itself is meaningful." Located on three acres of land, the Sou'Wester also offers camping sites and RV hookups with hot showers and laundry facilities.

Apartments and rooms in the main lodge are supplemented by four beach cabins, which have kitchens but no fireplaces. Guests may prefer the TCHP (trailer class hodge-podge) accommodations: self-contained recreation vehicles that are reportedly very satisfactory for families.

The Atkins left South Africa in 1951 to study A.S. Neill's method of children's self-government in England. From 1951 to 1966 they worked in Israel, where Len was co-director of "Neve Zeilim," the Residential Therapy Facility for the treatment of emotionally disturbed kibbutz children. While there, he was invited by Bruno Bettleheim to join the faculty of the University of Chicago Orthogenic School. They hold "Oceanside Retreats for Parents" which are an outgrowth of these experiences.

 PARENT COMMENTS: *"The drawing card here is the owners— they are wonderful—and were great to our kids."*

The best accommodations for the Long Beach area may be in

a tent, **camping at Fort Canby State Park** (360/642-3078). Located right at the mouth of the Columbia, Fort Canby is one of the best (and busiest) campsites in the state park system. Be sure to make reservations for a campsite early, and try to get a spot close to the beach. Reservations are only taken by mail (must be postmarked after January 1) or in person (after April 1). Write PO Box 488, Ilwaco, 98624.

PLACES TO EAT

THE ARK
360/665-4133; 273rd & Sandridge at the docks, Nahcotta
Hours: Seasonal, closed Jan-Feb
Essentials: Credit cards; highchairs

Out in the middle of nowhere sits this fine little restaurant that enjoys a well-deserved national reputation for outstanding cooking. At night the lights illuminate the grassy marsh of Willapa Bay, and the mood is casually elegant. The dinner menu is not child-oriented (salmon with chanterelles, scallops with sun-dried tomatoes, and such). If you want to go with children, however, we recommend the magnificent breakfast—there is often a guitarist and the mood is less subdued than it is at dinner. Hot honey-bran muffins with cranberry butter start the meal.

If you don't want to stop for a sit-down meal but are headed out to Leadbetter Point or the historic town of Oysterville, treat yourself to the out-of-this-world cinnamon rolls, muffins, cookies and other treats, which can be purchased for take-out at the front of the restaurant.

During summer months, reservations are essential.

42ND STREET CAFE
360/642-2323; 42nd St & Pacific Hwy, Seaview
Hours: Lunch Wed-Sat, dinner Wed-Mon
Essentials: Credit cards; highchairs

The atmosphere is crowded and homey, and the food is scrumptious. Tables are so close together that a hungry toddler with a good reach could snatch bread off the neighbor's plate, so keep this in mind if you have a high-energy tyke.

Food is basic American (i.e., kids will like it), servings are plentiful, and prices are very reasonable. If you have room for dessert, you won't be disappointed.

THE LIGHTSHIP RESTAURANT
360/642-3252; at Nendel's Inn at S 10th

Hours: Lunch and dinner daily; breakfast Sat and Sun only
Essentials: Credit cards; highchairs

Just a look at the nondescript Nendel's Inn would not entice you to try out its top-floor restaurant, which just goes to show that looks can be deceiving. The fare at the Lightship is a delicious surprise: the creatively prepared seafood and pasta dishes at dinner are superb; breakfasts are equally tasty.

MY MOM'S PIE KITCHEN

360/642-2342; Hwy 103 & 12th S, Long Beach
Hours: Lunch Tues-Sun
Essentials: Credit cards

The pies are excellent—banana cream, rhubarb, raspberry and so on, depending on the season—but don't overlook the rich crab quiche, steamy clam chowder or chili dogs for the kids. Prices are very reasonable.

WHAT TO SEE AND DO

THE CAPE DISAPPOINTMENT COAST GUARD STATION is located near the mouth of the Columbia, where the bar between the river and the ocean creates treacherous waters that have wrecked hundreds of ships.

The Coast Guard Station conducts a one-of-a-kind rescue boat handlers school that draws applicants from around the country. Occasionally visitors will witness boats being launched through the heavy surf to practice rescue missions.

Located about 4 miles southwest of Ilwaco. Open to visitors weekday afternoons and all day Sat and Sun.

Just below Cape Disappointment sits **Fort Columbia State Park**, an abandoned military outpost from the Spanish-American War of 1898. This 554-acre park includes a historical museum, abandoned gun batteries and old buildings.

THE ILWACO HERITAGE MUSEUM in Ilwaco offers an excellent overview of local history from early Native American culture through European exploration, pioneer settlement and the early 20th century.

115 SE Lake St; 360/642-3446. Open Mon-Sat, 10 am-4 pm. Cost: $1.25/adult, $.50/child 6-12, free for children under 6.

Perched on the cliffs above the cape is the **Lewis and Clark Interpretive Center**, with displays about the explorers' route from St. Louis to the Pacific in 1805-1806. About 230 ships have been wrecked near Cape Disappointment. It is a well-designed museum which also has spectacular views of the ships and fishing boats heading up and down the Columbia. Well worth a visit. *Fort Canby State Park; 360/642-3029. Hours vary. Free.*

At the northern tip of the peninsula is **Leadbetter Point** and the **Willapa National Wildlife Refuge** (located at Hwy 101 & Hwy 101A, Ilwaco; 360/484-3482), which has over 20 varieties of birds and numerous easy foot trails through pine forest and sand dunes.

THE WORLD KITE MUSEUM AND HALL OF FAME in Long Beach has rotating exhibits of more than 600 kites from around the world, along with displays of stunt kites, military kites and such. *Third St NW at Rte 103; 360/642-4020. Hours are seasonal. Cost: $1/adult, $.50 under 17.*

CALENDAR

MARCH: Whale watching, Long Beach Peninsula & Westport
APRIL: Ragtime Rhodie Dixieland Jazz Festival, Long Beach
MAY: Loyalty Weekend Celebration and Parade, Long Beach
JUNE: World's Longest Beach Walk/Run, Long Beach
JULY: Sand-sations, sand sculpture contest, Long Beach
AUGUST: International Kite Festival, Long Beach
SEPTEMBER: Arts & Craft Festival, Ocean Park
OCTOBER: Cranberry Festival, Long Beach

RESOURCES

LONG BEACH PENINSULA VISITORS BUREAU
PO Box 562, Long Beach, 98631
360/642-2400 or 800/451-2542

SEATTLE

No question—Seattle is one of the best cities in the U.S. to visit with kids. Whether you come to explore the colorful Pike Place Market and nearby waterfront, experience the world-class zoo, take in a play at the award-winning Children's Theater, ride a ferry or hike, boat, ski, river raft or fish in the great outdoors, you will never lack opportunities for a good time.

GETTING THERE

Interstate 5 is the main route into Seattle from the north and south; Highway 520 or I-90 will get you there from the east. Seattle-Tacoma International Airport is about 16 miles from downtown. The Amtrak station (800/USA-RAIL) is at Third and Jackson, at the south end of downtown. Amtrak operates six trains a week along the Seattle-Portland corridor, as well as trains north to Vancouver, B.C. and east over the Cascades to Montana and beyond.

PLACES TO STAY

EDGEWATER
206/728-7000; Pier 67, Alaskan Way
Rates: Expensive
Essentials: Credit cards; cribs
Extras: Restaurant; TV; exercise room

The location, smack dab on the waterfront and within easy walking distance of the Seattle Aquarium, the *Victoria Clipper* terminal and the Pike Place Market, can't be beat.

The decor is Northwest, comfy and not-too-fragile. For a small fee you can use the Seattle Club about five blocks away. It is a well-equipped health club that welcomes kids and includes a swimming pool and basketball court.

 PARENT COMMENTS: *"Fun location! My kids loved sitting in our waterside room and watching the constant boat traffic."*

FOUR SEASONS OLYMPIC
206/621-1700; 411 University St, Seattle, 98101
Rates: Expensive
Essentials: Credit cards; cribs
Extras: Indoor pool, Jacuzzi, exercise room; restaurants, TV, babysitting service; strollers, toys; pets OK with prior notice.

If you want to be in the heart of downtown Seattle and go first-class, you can rest assured you and your children will be well taken care of at the grand old Olympic. When you make a reservation tell them the ages of your children and they'll have suitable toys waiting when you arrive.

Whatever child-related paraphernalia you need—bibs, strollers, playpens, car seats, kids' videos, even Nintendo—will be provided. The children receive a fun gift when they arrive and at check-out there's cookies and milk for the road. They even welcome the family pet!

The pool and huge Jacuzzi are as lovely as you'll ever find in a hotel and the dressing rooms are wonderful for small kids—warm and comfy with an endless supply of big, soft towels. The food and service at the three restaurants in the hotel are also four-star and they all have a children's menu. The Garden Court, an enormous skylit room with massive potted plants, serves an elegant High Tea and a special Children's Tea.

PARENT COMMENTS: *"We live in Seattle, but we have taken several "vacations" at the Four Seasons. We catch a bus downtown with our three children and check in for a night of relaxation and indulgence."*

"Amazing! A four-star hotel that treats children as well as they treat the adults!"

MARRIOTT RESIDENCE INN
206/624-6000; 800 Fairview Ave N, Seattle, 98109
Rates: Moderate to expensive
Essentials: Credit cards; cribs
Extras: Full kitchens with microwave (no conventional oven), refrigerator, dishwasher and stove; swimming pool, hot tub, exercise room; babysitting; free continental breakfast buffet; shuttle; grocery delivery, coin-operated laundry facilities, TV; pets OK ($10/night)

The Inn is geared to the business traveler who has to stay awhile, but works exceptionally well for families. While not in the heart of downtown, the location is nice because you can stroll about at the south end of Lake Union, jump in your car and get on I-5 or use the free Inn shuttle to get to the downtown, Seattle Center or waterfront.

There is an open lobby and the majority of rooms face onto the lobby, so you can sit in the lobby and watch your kids go up the elevator then walk to their room. The rooms are spacious and kitchens are fully equipped with dishes, utensils and a packet of microwave popcorn. The pool, hot tub and exercise room are all situated in one area so you can be on an exercise machine while watching kids in the pool. The free continental buffet breakfast includes sweet rolls, bagels, muffins, fruit and cereals. The lobby has plenty of tables and sitting areas for dining or you can take food back to the room. A free dessert is served Thursday through Tuesday in the lobby at 7 pm.

With four hours notice the free shuttle will transport you anywhere within a 2 1/2 mile radius which includes the downtown, waterfront and the Seattle Center.

PARENT COMMENTS:*"We stayed here with three school-kids and it worked out very well. We didn't feel cramped for space."*
"It was relaxing to use the free shuttle to get to downtown and the Seattle Center and not hassle with driving and parking."

SILVER CLOUD INNS

206/526-5200; 5036 25th Ave NE, Seattle 98015
206/775-7600; 19332 36th Ave W, Lynnwood, 98036
206/746-8200;15304 NE 21st St, Redmond 98052
206/821-8300; 12202 NE 124th St, Kirkland 98034
206/241-2200/13050 48th Ave S, Tukwila 98168
Rates: Moderate
Essentials: Credit cards; cribs
Extras: Kitchens (in some units); swimming pool (except Redmond), fitness center; laundry facilities

Silver Cloud Inns are well-suited to families. All in the Seattle area (except Redmond) have an indoor or outdoor swimming pool. All have refrigerators in the rooms and most have the option of either a "kitchenette" (microwave, wet bar, refrigerator) or a full kitchen. All serve a free continental breakfast. Best of all, they are moderately priced. At the Seattle location a unit with a king bed plus queen hide-a-bed and a kitchenette runs $84-$89 for two adults with kids under 12 free. At the Redmond location, a one-bedroom suite with a king and queen-sofa bed and full kitchen is $95.

The new Silver Cloud near University Village Shopping Mall and the University of Washington is an excellent location if you are travelling by car. It is a 10-minute drive to downtown, Woodland Park Zoo and most other attractions and sits next to the outstanding Burke-Gilman bike trail so bring your bikes.

PARENT COMMENTS:*"We save the big hotel splurges for when we travel without the youngsters. Silver Cloud is our favorite in-city hotel when travelling with the kids."*
"Very clean, comfortable, good locations, family-friendly service and reasonable prices."
"Usually located near a shopping mall, which is convenient."

WESTIN

206/728-1000; 1900 5th Ave, Seattle, 98101
Rates: Moderate to Expensive
Essentials: Credit cards; cribs
Extras: Westin Kid's Club; refrigerators; step stools; potty seats; indoor pool and jacuzzi, exercise room; TV; free breakfast for kids

12 and under at the Market Cafe during summer months.

Like many other hotel chains, the Westin recognizes that catering to families is good business. Since 1994 they have offered the Westin Kid's Club to make your stay with kids hassle-free. Strollers, stepstools and potty seats are yours for the asking. Upon arrival kids receive a Kid's Club kit that includes a sports cap for ages 8 to 12 and a plastic drinking cup for younger kids. Parents get a safety kit that includes a safety i.d. bracelet, electrical outlet covers, bandaids and local emergency numbers. In the hotel restaurants, parents are given preferred reservations and express meal service (call in advance and your meal will be waiting when you arrive.)

During the summer months, there are even more good deals for families. The Westin Summer Package includes valuable discount coupons to the major local attractions, including the Science Center, Zoo and Aquarium. Even better, in the summer kids under 12 eat free in the highly recommended Market Cafe at the hotel.

PARENT COMMENTS: *"The staff was very helpful about providing the little touches that make travelling with a baby easier."* *"The room was standard, we'd give the pool a B+, but the free meal deal for kids at the Market Cafe (available only in the summer) was a GREAT deal. The food is excellent and we saved a bundle eating there with our three school-age kids."*

THE WILLIAMS HOUSE

206/285-0810; 1505 4th Ave N, Seattle, 98109
Rates: Moderate
Essentials: Credit cards; crib
Extras: Breakfast

Doug and Sue Williams have school-age children of their own and they welcome families to their charming bed and breakfast on the south slope of Queen Anne Hill. The location— a five minute drive or bus ride to downtown and an easy walk to the Seattle Center—is well-suited to families in town to see the sights. There are five guest rooms, four with views and two with private baths. One room has a king bed and a double futon and the Williams have a rollaway bed available for the other rooms. A full breakfast is served.

PARENT COMMENTS: *"It was very relaxing and pleasant to be staying in a B&B with young children in a nice neighborhood so close to the city."*

WESTCOAST PLAZA PARK SUITES HOTEL
206/682-8282; 1011 Pike St, Seattle, 98101
Rates: Expensive
Essentials: Credit cards; cribs
Extras: Free continental breakfast; kitchens; TV; outdoor
swimming pool, sauna, fireplaces and jacuzzi in some rooms.

   The one-bedroom suites have a living room with fold-out sofa, a comfortable bedroom (with a second TV) and a kitchen. Some suites come with fireplaces and Jacuzzis. While clearly aimed at the business traveler, the comforts of home that the Plaza Park provides are lovely for travelling families, too—especially the fully-equipped kitchen that includes a two burner stovetop, microwave oven, toaster and dishwasher. The outdoor pool is open year-round. The location, next door to the Convention Center, puts you within easy walking distance of downtown. However, you will pay dearly for the comfort and location—a one-bedroom suite runs about $200 per night.

PARENT COMMENTS: *"We stayed at the Plaza Park when we travelled with my spouse on business because we wanted to be downtown in a two-room unit with a full kitchen. It was expensive but we saved on money and hassle by not taking our two preschoolers out to eat and not renting a car, which we would have done if we'd stayed out in the suburbs in a less expensive motel. Public transportation worked fine for us."*

THE VERMONT INN
206/441-0101; 2721 4th Ave, Seattle, 98121
Rates: Inexpensive (weekly only)
Essentials: Credit cards
Extras: Kitchens; TV; weekly maid service

   If you are going to be in Seattle for at least a week, consider renting a unit in this inn-apartment located just one block from the Seattle Center. One and two-bedroom units are available; cost is about $250 per week. In addition to the reduced expense of your lodging, you will save money and hassle by being able to prepare meals.

THE HOTEL ALTERNATIVE
206/867-9200
PACIFIC COAST SUITES
800/962-6620

   Staying in a hotel is expensive and not very practical for families. Renting a condo will give you more space and the convenience of your own kitchen. Even if you want to give yourself a vacation and eat dinner out, you can save significant hassle and cost by fixing lunch and breakfast yourself.

Both of these services rent condominiums throughout the greater Seattle area. The staff is helpful about recommending a location that suits the needs of your family. All have kitchen facilities, many have pools, VCRs and other conveniences. A minimum stay is usually required.

ON THE EASTSIDE

BEST WESTERN BELLEVUE INN
206/455-5240; 11211 Main St, Bellevue, 98004
Rates: Moderate
Essentials: Credit cards; cribs
Extras: Swimming pool (outdoor); restaurant.

Nothing fancy here—which is why this is a good bet for families staying in Bellevue. The two-story, clean and comfortable motel is arranged around a lawn and outdoor heated pool. The location—just off Hwy 405 on "Hotel Row"-gives you easy access to the freeway to Seattle.

PARENT COMMENTS: *"We spent one day in Seattle at the Pike Place Market and one day school shopping on the Eastside. The kids loved cooling off in the pool at the end of the day."*

LA RESIDENCE SUITE HOTEL
206/455-1475; 475 100th Ave NE, Bellevue 98004
Rates: Moderate
Essentials: Credit cards; cribs
Extras: Kitchens; laundry facilities

The rooms have complete kitchens (full refrigerator, stove, oven, microwave, dishwasher) and separate bedrooms so they work well for families who can use some extra space and don't want to eat out every meal. The location—across the street from Bellevue Square, the best shopping center in the region—offers easy entertainment and several reasonably-priced eating options. Downtown Seattle is an easy 15-minute freeway drive away.

PARENT COMMENTS: *"The rooms are spacious and worked well for our family of two adults, a fourteen-year-old and an eleven-year-old. The kids were in heaven because we let them go wander Bellevue Square alone while we stayed at the hotel and read."*

See also **Silver Cloud Inns** under Seattle-Places to Stay.

PLACES TO EAT

EL PUERCO LLORON ("THE CRYING PIG")
206/624-0541; 1501 Western Ave on the Hillclimb
Hours: Lunch and dinner daily
Essentials: Credit cards; highchairs
  This cheerful hole-in-the-wall sits on the Hillclimb, between the Pike Place Market and the waterfront. The style is loose and easy—cafeteria-style, metal card tables, cha-cha music. All the dishes are handmade from fresh ingredients, including the hot-off-the-griddle corn tortillas. Delicious and inexpensive.

CHINOOKS
206/283-4665; 1900 W Nickerson St
Hours: Lunch and dinner daily, breakfast Sat and Sun
Essentials: Credit cards; highchairs
  Chinooks is a good place to look at a working marina and eat well-prepared seafood without emptying the wallet. Kids will find plenty to see through the large windows that enclose this attractive bustling restaurant in Fishermen's Terminal near Ballard—about 10 minutes by car from downtown Seattle. There's a wide selection—over 125 items on the dinner menu plus daily specials (fish off the daily specials is a good way to go) along with a decent children's menu. Dinner entrees for adults run $7.95-$14.95.
  There is often a short wait for breakfast on the weekends, but once you are seated, a basket of scrumptious fresh-baked scones will arrive at your table, along with orange butter. If you want to work off your meal afterwards, drive a few blocks west to Discovery Park, the largest park in the city (see Parks below for more details).

CUCINA!CUCINA!
206/447-2782; 901 Fairview at the south end of Lake Union
206/637-1177; 800 Bellevue Way, Bellevue
206/575-0520; 17770 Southcenter Pkwy, Tukwila
Hours: Lunch, dinner daily
Essentials: Credit cards; highchairs
  Here you'll find a good view of Lake Union, two-star Italian food at moderate prices and a lively staff that will give you and your kids a good time. Upon entering Cucina!Cucina! your child is offered a balloon—an instant hit. Crayons and a color-in menu

follow, and if that isn't enough, your table is covered with white butcher paper, so that the coloring can extend onto the table. The child's menu offers individual pizzas ($2.95 includes milk or soda) plus a good selection of pasta dishes. The adult menu has a decent selection of pastas, pizzas and salads.

FRESH CHOICE
206/440-8136; 463 Northgate Mall, Seattle
206/822-2548; 10733 Northup Way, Bellevue
Hours: Lunch, dinner daily
Essentials: Credit cards, highchairs
It had to happen sooner or later—an all-you-can-eat restaurant that offers healthy fare. At this cheery cafeteria, salads are the star of the show. Diners choose from several varieties of freshly prepared, pasta, legume, spinach, potato and fruit salads with all the accoutrements you can imagine. A pasta and baked potato and dessert bar round out the meal. Everybody finds something they like—and the parent smiles about the prices.

GREEN VILLAGE
206/624-3634; 721 S King St, International District
Hours: Lunch, dinner daily except Tues
Essentials: Credit cards; highchair
At Green Village your toughest moment will be choosing from the menu of over 100 items. Don't agonize too much though: we haven't found a bad choice yet. The style is mostly Szechuan so you will need to be careful not to order foods that will be too spicy for young palates. For a tasty thrill, order sizzling rice soup—a waitperson brings a big bowl of broth, vegetables and shrimp to your table, ceremoniously dumps in hot fried rice and it does sizzle. All the noodle dishes are wonderful: the seafood dishes are also exceptional, but more pricey. There are several big round tables that can comfortably seat a big group.

GREEN VILLAGE 2
206/621-1719; 514 6th Ave S, in the International District
Hours: Lunch, dinner Mon-Sat
Essentials: No credit cards, no highchairs
If you hanker for Chinese food but want a quicker, low budget alternative, head down to this little hole-in-the-wall with a barebones dining area and a very limited but tasty menu (House Special Rice Noodles, $4.50; Three Types of Seafood Noodles, $4.95; Vegetables over Rice $4.25). After your meal, walk across the street for some fun browsing at the Uwajimaya store—stuffed

with Asian imported goods.

HUONG BINH
206/720-4907; 1207 S Jackson St
Hours: Lunch, dinner daily
Essentials: No credit cards or checks; highchairs
You can dine-in or take-out at this busy spot just north of the International District, but if you aren't very familiar with Vietnamese food we suggest you eat on the premises so the friendly staff can give you some tips on what to order and how to proceed once your food arrives. Vietnamese food often comes with a little of this and a little of that and kids may not eat the interesting herbs and sauces but they will probably find something to nibble and enjoy the novelty. See what they think of bahn hoi chao tom (grilled shrimp served on a sugar cane)—at worst you can eat the yummy shrimp and let them suck on the sugar cane.

IRON HORSE
206/233-9506; 311 3rd Ave S near Pioneer Square
Hours: Lunch, dinner daily
Essentials: Credit cards, high hairs
We break a few of our own rules by including this place—like rule number one: the food must be good. The food is not bad here, just mediocre. But go for lunch anyway, because every child deserves to have the experience of getting his hamburger delivered by a model train. Fare is standard—salads, burgers, sandwiches and there isn't speedy delivery, but when your preschooler's face lights up as the train pulls up with the food, you'll be glad you came.

IVAR'S ACRE OF CLAMS
206/624-6852; Pier 54 on the downtown waterfront
Hours: Lunch, dinner daily
Essentials: Credit cards; highchairs
IVAR'S INDIAN SALMON HOUSE
206/632-0767; 401 Northlake Way, north side of Lake Union.
Hours: Lunch Mon-Fri, brunch Sun, dinner daily
Essentials: Credit cards; highchairs
With a child's menu that doubles as a colorful Indian mask, friendly waitpersons who go out of their way to make kids feel welcome and good food at reasonable prices (salmon, cornbread and slaw for $6.75), Ivar's is the place to go if you want a look at Northwest Indian culture and good fish.
Both restaurants are located on the water—the Salmon House

on Lake Union and Acres of Clams on Puget Sound— so there's always a good view of the boat traffic. Both also have a take-out counter—a good option on a nice day.

Our favorite is the Indian Salmon House on the north side of Lake Union. It is located in a replica of an Indian Longhouse, with magnificent canoes, masks and photographs decorating the dining area. Cod and salmon are prepared over a smoky alder fire which kids will enjoy watching.

MARKET CAFE AT THE WESTIN HOTEL

206/728-1000; Westin Hotel
Hours: Breakfast, lunch, dinner daily
Essentials: Credit cards; highchairs

It is surprisingly difficult to find a decent meal in downtown Seattle that will satisfy both the adults and the children without breaking the budget. This isn't a fancy place—just a brightly decorated coffeeshop located off the lobby of the hotel. However, the food is exceptionally well prepared and the menu offers a wide variety of healthy and delicious choices likely to meet the food preferences of all ages at your table.

On the breakfast menu the fresh muesli cereal (hand mixed in the kitchen with loads of fresh fruit) and the french toast are exceptional. At all meals the kitchen is happy to accomodate special requests. Crayons are provided and service is excellent.

THE OLD SPAGHETTI FACTORY

206/441-7724; 2801 Elliott Ave
Hours: Lunch, dinner daily
Essentials: Credit cards; highchairs

The first clue that this place is good for familes is its name: "Factory" is not a word usually associated with elegant dining. Even so the Spaghetti Factory has manged to create a festive atmosphere, with Victorian style decor, a beautiful old weighing scale (only kids like to weigh themselves before and after dinner) and a real caboose that sits in the middle of the main dining area. The food is good and very reasonably priced (spaghetti with clam sauce, $5.35; meatballs and spaghetti, $6.25.) All dinners include salad, a loaf of sourdough bread and spumoni for dessert. Kids get a paper train conductor cap and choice of special meals that come on a plastic dinosaur plate. A typical kid meal includes spaghetti, applesauce, beverage, dinosaur cookie and frozen treat for $2.95. A junior meal, for bigger or hungrier children, costs $3.75 and includes spaghetti, salad, bread, beverage and spumoni. Since you aren't the only parent looking for good food and fast service at great prices in a fun setting, plan to go early (before 5:30 pm) if you want to avoid a wait. Reservations are not accepted.

TESTAROSSA
206/328-0878; 210 Broadway E, Seattle
Hours:Lunch, dinner daily, Sunday brunch
Essentials:Credit cards; highchairs
It is worth a trip to Broadway on Capital Hill to experience the delectible deep-dish pizza served in this snazzy Italian spot. Kids are cheerfully welcomed. The salads are also extraordinary.

PARENTS NIGHT OUT
Even if you are on a "family" vacation, it would be a shame to visit Seattle without experiencing a meal at one of the many four-star restaurants. One night leave the kids back at the hotel with a sitter. You can't go wrong at: **Adriatica, Chez Shea, Dahlia Lounge, Etta's Seafood, Ponti Seafood Grill, Prego, Ray's Boathouse, Saleh al Lago, Wild Ginger.**

WHAT TO SEE AND DO

STROLL & BROWSE
Downtown Seattle has four areas that are well-worth exploring on foot with the kids: the waterfront, Pioneer Square, the Pike Place Market and Seattle Center. Seattle's hills are steep. While walking between Pioneer Square, the Pike Place Market and the waterfront is possible for an older child or an adult, younger people will quickly run out of steam, so take advantage of the **Bus Ride Free Zone** that Metro offers. It extends from Jackson Street—near the Kingdome on the edge of the International District—up to Battery Street and from Interstate 5 to the waterfront. Try to take at least one ride in the buses that go under downtown Seattle—the underground stations are resplendent with colorful murals. Metro has other good deals for families, like the weekend Family Pass.
Metro Information: 206/553-3000
The **elevated monorail** will thrill the kids and it is a convenient way to get from downtown to the Seatte Center. It departs from Westlake Mall about every fifteen minutes and whisks riders to the Center where the Pacific Science Center, the Seattle Children's Museum and other attractions are located.
Vintage trolleys, another fun mode of transportation, run frequently along the waterfront to Pioneer Square and the International District.

THE WATERFRONT

The Seattle **downtown waterfront** is a helter-skelter mix of magnificent views, schlocky tourist shops, a first-class aquarium, historical landmarks and colorful maritime traffic. It is a splendid place to spend an afternoon with the kids. If you are driving, park your car any place you can find a meter beneath the monstrous Alaskan Way Viaduct that runs parallel to the waterfront. It works well to park near the Pike Place Hillclimb, across from the aquarium, and then take the southbound trolley to the Washington St. station and cross the road to Pier 50. If you are walking from the center of downtown, kids will enjoy descending next to the waterfalls on the attractive new Harbor Steps between First and Western avenues at University Street. Once you reach the waterfront, watch the kids carefully: The guardrails next to the water are not childproof.

Pier 50 marks the beginning of **Colman Dock**, the terminal for ferries to Bremerton on the Kitsap Peninsula, Bainbridge Island and Vashion Island (passenger only). For a fabulous look at the city from the water and the great fun of a ride on these magnificent craft, walk on one of the ferries for a round-trip ride. (Information: 464-6400.) Just north of the terminal on Pier 53 sits Fire Station #5, home port for two splendid fireboats, the Alki and the Duwamish. You might get lucky and see the boats out in the bay spraying their hoses up towards the sky for one reason or another.

Further north, at Pier 54, don't miss **Ye Olde Curiosity Shop**. Since 1889, this one-of-a-kind place has been a Seattle fixture. Look for the fully dressed fleas, two shrunken heads, two real mummies and a navy bean that holds 10 ivory elephants. Kids also like to shop at **Watermark Landmark** on Pier 55. For just $.50, they can take home a scoop of beautifully colored rocks and tiny shells. Across the way, **Jonah's Glass Shop** sells very pretty and very fragile glass figurines (For under-control kids only).

If the stomachs are starting to growl, you can find good fast food at **Ivar's Fish and Chips**, the **Red Robin Express** or **The Frankfurter** at Pier 54 and Pier 55.

Tucked inside The Pavilion at Pier 57, you'll be surprised to find a grand old **carousel**—rides $1. Next door, **Waterfront Park** on Pier 59 offers an unparalleled view of the water and Olympic Mountains. Just north of the park sits the outstanding **Seattle Aquarium**. (see Animals, Animals for details).

The area between the aquarium and Pier 70 is not as interesting for walkers. If you hop back in your car and drive just beyond the shops at Pier 70 to the parking area, you'll discover **Myrtle**

It is easy to hop a trolley from the waterfront to Pioneer Square.

Edwards Park, a scenic strip along Elliott Bay that has paths for bikers, walkers and runners (about 8 miles round-trip) and a fishing pier and bait shop (the Happy Hooker) at Pier 86. The bike path is also excellent for roller blading. The first section of the path includes a small beach, spectacular views of Elliott Bay and the Olympic Mountains and a close-up look at gargantuan grain elevators loading freighters from all parts of the globe. Beyond the northern parking lot the path circles around a huge parking lot with rows and rows of imported cars awaiting delivery and a close-up view of a railway yard. At the turnaround point you'll be rewarded by the best vantage point in town for viewing the downtown skyline.

If being close to the water just isn't enough, extend your adventure by hopping on one of the ferries or tour boats taking off from the various piers.

Walking on board the **Winslow ferry** at Pier 50 for the half-hour ride to Bainbridge Island is a fine way to view the Seattle skyline and kids will be thrilled with the ride. Take a morning boat and enjoy a scrumptious breakfast at the **Streamliner Diner** in the tiny town of Winslow. *Ferry information: 464-6400 or (800)843-3779*

Argosy Tours depart from Piers 55 & 57. Both kids and adults will probably enjoy one of their boat tours of the city. Narratives are informative and lively. The 2 1/2 hour Cruise the Locks tour is the most interesting of the three. It includes the Chittenden Locks, Lake Washington and Elliott Bay on Puget Sound. *Information: 623-1445.*

For a boat ride and first-hand look at Northwest Indian culture, consider taking the four-hour **Tillicum Village Tour**. Just eight miles from Seattle across Puget Sound lies Blake Island, a Washington State Park with nearly 500 acres of forest, beaches and Tillicum Village. Once you reach the island you head for a huge cedar longhouse, where a complete salmon dinner—baked over an alderwood fire—awaits you. Following dinner, you and your family are treated to the outstanding Tillicum Village Native American production, with music, dance and legends of Northwest Coast Indians. During the summer there's also a Hike Special, offering an additional 2 1/2 hours of time to explore the island's 16 miles of hiking trails. *Information: 443-1244.*

Finally, near the north end of the waterfront, at Pier 69, there's the loading dock for the **Victoria Clipper**, a hydrofoil craft that carries passengers to Victoria, B.C. It is a highly recommended day trip for kids ages eight and up—the outstanding Royal British

Columbia Museum alone is worth the trip. (See Victoria, BC. for more details.) *Information: 448-5000.*

Recommended family restaurants in the area: **Ivar's** and **The Spaghetti Factory**. See Places to Eat for more details.

PIONEER SQUARE

A visit to **Pioneer Square**, a block off the waterfront at the southern end of downtown, offers a glimpse of Seattle history along with many interesting galleries and shops. During the summer months, an information booth at Occidental S and S Main is open from 10 am-4 pm, Monday through Saturday, providing directions and tips about the area.

From the city's incorporation in 1869 to the late 1880s, Pioneer Square was a thriving business district, where most of Seattle's 40,000 residents lived and worked. But on June 6, 1889 a furniture maker left a pot of glue on a hot stove unattended resulting in the biggest fire in Seattle history—one that burned the young city to ashes. The real capper is that you and your family can still visit what remains of the old town. **Seattle Underground Tours** offers 1 ½-hour tours daily throughout the year (not wheelchair or stroller accessible). The lively guides are full of history trivia and corny jokes and most adults enjoy the experience but many kids don't consider this fun—too much history and too dark and dank. *Call 682-4646 for details.*

For more regional history, drop by the **Klondike Gold Rush National Historical Park** at 117 Main. This little museum, using maps, photos, slides and films, tells the dramatic story of the Alaska Gold Rush and its enormous impact on the City of Seattle.

553-7220; Open daily, 9 am-5 pm. Free.

The children's (and parenting) book selection is outstanding at Elliott Bay Book Company in Pioneer Square.

SHOPPING. The art galleries and antique rug stores in this area are not suitable for most kids, but the following places are likely to interest the younger shopper:

The Elliott Bay Book Company *(1st Ave & S Main)* is a favorite bookstore among local literary buffs. It boasts a large, outstanding kids' books section and a two-story castle where kids can relax and read their selections. Downstairs there's a delicious cafe/deli—a nice stop for lunch or a snack.

Grand Central Shops at the Park is a two-story complex just north of Elliott Bay Books. Kids will enjoy watching the blacksmith at work in **The Blacksmith Shop** and the sticker/stamps collector in your group will appreciate **Paper Cat Rubber Stamps.**

Great Winds Kite Shop (*402 Occidental S*) has a dandy kite selection, nice to fly and dandy for decorating a child's room. **Magic Mouse Toys** (*1st and Yesler, at the north end of Pioneer Square*) is a first-class toy store. In addition to the usual gadgets, gizmos, dolls and balls, they have an exceptionally good selection of books and arts supplies.

PLACES TO GET A SNACK. At **Waterfall Garden** (*Second Ave S and S Main St.*) a real waterfall and benches to eat your take-out lunch offers a soothing escape from the city hustle and bustle. For a quick snack, check out **Bagel Express** (*205 1st*), across the street from Elliott Bay Books or **Walter's Waffles** (*106 James St*), about a block up the hill from Magic Mouse Toys. The basic yummy waffle snack is $1.25.

PIKE PLACE MARKET

PIKE PLACE MARKET, located at Pike St and 1st Ave, doesn't attract over nine million shoppers a year for its farm fresh goods alone—although they are certainly a main attraction. Opened in 1907, the market has grown to encompass a wide variety of merchants and wares, plus over a dozen ethnic groceries and bakeries, numerous restaurants and novelty shops. It is an ideal place for a family outing, because there is something to interest every age.

The area is a hodge-podge of stairways and halls so the shops and eateries that we recommend may be difficult to find: make your first stop the **Market Information Booth**, located at 1st Ave and Pike St. It offers shopping and restaurant brochures, maps, tour information and discount theater tickets. It is open daily 10 am-6 pm.

Parking can be frustrating in the Market area, especially on sunny summer days. Whatever you do, don't get stuck driving on Pike Place (the road that goes through the Market). Though you may find a parking space, you will surely lose your sanity. Take a bus to the area or opt for parking in one of the many garages or lots located along Western Ave, just below the Market.

Most kids (and adults) will find covering the market and the waterfront in one day is too much, but if you choose to continue your outing with a trip to the waterfront, you can take the elevator from the Public Market Parking Garage, just south of Virginia St, or use the stairs (steep and long) located at the southern end of the Market in an area called the Pike Place Hillclimb to get down to the waterfront.

The **Main Arcade** is the heart of the Market: find it by listening

Don't transport young ones through the Market in a stroller— crowded aisles make navigation very difficult. A backpack will be easier and give your child a better view of the action.

for the shouts of fish mongers and the wet slap of fish being tossed around. You'll also find rows of meticulously arranged fruits and veggies, handmade children's clothing and toys, seasonal fresh-cut flowers, hand-crafted jewelry and pottery and if that isn't enough of a sensory feast, there's always a variety of musicians, balloon sculptors, puppeteers and magicians offering their entertainment to anyone who will take the time to watch. Point out to the kids that the 46,500 tiles that make up the floor each bear the name of somebody who gave money to replace the old wooden floor back in the 1980's.

Don't forget to explore the shops tucked away on the floors below the Main Arcade. The places likely to interest kids include: the **Craft Emporium**, selling beads, feathers, sequins, etc.; **Pike Place Magic Shop**, with a very knowledgeable staff selling all levels of tricks; **Silly Old Bear**, carrying stuffed bears, gnomes and other creatures and **Seattle Market Parrot and Reptile House**, where a $.50 browsing fee will get you a close look at a variety of exotic birds, iguanas, lizards, snakes, pythons, the Fuzzy Baboon Tarantula and the Tomato Toad.

If all this exploring whets appetites, take advantage of the bountiful eating opportunities at the Market. Some of the tastiest food and best bargains are found at the following: **The Crumpet Shop** (delicious toppings on fresh baked crumpets), **Burrito Express** (walk-up window, no place to sit down, generous servings), **Biringer Farm and Bakery** (fresh berry pie and shortcake to die for, plus yummy sandwiches and soups), **Delaurenti's Pizza Window**, (good pizza by the slice) the **Popcorner** (a zillion kinds of popcorn), **Three Girls Bakery** (friendly, cozy spot with delicious salads and soups), **Rasa Malaysia** (stirfry noodles with vegies and chicken) and **El Puerco Lloron**, (fresh tortillas, tacos, tamales and so on) at bargain prices on the Hillclimb.

SEATTLE CENTER

On the northern border of downtown, near the foot of Queen Anne Hill, sprawls the 74-acre **Seattle Center**. Constructed for the 1962 World's Fair, its vast expanse offers a multitude of indoor and outdoor activities along with numerous fine arts and sports facilities, including the Seattle Symphony, Seattle Opera, Seattle Supersonics basketball team, Intiman Theatre, Pacific Northwest Ballet, and the Seattle Repertory Theatre. Of greater interest to anyone traveling with children, the Center is also home to three outstanding places to take the kids: the **Pacific Science Center**, the **Seattle Children's Theater** and the

Children's Museum. And if that isn't enough to keep you busy, there's also the Space Needle and carnival rides at the Fun Forest.

There are ample parking lots near the center, except on the south side. If you are heading to the center from the downtown area, opt for taking the **Monorail** (684-7200) from Westlake Center—the ride is just under two minutes, and it will bring you right to the center of the action.

If you have children under the age of eight, don't pass up a visit to the **Children's Museum**, on the lower floor of the Center House. It is one of the best museums for children in the country. Allow plenty of time—this is a place where the kids should not feel rushed— parents can sit back and relax while keeping an eye on their child absorbed in creative play.

441-1768; Tues-Sun, 10 am-5 pm; daily during summer months. Cost: $3.50/person; children under 12 months free. As of Oct. 1, 1995 – $4.50/person; children under 12 months free.

At the **Pacific Science Center** adults will likely have as much fun as the kids. Visitors roam from exhibit to exhibit, testing their physical and mental skills and discovering why the world is the place it is. A child of four and a teen-ager will both find more than enough to keep them busy in this veritable science playground so plan on staying several hours.

All exhibits at the Science Center are stroller and wheelchair accessible. A stroller is recommended rather than a backpack so you can easily let loose a curious child.

After a few hours of energetic exploration, the **IMAX Theatre**, in the upper west corner of the Science Center, is an excellent place to relax and have a truly unforgettable movie experience. The outstanding IMAX movies are shot on 78-mm film and shown on a screen three-and-a half stories high. You get a free movie with each admission to the Science Center or you can just go to IMAX. Cost for the movie alone is $5.50 /adult; $4.50 children 6-13; $3.50 ages 2-5. Watch out—popular movies fill up early on busy days.

The **Laser Fantasy** is another theater inside the Science Center. It is one of the few places in town that provides good evening entertainment for teen-agers. Viewers lie back in comfy chairs or stretch out on the carpeted floor to watch a laser light show accompanied by music. Evening shows feature music popular with teens; the daytime show is a space odyssey set to classical and popular music and provides a soothing break. Cost is $3 Tues; $6.75 Weds-Sun (closed Mon). (One free show is included with admission to the Science Center.) Call the Laser Hot Line at 443-2850 for schedule information.

Science Center Information:443-2001; Mon-Fri, 10 am-5 pm; Sat, Sun and Holidays 10 am-6 pm. Cost: $6.50/Adult; $5.50/ children 6-13 years; $3.50/children 2-5 years.

During the summer months, the **Fun Forest**, located in the shadow of the Space Needle, presents an assortment of carnival rides for pint-sized to full-grown thrill seekers. Tickets may be purchased individually or in books.

Thirty years after it was erected the **Space Needle** still is one of the best vantage points in Seattle. Visitors take the elevator 518 feet to the Observation Deck, for a panoramic view of the city and its surroundings. The Needle also has a restaurant at the top—good food but expensive.

Rated one of the top children's theater companies in the United States, **Seattle Children's Theatre**, located in a grand new facility on the southwest corner of the Center, presents some of the very best in family entertainment for ages four and up. Each production gives special attention to the young theater audience without losing its appeal to adults and teens. The season is October through May and performances usually run one to two hours in length. An after-show question-and-answer period, during which the audience has a chance to ask questions of the actors, is a big hit with the younger set. Also recently opened is a new theater in the same building intended for a preschool audience.

443-0807 Cost: $16/adult; $10/child. October through May.

PLACES TO SNACK: If your kids get hungry while you are visiting the Seattle Center, head for the **Food Circus**, a collection of restaurants offering a variety of take-out options on the cavernous first floor of the Center House. The prices are reasonable and the smorgasbord approach well suited to feeding kids and adults—everybody can choose a different meal. The stir-fry noodles at Cafe Loc are very popular with all ages.

At the southeast corner, across the street from the Center in the shadow of the Monorail track, is a **McDonald's**. At the northwest corner of the Center, across Mercer St, there is a new shopping/ restaurant complex that includes a state-of-the-art **Larry's Grocery** and another **McDonald's**.

MUSEUMS

BURKE MUSEUM, located on the north end of the beautiful University of Washington campus, is the state museum of natural history and anthropology. The well-presented exhibits include the only dinosaur skeleton on display in the Northwest, a collection of canoes of Native Northwest peoples and a discovery room for children to explore natural history.

17th Ave NE & NE 45th St, University of Washington Campus; (206)543-5590. Hours: Daily 10 am-5 pm, Thursday evenings until 8 pm. Suggested donation: $3/adult; $1.50/ages 6-18; 5 and under no charge.

CENTER FOR WOODEN BOATS. This floating museum and shop located at the south end of Lake Union features a collection of approximately 60 wooden boats, many of them moored along the docks, ranging from the smallest dinghy to a tall three-masted schooner. Children can climb aboard the Panesano, a Monterey fishing boat, work the wheel and imagine they are the captain of their own ship. The staff builds and restores water craft of a variety of sizes so there is always some interesting activity going on. During the summer, skiffs, sailboats, canoes and kayaks can be rented. On the Fourth of July weekend the annual Wooden Boat Festival at the Center includes small boat races, music, food, contests and exhibits for kids.

Also during the summer you'll find delicious fish and chips at **Benji's,** an outdoor fish and chip stand shaped like a tugboat located just outside the restaurant Benjamin's.

1010 Valley St; (206)382-2628. Open year-round Wed-Mon, noon-6 pm, closed Tuesday. Free.

CHILDREN'S MUSEUM. See Stroll & Browse: Seattle Center

MUSEUM OF FLIGHT. This spectacular museum tells the history of flight from the earliest aircraft to the space stations of the future. Located within the museum's vast, open Great Gallery is the hangar exhibit, which features three aircraft, a variety of tools, spare aircraft parts and engines. There's also a full-scale mock-up of a Northrop F/A 18—56 feet in length with a wingspan of 40.5 feet. Children can climb into the cockpit and pretend they are part of the Blue Angels aerobatics team!

9404 E Marginal Way S, near Boeing Field;(206)764-5700. Hours: Open daily 10 am-5 pm, Thursday evenings until 9 pm. Cost: $6/adult, $3 child 6-15, under 6 free.

THE MUSEUM OF HISTORY AND INDUSTRY, located just south of the Montlake Bridge near the University of Washington, focuses on Seattle and Northwest history. It is a small, well-designed museum that is well-suited to children. Highlights include: the Great Seattle Fire of 1889 exhibit; a historical timeline of Seattle from 1850 to the present and the full-scale model of a section of First Ave in the 1880's.

After you visit the museum you can take a scenic walk over foot bridges and boardwalk through marshes on the Foster Island trail—part of the University of Washington Arboretum. The trail begins in the northeast corner of the museum parking lot. *2700 24th Ave E; (206)324-1126. Hours: Open daily, 10 am-5 pm. Suggested donation: $5.50/adult, $3.00/child 6-12, $1.00/child 2-5, under 2 free.*

PACIFIC SCIENCE CENTER. See Stroll and Browse: Seattle Center

ROSALIE WHYEL MUSEUM OF DOLL ART. What's big and pink and full of dolls? The Rosalie Whyel Museum of Doll Art. This 13,000-square foot baby-pink Victorian-style mansion is home to 1,050 dolls—Whyel's collection. The museum, which cost her $3.5 million to build, opened in Bellevue the fall of 1992 to tell the history, technology and artistry of doll making. The collection includes everything from two Egyptian tomb dolls dating back to sometime BC to Barbie.

1116 108th Ave NE, Bellevue; 455-1116. Hours: Mon-Sat, 10 am-5 pm, Thursday evenings until 8 pm, Sunday 1-5 pm. Cost: $6/adult, $4/child 5-17, children under 5 free.

SEATTLE ART MUSEUM. Seattle Art Museum (SAM) opened its new downtown building, just one block south of the Pike Place Market, in 1991. Kids will appreciate the famous 48-foot, 20,000 pound sculpture—Hammering Man—that guards the front entrance. The museum interior is spacious and bright, and the collection includes Native American art, European works, African art, modern art and photographs as well as an extensive Asian art collection. Exhibits are fully accessible to strollers but there are none to rent so bring your own.

100 University St; (206)654-3100. Hours: Tues-Sun, 10 am-5 pm, Thurs, 10 am-9 pm, select Monday holidays. Cost: $6/adults, children under 12 free, admission free first Tuesday of every month.

PARKS

Thanks to early city planners dedicated to preserving open spaces for public enjoyment, Seattle parks are numerous and well-maintained. Below are a few of the best to visit with kids:

DISCOVERY PARK is the largest and most diverse park in Seattle, boasting 534 acres of forest, meadows, cliffs and beaches, self-guided interpretive loops, short hiking trails, man-made ponds and a thriving population of birds and animals. (There are even bald eagles living there.) Located at the northern end of the Magnolia neighborhood, the park is about ten minutes from downtown Seattle. Enter at the west entrance and drive straight ahead to the parking lot and Visitors Center to get the lay of the land. Excellent free drop-in nature walks are offered every Saturday at 2 pm starting from the Visitors Center.

One highlight is **Daybreak Star Center**, a Native American cultural/education center located in the northwest corner. Twelve Native American artists were commissioned to create artworks for this beautiful building and most of the pieces are large murals and carvings depicting legends and traditions that children will find interesting. Daybreak Star's gift shop features a variety of Native American beadwork, baskets and dolls.

Daybreak Star Center hours: Mon-Sat, 10 am-5 pm 206/285-4425. No charge.

Discovery Park, 3810 W Government Way, 206/386-4236.

GASWORKS PARK. When park designers first presented the idea of leaving the old gasworks plant perched on the north side of Lake Union as an integral part of a new park, there were noisy critics galore. Today, the grotesque remnants have become a familiar part of the cityscape and Gasworks Park a premier spot to fly a kite and enjoy an unobstructed view of the city skyline. Look for a giant sundial built in the ground near the top of the grassy hill. Note: The playground at the park is quite challenging—best for ages six and up. Because of boat traffic and commercial activity, swimming is not recommended.

At Northlake Way and Meridian, north end of Lake Union.

GREEN LAKE. Many Seattlites exercise religiously, and Green Lake has become their Mecca. Situated just east of the Woodland Park Zoo (about fifteen minutes from downtown) the 2.8-mile paved trail that circles the lake is ideal for running, walking, skating and biking. There's also a good playground, (at the east main entrance), lifeguarded beaches from mid-June through Labor Day, a big wading pool (northwest corner), a community center and indoor swimming pool open to the public, boat rentals at the lake, bike and skate rentals just across the street and many places nearby to find a snack.

Greenlake Way N, northeast Seattle.

On a busy weekend the path around Green Lake is too crowded for young (wobbly) bicyclists.

HIRAM M. CHITTENDEN GOVERNMENT LOCKS. The difference

between the water levels of Puget Sound and Lake Washington varies from six to 26 feet. The Hiram M. Chittenden Government Locks enable boats to go from salt water Puget Sound into fresh water Lake Union and Lake Washington. The operation can be viewed at close range at the Locks and most people, regardless of age, are fascinated by the remarkable sight of boats and water rising and dropping right before their eyes. On a warm day, bring a picnic to enjoy on the grassy knoll above the locks and watch the boat traffic. There are also fish ladders with underwater viewing; although with the salmon shortage it is often hard to spot a fish.

3015 54th in Ballard; 783-7001. Open daily 7 am-9 pm Call 783-7059 for information about free public tours.

SPECTATOR SPORTS

The **Seattle Mariners** play baseball in the Kingdome from April through early October. The baseball club has made a special effort to make games affordable and fun for families, including a fireworks display when the M's hit a homerun.
206/628-3455

The popular **Seattle Sonics basketball** team plays at the newly remodelled Seattle Center Coliseum from October through April. These games are a treat for kids but tickets are pricey. During the regular season, special day-of-game discounts are available after 5 pm.
206/281-5850

The **NFL Seahawks** play football in the Kingdome from August through December. Tickets are expensive—no discounts are offered.
206/827-97766

Seattle Thunderbirds play hockey at the Seattle Center Arena and Coliseum from September through March. Games are fast-paced and fun to watch, although the crowd can get loud and obnoxious.Be prepared for the fights among the players that often take place in the rink. The Thunderbirds offer $1-off tickets for kids under 14.
206/448-PUCK.

THE UNIVERSITY OF WASHINGTON offers a host of sporting events featuring talented athletes and great competition at a fraction of the cost of the professional games. The UW Women's basketball team (November-March) is a top contenter in the Pac Ten and one of the most popular sporting events in town. Husky Football games (September-November) usually sell out. *206/543-2200*

ANIMALS/ANIMALS

THE SEATTLE AQUARIUM, located at Pier 59 on the downtown waterfront, is meticulously planned to optimize viewing and learning. It is an ideal outing for a group with a variety of ages. Your visit will begin with tanks exhibiting an exotic variety, including seahorses, leaffish and lionfish, followed by a favorite of the kids, the Local Invertebrates exhibit and a giant Pacific octopus. (Strollers are allowed but backpacks will give small children a better view of the tanks.)

Get kids past the life-size, great white shark model hanging overhead (Puget Sound is home to seven varieties of shark) and they'll be rewarded with an exceptionally good "touch tank" where they can feel starfish and other creatures. One of the most popular features of the Aquarium is the 400,000-gallon Underwater Dome, a glassed-in area where families can relax on comfortable benches and watch sea life circle overhead and all around. Even an infant will be mesmerized by the action in this "inside-out" aquarium. One of the last exhibits will probably be one of your children's favorites: both an underwater and above-water view of playful seals and otters.

Adjacent to the Aquarium is the **Omnidome Theatre**, featuring films that put you so close to the action, you're sure you are a part of it. The movie about the eruption of Mt. St. Helens is a first-rate education on this rare event but watch out, preschool kids may be overwhelmed by the fiery explosion depicted on the enormous screen at full volume.

Pier 59, Waterfront Park, Seattle Aquarium; (206)386-4320. Omnidome: (206)622-1868. Hours: Open year round. Labor - Day-Memorial Day, 10 am-5 pm, Memorial Day-Labor Day, 10 am-7 pm. Admission: $6.95/adults, $4.50/children ages 6-18, $2.25/ children ages 3-5, children under 2 free. Admission to Omnidome & Aquarium; $10.75 adults, $6.75/youth 13-18 years, $5.75/children 6-12 years, $4.30/children ages 3-5; children under 2 free. Omnidome only: $5.95/adults, $4.95/youth ages 13-18, $3.95/children ages 3-12, under 3 free.

WOODLAND PARK ZOO. Rated one of the 10 best zoos in the United States, the Woodland Park Zoo is an outstanding example of what a zoo can be with natural habitats where the animals roam free. Conveniently located just 10 minutes from downtown Seattle, the 92-acre zoo features an extensive collection of animals. Giraffes, zebras and hippos roam about the African savannah; elephants plod through the Asian Elephant exhibit; gorillas go native in their jungle home. The Tropical Rain Forest makes a vivid impression with an exhibit that takes visitors from the floor of the forest high up into the canopy. One of the exhibits that is a favorite with kids is the Nocturnal House, where bats, raccoons, lizards and others live in a nighttime environment. It is linked to the Reptile House, which is equally popular with kids, and likely to get a few oohs, ahhs and eeks. During July and August the zoo presents an outdoor summer concert series on the north meadow. These evening concerts are free for kids 12 and under when accompanied by an adult.

5500 Phinney Ave N ; (206)684-4800. Opens daily at 9:30 am year round, closing time varies with the season. Cost: $7/adults; $4.25/ children 6-17;$2.25/children ages 2-5; under 2 free.

The basement at REI has good bargains on outdoor clothing for kids.

OUTDOOR ACTIVE FUN

Many Seattle locals seize every opportunity to enjoy the great outdoors. Below are suggestions for ways to let the kids burn off excess energy while exploring the city and surrounding foothills.

Recreational Equipment Inc (REI) is one of the best stores in the country for outdoor equipment and clothing for both adults and kids. The flagship store, on Capitol Hill just five minutes from downtown Seattle, also has an extensive rental shop that includes hiking and cross-country skiing equipment and snowshoes in all sizes.

1525 11th Ave (Branches in Bellevue and Federal Way). 206/323-8333. Open every day.

BIKING

Despite the hilly terrain, bicycling is very popular in Seattle. The city and the county have worked with the many avid bicyclists in the area to develop an impressive network of bicycle trails. From May to September, on the third Sunday of every month, the Seattle Parks Department sponsors **Bicycle Sunday** when it stops auto traffic on Lake Washington Boulevard all the way to Seward Park. It's an ideal bike route for kids. The following additional routes are flat, very scenic and highly recommended for both kids and adults. Bicycle rental shops located near the bike trails are mentioned: be sure to call first to make sure they have the right size bikes available. Helmets are required—they should be provided by the rental shops.

ALKI. Alki Beach is a popular 2 ¹/₂ mile strip of saltwater beach in West Seattle with a spectacular view of the downtown skyline and fine beachcombing. It is also a good place to take a bike ride. The trail is safe and wide (about 10 feet) and features a separate six-foot path for pedestrians. Enjoy a beach fire or visit the Coast Guard-maintained **Alki Point and Light Station** (call 932-5800 for visiting hours.) The bike path continues past the beach to Lincoln Park—a large, wooded park near the Vashon-Fauntleroy ferry dock.

Alki Beach to Lincoln Park, West Seattle. Nearby bike rental: Alki Bicycle Company, 938-3222. Length one way. 6 miles.

BURKE GILMAN TRAIL & SAMMAMISH RIVER TRAIL. With the completion of the connection between the Burke Gilman Trail on the west side of Lake Washington and the Sammamish River Trail on the east, bicyclists can now enjoy a level, scenic trail from Gas Works Park at Lake Union, past the University of Washington, around the north end of Lake Washington and out to Marymoor Park in Redmond. The 25 mile route is too much for most kids (and adults) but there are numerous short stretches that are ideal, including the ride from the University of Washington to Gas Works Park (about 2 ¹/₂ miles) and the 3 ¹/₂ mile stretch from Marymoor Park on the east side of Lake Washington to the lovely Chateau Ste. Michelle winery.

Nearby bike rentals in Seattle: Al Young Bike and Ski, 524-2642; The Bicycle Center, 523-8300. Bike rentals on the Eastside: Redmond Cycle, 885-6363; Bothell Ski & Bike, 486-3747. Length one way: 25 miles.

ELLIOTT BAY BICYCLE PATH. This trail is rarely crowded, except at noon on weekdays when it attracts a large number of downtowners trying to get some exercise and fresh air at lunch. Even then, the runners are on a separate path so it doesn't get too busy for bicyclists or skaters. The route begins at Myrtle Edwards Park, at the north end of the downtown waterfront, and winds past grain elevators and other interesting port activities. Views are spectacular.

Pier 70, north through Myrtle Edwards Park. No nearby bike rentals. Length one way: Approx 3 miles.

GREEN LAKE. The trail around the lake is flat and paved, and there are endless good places to stop along the way. On sunny days the loop gets crowded with cyclists, runners, skaters, walkers and other folks having a good time, so try going on a weekday or

get started early on a weekend.
*Northeast of Woodland Park Zoo. Nearby bike (and skate) rentals:
Gregg's Greenlake Cycle, 523-1822. Length: 2.8 mile loop.*

BOATING

Seattle is one of the largest boating areas in the country. If you
want to rent a small craft while you are in town, there are ample
opportunities.

THE CENTER FOR WOODEN BOATS, located at the south end of
Lake Union (five minutes from downtown) rents rowboats,
paddleboats, canoes and sailboats year round. With houseboats
lining parts of the shore and seaplanes coming and going, Lake
Union is a fun place to explore by boat. Before being allowed to
take out sailing craft, your boat handling skills will be checked
out. Cost to rent sailing craft starts at $10 per hour; rowing and
paddling craft cost $8-$12 per hour.
*1010 Valley St; 206/382-BOAT. Open daily year round 12-6 pm,
except Tuesday. Rentals available starting at $8/hour.*

GREENLAKE BOAT RENTALS, located at the east entrance,
offers rowboats, paddleboats, canoes and sailboards for rent from
mid-April through September. Reservations are recommended
during summer months.
*7351 E Green Lake Dr N; 206/527-0171. Rental rates range from
$8 to $12 per hour.*

NORTHWEST OUTDOOR CENTER. Rent a two-person kayak
from Northwest Outdoor Center and see Lake Union from a new
perspective. Paddle to Gas Works Park in 10 minutes, Ballard
Locks in about 45 minutes. Several models are available for
rental, seating one, two or three people. Kids sit in front, adults
in the rear steering position. Rentals are available by the hour,
half-day, full day and longer. No experience is necessary.
2100 Westlake Ave N; 206/281-9694. Cost: $10/hour.

UNIVERSITY OF WASHINGTON WATERFRONT ACTIVITY CEN-
TER. Enjoy a leisurely paddle through the University of Washington Arboretum in a canoe or rowboat rented at the Canoe
House. The Foster Island area is full of byways and foot bridges to
navigate through and under, a multitude of interesting birds to
observe and unlimited places to hop ashore and enjoy a picnic.
Canoes seat up to three people and rowboats up to four. Life vests
are available for children as small as 25 pounds. Boats available

on a first-come basis—on a sunny weekend canoes are in high demand. You'll be asked to leave a driver's license at the rental shop.

University of Washington, on the water between Husky Stadium and the Montlake Bridge; 206/543-9433. Hours: Feb-Oct, 9 am-dusk. Cost: $4.00/hour per boat.

HIKING

When you think of hiking with the kids, do you picture the family in lederhosen, yodeling together up the mountain? Or do you imagine yourself dropping a trail of jelly beans just to get your kids up the hill? Maybe the second scenario is a bit more realistic, but don't get discouraged. There are hundreds of easy day hikes within a short drive of Seattle that will no doubt convert your couch potato to an avid fan of Mother Nature. Remember to be generous with praise and snacks, and set a pace and a goal that are realistic. Try one of the following to get started:

GEOLOGY ADVENTURES. This interesting organization offers hikes that teach the geology of the Cascade foothills, about 30 minutes from downtown Seattle. The adventures are especially geared to parents and kids, and the guides provide a wealth of information, as well as hands-on activities, including gold panning and fossil hunting. *Phone: 255-6635*

ISSAQUAH ALPS TRAIL CLUB. This club's members lead free hikes for all ages and skill levels year-round on the mountains and plateaus in the greater Issaquah area. No reservations are necessary and no special gear is required. Each hike is rated by length and climbing difficulty. Hikers meet at the Issaquah City Hall (about 30 minutes from downtown Seattle) at an appointed time, and carpool to the trail head. Call Issaquah Alps Hotline for more information and complete hike schedule. *24-hour hotline: 328-0480*

THE MOUNTAINEERS is the largest outdoor organization in the region, currently comprising 14,000 members. The club is dedicated to offering a wide range of outdoor activities for all ages including hiking, cross-country skiing, backpacking trips, kayaking and more. Mountaineer Books publishes two excellent guides for families that want to hike together: *Best Hikes with Children in Western Washington & the Cascades, Volume 1 and 2.* They are available at local bookstores. *For additional information call 284-6310.*

Ten essentials for ANY dayhike:
1. Extra clothing
2. Extra food
3. Sunglasses
4. Knife
5. Firestarter
6. First-aid kit
7. Matches
8. Flashlight
9. Map
10. Compass
—compiled by The Mountaineers

EXCURSIONS

There's more than enough to keep you busy in the city but if you want to venture out of town for the day, the following places are well worth checking out:

BOEING TOUR CENTER. Free tours of the Boeing Everett Plant are offered for ages 10 and up on weekdays on a first-come basis. The tour begins with a half-hour video presentation in the plant's theater, and continues at a moderate pace through the factory, covering about one-third of a mile, including some steep stairs. Tours are very popular so arrive at least one hour prior to desired time. (The 9 am and 1 pm tours accommodate up to 90 people; the others are limited to 45).

Boeing Everett Plant, Exit 189 from I-5; 206/342-4801. Public Tours, Mon-Fri, 9 am, 10 am, 11 am, 1 pm, 2 pm & 3 pm. Free.

ENCHANTED VILLAGE AND WILD WAVE PARK. Pack a picnic and spend the day enjoying the 50 acres of family fun. The price of admission is steep and there's plenty to keep kids busy, so plan to get there early to get your money's worth. Enchanted Village is a magical place for young children. It is a quiet, forested setting—a pleasant switch from the carnival atmosphere of most amusement parks. It offers several attractions likely to drive any kid to delirium, including 14 amusement rides, a giant wading pool, bumper boats and a tiny zoo area. And best of all, the price of admission covers all the rides so parents can relax and let the kids enjoy the same ride as many times as they like. There are a few rides that will thrill older kids, but this place is ideally suited for kids under age 8. Older kids will likely gravitate next-door to Wild Waves, the Northwest's largest water park—20 acres of water mania including giant water slides and a 24,500 -square foot wave pool.

36201 Enchanted Pkwy S, Federal Way ; 206/661-8001. Hours: open mid-April-Labor Day; seasonal hours vary. Admission: Enchanted Village only. $9.00-$11.00; Wild Waves & Enchanted Village combination $16.00-$18.50 (no admission to Wild Waves only).

STE. MICHELLE WINERY. The award-winning Ste. Michelle Winery presents a variety of activities throughout the year in addition to its own cellar tours and wine tasting, which occur daily. Though your children won't be able to participate in the wine tasting, they are allowed to take the tour which lasts about 45 minutes and is free of charge. Cellar tours leave the lobby about every half-hour and are stroller/wheelchair accessible.

During the spring and summer months, the park-like grounds of Ste. Michelle are host to a wide assortment of outdoor concerts, including jazz, classical and contemporary music. Many of these events are free. For a complete events schedule call 488-3300.
14111 NE 145th, Woodinville; 206/488-1133. Hours: Open year-round, Mon, 10 am-4:30 pm & Tues-Sun, 10 am-6 pm. Admission and tours are free.

SNOQUALMIE FALLS PARK. This scenic park, located in the foothills of the Cascade Mountains, is a fine place to get out in the woods and view a waterfall. Just outside the town of Snoqualmie (about 35 minutes east of Seattle on I-90) the Snoqualmie River plunges 270 feet in a rock gorge. The park's grounds feature observation platforms to view the falls, picnic areas, a gift shop and cafe. For the ambitious, the half-mile River Trail leads down to the river's edge, for an upclose view of the cascading falls. The trail is steep, however, so be prepared to help the little one on the trip back up. The falls are lovely and in late spring when the snow is melting they are quite impressive.
Located 25 miles east of Seattle; take Exit 27 from I-90. Open year-round. Free.

MT RAINIER SCENIC RAILWAY, vintage steam locomotive, departs Elbe for an 1 1/2 -hour steam train excursions through the foothills of Mt. Rainier, 14 miles to Mineral Lake. If the extraordinary scenery doesn't keep your kids entertained, the live music surely will. No reservations required for this ride. If you want to give an older child a treat, the Cascadian Dinner Train offers a complete five-course prime rib dinner during a four-hour train ride from Elbe to the logging town of Morton.
Located about 40 miles south of Tacoma on Hwy 7 in Elbe; 206/ 569-2588. Departs daily, mid-June through Labor Day, plus three times per day on weekends from Memorial Day through the end of September. Prices: $8.50/adults; $5.50/children 2-11 years; children under 2 free.

PUGET SOUND AND SNOQUALMIE VALLEY RAILWAY. Travel aboard the historic Puget Sound and Snoqualmie Valley steam train for a 1 1/4 -hour trip through the scenic Snoqualmie Valley. Train runs every weekend from Memorial Day through Labor Day, as well as select days during the spring and fall. No reservations are necessary.
In the town of Snoqualmie; 206/888-0373 or 206/746-4025 Weekends only, April-October, call to confirm departure times. Cost:

$6/adults, $4/children; under 3 free.

NORTHWEST TREK AND WILDLIFE PARK. In 1971, Dr. and Mrs. David T. Hellyer donated 600 acres of beautiful forest, lake and meadow land to the Metropolitan Park District of Tacoma to create a protected place where Northwest wildlife could roam free. The result of their generosity is a unique park ideally suited to children. Tram tours led by expert naturalists depart hourly, taking visitors through 435 acres of free-roaming habitat, which is home to bison, bighorn sheep, elk, caribou, water fowl, moose, mountain goats, blacktail deer and many others. Don't be surprised to see a curious caribou walking alongside the tram or a herd of bison calmly grazing in the thicket—so close that your child can almost reach out and pat their heads! Allow at least three hours for your visit.

Located 55 miles from Seattle. Get on I-5 south, take Exit 142B from I-5 and travel south on State Route 161. Northwest Trek is 17 miles south of Puyallup on SR 161. 800/433-TREK. Open year round; seasonal hours vary. Cost: 7.85/adults; $5.50/children 5 -17 years; $3.50/children 3-4 years;3 and under free.

CALENDAR

JANUARY: Science Circus, Science Center
MARCH: Children Hospital Health Fair
St Patrick's Day Parade
Whirligig, Seattle Center
MAY: Opening Day of Boating Season
Seattle International Children's Festival
Northwest Folklife Festival
Pike Place Market Festival
Bicycle Saturdays & Sundays (through September)
JUNE: Fire Festival
Seattle Maritime Week
KidsDay
JULY: Bellevue Jazz Festival
Flight Festival & Air Show
Marymoor Heritage Festival
Paine Field International Air Fair
Seafair
Wooden Boat Festival
AUGUST: KOMO Kidsfair
Seafair
SEPTEMBER: Bumbershoot

St. Demetrios Greek Festival
OCTOBER: Issaquah Salmon Days, Issaquah
NOVEMBER: Peter Pan, Intiman Theater
The Nutcracker, Pacific Northwest Ballet
Model Railroad Show, Pacific Science Center
DECEMBER: KING 5 Winterfest, Seattle Center
Festivals of Light, Seattle Childrens Museum
Seattle Civic Christmas Ship

RESOURCES

KIDSTAR AM 1250. When stuck in Seattle traffic, turn the car
radio to KIDSTAR, 1250 AM, the lively, award-winning radio
station with music, weather, news and storytelling just for kids.

CHILDREN'S RESOURCE LINE, operated by Children's Hospital and Medical Center, has nurses on call 24-hours a day to
answer questions about medical concerns and refer parents to
community physicians. *Call 206/526-2500.*

BOOKS/PUBLICATIONS. *Seattle's Child* and *Eastside Parent,*
monthly newsmagazines for parents, feature monthly calendars
of events and other useful information for parents visiting or
living in the area. *The Education Directory* is an annual
guide to public and private schools. *Summer Learning* is a
guide to summer classes and camps. *A New Arrival* is a guide
for new and expectant parents.*The Activity Guide* lists
enrichment activities for kids. *Out and About Seattle with
Kids* is a 210-page book about what to see and do with kids in
Seattle. Cost: $12.95. Available at area bookstores. Call 206/
441-0191 for more information.

VISITORS INFORMATION. Washington State Convention &
Trade Center, 8th Ave & Pike
206/461-5800

MT. RAINIER

At 14,410 feet, Mt. Rainier dominates the Western Washington skyline. Fortunately, you can get close enough to touch this
majestic ice cream cone in the sky without getting into mountain
climbing. All of the great peak and much of the surrounding
foothills lie within well-developed Mt. Rainier National Park.

GETTING THERE

Mt. Rainier National Park has four entrances: the **Nisqually**, off SR 706 in the southwest, is the closest to I-5 and the most popular entrance; the **Carbon River**, on Carbon River Road in the northwest; the **White River**, on White River Road off SR 410 in the northeast and closest to Sunrise; and the **Stevens Canyon Road** entrance in the southwest. Your route to the mountain will depend on whether you are approaching from the north, south, east or west, where you want to go inside the park and the time of year—only the Nisqually (southwest route that leads to Paradise) is open all year. All the other roads in the park are closed from late October or the first snowfall, whichever comes first, to somewhere between late April and early June, depending upon how fast the winter snow melts. Regardless of which route you choose and no matter what time of year you visit, be sure to check weather and road conditions by calling the 24-hour Park Information Service (360/569-2211).

ROADSIDE ATTRACTIONS. There are several ways to approach Rainier and a variety of worthwhile stops on the way to the mountain. If you are making it a day trip from Seattle, it is a long drive (2 1/2 hours one way). The following stops are good destinations for an outing, not places you can stop for a quick look. Consider allowing several hours for visiting them on your way home if you are planning to stay overnight at the mountain.

See **Seattle**: What to See and Do: Excursions for details about the following places:

Northwest Trek
Mt. Rainier Scenic Railway

PLACES TO STAY

There aren't any places to stay in or around Mt. Rainier National Park that offer first-rate accommodations for families. But this awesome mountain is too much to explore in just a day, so we urge you to spend at least a night in the area at one of the places listed below.

Camping at any of the five National Park campgrounds is also a good option for families. However, expect to be in close quarters with your fellow campers. Try to avoid the weekends: no reservations are possible and campgrounds fill early on Fridays.

ALEXANDER'S COUNTRY INN
360/569-2300; 37515 State Rd 706, Ashford, 98304

Rates: Moderate
Essentials: Credit cards; cribs
Extras: Free breakfast; restaurant; hot tub

This is a renovated 1912 country inn that is located just one mile outside the Nisqually entrance to Mt. Rainier National Park. It's a good place to stay if you want comfort and a good meal and want to be close to the mountain. Most rooms have a shared bath, but facilities are immaculate and there is a pleasant, large "living room" on the second floor that is a nice place for the kids to play board games or read.

The free breakfast includes juice, fruit, muffins, omelette or French toast. The restaurant at the Inn is excellent and accomodating with children—see Places to Eat.

PARENT COMMENTS: *"I went to Alexander's Country Inn with my eight-year-old daughter for a mother-daughter get-away. We visited Paradise and took a hike during the day, ate a fabulous meal in the restaurant at the Inn and spent the night in the elegant Turrent Room. On the way home the next day we visited Northwest Trek."*

"Too close quarters if you have rowdy kids."

NISQUALLY LODGE
360/569-8804; 331609 Rt 706, Ashford, 98304
Rates: Moderate
Essentials: Credit Cards; crib ($5)
Extras: Hot tub; continental breakfast; TV

The name of this place suggests a grand mountain lodge in a breathtaking setting, but be prepared to find your basic two-story motel sitting just off the highway. But even if the location isn't scenic, it is just five miles down the road from the south entrance of the park and there is a grand stone fireplace in the lobby. There's also a hot tub outside that feels good on aching muscles after a big day outdoors. Pastries, juice and coffee are served in the lobby every morning.

PARENT COMMENTS: *"It is tough to find a good place to stay near Rainier but the park is without question one of the finest areas in the state to explore with kids. We wanted to stay in a cozy log cabin in the woods with a fireplace. There are numerous accommodations in the area that tempted us when we read their brochures but once we got there they were too "rustic" for our standards (unsafe and dilapidated). So we were glad to find the comfortable, new Nisqually Lodge so close to the park entrance."*

INN AT LONGMIRE
PARADISE LODGE
360/569-2275
Rates: Moderate to expensive
Essentials: Credit cards; crib
Extras: Restaurants, snack bar at Paradise

The Mt. Rainier National Park Service maintains two places to stay inside the park, Inn at Longmire and Paradise Lodge. Neither is great for families—small rooms, no kitchens, relatively high prices for what you get in accommodations—but you will be able to jump out of bed and hit the trails right outside your door in the morning. For reservations and information, talk to Mt. Rainier Guest Services at 360/569-2275. Rainier is one of the most popular tourist attractions in the Northwest and the summer season is short so it is difficult to get reservations in the summer unless you call early.

NATIONAL PARK INN at Longmire had a major renovation in 1990, expanding the Inn from 16 to 25 rooms by adding a side wing. It sits just inside the Nisqually entrance, at the base of the mountain. Rooms are available with or without a private bath, two single beds, two double beds or a queen bed. The most spacious option is the two-room unit with a bath ($106). The lounge downstairs, with a lovely river rock fireplace, is small but a comfy spot to play a board game or enjoy a book. The first inn at the park was a log cabin built by the Longmire family in 1884—you'll see what remains when you walk the Trail of the Shadows across the road.

Meals at the restaurant are basic—including burgers, sandwiches, salads and soups.

One of the attractions of the Inn is the chance to appreciate some of the history of the area. Most of the buildings at Longmire date back to the 1910s and 1920s including tiny Longmire Museum.

PARADISE INN was first opened in 1917 and has the feel of all such national park edifices, including the massive lobby with huge beams and big stone fireplaces at each end. This is a busy place during the day, as there are lots of daytime tourists. Accommodations are comfortable but in no way roomy or fancy. Some of the rooms in the front part of the lodge are tastefully furnished but the rooms in the annex have not been redecorated since the 1960s and show it—cheap wood panelling and lime-green carpet. A two-room unit with bath costs $106. A few board games can be checked out from the desk and there's a gift shop to browse, but the real entertainment is located just outside the door, where at 5,400 feet the views are spectacular and numerous trails beckon.

There is a small snack bar and dining room at the Paradise Lodge. Food in the dining room is pricey and nothing special but children are well-tolerated. Consider heading down the mountain to the Wild Berry Restaurant or Alexander's (see Places to Eat below) or bringing a picnic.

> **PARENT COMMENTS:** *"The rooms at Paradise aren't very nice but since we only used them to sleep it really didn't matter."*
> *"Be sure to check the weather! One June we took a nephew who was visitng from the east coast to Paradise to show him the mountains of the west and we couldn't see a thing through a blizzard."*
> *"We wanted to stay at Paradise but it was full so we went to Longmire. We were glad we did because it was less crammed with tourists and the rooms were nicer because they were recently renovated."*

PLACES TO EAT

BAUMGARTNER'S
360/825-1067; Junction of State Routes 169 and 410, Enumclaw
Hours: Lunch and early dinner, 10 am-6 pm
Essentials: Credit cards; highchairs

Who wants to spend your precious time on the mountain inside a restaurant or at a snack bar? A picnic at Rainier is a grand idea—in the summer you can enjoy your meal in a meadow of wildflowers and in the winter a snow picnic will be a certain hit (bring plastic bags so you can sit on the snow). And don't worry if you didn't get it together before you left town, Baumgartner's in Enumclaw is the place to stop for a bountiful selection of delicious deli meats, salads, desserts, sandwiches, etc. They also have a small dining area if you don't want to take it with you.

WILD BERRY RESTAURANT
360/569-2628; 4 miles east of Ashford on Route 706
Hours: Breakfast, lunch and dinner
Essentials: Credit cards; highchairs

Surprisingly tasty food at reasonable prices. (Adults can get a decent dinner for $5). Excellent sandwiches and pizzas, the usual breakfast stuff plus burritos, yummy desserts.

ALEXANDER'S
360/569-2000; In Alexander's Country Inn, Ashford
Hours: Breakfast (summer only), lunch, dinner daily (weekends

only Nov 1-June 1)
Essentials: Credit cards; highchairs
Food is fresh, gourmet and not overpriced. There is a children's menu and kids are well-tolerated. The best restaurant in the area.

WHAT TO SEE AND DO

It is easy to introduce your children to the mountain by covering some of the 300 miles of backcountry trails in the park. There are four entrances around the park's perimeter, making the area very accessible. Visitor centers with tips on trails, camping and interpretive programs are located at the four major areas of the park: Paradise, Longmire, Ohanapecosh and Sunrise. The interpretive hikes and evening programs offered at each of the Visitors Centers are ideal for families with young children. The hiking season normally extends from mid-July to Mid-October and there are many short, easy hikes that work for young children, such as the Grove of the Patriarchs. Admission to the park is $5 per car per day.

The most popular destination for visitors to the park is **Paradise**, at 5,400 feet. The Henry M. Jackson Memorial Visitors Center is open 10 am-5 pm on weekends and holidays until mid-April when it opens daily for extended hours. The Center offers a cafeteria, nature exhibits and slide shows, as well as guided hikes. The 1917 historic Paradise Inn is open from late May through the first week in October (Sunday brunches are served all summer). See Places to Stay.

Many trails that school-age children can enjoy branch out from Paradise. Some of the best wildflower viewing is here in July and August, and in September the fall foliage is spectacular. In winter, Paradise is open as a cross-country skiing, inner-tubing and snow-shoeing area. Park naturalists lead snowshoe hikes for those 10 years and older to explore winter ecology on weekends from January through mid-April. (Snowshoe rental is available in Seattle at REI and at Paradise).

Just east of Paradise at the end of Stevens Canyon Road is **Ohanapecosh**. The most impressive stands of old growth trees are here. Two good hikes for young children in this area are a 2-mile loop to **Silver Falls** and **Grove of the Patriarchs**, a 1 1/2-mile stroll through massive 1,200-year-old Douglas firs, red cedars and western hemlocks.

At 6,400 feet, **Sunrise**, on the northeast flank of the park, is the highest point you can reach by automobile and is open only

> "What my kids remember about Mt. Rainier is the game of spotting the 6-inch banana slugs."

during the summer months. On a 17-mile spur road off State 410, there is a Visitors Center that opens July 1 and has displays explaining the volcanic history of Mt. Rainier and a sweeping view of the mountain and other Cascade volcanic peaks. This is a good spot to watch climbers on difficult climbing terrain. There are also walk-in picnic sites, a ranger station and snack bar. A campground with 10 sites is a half-mile walk away.

Surrounded by alpine meadows, Sunrise is also a good place for viewing the wildflowers and taking a hike. The **Mt. Fremont** trail is especially fun for kids because it leads to the Mt. Fremont Lookout station, one of the few lookouts in the state still staffed. When you enter the park at the White River entrance, ask if a ranger is at the lookout. The trail begins in the Sunrise parking lot, is 2 3/4 mile one way, is steep in places and covers some rough terrain so should only be tackled by a child who has staying power on the trail. Once you get there, if there is a ranger at the station, the kids can ask him or her about life at the lookout and the ranger's responsibilities. Even if the station isn't manned at the time you visit, on the way up you will have crossed meadows exploding with wildflowers and once you reach your destination the kids will enjoy climbing around the empty little building and taking in the panoramic view of the south side of Mt. Rainier, with a glimmer of Puget Sound and the Olympics in the distance.

Tell the kids they are standing on a volcano that is over one million years old!

In the southwest corner of **Longmire**, you can browse through the small historical museum, and visit the Hikers Center—an excellent source for information about hiking in the Park. Hours at the Museum and Hiking Center are 9 am-4:30 pm daily, year-round. There is a small inn here that has been renovated recently. See Places to Stay.

Just across the road from the Inn at Longmire, a pleasant ³/₄ mile walk up the **Trail of the Shadows** winds through lowland forest to bubbling Soda Springs, a beaver dam and James Longmire's homestead cabin. Up from Longmire is Cougar Road campground and an easy two-mile loop to **Cougar Falls**. During the winter, Rainier Ski Touring, at Longmire, provides rental equipment and trail maps for cross-country skiing and snow shoeing, but the trails for winter sports are too difficult for inexperienced young skiers.

If you plan to camp in the park, don't overlook the **Carbon River** entrance. Although it is the least visited, this area, located in the northwestern corner of the park, offers excellent hiking and camping opportunities for families. To get there, you take State 165 through several picturesque old coal-mining towns. **Mowich Lake**, at the end of State 165, is popular with canoeists and a starting point for several easy hikes. At Carbon River, if you can steel your nerves to cross a 50-foot-high suspension bridge, you can walk almost to the terminus of a glacier.

CROSS-COUNTRY SKIING. There are several trails that leave from Paradise but they are hilly and not recommended for novices. **Mt. Tahoma Scenic Ski Trails Association** has developed over 90 miles of trails through a spectacular area south and west of Mount Rainer Natonal Park as well as two eight-person overnight huts. Call 360/832-8338 for more information.

RESOURCES

MT. RAINIER NATIONAL PARK INFORMATION
Includes Visitors Centers hours, information about hiking, skiing and snow shoeing, food and lodging, camping, weather and road conditions.
360/569-2211

PARK RADIO INFORMATION
Approaching the Nisqually entrance tune to 1610 AM on your radio for useful park information.

BOOKS/PUBLICATIONS
Mt. Rainier Offical Map and Guide locates roads, campsites and trails and provides a short introduction to the park's attractions. Available free at park entrances.
Two newspapers—*Tahoma* in the summer and *Snowdrift* in the winter—give details on seasonal activitities in the park. Available free at the visitors centers.
Best Hikes with Children in Western Washington and The Cascades, **Part 1 and Part 2**, Mountaineer Books, $12.95.

LEAVENWORTH

Once a booming mill and railroad town, Leavenworth made a successful transition to tourism in the early 60's. Believing the town's primary selling point is its gorgeous alpine setting, boosters took advantage by adding a Bavarian touch to virtually every structure. While some claim the theme is overdone, most children delight in the "fairytale" charm.

Located just beyond the Seattle "rain zone," Leavenworth boasts a dependable climate: cold, crisp and generally clear in winter, hot and clear in summer. With a festive, holiday atmosphere all year round and easy accessibility to a wide assortment of outdoor activities, Leavenworth is one of the best family vacation spots in the Northwest.

GETTING THERE

The direct route to Leavenworth from the west side is via Stevens Pass on US Highway 2. An alternative route is I-90 over Snoqualmie Pass. Turn off I-90 at Exit 85 near Cle Elum, to Highway 970 (shortly becomes Highway 97) through Blewett Pass. Highway 97 connects with Highway 2 just east of Leavenworth.

REFUELING. If you travel via Stevens Pass, you may want to start your trip with an empty stomach, so you'll be good and hungry when you reach the small town of Startup (about 45 miles from Seattle). **The Brick Pit** (509/793-2778), a log cabin-style restaurant on the south side of Highway 2, features great barbecue. The inexpensive fare includes tangy, tasty sandwiches of beef, chicken or pork with baked beans, coleslaw and curly fries. Save room for a thick shake or an ice cream cone (child's size available).

If weather permits, eat out in the backyard and watch for the restaurant's adopted mom-cat, who seems to have a new litter no matter when you visit. This stop requires a relaxed time schedule, though; the service is just as informal as the atmosphere.

ROADSIDE ATTRACTIONS. Both **Stevens** and **Snoqualmie** are popular ski areas with complete facilities. At other times of the year, you'll find food service, restrooms and opportunities to stretch your legs on trail walks.

PLACES TO STAY

ENZIAN MOTOR INN
509/548-5269 or 800/223-8511; 590 Highway 2, Leavenworth, 98826

Rates: Moderate to expensive
Essentials: Credit cards; cribs, hide-a-beds (some units)
Extras: Free breakfast; cable TV, fireplaces, free wood (some units); outdoor pool (heated May to Sept), indoor pool, hot tubs, spas (some units); racquetball court, ping-pong room, exercise equipment, complimentary cross-country skiing equipment
Don't let the name fool you; this spot is much more than a

motel. From the authentic Bavarian furnishings to the two swimming pools, The Enzian offers a luxurious experience. The only downside of the motel is that it sits on the main highway, which in this spectacular natural setting is unfortunate. However, if you are willing to trade a more sylvan setting for the excellent accommodations, you will likely be well satisfied.

A short walk from downtown, The Enzian has 104 units, all with queen beds. Many rooms have sliding doors that close off the master bedroom from shared areas, a real plus for families. The European buffet breakfast is more than ample: omelettes to order, pastry, a potato dish and fresh fruit.

PARENT COMMENTS: *"The indoor pool is exquisite— large and very beautiful. The kids had a great time swimming and splashing in one part of the pool; my husband and I were in a whole different part. It was* almost *romantic!"*
"A very nice place, but next time we'll stay in a smaller inn or B&B to get better experience of Leavenworth."

HAUS LORELEI INN
509/548-5726; 347 Division St, Leavenworth, 98826
Rates: Moderate to expensive
Essentials: No credit cards; cribs
Extras: Breakfast; two TVs in shared areas; hot tub overlooking the river (adults only); sandy swimming area on river, sledding hill, tennis courts

This is a rare find for families: a spacious, beautifully-appointed B&B where children are truly welcome. Located on two acres overlooking the Icicle River, the inn feels secluded, though it is only a few blocks from the center of town. The relaxed, European feel is accentuated by the careful attention of hostess Elizabeth Saunders.

Each of the six rooms has a private bath, and several are appropriate for families. A large, cheerful sunroom (complete with two chatty parakeets) serves as sitting area, game room and breakfast spot; a hearty, sumptuous breakfast is served. Several large sitting areas, and two fireplaces, give families plenty of room to move without worrying about disturbing other guests.

PARENT COMMENTS: *"We loved the River Room, which has gorgeous views from the master bedroom and two kids' alcoves adjoining the bath. The hosting family was really friendly toward our girls—they even loaned us a new-fangled sled to take to the sledding hill."*

HAUS ROHRBACH PENSION
509/548-7024; 12882 Ranger Rd, Leavenworth, 98826
Rates: Moderate to expensive
Essentials: Credit cards; cribs
Extras: Outdoor swimming pool (summer only), hot tub; sledding hill (equipment available on loan), well-equipped game room, badminton, croquet

This is a true pension, with its small rooms, thin walls and shared baths. But it is a charming place, managed by friendly, helpful hosts.

A two-minute drive from downtown, the pension is located at the base of Tumwater Mountain, and offers beautiful views of farms and pastures nestled in the valley. Most of the rooms open onto balconies and in fine weather the scrumptious breakfasts are served *al fresco*.

 PARENT COMMENTS: *"The nearby sledding hill was fun!"*

MOUNTAIN SPRINGS LODGE
509/763-2713; 19115 Chiwawa Loop, Leavenworth, 98826
Rates: Expensive
Essentials: Credit cards; cribs
Extras: TV, VCR, videos (on request); kitchen (some units); wood-burning stove, free wood (some units); outdoor hot tub (some units); washer and dryer (some units); sun deck

Mountain Springs Lodge is located on a homestead dating to the late 19th century. The main lodge, a remodel of the original farm house built of Douglas fir and Ponderosa pine, offers cozy rooms, each with a private bath. But families are likely to be most comfortable in the guest lodges, which accommodate up to eight people and are complete with kitchen, washer and dryer, wood stove, sun deck and private outdoor hot tub.

This is a wonderful family place, owned and operated by a friendly, hospitable family. Located 20 minutes from Leavenworth, it offers a choice of secluded relaxation or in-town activities. For outdoor fun, there are acres of meadows and trails for skiing and hiking, a catch-and-release trout pond (bring your own pole!) and guided tours on horseback.

PARENT COMMENTS: *"A beautiful lodge in a gorgeous setting with top-notch hosts! The ideal mountain getaway."*
"Our kids loved fishing, playing baseball and football on the playfield outside our front door, exploring wooded paths along the creek, and relaxing in our very own hot tub after a long day."

PLACES TO EAT

CASA MIA
509/548-5621; Highway 2 across from the Fire Department
Hours: Lunch and dinner
Essentials: Credit cards; highchairs

When you've had enough of the Bavarian atmosphere, Casa Mia can spell relief. Kids are more than welcome at this Mexican restaurant, which offers fast and friendly service. There is a kids' menu with combinations (i.e. taco, enchilada and burrito) around $5. Portions are generous enough to share.

EDEL HAUS INN CAFE
509/548-4412; 320 Ninth St
Hours: Lunch and dinner
Essentials: Credit cards; highchairs

Located in a classic old home overlooking the Wenatchee River (and the sledding hill), the Edel Haus serves fresh pasta, seafood and vegetarian meals with an emphasis on nutrition. The menu includes some traditional kid foods, such as hot dogs and half-portions of pasta. Mom and dad might enjoy the chicken picata or vegie lasagna accompanied by a selection from the complete wine and beer list.

For a little extra privacy, request the "green room," which has three tables separate from the main dining area. In nice weather, meals are also served outdoors.

THE GINGERBREAD FACTORY
509/548-6592; 828 Commercial St
Hours: Summer, 7 am-7 pm; winter, 7 am-6 pm
Essentials: Credit cards; highchairs, "child's table"

This small, informal spot is a great place to enjoy a morning espresso, pick up deli foods for a picnic lunch or relax with a warm drink in the afternoon. Featured are authentic gingerbread cookies, assorted pastries, soups and deli salads. If you like to browse, there are gingerbread houses and related utensils, books, cards and t-shirts. The gingerbread houses are also available by mail; ask for a catalogue.

HOMEFIRES BAKERY
509/548-7362; 13013 Bayne Rd
Hours: Wed-Mon, 9 am-5 pm
Essentials: No credit cards

Worth the short, scenic drive from town, the Homefires Bakery features a German-style, wood-fired oven that turns out a great loaf of bread. (The nine-grain, dark rye and cinnamon swirl are favorites.) They also have a small assortment of pastries, coffee and juices. There's no indoor seating, but if the weather is agreeable you can enjoy the outdoor picnic table.

KRISTALL'S RESTAURANT
509/548-5267; 280 Highway 2
Hours: Breakfast, lunch and dinner
Essentials: Credit cards; highchairs

Kristall's is the quintessential "family" restaurant—full of comfortable booths and tolerant servers. The menu is extensive, with several selections just for kids; it's a rare child who won't find something to love. If you arrive with hungry, impatient little ones, order the cheese bread while you peruse the menu.

Our reviewers found the food good, the service fast and the server willing to split orders or adapt combinations to suit everyone's taste.

THE SOUP CELLAR
509/548-6300; 725 Front St
Hours: Lunch and dinner
Essentials: Credit cards; highchairs

For a quick, cafeteria-style meal, duck downstairs to The Soup Cellar, featuring a variety of sandwiches, salads and soups (billed as the "home of famous white chili.") The decor features family-sized booths, spill-proof tablecloths and a collection of dollar bills that paper the beams and provide a conversation piece.

WALTER'S OTHER PLACE
509/548-6125; 820 Commercial St
Hours: Dinner only
Essentials: Credit cards; booster seats

This comfortable little restaurant features Greek and Italian specialties, and is best known for its generous and tasty pastas. Though not a "crayons on the table" sort of place, it might be appropriate for an older child who can appreciate a finer dining experience. There are several booths toward the back of the dining area which are worth requesting if a child is in tow.

WHAT TO SEE AND DO

Regardless of the season, the Leavenworth area offers an array of outdoor activities and beautiful scenery. In winter, it can be a winter wonderland or slush city, depending on the temperature. But don't let moderate temperatures stop you—a short drive will usually net a decent ski or sledding area. In summer, the weather tends to be hot and dry, with myriad opportunities for outdoor fun. When you've had enough serious exercise, consider browsing the shops, taking a factory tour or just relaxing.

STROLL AND BROWSE

If its Bavarian, chances are its for sale somewhere in Leavenworth. But there are shops offering other types of merchandise, including hand-crafted goods and imports.

Leavenworth is a small town, and the shopping district is contained within a few square blocks. If your family is into browsing, you'll find something here for everyone. Those who lose interest early can stop for a lemonade or hot chocolate.

At **Alpen Bear** (downstairs at 827 Front Street), mom and dad can enjoy a cup of gourmet coffee or tea while the younger set inspects the selection of stuffed bears and related paraphernalia.

Nearby, **Alpen Haus** (807 Front Street) offers an interesting collection of imported nutcrackers and steins and, downstairs, miniatures and doll houses.

A "must stop" if you're strolling Front Street is **Die Musik Box**, featuring more than 2,500 music boxes from around the world (yes, they're breakable, but there are lots of clerks to help parents control those little hands). Around the corner at **A Book for All Seasons** (on Ninth St near Commercial), you'll find a small but good selection of books and activity books guaranteed to entertain little hands and minds.

If you have a child who's into trains, stop by **The Train Shop** at 217 Ninth St, in Alpenhoff Mall. This shop has toy trains, drawings and railroad memorabilia. For wooden toys, try **The Wood Shop**, an eclectic and inexpensive collection of handmade toys and Christmas ornaments. **The Black Swan** (827 Front Street) is a good spot to find the souvenir or novelty t-shirt (child and adult sizes) you promised someone you'd bring.

PARKS

LAKE WENATCHEE STATE PARK has a wide variety of recreational activities in any season. In summer, families can enjoy camping (199 sites) or swimming at the sandy beach on Lake Wenatchee. The lake is also good for boating, fishing and sailboarding. Families with older children can explore area hiking trails; for a great family memory, rent horses for a backpacking trip.

In winter, the area offers a maze of groomed Nordic trails and a popular sledding hill (at Nason Creek Campground). Sno-park permits are required in the area.

Located 20 miles northwest of Leavenworth. Take Highway 2 west to Route 207. Head north, watching for park signs.

THE OHME GARDENS COUNTY PARK provides a low-key outdoor excursion. This scenic area covers nine acres of lush mountain beauty on a rocky bluff overlooking the Wenatchee Valley. Family members who are not interested in scenery or plants will still enjoy the nine acres in which to run and play.

Located three miles north of Wenatchee on Route 97 (about 35 minutes from Leavenworth). Open daily, Apr 15-Oct 15; 9 am-7 pm (between Memorial Day and Labor Day); 9 am-6 pm (before Memorial Day and after Labor Day). Cost: $5/adult, $3/children 7-17, free for children under seven.

THE GREAT OUTDOORS

BIKING. Summer in Leavenworth offers some of the finest bicycling in the Northwest. For information about mountain biking in the area, contact the Lake Wenatchee Ranger District, 509/763-3103. Rental bikes are available at **Der Sportsmann**, (837 Front St, 509/548-5623). **Gator's Gravity** provides a 17-mile bicycle tour descending more than 2,000 feet along the Icicle River Canyon (reservations, 509/548-5102).

HIKING. The sights, sounds and smells of wilderness make hiking a popular pastime in the Leavenworth area. A list of relatively short, easy hikes in the Leavenworth Ranger District is available from the Chamber of Commerce (Highway 2 & Sherbourne St).

The **Black Bird Island Trail** is an easy 2 1/2 -mile walk along the Wenatchee River.

Drive west on Highway 2 and turn left at the yellow blinking light. Turn right on Commercial St for two blocks to parking lot.

The 1 1/2-mile **Old Pipeline Bed/Tumwater Canyon** trail affords views of the cascading Tumwater River and access to small sandy beaches perfect for wading.

Drive 1.7 miles west on Highway 2 and turn left at the public fishing/picnic area. Cross the old foot bridge and hike upstream.

HORSEBACK RIDING. Spring and summer is the time for an adventurous family to explore the local terrain on horseback. **Eagle Creek Ranch** (509/548-7798 or 800/221-7433) and other area outfitters offer hourly and daily trail rides, hay rides and "high country" pack trips.

RIVER RAFTING. Some of Washington's most thrilling white-water rafting tours start at Leavenworth and take enthusiasts down the Wenatchee River in spring and early summer. Although most companies don't recommend rafting for children under 10, older children just might enjoy the ride of their lives. A list of river runners and outfitters is available from the Chamber of Commerce (509/548-5807).

CROSS-COUNTRY SKIING Winter in Leavenworth affords plenty of opportunity for Nordic skiing, with several trails designed specifically for families and beginning skiers. The **Icicle River** trail (8K) meanders gently along the Icicle River and offers beautiful scenery and occasional glimpses of wildlife. At the **Leavenworth Golf Course**, skiers will find 12K of groomed trails over gently rolling terrain, with breathtaking views of the Wenatchee River and Cascade Mountains.

To get to either of these trails, drive west on Highway 2 and turn left onto Icicle Road (west end of town). The golf course 1/2 mile on your left; the Icicle River Trail is two more miles down the road (there is a small parking area).

For information on trails, conditions and fees, or about Kids Day, an annual cross-country ski event for families, call the **Leavenworth Winter Sports Club**, 509/548-5115. There are several places in town to rent skis.

SLEDDING. As long as snow is on the ground, no matter what time of day, you'll find kids sledding on a small but steep hill, on the main street of town. It is fun to sled in the early evening, before you go to a nearby restaurant for dinner.

If you're up for a drive, try **Nason Creek Campground** in the Lake Wenatchee area (west on US 2, then north on Route 207 and follow signs to campground). Parking in this area requires a Sno-park permit.

SLEIGH RIDES. Old-fashioned sleigh rides are a wintertime tradition in and around Leavenworth. Most go over pastures and through woods for 45-60 minutes and stop for a campfire and hot cider. Others return to a lodge area for a warm-up following the ride. Reservations are recommended. Phone **Eagle Creek Ranch** (509/548-7798 or 800/221-7433) or **Red Tail Canyon Farms** (509/548-4512 or 800/678-4512).

SNOWMOBILING is enjoying increased popularity among families with older children. Snowmobile trails abound in the Lake Wenatchee Ranger District (509/763-3103). To check avalanche conditions, phone 509/526-6677.

EXCURSIONS

THE APLETS AND COTLETS CANDY KITCHEN offers continuous 15-minute tours and samples of their famous confections. Browse in the Country Store, featuring homemade fruit products, souvenirs and an assortment of Washington State wines.
Located just off Highway 2, in Cashmere (15 miles east of Leavenworth); 509/782-2191. Tour hours: (May-Dec) Mon-Fri, 8 am-5:30 pm, Sat and Sun, 10 am-4 pm; (Jan-Apr) Mon-Fri, 8 am-noon, Sat and Sun, 1-5 pm. Free.

LEAVENWORTH NATIONAL FISH HATCHERY. Don't tell the kids, but this is a fun outing that's also educational. Established in 1940 to help salmon in the Columbia River following construction of the Grand Coulee Dam, the hatchery has exhibits identifying the fish and describing their habitats and environmental needs. Pick up a trail guide and walk the one-mile interpretive trail that covers the history, environment and wildlife of the area.
Turn south from Highway 2 on Icicle Rd (west end of town) and continue 1 1/2 miles. Turn left at the sign. 509/548-7641. Open daily 7:30 am-4 pm.

ROCKY MOUNTAIN CHOCOLATE FACTORY is another popular stop for families. Here you can watch candy makers hand fashion chocolates and sample their yummy fudge.
In the Brewery Building, 636 Front Street; 509/548-6525 or 800/272-9775.

ROCKY REACH DAM. When weather permits, this hydroelectric project dam makes an interesting outing. Take a picnic and stroll the floral gardens, turn the little ones loose in the playground and visit the fish-viewing room. Exhibits tell the history of the Columbia River area.
Five miles north of Wenatchee on Highway 97A (35 minutes from Leavenworth); 509/663-8121. Open daily 8 am-6 pm.

CALENDAR

JANUARY: Great Bavarian Ice Fest

MAY: Maifest
JUNE: Kinderfest,
International Folk Dance Festival
SEPTEMBER: Washington State Autumn Leaf Festival
OCTOBER: Wenatchee River Salmon Festival
DECEMBER: Christmas Tree Lighting & Bavarian Ice Fest

RESOURCES

LAKE WENATCHEE STATE PARK
509/763-3101

LEAVENWORTH CHAMBER OF COMMERCE
894 Clocktower Building
P.O. Box 327, Leavenworth, 98826
509/548-5807

LEAVENWORTH RANGER DISTRICT
509/782-1413

LEAVENWORTH WINTER SPORTS CLUB
P.O. Box 573, Leavenworth, 98826
509/548-5115

LINK (509/662-1155 or 800/851-LINK) is a free transit system serving Chelan and Douglas counties. Buses operate weekdays 6 am-8 pm and Saturdays 8 am-8 pm.

SNOQUALMIE PASS

Forty-seven miles from Seattle on four-lane Interstate-90 is Snoqualmie Pass in the Cascade Mountains. For families living in the Seattle-Tacoma area who want to hike, mountain bike, snowshoe, cross-country or downhill ski, the area offers terrain for all ages and abilities.

GETTING THERE
Snoqualmie Summit is at 3,100 feet on I-90.

PLACES TO STAY

SNOQUALMIE SUMMIT INN
206/434-6300; PO Box 163, Snoqualmie Pass, 98068

Rates: Moderate
Essentials: Credit cards; crib
*Extras: Outdoor heated pool, playground, sauna, whirlpool;
restaurant; TV*

For years, there wasn't a place for families to stay at Snoqualmie Summit, unless you were lucky enough to own (or know someone who owned) a private cabin. In 1989, Best Western built this pleasant motel, giving travelers a place to stop-over when headed over the mountains as well as a place to stay for a weekend of outdoor fun. The pool is small but outdoors and open year-round, so your kids (and you if you're a hardy type) can experience the thrill of swimming while it is snowing.

The Family Pancake House Restaurant attached to the Inn does the job nicely and you are no more than a few minutes from all four ski areas and hiking trails galore.

PARENT COMMENTS: *"My eight-year-old and four-year-old were just learning to ski so we went to the Summit Inn for a Saturday night in January. Accommodations were nothing fancy but comfortable and my kids loved swimming in the outdoor pool in the snow."*

"I wanted to get my five-year-old into hiking so I bribed him: you take a five-mile hike with dad and we will spend a night at a motel with a pool in the mountains. He made it and we both had a memorable time."

WHAT TO SEE AND DO

HIKING

There are hiking trails approaching and at the summit of Snoqualmie that will suit all age and energy levels. For specific trail suggestions consider the following:

SNOQUALMIE PASS VISITOR INFORMATION CENTER, operated by the National Forest Service, has a wealth of good information about hiking in the area. The folks operating the center are very friendly and familiar with the area and will tell you about specific hikes suited to your group.

Exit 52 off I-90; 206/434-6111. Open 8:30 am-4:45 pm, Thursday through Sunday in the winter and summer; weekends only during the spring and fall.

SKI ACRES MOUNTAIN BIKE AND HIKING CENTER. For a jump start on your hike, ride the chair lift up the mountain. The Center at Ski Acres can tell you about trails that will bring you back down the mountain—or you can buy a round-trip ticket and take the easy way down. Chair lift rates are $2.50 for a one-way ride—

kids under five ride free.

GEOLOGY ADVENTURES. This interesting organization offers hikes that teach about the geology of the Cascade foothills, about 30 minutes from downtown Seattle. The adventures are especially geared to parents and kids, and the guides provide a wealth of information, as well as hands-on activities, including gold panning and fossil hunting.

Phone: 255-6635

ISSAQUAH ALPS TRAIL CLUB. This club's members lead free hikes for all ages and skill levels year-round on the mountains and plateaus in the greater Issaquah area. No reservations are necessary and no special gear is required. Each hike is rated by length and climbing difficulty. Hikers meet at the Issaquah City Hall (about 30 minutes from downtown Seattle) at an appointed time, and carpool to the trail head. Call Issaquah Alps Hotline for more information and complete hike schedule.

24-hour hotline: 328-0480

THE MOUNTAINEERS is the largest outdoor organization in the region, currently comprising 14,000 members. The club is dedicated to offering a wide range of outdoor activities for all ages including hiking, cross-country skiing, backpacking trips, kayaking and more.

For more information: 284-6310

CROSS-COUNTRY SKIING

This fun sport grows more popular with families each year and it is easy to see why—it is much less expensive and easier to learn than downhill and gets you away from the crowd and into the woods. It is a sport you can quickly learn alongside your kids.

SKI ACRES CROSS-COUNTRY CENTER is an excellent facility for kids and others just getting acquainted with the pleasures of cross-country skiing. You can rent equipment, take lessons, go on guided treks and enjoy 75 kilometers of trails (3 kilometers are lit for night skiing).

East end of Ski Acres Parking lot; 206/434-6646.

DOWNHILL SKIING/SNOWBOARDING

Your options at Snoqualmie Summit are numerous. There are four areas: Hyak, Ski Acres, Snoqualmie and Alpental. A free shuttle bus runs between the areas on weekends. Snoqualmie has good instruction for all ages and is the best hill for beginners. Downhill telemarking is popular at Hyak; Alpental has the most challenging runs.

Information:360/434-6161.

MOUNTAIN BIKING

Taking a bike out on the mountain trails is one more fun outdoor activity that works well for all ages—the only requirements are that you have to be a decent bike rider and enjoy a bumpy ride.

SKI ACRES MOUNTAIN BIKE AND HIKING CENTER was recently rated the third largest mountain biking center in the country. You strap your bike to the back of the chair lift and ride to the top, where you can take the speedy route or the slow, scenic route back down, choosing from 35 miles of trails. Lessons and bike rentals are available. Helmets are required and can also be rented.

206/434-7669; ext. 3372; east end of Ski Acres Parking Lot, take exit 52 from Seattle, Exit 54 from Ellensburg. For recorded information about lessons, chair lift rates, and hours call 206/236-1600. Open late May thru Labor Day, Friday through Sunday and holidays.

TUBING AND SLEDDING

You can bring along your own sleds and tubes and find your own hill (along the road to the Alpental Ski area there are several good spots) or at **Snow Flake Tubing and Snow Play** kids can rent or bring their own inner tubes, and have the option to take a rope tow up the hill. There is also a small area for sledding, though sleds are not rented. Admission is charged whether or not you supply your own tube. Warning: Snow Flake gets crowded on weekends.

Snoqualmie Pass, east corner of Ski Acres parking lot. 206/285-TUBE. Admission $5.40/person (under 5 free); tube rental $4.50.

SNOQUALMIE FALLS PARK

This scenic park, located in the foothills of the Cascade Mountains, is a fine place to get out in the woods and view a waterfall. Just outside the town of Snoqualmie (about 35 minutes from Seattle on I-90) the Snoqualmie River plunges 270 feet over a rock gorge. The park's grounds feature observation platforms to view the falls, picnic areas, a gift shop and cafe. For the ambitious, the half-mile River Trail leads down to the river's edge, for an upclose view of the cascading falls. The trail is steep, however, so be prepared to help the little one on the trip back up. The falls are not really spectacular, but in late spring when the snow is melting they are quite impressive and the surrounding park is lovely.

Located 25 miles east of Seattle; take exit 27 from I-90. Open year-round, free admission.

PUGET SOUND AND SNOQUALMIE VALLEY RAILWAY

Travel aboard the historic Puget Sound and Snoqualmie Valley steam train for a one-and-a-quarter hour trip through the scenic Snoqualmie Valley. Train runs every weekend from Memorial Day through Labor Day, as well as select days during the spring and fall. No reservations are necessary.

In the town of Snoqualmie; 206/888-0373 or (206)746-4025 Weekends only, April-October, call for departure times and prices.

RESOURCES

WASHINGTON STATE DEPARTMENT OF TRANSPORTATION
PASS INFORMATION LINE
206/455-7900 (Nov-Apr)
Like on any mountain, weather and road conditions can deteriorate rapidly in the winter. Always carry chains and check the road report before departing.

SKI ACRES MOUNTAIN BIKING AND HIKING CENTER
206/236-1600

VISITORS INFORMATION
206/434-6111
Exit 52 off I-90; open 8:30 am-4:45 pm, Thursday through Sunday in the winter and summer; weekends only during the spring and fall.

Best Hikes with Children in Western Washington & the Cascades, Volume 1 and 2, by Mountaineers Publishing.

CLE ELUM/ELLENSBURG

Cle Elum sits in the foothills of the eastern side of the Cascade Mountains on Interstate 90. Gateway to the Alpine Lakes Wilderness, it is a rapidly developing recreation area——with abundant opportunities for fishing, camping, boating, horseback riding, bicycling, hiking, Nordic skiing and snowshoeing.

Ellensburg, 108 miles east of Seattle on I-90, is a charming mix of college and cowboy. Cattle ranching and horses are prevalent in this area—two of the recommended places to stay are ranches.

GETTING THERE
Both Cle Elum and Ellensburg are located on Interstate-90.

ROADSIDE ATTRACTIONS. See Snoqualmie Pass: What to See and Do.

PLACES TO STAY

BEST WESTERN ELLENSBURG INN
509/925-9801; 1700 Canyon Rd, Ellensburg, 98926
Rates: Inexpensive to moderate
Essentials: Credit cards; cribs
Extras: Indoor pool, wading pool, sauna, whirlpool; restaurant;
TV, free movies; refrigerators in some rooms; pets OK
   Located at exit 109 off I-90, this is a good choice for a motel if you are passing through town or here for a couple days—especially if the family dog came on your trip.

   PARENT COMMENTS: *"The Best Western worked well for us when we went to the rodeo Labor Day weekend. Our only disappointment was no outdoor swimming pool—in this hot climate that would be nice."*

HIDDEN VALLEY RANCH
509-857-2344; 3942 Hidden Valley Rd., Cle Elum, 98922
Rates: Moderate to expensive
Essentials: Credit cards; cribs
Extras: All meals plus snacks included; outdoor pool (year-round);
recreation room (books, piano, pool table); hot tub; horseback
riding; hiking trails; sport court; cross-country skiing trails and
instruction; fishing; babysitting (by pre-arrangement)
   Hidden Valley is quite a spread—800 acres of ranch, field, river and gently rolling hills. The ranch house sits on a hill with a gorgeous vista from every side of the wraparound porch. There are hammocks on the porch for dreaming in and friendly ranch cats and a ranch dog.
   The outdoor swimming pool is heated and open all year. The large recreation area at the lodge is a popular place for guests to gather. There's a fireplace, a pool table and ping-pong table and a good collection of books. Outside, the firepit is a popular spot for evening fireside socials.
   Fishing in Swauk Creek, which runs through the ranch property, is popular. Horseback rides are offered several times a day. Children must be six years old and accompanied by a paying adult. (Bring bike helmet for the ride.) Price is $25 for a 1 1/2-hour ride. Younger children can be led on a horse around the corral.

The trail riding program is exceptionally good. Childcare for ages two to five is available at the 9 am ride.

The food is hearty and delicious. Meals are buffet-style, all-you-can-eat, but the cook is eager to meet special needs of the guests. Snacks for munchers are available at all times.

Cabins are "comfortable rustic." They all have electric heat and showers. Floor plans vary slightly so ask the manager to recommend the right cabin for your group. Rates include meals, lodging, and the use of all other ranch facilities and activities except trail rides, hay rides, and a few other special services that cost extra. There's a minimum stay of two days on weekends; guests who stay for one or more weeks are entitled to one free day per week. In the winter, the ranch has Nordic skiing weekends, with skiing on the fields, meadows and trails of the ranch or nearby Blewett Pass.

> **PARENT COMMENTS:** *"Visiting here is like stumbling onto the set of a John Wayne movie."*
>
> *"I like to visit in the spring. The days are sunny and the hills are green and inviting. The staff is very friendly and helpful."*
>
> *"Even in the summer the nights can get cold so pack accordingly. "*
>
> *"Our children were charmed. They loved watching the wranglers work the horses in the corral and feeding the horses grain through the fences. They found a rope and pretended to rope each other for two hours."*
>
> *"Except the space heater in the cabin, the rooms were fairly childproof. We left it off when our toddler was in the room."*
>
> *"After dark, we had star-filled chats around the outdoor fireplace with other guests. Bring a star chart!"*
>
> *"Ranch vacations are wonderful and ranch vacations are expensive! In July it cost us $190 for each adult, $100 for our seven-year old and $50 for our two-year-old for a two-night stay in the summer. Plus horseback riding! Next time just mom and the seven-year-old—the two horse lovers—will go."*

CIRCLE H RANCH
509/964-2000; Rt 1, Box 175, Thorp, 98946
Rates: Moderate to expensive
Essentials: Credit cards; cribs
Extras: All meals; kitchenettes; pond; horseback riding; Petunia the donkey, goats, rabbits; hay rides; campfires; fishing; babysitting available by pre-arrangement; pets okay

Circle H Holiday Ranch is a picturesque cluster of buildings on 58 acres of pasture and forest and adjacent to the 100,000 acres of the LT Murray Wildlife Recreation Area. The ranch is a fine place to take kids who like the outdoors, farm animals and horseback riding. The five cabins, small but comfortable (they were originally cowboy bunkhouses), are filled with wonderful memorabilia collected by owner Betsy Ogden—more of which can be seen in the main house.

Each cabin has a sitting room, kitchenette (refrigerator and microwave), bedroom and bath. They are clean, with numerous "little touches" to make guests comfortable—including coffee, cocoa and microwave popcorn. Four cabins are connected by doors which is convenient if you are with another family: Tonto connects with Lone Ranger, Dale Evan with Roy Rogers. Gene Autry is bigger—it was once the caretaker's house. It has a full kitchen and a tiny back room with a daybed just right for a child.

Meals are served in the main house where there is also a TV and VCR available for guest use. The pond, tether ball and farm animals are located close to the cabins which is convenient for keeping your eye on the kids. Horseback rides are $12.50/hour.

From Memorial Day through Labor Day Circle H operates as a full guest ranch with all meals included in the price. During the balance of the year, the ranch operates as a bed and breakfast, with a reheatable breakfast delivered to each cabin the night before. Off-season rates are considerably lower.

PARENT COMMENTS: *"Six moms took our eight daughters for a "ladies weekend" at Circle H. We ALL thought it was a great place."*

"We visited Circle-H in early June. There weren't many guests and the whole experience was slightly off—like we were invading a private home. The meals were so-so—hamburgers and curly fries one dinner, lasagna the next night. Even though the hostess was very gracious and the cabins fine, it was an expensive weekend and we thought we should have had really good food for the prices. However, our kids, ages 11, eight and six adored Circle H. My son caught his first fish in the trout pond and our daughters were enchanted with the horses, the farm animals and most of all, the memorabilia in our cabin."

"The wrangler was super nice to our kids. They got up early so they could help him feed the horses."

STEWART LODGE
509/674-4548; 805 W First St; Cle Elum, 98922
Rates: Inexpensive
Essentials: Credit cards; cribs
Extras: Outdoor heated pool open seasonally; TV; refrigerators in

some rooms; small pets okay

If you are looking for a basic motel to serve as your home base so you can explore the great outdoors in this part of the state, the Stewart Lodge, located at the west end of Cle Elum, will do the job. There are outside corridors on the two-story building; rooms have an attractive country motif.

PARENT COMMENTS: *"We spent a night here when we came over from Seattle to raft on the Yakima in July. It was very hot and the outdoor pool was a nice bonus."*

PLACES TO EAT

THE VALLEY CAFE

509/925-3050; 105 W. 3rd St, Ellensburg
Hours: Breakfast weekends; lunch and dinner every day
Essentials: Credit cards; highchairs

Even if you are just passing through, it is worth timing your drive past Ellensburg so that you stop at this attractive and delicious take-out or sit-down restaurant. Salads are fresh and reasonably priced, sandwiches hearty and delicious. Breakfast and dinner selections are also interesting and well-prepared. If you don't want to take the time for a full meal, pick up a picnic at the take-out counter next door.

WHAT TO SEE AND DO

DICK AND JANE'S DRIVE-BY ART. Give the family material for a lengthy car discussion by driving them past this remarkable "yard art." Even the preschooler will be impressed by 20,000 bottle caps, 15,000 bike reflectors and tons of other random items assembled in what the owners/creators describe as their means to encourage "peace through art."
101 N. Pearl St, Ellensburg; 509/925-3224

CHIMPOSIUMS. Central Washington University Chimpanzee & Human Communication Institute offers one-hour, educational workshops involving their world-renowned signing chimpanzees. Located on the Central Washington University campus in Ellensburg, the institute is designed to facilitate research on primate communication. Washoe and the other four signing chimpanzees have acquired extensive American Sign Language vocabularies. Visitors learn about the research being done at the Institute as well as observe the chimps conversing with each other and their human teachers.

Corner of Nicholson Blvd & "D" St, Ellensburg; 509/963-2244. Saturdays, 9:15 & 10:45 am. Sundays 12:15 & 2:15 pm. Admission: $10/adult; $7.50/under 18.

THE CLYMER MUSEUM & GALLERY in historic downtown part of Ellensburg features the work of the Western illustrator and artist and Ellensburg native son, John Clymer, known for the storytelling quality and fine detail of his work. Parents may recognize some of the 80 examples of covers of *The Saturday Evening Post* drawn by Clymer.

416 N. Pearl St, Ellensburg; 509/962-6416. Hours: weekdays, 10 am-5 pm, weekends noon-5 pm. Admission: $2/person.

CROSS COUNTRY SKIING. Trails in Iron Horse State Park once used as railroad tracks are now used as paths for cross-country skiing and snow shoeing. The John Wayne Pioneer trail winds through the forests of Easton to the rolling farmland of the Upper Yakima River Valley.

Located at the foot of 4th St. in South Cle Elum; 509/656-2230.

The Forest Service will provide maps of other ski trails in the area, as well as Snow Park permits.

803 W. 2nd S., Cle Elum; 509/674-4411

THE ELLENSBURG CHILDREN'S ACTIVITY MUSEUM has a mini-city with bank, post office and other important stops. Special events for children are staged throughout the year.

400 N. Main; 509/925-6789;Thurs-Sat, 10 am-5 pm, Sun 1-5. Admission: $2.50/person.

THE ELLENSBURG RODEO has been happening every Labor Day weekend since 1923. It is rated one of the top ten rodeos in the country and the **Kittitas County Fair** happens the same wild weekend, so Ellensburg is jam packed with tourists and entertainment. Admission to the rodeo ranges from $8-$17, depending on your seat; a family ticket (two kids and two adults) is available for $29.95. Lodging and tickets go quickly, so make your plans early.

Every kid should see wild bronco riding and the magic of cow roping at least once, but you might opt for the Saturday-night rodeos staged in Ellensburg in July and August instead of the huge Labor Day extravaganza. They are a much smaller version, but will give your family a chance to experience the thrill of the rodeo without the crowds and expense of the major event.

For information about the Labor Day Rodeo call 509/962-7831 or 800/637-2444. Call the Chamber of Commerce for exact dates of the Saturday night rodeos. (509/925-3137).

ELK FEEDING. Once the snow is deep enough to cover natural forage, the Department of Wildlife feeds some 750 elk a day at Joe Watt Canyon, fifteen miles northwest of Ellensburg. Be there by 8 am to see these spectacular animals and dress warmly.

From Ellensburg travel west on I-90 to the Thorp Exit 102, proceed left over the freeway approximately ¼ mile to the top of the hill. Go right on Old Thorp Cemetery Road and continue to the Joe Watt Canyon Road. Turn left here and proceed to the end of the road (approximately 1 mile) where you will see the elk feeding station.

GINKGO PETRIFIED FOREST STATE PARK is located near the geographic center of the state where Interstate 90 crosses the Columbia River at Vantage. One of the most unusual fossil forests in the world is located here. The park is located on what was a region of lakes and swamps 15-20 million years ago. The Heritage Center, which houses the park's Interpretive Center, has over 50 varieties of petrified wood on display. There is also a ³/₄ mile interpretive trail following an exposed prehistoric lake bed and a ¹/₂ mile hiking trail through the sagebrush terrain.

Heritage Center open daily 10 am to 6 pm, May 15 through September 15. Free.

HIKING. For families that want to hike in this beautiful section of the state, the wilderness area awaiting exploration is unlimited.

For information about trails and campgrounds around Cle Elum and Ellensburg, contact the Cle Elum Ranger Station at 803 W. 2nd St., Cle Elum, 98922. 509/674-4411.

HORSEBACK RIDING. You don't have to be a guest at the Circle H Holiday Ranch or Hidden Valley Ranch, to ride their horses. Trail rides start at $20 for 1 ¹/₂ hour rides at Circle H, $25 for the excellent 1 ¹/₂ -hour ride at Hidden Valley.

509/964-2000, Circle H Ranch. 509/857-2087, Hidden Valley Ranch.

OLMSTEAD PLACE STATE PARK is a heritage site that celebrates the legacy of the family farm. In 1875, Sarah and Samuel Olmstead crossed the Cascade Mountains on horseback with their young family. Their farm was one of the first homesteads in the valley. In 1908 a red barn was constructed and a new residence was built. The Seaton Cabin Schoolhouse was built in the 1870s and was reconstructed at Olmstead place in 1980. All of these buildings can still be seen at Olmstead Place. *Located 4-¹/₂ miles southeast of Ellensburg at I-90 & Squaw Creek Trail Road. 509/925-1043. Free.*

RIVER RAFTING ON THE YAKIMA is a do-it-yourself rafting adventure well-suited to families. The river is gentle you don't need previous rafting experience or a guide for a successful trip. Equipment can be rented near Cle Elum at **River Raft Rentals.** The trip is fun with a group and taking two or more cars lets you shuttle from the finish. The canyon has no tourist facilities other than portable toilets at the Roza Dam and Umtanum access area. Most of the river's forty miles from Cle Elum to Roza Dam can be floated. Ask at River Raft Rentals for a map that gives river access information.

You can transport the rafts inflated or deflated (rafts come with pumps). For a half-day float, drop a car in the parking lot at Roza Dam access area, 21 miles south of Ellensburg on State Highway 821. Drive 9 miles north to Umtanum access area, where there is a parking lot off the road to the left. Or for a float about half as long, start at Squaw Creek access area 5 miles south of Umtanum. Unload your raft and start down the river. Around three or four hours later, you'll be back at Roza Dam.

The river gets crowded on weekends in the summer. If you don't bring your own tubes or rafts, reserve a rental at least one day in advance.

Tips: Wear a lifejacket. From May on the sun is scorching: bring sunscreen lotion, sunglasses, a cover-up to wear over your bathing suits and old tennis shoes to protect your feet from the rocky bottom. Keep a dry change of clothes and food in large plastic bags.

River Raft Rentals, 509/964-2145; Route 4, Box 275, Ellensburg 98926. Located seven miles northwest of Ellensburg off State Highway 10. Eight- person raft costs $30/day weekends; $20/day Mon-Thurs. Inner tubes $3/day. Prices include life jackets.

TELEPHONE MUSEUM. The only telephone museum west of the Mississippi is in Cle Elum. Kids who think nothing of mom using a car phone might be interested in seeing the 1901 switchboard and collection of old, crank-style telephones.

221 East First Street; 509/674-5702; open Memorial Day through Labor Day.

A WALK AROUND THE ELLENSBURG DOWNTOWN HISTORIC DISTRICT will give kids a chance to see the **Cowboy Sculpture** by Dan Klennert while parents enjoy the eclectic mix of cowboy and expresso that characterizes this historic part of town. The lanky cowboy stands with his six-guns at his side guarding the corner of Fifth Ave and Pearl. While you're there, you can't miss the droll **Ellensburg Bull** by artist Richard Beyer, lounging on a bench, cowboy hat in lap.

CALENDAR

SEPTEMBER: Ellensburg Rodeo, Labor Day weekend Threshing Bee, Olmstead Place Park
NOVEMBER: Celebration of Lights, Ellensburg.

RESOURCES

CLE ELUM CHAMBER OF COMMERCE
509/674-5958
221 E 1st St, Cle Elum, 98922

ELLENSBURG CHAMBER OF COMMERCE
509/925-3137
436 Sprague, Ellensburg, 98926

CLE ELUM RANGER STATION.
509/674-4411
803 W 2nd St, Cle Elum, 98922

GRAND COULEE DAM/DRY FALLS

North of Soap Lake, Coulee City is the former junction for railroad and stagecoach lines running along the Columbia River. According to Guy Waring, a 19th-century author/pioneer from Massachusetts, the trains and and coaches were deliberately scheduled not to connnect with each other, forcing passengers to spend the night in town. Today, what will bring you through the little town of 600 inhabitants will most likely be a trip to Grand Coulee Dam or a vacation at nearby Coulee Lake Resort.

GETTING THERE
Take I-90 to Soap Lake, then drive 15 miles north on Highway 17. The resort is located on Blue Lake.

ROADSIDE ATTRACTIONS. See Snoqualmie Pass and Cle Elum/ Ellensburg: What to See and Do

WHERE TO STAY

COULEE LODGE RESORT
509-632-5565; 3017 Park Lake Rd. NE, Coulee City, 99115
Rates: Inexpensive
Essentials: Credit cards; cribs
Extras: Kitchens; Jet skis, boats; laundromat; store

Coulee Lodge Resort is located on quiet, uncrowded Blue Lake, in the scenic "Little Grand Canyon" of Washington in the Lower Grand Coulee. The lake is 3 ½ miles long and stocked with rainbow trout. The dry, hot climate and clear, cool lake are ideal for swimming and water skiing.

The comfortable, low-key resort offers air-conditioned cabins, a great swimming area with raft, boat rentals, and a little store. The owners are friendly and very helpful.

The kitchens are well-equipped. You will probably want to cook most of your meals but if you hanker for a night out, there are several family-friendly restaurants in Soap Lake, about 15 miles away.

PARENT COMMENTS: *"We've been there two years in a row and plan to return next year. The kids love it and so do we!"* *"Just what we wanted—a not-fancy, comfortable place to relax with the kids and at an affordable price."*

WHAT TO SEE AND DO

DRY FALLS, located 4 miles southwest of Coulee City on Route 17, is a good place to show kids the mighty force of nature. The Columbia River once cascaded over this cliff 3 miles wide and 400 feet high that was formed by ice age floods. There's an interpretive center that does a good job explaining the fascinating geology of the area. An awesome sight well worth a stop.
Park open year-round. Interpretive Center open Wed-Sun, 10 am-6 pm, in summer; 509/632-5583.

GRAND COULEE DAM harnesses the Columbia River for irrigation, power and flood control. It is a "must-see" if you traveling in Eastern Washington. Adults and kids alike will be awed by the massive size of the dam, said to be the largest concrete structure in the world. Usually the water flows through pipes to turbines inside the dam. Try to time your visit to see the water spill (1:30-2 pm) over the dam into the river below.

There are several ways to get to the dam. The most direct is U.S. 2 to Route 174 from Spokane, or U.S. 2 to Route 155 from Wenatchee or Seattle. Allow about two hours for a visit. Self-guided tours are available in the summer. A Visitor Center provides a good history of the geology of the area and the construction of the dam. The hour-long laser show that illuminates the dam nightly during the summer is remarkably beautiful.

Visitor Center open daily 8:30 am-10 pm, Memorial Day-Labor Day; 9 am-5 pm rest of year. Hour-long laser light show presented nightly at 10 pm, Memorial Day weekend-July 31; 9:30 pm, Aug; 8:30 pm, Sept. Free. 509/633-9265.

SPOKANE

Spokane is the second largest city in Washington state, but you'd never know it. Full of charming parks and pleasant neighborhoods, it still feels like a small town. Riverfront Park, developed for Expo '74 and covering more than100 acres along the Spokane River, will no doubt be a major focus of your visit, but you'll find many other interesting attractions to explore with the kids.

GETTING THERE

The drive from Seattle to Spokane is east on I-90, over the Cascade Mountains. You'll cover about 290 miles, so count on at least one good rest stop.

Amtrak (800/872-7245) has a train running from Seattle to Spokane daily, but the schedule isn't convenient for families. It departs Seattle at 4:50 pm and arrives in Spokane at 12:05 am. The return trip leaves Spokane at 2:15 am and arrives Seattle at 10:25 am. Cost is $65 one way; kids two to15 are half-price when traveling with an adult.

Shortly after you cross the Columbia River, look to your right for a sculpture — a thundering herd of bronze horses — tucked in among the hills.

REFUELING. On the west side of the Columbia River is Vantage — a good place to refuel and refresh. There's a restaurant on the bluff that has okay food. If the weather is suitable, a picnic lunch would be ideal, either at the river's edge or up the hill in Gingo Petrified Forest State Park.

If you want to push on a little further before you stop and feed the group, there are numerous restaurants and picnic areas in the town of Moses Lake, about 40 miles from Vantage. But watch out if you eat outdoors: we saw a sea gull snatch a toddler's burger right off his plate!

ROADSIDE ATTRACTIONS. The Vantage exit on I-90 is a good place for bathroom breaks, picnicking, leg-stretching and sightseeing. Follow signs to **Ginkgo Petrified Forest State Park** for spectacular views of the Columbia River. The Interpretive Center (509/856-2700) has Indian artifacts, fossils and petrified wood. Take one of the short trails through the sagebrush to see petrified logs. There are picnic tables, restrooms and, just down the road, a gift shop with rocks, crystals and other treasures.

If the weather is hot, stop at the **public beach at Vantage** (on the right side of the road, just before of the bridge) for a refreshing dip in the Columbia. There are dressing rooms and picnic tables, as well as a grassy park where you can toss a Frisbee.

Another good stop is **Moses Lake State Park** (off the freeway at exit 175). You'll find a playground, picnic tables, restrooms, concessions and a swimming beach. Your future aviator may be more interested in the 747s overhead, however—Japan Airlines trains pilots at the nearby Grant County Airport.

At exit 174 is another interesting attraction: the **Sand Dunes ORV Area** (known locally as "Four Wheel Drive Park"). With 280 acres, the park provides room for hikers, picnickers, fishermen and four-wheelers to coexist peacefully (if not quietly).

See the "Cle Elum/Ellensburg" section for more roadside attractions and places to eat on the way.

> You're in rattlesnake country, so make sure the kids stay on the trails and out of the brush.

PLACES TO STAY

CAVANAUGH'S RIVER INN
509/326-5577, 800/843-4667 for reservations; N 700 Division, Spokane, 99202
Rates: Inexpensive to moderate (Entertainment cardholders get 50% off rates, depending on availability)
Essentials: Credit cards; cribs
Extras: Restaurant; TV; two outdoor swimming pools (one covered with a bubble in the winter months), Jacuzzi; game room; playground; tennis court, putting green; pets OK

There are four Cavanaugh hotels in Spokane. Two of them, the River Inn and the Inn at the Park, are ideally located near Riverfront Park. For families we recommend the River Inn for these reasons: the rates are generally lower; the facilities are better for children, with a game room, outdoor playground, tennis courts and putting green. The layout and atmosphere are friendly to families (the Inn at the Park has a more corporate feel). River Inn guests enjoy full access to the fabulous outdoor pools at Inn at the Park, just a block and a half away (pools are open during summer months only).

The design of the River Inn complements the nearby river, offering easy access and lovely views. Be aware, however, that the river banks are steep. Kids must be supervised—playground and pools are near the river and unfenced.

The restaurant at the River Inn, Ripples, is kid-friendly. The children's menu is affordable, portions are large, and highchairs are available. Most important, our young reviewers loved the food. Parent reviewers also praise Ripples for great service, reasonable prices, pleasant river views and good, fresh food.

PARENT COMMENTS: *"The Inn at the Park is located a little closer to Riverside Park, but for us that's not enough to justify the higher price. We stay at the River Inn and take the kids to swim at the Inn at the Park at least once. They love the wonderful pool slides built into the landscaping."*

COURTYARD BY MARRIOTT
509/456-7600; N 401 Riverpoint Blvd, Spokane, 99202
Rates: Inexpensive to moderate
Essentials: Credit cards; cribs
Extras: Cafe; TV; mini-refrigerators (some units); indoor pool, whirlpool; exercise equipment

Located on the south side of the river, across from Cavanaugh's River Inn, the recently opened Courtyard offers the same advantages as the Cavanaugh hotels—excellent river views and proximity to Riverfront Park. Suites, each with a bedroom and separate living area, have mini-refrigerators but no microwaves.

PARENT COMMENTS: *"This is one of the newest hotels in the area and one of the best values. Winter rates are excellent. However, it is often hot in Spokane in the summer, so when we visit during July or August we opt to stay at a place with an outdoor pool."*

HAMPTON INN
509/747-1100, 800/426-7866; 2010 S Assembly Rd, Spokane, 99204
Rates: Inexpensive to moderate
Essentials: Credit cards; cribs
Extras: Free buffet breakfast; TV; indoor pool

Located five minutes from downtown and five minutes from

the airport, the Hampton Inn is moderately priced and family-friendly. One of its best features is the indoor, 24-hour pool.

The breakfast is also well-suited for families. Served buffet-style (no waiting), choices include cold cereals, muffins, English muffins, toast, doughnuts, yogurt, fruits, oatmeal, juices, hot chocolate and coffee. A deli at the Inn serves lunch and dinner at reasonable prices in a relaxed atmosphere. Menu choices include many kid favorites, such as chicken pot pie, pizza, sandwiches and soup.

PARENT COMMENTS: *"We got back to the Inn about 8 pm one night and appreciated being able to get a quick, reasonably priced meal at the deli."*
"With the pool open 24 hours we could take a swim very early if our kids woke up at the crack of dawn and at the end of the day to relax."

QUALITY INN VALLEY SUITES
509/928-5218; E 8923 Mission Ave, Spokane, 99212
Rates: Inexpensive to moderate
Essentials: Credit cards; cribs
Extras: Free breakfast; TV; mini-refrigerators, microwaves; indoor pool; deluxe suites with Jacuzzis; exercise equipment; pets OK

This is a bright, clean, modern, full-service hotel, located off I-90, about 10 minutes east of Spokane. Though it's not in a notably scenic location, the rooms are pleasant and the indoor pool is a big hit with the kids. Also, there are mini-refrigerators and microwaves in every room—a real cost-saver for traveling families. Perhaps the only real drawback is the 11 am checkout time.

Large families, and those who don't want to be limited to sitting (or eating) on the beds, should consider getting a suite. The rates are more reasonable off-season.

The hotel provides a complimentary continental breakfast that is convenient and adequate for most younger kids' morning appetites. The dining room at the hotel is open for dinner 5-10 pm, and the atmosphere is rather dark. Opt instead for Perkins Restaurant, which adjoins the hotel—it's kind to kids, palates and wallets. The nearby Longhorn (509/924-9600; N 2315 Argonne) serves outstanding barbecue, including take-out.

Quality Inn is close to Dishman Hills, a good area for hiking, and the Centennial Trail, great for both hiking and biking (see "What to See and Do"). If the weather is lousy and the kids have energy to burn, consider a trip to Discovery Zone (509/924-0023; N 1445 Argonne Rd), a snazzy indoor playground where kids can safely jump, swing and slide. (Open daily, hours vary. Cost is $5/ child, age 18 months and over, for unlimited play. Parental supervision is required; no childcare is available.)

> **PARENT COMMENTS:** *"Quality Inn is an ideal place to stay if you are passing through Spokane on your way to Yellowstone or Schweitzer or if you don't want to stay right in the city."*

PLACES TO EAT

AZTECA
509/456-0350; W 200 Spokane Falls Blvd
Hours: Lunch and dinner
Essentials: Credit cards; highchairs
Western Washington residents will recognize this restaurant chain and can expect the same tasty Mexican fare, good service and good value. In keeping with its family-oriented reputation, Azteca has an exceptional "Little Amigos" menu. An added advantage is its proximity to Riverfront Park.

CLINKERDAGGERS
509/328-5965; W 621 Mallon
Hours: Dinner daily, lunch Mon-Sat
Essentials: Credit cards; highchairs
This is the place to go if you want to take the kids out for a special dinner. (Many Spokane grownups also consider it a favorite). The food and service are consistent; the views of the Spokane River are spectacular. Kids will enjoy the Old English atmosphere and the extensive children's menu (prices range from $3 to $4; a kid-sized prime rib dinner is $6). Parents will appreciate the warm reception given their kids, along with the good food. Reservations are recommended, especially if you want a table near a window with a view of the river.

Clinkerdaggers is located in the Flour Mill, which houses a variety of shops and merits an after-dinner stroll.

CYRUS O'LEARY'S
509/624-9000; W 516 Main
Hours: Lunch and dinner
Essentials: Credit cards; highchairs
Located downtown across from Riverfront Park, Cyrus O'Leary's has a fun atmosphere and an extensive menu. Homemade pies are the claim to fame, but they also serve sandwiches, salads, soups, pasta, and inexpensive children's entrees. Two recom-

mendations: bring your own crayons and paper (they aren't provided), and ask for a booth or table near a window.

GINGER'S ON THE SKYWALK

509/456-8622; 221 N Wall
Hours: Lunch, Mon-Fri,10 am-5 pm; Sat,11 am-5 pm
Essentials: Credit cards; highchairs

With a scenic location (overlooking Riverfront Park from the downtown skywalk) and good, basic food (soups, salads, sandwiches, muffins, brownies), this cafe is a fine lunch spot for sightseeing families. Menu items are available for take-out, so if the weather permits, take a picnic to the park below.

MAMMA MIA'S RISTORANTE

509/482-7162; N 7706 Division
Hours: Lunch and dinner Mon-Sat, dinner Sun
Essentials: Credit cards; highchairs

Huge portions of scrumptious homemade pasta and pizza have earned Mamma Mia's a well-deserved reputation as an outstanding family eatery.

WHAT TO SEE AND DO

STROLL & BROWSE

Downtown Spokane is good for walking and window shopping. Pick up a Spokane tour map at the **Visitors' Bureau** (Sprague Ave & Monroe St) or in one of the downtown stores. Check out the historic Davenport Hotel (Sprague & Post), which has recently undergone major renovations.

The downtown skywalk shopping area includes 15 blocks of second-story shopping, all connected by skywalks. You'll find many little shops (see "Shopping"), restaurants and places to sit and rest, as well as the downtown Bon Marche and Nordstrom department stores. The skywalks are wide and easily accommodate strollers. In inclement weather, you can park the car indoors and ride an elevator to the shopping level, without setting foot outside.

THE FLOUR MILL is a 100-year-old building that once used the Spokane River's energy to mill wheat. These days it's filled with unique shops and restaurants, as well as historical displays of its milling days. Unless you have older, extremely well-behaved (hands-in-pockets) kids, stick to window shopping until you come to **Positively Tooney**, a small store packed with cartoon characters, clothing, toys and related kitsch. Another interesting shop is **The Books and Game Company**, with its large assortment of games, puzzles and books for kids and adults. *Located on the north side of the river, connected by foot-bridge to Riverfront Park.*

PARKS

CENTENNIAL TRAIL. This 39-mile, 8-foot-wide paved trail follows the Spokane River from Spokane to Coeur d'Alene, Idaho, and is ideal for running, walking, biking, skating or pushing a stroller. It begins at Riverside State Park and is also accessible from Riverfront Park.

MANITO PARK features a large, modern playground that will entertain young children for hours. If you happen to visit during snow season, the hills offer the best sledding and tubing in town. There's also a duck pond at the park, which often freezes over in the winter, providing a good, though ungroomed, skating surface for adventurous skaters. (In the summer, bring bread crumbs for the ducks.) Concessions and a cafe are available seasonally.

For the flower lovers in the family, Manito Park has a conservatory and beautifully groomed gardens in season, including a rose garden, lilac garden and Japanese garden. *Located on the south hill, at Grand Blvd & 18th. Open daily. Free.*

Check out the sculpture of runners on the southeast side of Riverfront Park. It's a tribute to the runners in Spokane's annual Bloomsday Run.

RIVERFRONT PARK, on the former site of Expo '74, is Spokane's centerpiece. Located along the Spokane River on Native American fishing grounds, the park features year-round attractions and activities, including the intricately carved 1909 Looff Carousel, a suspension bridge over the river, a gondola ride above Spokane Falls and, during summer months, carnival rides and outdoor concerts. The clock tower, four-story IMAX theater, opera house, convention center and Ice Palace (an outdoor skating rink) are also located in this 50-acre park. A no-cost attraction, which is very visible from Spokane Falls Blvd, is a big red wagon that has a long slide for a handle. For those who enjoy simpler park pleasures, there are plenty of paved pathways to explore on foot, bike or roller blade. Skate and bike rentals are available seasonally. **Quinn's Wheel Rentals** (509/456-6545; near Howard Street Bridge at Riverside Park) rents all sorts of fun wheeled toys, including roller blades, bikes of all sizes, tandem bikes and surreys — pedal-propelled cars that will seat five to eight persons.

If the gang gets hungry, concessions are available at the park. Restaurants are not far away (downtown to the south on Spokane

Falls Blvd and in Flour Mill shopping area, north on Mallong Rd).
*509/625-6600, 800/336-PARK. Hours vary depending on the
season. Tickets range from $1/carousel ride to $3-$5/ice skating or
admission to the IMAX theater. A $9 day pass buys a gondola ride,
a ride on the Looff Carousel, admission to an IMAX film, and carnival
rides or ice skating.*

ANIMALS, ANIMALS

CAT TALES ENDANGERED SPECIES EDUCATION CENTER is a
family-oriented center that features 26 big cats, including lions,
tigers and leopards. Take a tour or enjoy the wildlife on your own.
The gift shop is worth a browse.

*N 17020 Newport Hwy, Mead; 509/238-4126. Located five miles
north of Spokane on Hwy 2. Hours: Wed-Sun, 10 am-4 pm (winter),
10 am-6 pm (summer). Cost: $3/adult, $2/children 12 and under.*

TURNBULL NATIONAL WILDLIFE REFUGE. Just a half-hour's
drive from Spokane, this 17,000-acre refuge is full of lakes, ponds,
marshes and all the wildlife characteristic of this landscape
(especially waterfowl). Visitors can bike, walk or drive through
the refuge on various trails.

*26010 S Smith Rd; 509/235-4723. To get there, drive four miles
south of Cheney on Cheney-Plaza Rd, then two miles east on Smith
Rd. Cost: $2/vehicle.*

WALK IN THE WILD ZOO is a natural wildlife zoo, home to both
native and exotic animals. Covering 240 acres, it includes a
children's zoo and features traveling educational exhibits from
Seattle's Pacific Science Center as well as special events, such as
"Zoo Lights," during the winter holidays.

*E 12600 Euclid; 509/924-7221. Take the North Pines exit from I-
90 (about 12 miles east of downtown), travel north about 1 mile to
Euclid, and turn right. Hours: daily 10 am-4 pm (winter), 10 am-6
pm (summer). Cost: $4/adult, $3.50/youth, $3/child age 2-5.*

MUSEUMS

BROADVIEW DAIRY MUSEUM. Housed in the original Broadview
Dairy, this museum offers visitors a chance to see an old-time
milking barn and horse-drawn wagon preparing for milk deliver-
ies. Learn about different kinds of cows and how modern dairy
plants work. There are no live cows here, but the museum offers
an entertaining explanation of where milk comes from. There is
a gift shop, but no restaurant.

W 411 Cataldo; 509/324-0910. Hours: Tues-Sat, 12-5 pm. Free.

CHENEY COWLES MUSEUM. This small museum does an excellent job of providing a historical perspective on this region. Exhibits include a lively presentation of regional history, local artists and Native American artifacts. Kids will find the lifelike displays in the adjoining Campbell House (an old mansion from Spokane's mining days) particularly interesting. *2316 W First Ave; 509/456-3931. Open Tues-Sat, 10 am-5 pm; Wed, 10 am-9 pm; Sun, 1-5 pm. Cost: $7.50/family, $3/adult, $2/ child over 6; on Wed admission is half-price 10 am-5 pm, free from 5-9 pm.*

SHOPPING

If shopping is part of your plan, you'll find a number of options in the Spokane area. **Auntie's Bookstore** (402 W Main; 509/ 838-0206) is a cozy place for browsing. This spot, which just won "Best Family Bookstore" in a local parenting magazine readers poll, has a fine selection of children's books. **Whiz Kids** (W 518 Riverside; 509/456-6536) is an educational store for kids, parents and teachers. It offers a good selection of toys, books, puzzles, and science and nature items.

If you're visiting the River Park Square Mall, there are two stores in which you'll want to wander. **Anakko Toys**, a spacious, attractive store conveniently located in the skywalk, offers a large selection of toys, games, puzzles, music, stuffed animals and more (W 814 Main; 509/456-0982). Another attractive store is the **Children's Corner Bookstore** (W 814 Main; 509/624-4820), which carries an extensive array of books.

FRED MEYER may sound like run-of-the-mill shopping, but this superstore has a special feature that makes it the perfect place to pick up ice chests, swimming suits and other vacation supplies. Freddy's Playland is an in-store play area for preschoolers (ages two to six). There's no charge, and safety and health rules are strictly enforced. Parents and kids get numbered ID bracelets, and parents also carry a pager. Located 15 minutes east of downtown, it's actually on the way if you're heading into northern Idaho (15609 Sprague, Veradale; 509/921-5350).

EXCURSIONS

COEUR D'ALENE, IDAHO is only 33 miles from Spokane on I-90. It is fast becoming a vacation mecca in the Northwest and is well worth a day trip, if you're planning an extended stay in Spokane. Some families stay in Spokane and drive to Silver Mountain outside Coeur d'Alene to ski. See "Idaho: Coeur d'Alene" section for details.

DISHMAN HILL NATURAL AREA. This 400-acre preserve is home to nearly 40 plant species and 100 species of birds. The area is filled with hikes of varying degrees of difficulty. Northwest Map Service (525 Sprague Ave; 509/455-6981) sells a good map of these trails.

To get to Dishman Hill, take I-90 east from Spokane to the Sprague Ave exit, go east 1 ¹/₂ miles to Sargent Rd, turn right and continue for one half mile.

FORT SPOKANE. This late-19th century-fort was built to maintain peace between settlers and Native American tribes, but it never saw any real action during 20 years of use. Today, the fort houses both visual and audio displays that provide a history of the area. Tours of the grounds are also offered.

It's a bit of a drive from Spokane, but certainly a scenic one. The small town of Davenport has a nice city park that surrounds a natural spring — a good spot for a picnic before or after visiting the fort. Kids can play on the playground equipment and maybe even take a dip in the city pool. This is an excellent excursion for budget-minded families who enjoy getting out and exploring small towns and regional history.

Located 58 miles northwest of Spokane; 509/725-2715. To get there, go east on I-90 to the Hwy 2 exit (about two miles), then travel about 35 miles on Hwy 2 to the town of Davenport. From Davenport, proceed north on Hwy 25 about 15 miles. The Fort Spokane Visitors Center is open Memorial Day-Labor Day, 9:30 am-5:30 pm. Free.

GREEN BLUFF. This small farming community, 10 miles north of Spokane, is especially picturesque at autumn harvest time. The fields and orchards of Green Bluff are filled with u-pick vegetables and fruits. On an October visit, pick an Eastern Washington pumpkin to take home or pluck some apples off the tree. Several of the farms have gift shops where you can buy a jar of apple butter or honey to take home, or some apple cider to sit and sip as you enjoy the scenery.

To get there, take Hwy 2 to Day-Mount Spokane Rd, then turn east.

RIVERSIDE STATE PARK. You'll find places to hike, picnic, fish and camp in this 7,300-acre park located along the Spokane River, northwest of the city. One trail takes you through a 17-million-year-old fossil forest, set in Deep Creek Canyon. Two easy family hikes begin near the Bowl and Pitcher rock formation, located close to the suspension bridge that crosses the river. Bear right past the picnic shelter to hike the downstream section of the trip (five miles roundtrip) or left at the picnic shelter to hike the shorter upstream section (two miles roundtrip).

The park office is open Wednesday through Friday for trail information. Horseback riding is also available at the park (**Indian Canyon Riding Stables**, 509/624-4646). There is no food available, so bring your own picnic or plan to barbecue.

N 4427 Aubrey L. White Pkwy; 509/456-3964. To get there, travel north on Division to Francis, then west on Francis to Assembly Street, where Francis becomes Nine Mile Rd. Continue northwest on Nine Mile about ³/₄ mile to Rifle Rd and turn left onto Aubrey L. White Parkway. Go approximately two miles to entrance of Bowl and Pitcher recreation area.

SILVERWOOD THEME PARK. Northeast of Spokane in Athol, Idaho you'll find a turn-of-the-century theme park, complete with rides, air shows and live entertainment. Come early and plan to stay all day. The admission rates may seem steep, but those with patience for the inevitable lines will certainly get their money's worth.

Northern Idaho is rich in mining history, and Silverwood recreates the atmosphere of an old mining town—with several modern twists, of course. Besides rides, rides, rides (pony, train, water, roller coaster, Ferris wheel and old-time carnival rides), enjoy live entertainment daily. Look for vintage biplanes performing stunts overhead, jugglers tossing all sorts of things on Main Street, and snacks everywhere.

Located one hour northeast in Athol, Idaho; 208/683-3400. Open daily June-Labor Day: Sun-Thurs, 11 am-9 pm; Fri-Sat, 11 am-10 pm. Weekends only mid-May through early June and Labor Day through early Oct, 11 am-8 pm. Take I-90 east about 30 miles to Hwy 95, then north 15 miles. Cost: $18/adult and children age 8 and older, $9/children age 3-7, children under 3 free.

CALENDAR

JANUARY: Northwest Bach Festival
MARCH: St. Patrick's Day Parade
MAY: Lilac Festival & Bloomsday Run
Spokane Music and Arts Festival
Armed Forces Torchlight Parade
JULY: Cheney Rodeo, Cheney
SEPTEMBER: Spokane Interstate Fair
OCTOBER: Family A-Fair
Green Bluff Apple Festival

RESOURCES

SPOKANE TRANSIT AUTHORITY
509/328-7433

SPOKANE REGIONAL CONVENTION AND VISITORS BUREAU
926 W Sprague, Suite 180, Spokane, 99204
509/747-3230

Inland NW Family Magazine is available at most children's shops, grocery stores and libraries.

Kidsline provides a taped message about activities for children. 509/458-8800, ext 3020

REI store has hike information.
N 1125 Monroe; 509/328-9900

100 Hikes in the Inland Northwest, by Rich Lander, Ida Rowe Iophin and the Spokane Mountaineers. Published1987 by Seattle Mountaineers.

LAKE CHELAN

It is no surprise that Lake Chelan is one of the most popular vacation places in the state for families—the combination of fine weather, a lively little resort town, a beautiful lake and access to some of the most spectacular wilderness in the country is unbeatable.

It's not just Chamber of Commerce talk that established Lake Chelan as "a place in the sun." Whatever the weather may be west of the Cascades, it is a good bet that in spring, summer and fall, the four-hour drive to Lake Chelan will produce warm, cloudless, sunny skies. Be prepared with hats and plenty of sunscreen.

GETTING THERE
From the Seattle area there are two main routes with about equal travel time of 3 $^1/_2$ to 4 hours.

One route goes through Stevens Pass. Follow I-5 for 27 miles north from Seattle and take Exit 194 to U.S. 2. Or, take Highway 405 on the east side of Lake Washington to connect with Highway 522 near Bothell and follow 522 to the junction with

U.S. 2 at Monroe. Near Wenatchee, turn north on U.S. 97 and follow it into Chelan.

The second route goes through Snoqualmie Pass. Take I-90 from Seattle to Exit 85 near Cle Elum. Follow Highway 970, merging with U.S. 97 in a few miles through Blewett Pass to connect with Highway 2. Turn north on U.S. 97 near Wenatchee.

From Portland, take I-84 east along the Columbia River to U.S. 97 at Biggs. Cross the Columbia and follow U.S. 97 north through Goldendale, Yakima, and Ellensburg through Blewett Pass to U.S. 2 and Wenatchee.

ROADSIDE ATTRACTIONS. Both **Stevens Pass** and **Snoqualmie Pass** summit areas are popular skiing developments with complete winter sport facilities. At other times of the year both areas offer good rest stops with trail walks and food service. Both routes also provide numerous opportunities for picnics as you drive over the Cascade mountains.

The Stevens Pass route goes through the Bavarian-style town of **Leavenworth**. See Leavenworth: Places to Eat and What to See and Do for details.

The Snoqualmie and Stevens Pass routes join just west of the town of Cashmere. This spic-and span early American town celebrates apples and pioneers. A popular stop is the **Aplet and Cotlet Candy Kitchen** where the unique fruit and nut confections have been made for 60 years. Visitors are welcome and kids like the samples.

The Ohme Gardens, located three miles north of Wenatchee on U.S. 97, were developed on a high rocky bluff overlooking the Columbia River and the Wenatchee Valley. It took 50 years by a dedicated family to build this nine-acre, alpine-style garden rated one of the outstanding gardens of its kind in the nation. Kids longing to stretch their legs after a long car ride will like exploring the stone pathways, a wishing well, numerous pools and rustic shelters.

Open 9 am to dusk, mid-April to mid-October; Admission $5/ adults; $3 ages 7 to 17. 509/662-5785.

Children will likely enjoy even more a visit to **Rocky Reach Dam**, located close by on U.S. 97. The fish ladder viewing room is where you can observe at close range the salmon swimming up to return to their spawning grounds. There are also good geology exhibits and the story of electricity with hands-on gadget for kids to operate. With 15-acres of beautiful landscaped gardens and a good playground, this is an ideal spot to have a picnic.

Admission is free; open daily dawn to dusk.

REFUELING. Two similar eateries that combine the economy of fast-food with the charm of an outdoor picnic are good stopping-off places on the way to Eastern Washington and Chelan. Both offer decent food and picnic tables in an area where the kids can stretch out and play.

McKean's Giant Hamburgers is at the eastern outskirts of Cle Elum on the north side of the road. (Get off I-90 and drive through the main street of town.) The menu includes a good sandwich selection.

Rusty's is your classic burgers and shakes drive-in. It sits on the western edge of Cashmere on the south side of the highway, just as you enter town.

The Cle Elum Bakery, located in the center of town on Main Street, has wonderful rolls, breads and breakfast muffins.

PLACES TO STAY

DARNELL'S RESORT MOTEL
509/682-2015 or 800/967-8149; 901 Sader Rd, PO Box 506, Chelan, 98816
Rates: Expensive
Essentials: Credit cards; cribs
Extras: Kitchens; fireplaces (in some units); outdoor pool (seasonal), whirlpool (seasonal), sauna, exercise room; lighted tennis courts; 9-hole putting greens; boats, badminton; bicycles

Darnell's sits on 300 feet of lakefront, a few blocks southwest of the center of town. It is a family-oriented place with plenty of amenities. Parents will especially appreciate that all the extras—boats, golf, —are free of charge. Units are large and comfortable.

> **PARENT COMMENTS:** *"A very family-friendly place. We loved having so much for our school-age kids to do right on the premises at no extra charge."*
> *"The lake is very busy at this end—lots of noisy ski boats, jet skis, etc. But it was nice to be able to walk into town for dinner and shopping."*

KELLY'S RESORT
509-687-3220; Rt 1, Box 119, Chelan, 98816
Rates: Moderate to expensive
Essentials: Credit cards
At a Glance: Kitchens, boats; playground; pets OK in cabins; ping-pong; playpen (need to reserve); fireplaces; babysitting (by pre-arrangement)

Kelly's has been operated by the Kelly family for more than 45 years. It is the kind of place where families return year after year and lifelong friendships are formed. Located north of the State Park, 13 miles from Chelan, Kelly's attracts a crowd that wants to avoid the jet-ski atmosphere at the southern end of the lake. It is more laid-back and less crowded than the better-known and expensive resorts in Chelan, but close enough to town that you can easily drive in for dinner or a day at the waterslides. The beautiful setting, comfortable accommodations and hospitable owners make it an ideal getaway for families.

The pine-paneled cabins are located in the woods across the road from the lake. They have a living room, Franklin fireplace, deck, full kitchen, and bathroom with shower. The larger cabins also have a screened sleeping porch. There is a small playground near the cabins.

The four new lakeside units sit right at the water's edge with decks over the water. All these units have full kitchens; two have fireplaces.

The cabins are less expensive and more private than the lakefront units. They are located near a road that is busy during the day and you can't see the lake from the cabin, so you will need to load up books, toys and beach towels and walk the youngsters down to the beach. The playground, however, is located near the cabins, which is convenient. The lakefront units are right at the beach, so you can stay at your unit and keep an eye on the kids, but the easy access to the water might be nerve wracking if you have young non-swimmers in your group.

All accommodations are immaculately maintained. Summer reservations should be made at least six months in advance.

Summer activities center around the well-designed lakefront that has a concrete-enclosed swimming area that is ideal for young children. There is also a roped swimming area with a diving board for stronger swimmers. The water is crystal clear and cold. There is boating in rowboats and canoes; many families bring ski boats with them. In the evenings, families often congregate in the lodge where there is a large fireplace, an old bowling machine, a ping pong table and a little store.

Two of the cabins and four of the lakeside units are now open year round. They offer a quiet, scenic place to stay while enjoying the winter sports available in the area.

PARENT COMMENTS: *"Many families start coming here when their children are young and continue coming through the teen-age years."*
"Our kids love the little store at the resort where they get to buy one

treat a day. One night during our visit we always go to Lake Chelan State Park, which is a five-minute drive away, play miniature golf, eat burgers at the drive-in across the street, and when it gets dark sit on the lawn and watch a movie and listen to a lecture about the geology of the area."

"It's a bit of a trek from the cabins down to the beach and store, including crossing a road, so you can't let young children run back and forth between the cabin and the beach."

"The beachfront units are lovely but we were on the ground-level units and even though my two-year-old had a lifejacket on practically 24 hours a day, I couldn't really relax knowing he could be out the door and in the water in a matter of seconds."

WAPATO POINT

1-800-572-9531 or 509-687-9511. PO Box 426, Manson, 98831
Rates: Moderate to expensive
Essentials: Credit cards; cribs
Extras: Kitchens; TV; restaurant, hot tub; outdoor and indoor swimming pools; miniature golf course; fishing; sports equipment rentals; boat rentals; bicycle rentals; cross country ski rentals; playground; organized activities for children; babysitting (by arrangement); ice skating rink in winter; tennis

This is an extensive condo development located nine miles north of Chelan on a point of land that juts into Lake Chelan. There are numerous options for recreation in and on the water. The resort has two miles of private waterfront and well-designed indoor and outdoor swimming pools.

The resort condominiums differ in floor plans, although most have two floors. Units have kitchens with dishwashers, and each is equipped with a Weber grill. In addition to all the activities around the water, kids can fish in the fishing pond, ride bikes, play miniature golf, basketball, horseshoes and tennis, or play at the two good playgrounds. There are usually organized activities for kids including arts and crafts sessions and evening movies.

During the winter, children can swim in the indoor pool, skate on the outdoor ice rink, and cross-country ski at the resort or at nearby Bear Mountain or Echo Valley.

Grocery shopping is convenient in nearby Chelan. The restaurant at Wapato has a good children's menu, good service, moderate prices and above-average food.

PARENT COMMENTS: *"We like to visit here in the late spring or early fall. The weather is not so hot, it is less crowded and prices are lower."*

"The one-bedroom unit we rented had a spiral staircase between living area and bedroom; not great for our toddler."

" For a family, I think this is a great place. It is completely furnished— all you need to bring is your food. And if you don't want to cook, the Wapato Cafe, at the entrance to Wapato Point, serves a good selection of favorites."

"There is a lot of room on the grounds of the resort for older kids to explore. Nearly all the visitors have families so you have a real sense of safety and the children find playmates easily."

PLACES TO EAT

CALICO COW
509/682-4064; on Hwy 97A near Lakeside Park
Hours: Breakfast, lunch, dinner
Essentials: Credit cards; highchairs

Chelan doesn't allow fast food franchises—you will have to take the kids to Wenatchee for a McDonald's or Burger King meal. But at Calico Cow you'll find a delicious burger, and thick shakes. This cheerful place on the north side of town has dining inside or out. Breakfasts are hearty and delicious—the home-made biscuits are a highlight. The lunch and dinner menu is just good casual fare. What makes Calico Cow worth visiting is the large outdoor eating area that is especially pleasant for breakfast before the weather gets hot.

GOOCHI'S
509/682-2561; across from Campbell's Lodge on E Woodin, Chelan
Hours: Lunch, dinner
Essentials: Credit cards; highchairs

When you long for a good fresh salad or a flavorful cup of soup, take a break at this casual restaurant around the corner from Riverfront Park. Kids who have overdosed on vacation fare of burgers and pizza will likely welcome the yummy pasta selections. Grown-ups will choose between a daily seafood and chicken special, Chinese Joe's Special, an oyster loaf sandwich and other tempting dishes.

WHAT TO SEE AND DO

The friendly town of Chelan has much to offer a family looking for vacation fun. Several stores will supply the water toys, bathing suits, sandals and sun screen you might have forgotten.

All the restaurants are "family-friendly" and if you want a break from swimming and boating there are numerous other diversions.

BOATING RENTALS are easy in Chelan. If you didn't bring a boat with you, chances are good that at some point during your summer visit, you'll want to get out on the water. Ski boats, jet skis, fishing boats, Hobie cats, sailboards, canoes, rowboats and paddle boats are available at one or both of the following places located right in town:

Chelan Boat Rentals, 1210 W Woodin Ave; 509/682-4444
Ship 'n Shore Drive Inn, 1230 W Woodin Ave; 509/682-5125.

DON MORSE MEMORIAL CITY PARK, just past the Red Apple Market on Manson Highway has an excellent swimming beach and good playground equipment, plus bumper boats, go-karts and miniature golf.

SLIDEWATERS, located just off Highway 97A on the south side of Chelan, is one of the largest waterslide parks in the Northwest. With nine major slides, a 60-person hot tub, a fabulous inner tube river ride and a large pool and slides for preschoolers, there is enough here to keep all ages entertained for most of a day.

Best of all, the staff to visitors ratio is high and friendly employees are present at all times giving careful instructions to children before they zip down the slides. The safe atmosphere allows parents to relax and have fun right along with the kids.

There is a snack bar inside the park with limited selection; no other food or drink is allowed on the premises. Plan to feed the group before you go into the park and/or budget snack money.

Taking a family to Slidewaters is an expensive outing; one way to cut the cost is to go at 5 pm when prices are reduced, the crowds have thinned and the lines are much shorter. Give everybody a late lunch that day and plan to eat pizza in town after you leave the slides at 8.

Open daily 10 am to 8 pm, Memorial Day thru Labor Day; 509/ 682-5751. Admission $9.95 adults, $6.95 children 4 to 7, under 3 free. Reduced admission, 5 pm to 8 pm, $6.95 adults, ¹/₂ price for children 4 to 7.

HIKING. The vast and varied wilderness that stretches out from the northern end of Lake Chelan is laced with hundreds of miles of trails that give access to mountain glaciers, high country lakes and alpine meadows. Including Wenatchee National Forest, the North Cascades National Park, Lake Chelan National Recreation Area, Okanagan National Forest and Mt Baker-Snoqualmie National Forest, the best hiking terrain is accessible up the lake only by boat. For the visitor without a boat, the *Lady of the Lake* passenger boat will on request drop and pick up campers and hikers. For information about maps, trails and guides in this region, contact:

Chelan Ranger District office, 428 W Wooden Ave, Chelan; 509/ 682-2576. Open 7:45 am-4:30 pm, weekends, daily in summer.

CROSS COUNTRY SKIING is available at nearby Bear Mountain. Although lack of snowfall can sometimes be a problem, there are 55 kilometers of trails and warming huts with picnic tables. The gently rolling terrain is good for beginners.

Located 5 miles west of Chelan off Highway 97A; 509/682-5444.

STEHEKIN. At the northern head of the lake sits the tiny community of Stehekin, only accessible by boat or plane. For most people, experiencing the remote reaches of Lake Chelan means a scenic excursion on the *Lady of the Lake II* or the newer *Lake Express.* The company's dock is less than a mile from downtown Chelan.

See Stehekin: Getting There for details.

CALENDAR

JULY: Chelan Rodeo
Arts and Crafts Fair

RESOURCES

CHAMBER OF COMMERCE
509/682-3503 or 800/4-Chelan
P.O. Box 216, Chelan, 98816

STEHEKIN

Stehekin, located at the head of Lake Chelan, is an isolated village perched on the edge of magnificent North Cascades National Park. It has no phone service and is not accessible by car, but as the only town within the Lake Chelan Recreation area, Stehekin is the starting point for the hiking, camping, backpacking, mountain biking, boating, canoeing, rafting, guided horseback trips, bicycle trips and fishing that take place in the region. The National Park Service operates a $3 shuttle ride along the Stehekin River Road, linking Stehekin and the lakeshore to the national park. The lectures and guided nature walks provided by the Park Service are excellent.

GETTING THERE

Stehekin is only accessible by boat, plane or on foot.

CHELAN BOAT COMPANY has two passenger excursion boats: the 350-passenger *Lady of the Lake II* and *Lady Express* provide round-trip service to Stehekin and the Lake Chelan Recreation Area. The dock is one mile south of the town of Chelan on U.S. 97 or you can board about 30 minutes later up lake at Fields Point Landing. No pets are allowed on the boats and regular service is for passengers only. Both boats have a snack bar, indoor and outdoor seating.

THE *LADY OF THE LAKE II* leaves Chelan at 8:30 am and returns at 6 pm, with a 90-minute layover in Stehekin. It departs daily from May 1 through mid-October. The ride is popular as a day outing but despite the magnificent scenery, it is a long and tedious ride (four hours one way) for kids so bring along crayons, games and snacks. *Lady Express* is a smaller and faster boat. It departs daily at 8:30 am and returns from Stehekin at 2 pm. If you want more time in Stehekin, you can take the *Express* up the lake and return on the *Lady of the Lake II* at 6 pm for a three-hour visit in Stehekin. Reservations are not necessary for the *Lady of the Lake II* because of its large seating capacity but reservations are strongly advised for the *Lady Express*. The boats run less frequently during winter months; call for details.

Lake Chelan Boat Company, PO Box 186, Chlean, 98816; 509/ 682-2224. Lady of the Lake II round-trip fare is $21/adult, $10.50/ child 6-11, under 6 free. Lady Express round-trip fare May 15-Sept 30 is $39/adult, $19.50/child, under 2 free. Express fare Nov-April is $21/adult, $10.50/child 2-11. It costs $38.50 round trip to take the Express up lake and the Lady II back.

Parking your car at the Boat Company parking lot will cost $4/day in Chelan or $3/day and $15/week at Field's Point.

CHELAN AIRWAYS (509/682-5555) will take you to the top of the lake in 30 minutes. Cost is about $75 round trip for adults, half-price for children ages 2 - 12 and children under two fly free. It is an unforgettable half-hour ride. Reservations are a must.

THE HIKE OVER THE NORTH CASCADES INTO STEHEKIN is a wonderful two- or three-day hike for a family of reasonably-fit walkers. For information contact the Chelan Ranger Station at 509/682-2576.

PLACES TO STAY

NORTH CASCADES LODGE
509/682-4494 Write to P.O. Box 457, Chelan, 98816
Rates: Moderate to expensive
Essentials: Credit cards; cribs
Extras: Kitchens; TV (in lounge); restaurant; hot tub; bicycle,
fishing, snowshoe and boat rentals

The North Cascades Lodge is located down valley (near the Stehekin dock) and it isn't fancy or imaginative, but the accommodations are satisfactory and will give you a home base for exploring the beautiful surroundings. There are lodge rooms and cabins; some units have housekeeping facilities. All are comfortable and simply appointed. Maid service is prompt and the staff is friendly and helpful.

In the winter, the lodge is open for cross-country skiing, which is excellent (average snowfall November-March is four feet), but during the off-season the boat only goes up the lake two or three times a week, so plan your trip carefully.

If you rent a housekeeping unit, be sure to bring your food with you, as groceries at Stehekin are limited. The restaurant at the lodge serves breakfast, lunch and dinner.

PARENT COMMENTS: *"Stehekin has a wonderful calm atmosphere. The Lodge acts as a comfortable, friendly base from which we were able to pursue various activities. The Lodge isn't the focal point of the trip, but rather a starting point for some super wilderness experiences."*

"We hiked into Stehekin from the west side of the mountains. Our party had five adults and seven kids, ranging in ages from 9 to 16. We spent a night at the lodge, then took the boat down to Chelan where we had arranged to leave our cars. It is fair to say we all treasure the memories of a great experience."

SILVER BAY INN
509-682-2212; P.O.Box 43, Stehekin, 98852
Rates: Moderate; five night minimum in cabins
Essentials: No credit cards
Extras: Continental breakfast; kitchens; woodstoves; bicycles;
canoes, croquet

No TV, no phone and steps away from rugged wilderness—a vacation at the Silver Bay is a comfortable way to get away from it all. The Inn is heated by passive solar heat and sits on 700 feet of waterfront with a broad expanse of green lawn that stretches to the water. There are two lakeside cabins (the main house has a bed and breakfast for adults only) that can be rented by families, as long as your children are ages 8 and up. Both cabins have woodstoves, private decks, and a beach area, and come fully equipped with dishes and linens. Kitchens even have microwaves and dishwashers. Kathy and Randle Dinwiddie are very helpful with suggestions for ways to explore the magnificent surroundings.

The Inn will arrange transportation to and from Stehekin Landing for your arrival and departure. It is also open in the winter for cross-country skiing.

PARENT COMMENTS: *"The Inn and cabins are right on the lake. They are attractive and very comfortable. The setting is spectacular."*

STEHEKIN VALLEY RANCH
509/682-4677; PO Box 36, Stehekin, 98852
Rates: Inexpensive
Essentials: No credit cards or cribs
Extras: All meals included; horseback riding, river rafting

If roughing it in the boonies interests you, but you don't quite have the nerve or energy to take the kids on an overnight backpacking trip, you can compromise by staying in one of the ten tent-cabins at this lovely ranch. Accommodations have a concrete floor, wood walls and a canvas roof and vary in the number and size of the beds. The cost includes transportation from the boat landing nine miles away, beds, a kerosene lamp, hot showers, and three excellent meals a day. Closed Sept 23-June 13.

PLACES TO EAT

STEHEKIN VALLEY RANCH
509/682-4677

Give the family a fun trip and the best meal in the area at the Stehekin Valley Ranch. The ranch will provide van service out and back or you can take a taxi. Dinner is served buffet-style with a different main dish every night, with hamburgers and steaks as alternates. The food is wholesome and delicious, including wonderful pie, and all guests eat together at long log tables. The kitchen and dining room have large, screened windows with a view of the corrals and alfalfa fields. Coffee is available at the woodstove. Kids are very welcome.

WHAT TO SEE AND DO

In the summer, good weather is almost guaranteed. The water is very cold for swimming, but riding, hiking and boating activities are endless. The National Park Service offers many free programs, including slide shows, bus service to scenic points, and nature walks. Some of the latter are specifically designed with children in mind—they're short, and include stops at the one-room schoolhouse and apple juice at the Ranger's house.

In the winter, it gets very quiet in this remote part of the state. Boat service is limited so you have to plan your trip carefully. Cross-country skiing and snowshoeing are a good way to explore at this time of year.

RESOURCES

LADY OF THE LAKE VACATION PLANNER (free)
Information about getting to Stehekin, accomodations and tours provided by Lake Chelan Boat Company.
509/682-2224

CHELAN RANGER STATION
Information on hikes, mountain biking and other activities in the Stehekin area.
509/682-2576

NATIONAL PARK SERVICE DISTRICT OFFICE
Located at the Stehekin dock, no phone service.
Information about routes, trail conditions, etc.

NORTH CASCADES

The rugged snow-capped mountains, glaciers, forests of tamarack and fir, alpine lake and waterfalls provide magnificent vistas for sightseers and abundant opportunities for excellent hiking.

GETTING THERE

Take Interstate 5 to exit 232 just north of Mt. Vernon. Follow Highway 20 to the North Cascades. The drive along the North Cascades Highway (Highway 20) is stunning once you pass Marblemount. The road was not completed until 1972. Winter snow closes the highway from late fall to spring from about six miles east of Diablo Lake.

PLACES TO STAY

CLARK'S SKAGIT RIVER CABINS

360/873-2250; 5675 Hwy 20, Rockport, 98283
Rates: Inexpensive to moderate
Essentials: Credit cards; cribs
Extras: 100 rabbits; kitchens; fireplaces in some cabins; restaurant; TV; laundry; pets OK

Don't come here expecting "a cozy cabin deep in the woods" or you will be disappointed. The tidy cabins at Clark's sit close to each other, about 100 feet back from the highway and across the road from the beautiful Skagit River. Nevertheless, Clark's provides an affordable and pleasant base for exploring one of the most beautiful regions in the Pacific Northwest.

The one-, two-and three-bedroom cabins are fully furnished and neatly kept. The kitchens are well-equipped and clean towels are provided each day. The restaurant offers a standard "drive-in" menu plus some fresh berry desserts.

One unique feature of Clark's will delight young visitors—rabbits everywhere. Especially in the morning and evening, a large assortment of rabbits can be found grazing on the lawns.

PARENT COMMENTS: *"Clark's is ideally located if you want to explore the west side of the North Cascades. We hiked and visited the dam at Diablo. We'll be back next year."*

"Our 2-year-old was enchanted by the rabbits that roam freely on the grassy yard at Clark's. They will often come close enough to be fed."

PLACES TO EAT

GOOD FOOD

This attractive fast-food stop on Highway 20, just before you enter Marblemount, is an excellent place to stop for a quick bite on your way over the mountains or if you are staying in the region. The food is fine but it is the location that is extraordinary—behind the restaurant there is a long, grassy lawn that ends on the banks of the Skagit. Kids have plenty of room to stretch and romp before and after their meal.

MOUNTAIN SONG RESTAURANT

360/873-2461; 5860 Hwy 20, Marblemount
Hours: Breakfast, lunch, dinner
Essentials: Credit cards; highchairs

There is indoor and outdoor seating at this comfy, cafeteria-style restaurant in the middle of the town of Marblemount. Food is fresh, healthy, hearty—and, best of all, delicious. There is a good assortment of microbrews, homemade pies, quiche and soups as well as hefty sandwiches.

WHAT TO SEE AND DO

CASCADIAN FARM ROADSIDE STAND. Yummy homemade ice cream, shakes and shortcake—loaded with organic berries—are sold at this cute little stand that sits at the edge of the Cascadian Farm. You can also buy fresh berries to take home July through September and sweet corn and pumpkins in September and October. There's also a picnic area.
Open daily May 1-Oct 31. On Highway 20 at Milepost 100 near Rockport; 360/853-8629.

HIKING. North Cascades National Park has more than 345 miles of trails. The ranger stations (see Resources below) provide trail maps and back country permits. Permits are necessary if you plan to spend the night in a wilderness area. It is also a good safety measure to check in with a ranger station before you take off on a hike. Many of the hikes begin off Highway 20.

LLAMA TREKKING. If you long to take the kids hiking into the Pasayten Wilderness as well as the western and eastern slopes of the North Cascades, but don't want to get stuck carrying the load, consider trekking with a llama. In 1980 Bob and Meriann Shapiro started a llama trekking operation and since then they have led over 50 expeditions into the North Cascades, with trekkers ranging from five- to 86-year-olds. The Shapiros provide all the food and camping amenities. The hikers just have to supply sleeping bags.
Deli Llama Wilderness Adventure, 306/757-4212; 1505 Allen Road, Boy, 98232.

NEWHALEM. Originally a company town for Seattle City Light, the name means "goat snare" in the Upper Skagit Tribal language, in honor of the mountain goats who gamboled through these hills. The general store here is the last store until you reach Mazama on the other side of the mountains. Kids can climb on Old Number Six, a retired steam engine from the early days of dam construction, and take the Trail of Cedars Nature Walk, a short walk through the forest to the historic Newhalem Powerhouse.

NORTH CASCADES INSTITUTE offers outdoor enthusiasts of all ages a wide variety of classes about the region. Most classes take place on the weekend in a setting that ranges from the North Cascades to the San Juan Islands. Experts share their knowledge of natural history. Some classes integrate the curriculum with backpacking, kayaking, rafting and sailing.

2105 Highway 20, Sedro Woolley, 98284; 360/856-5700, ext 209.

NORTH CASCADES VISITOR CENTER, staffed by the National Park Service, is well worth a visit. Located off the main highway west of Newhalem, the center features interpretive displays, a theater with an interesting slide show and a ranger on hand to answer questions. Daily programs at the center, as well as nature walks, are offered. The building, completed in 1993, is well-designed to integrate with the surroundings—a massive stone fireplace, skylights and giant open beams.

To reach the center, turn south off Highway 20 just west of Newhalem and cross the bridge across the Skagit River. Open 8:30 am-5:30 pm daily, Memorial Day thru Labor Day. Open weekends in the winter.

SEATTLE CITY LIGHT SKAGIT TOURS are a fun and educational outing with school-age kids. The main tour departs from the City Light Diablo tour center and lasts 4 1/2 hours. Highlights include a 560-foot mountain ascent and descent on a railway incline lift, a slide show, a boat cruise on Diablo Lake and a tour of the massive generating facilities of Ross powerhouse, followed by an optional, all-you-can-eat dinner. Shorter 90-minute tours, which are preferable with younger children, include a slide show, a tour of Diablo powerhouse and a lift ride.

Main tour (including dinner) $25/adults, ages 6-11 $10. Discount packages available for families for certain tours. Main tour without dinner $18/adults; $5 ages 6-11. The ninety-minute tour costs $5, under 6 free. If you just want the thrill of the ride up the railway lift so you can walk around near the dam, the ride will cost you $.25.

Reservations are recommended for meal tours. Contact Skagit Tours, 1015 3rd Ave, Seattle, 98104; 206/684-3030.

WILDFLOWERS. The myriad colors, shapes and fragrances of the mountain wildflowers can be found on the numerous trails that thread across forests and alpine meadows. The U.S. Forest Service provides hikes to see the flowers as part of the "Celebrating Wildflowers" observation that the agency conducts each summer to help promote both the appreciation and conservation of native plants. Walks begin in mid-June and end in late summer.

Information available at Mt. Baker-Snoqualmie National Forest Service offices.

On Highway 20 in Sedro-Woolley or Backcountry Ranger Station, Marblemount; 360/856-5700 or 360/873-4500.

RESOURCES

NORTH CASCADES VISITOR CENTER
360/856-5700 or 360/386-4495
Open 8:30 am-5:30 pm daily, Memorial Day-Labor Day. Open weekends during the winter. To reach the center, turn south off Highway 20 just west of Newhalem and cross the bridge across the Skagit River.

NORTH CASCADES NATIONAL PARK GENERAL INFORMATION
To get general information about the region write to: Superintendent, North Cascades National Park, 2105 U.S. 20, Sedro Woolley, 98284.

METHOW

Before 1972, when the North Cascades Highway was built through rugged mountain country, the Methow Valley was a dead end destination reached only from a southern approach. As such it was an isolated paradise known mainly to miners, ranchers and sportsmen. Today the miners are gone, but ranches, old orchards and horses are still there. Families are attracted by mountains, crystal-clear rivers, outdoor sports of all kinds and a unique mixture of pioneer nostalgia and modern comforts.

The valley has a four-season climate averaging 300 days of sunshine a year and about 16 inches of rain. Mean average summer temperature is 78 degrees and winter, 19 degrees. National forest and state range almost completely surround the valley.

Mountain biking, hiking, cross-country skiing, horseback riding and river rafting are the most popular forms of outdoor sport in the valley. But visitors can also helicopter ski, snowshoe, snowmobile, swim, fish and play tennis and golf.

Although there are several towns in the valley, Winthrop is the acknowledged hub. With wooden sidewalks and western-style turn-of-the-century buildings, the town's main street is interesting and lively. The town was started in 1891 by Guy Waring, a Harvard graduate, who named it for a colonial governor of Massachusetts, and Waring financed his trading company with money from Boston friends. A Harvard classmate, Owen Wister, visited Winthrop on his honeymoon, traveling by buggy from the railhead at Coulee City. While in Winthrop he wrote the first chapters of his famous western novel, *The Virginian*. Waring's log cabin is now Shafer Museum, a friendly little museum full of touchable things from early days.

From Winthrop, you can drive to Slate Peak, the highest point you can drive to in Washington, at 7,440 feet. Or, drive from the valley floor in Winthrop to Harts Pass, a 40-minute trip (be mentally prepared for a narrow road on a sheer cliff close to the top of Harts Pass). At the Forest Service lookout tower you'll get a 360-degree view right on the edge of the Pasayten Wilderness, with a peek into Canada. North of the Methow, the Okanogan Valley extends into Canada. While the Canadian side has been developed into a popular resort area (see B.C.-Okanagan section), on the U.S. side ranching and wilderness prevail.

GETTING THERE

From Seattle there are two main routes to this region of the state: State Highway 20, commonly called the North Cascades Highway, and U.S. 2. The North Cascades Highway, one of the most spectacular drives in the nation, is not open year round. Winter weather closes it from about mid-November until late April. To reach the valley for a winter outing, you need to use U.S. 2.

The North Cascades Highway begins at the junction of I-5 and Highway 20 north of Seattle at Burlington. Follow Highway 20 to Mazama and Winthrop. From Seattle it is 192 miles, four hours driving time.

Alternatively, you can take Stevens Pass over the Cascades on U.S. 2 to Wenatchee. Follow signs to East Wenatchee/Okanogan and take Highway 97 north to Okanogan. To reach the Methow, at Pateros turn onto Highway 153 (changes to Highway 20) and follow the road to Winthrop.

From Portland, take I-84 east along the Columbia River to U.S. 97 at Biggs. Cross the Columbia River, follow U.S. 97 north through Goldendale, Yakima, Ellensburg and Blewett Pass to U.S. 2 and Wenatchee. Follow directions above from Wenatchee to reach the Okanogan or Winthrop.

Or you can fly to Wenatchee and rent a car for the drive to

Winthrop or the Okanogan.

ROADSIDE ATTRACTIONS. If you travel U.S. 2 to reach the Methow, check the Leavonworth section. For information about what to see when you travel over the North Cascades Highway, see the North Cascades section.

PLACES TO STAY

MAZAMA COUNTRY INN
509/996-2681 or 800/843-7951; PO Box 275, Mazama, 98833
Rates: Moderate
Esssentials: Credit cards
Extras: Restaurant; hot tub; horseback riding; helicopter skiing; cross-country skiing

The tiny town of Mazama is fourteen miles west of Winthrop. The Mazama Country Inn is a wonderful getaway in an idyllic location. It is a fine place to go when you want to get away to the Methow without the kids. Prices are reasonable and meals at the Inn are well-prepared. In the summer, there are horses to ride and some of the best hiking in the state nearby. In winter cross-country trails begin at the front door or if you need a bigger thrill, a helicopter will whisk you off to a nearby peak.

However, children are not allowed at the Inn, which is just as well because it is a wonderful place to escape for some grown-up R & R. When you have the kids along, consider renting one of the cabins and houses managed by the Inn. These accommodations vary widely in location and size—the staff is very helpful with advising which place will best satisfy your needs.

PARENT COMMENTS: *"We snuck away to the Mazama Country Inn one weekend without the youngsters. When we walked into the lovely sitting room with the massive stone fireplace, we both heaved a big sigh and felt the tension of city life begin to slip away. It is a wonderful getaway—informal yet very attentive to your needs. We plan to return with the kids during the summer and rent a cabin on the premises."*

NORTH CASCADES BASE CAMP
509-996-2334; 255 Lost River Rd, Mazama, 98833
Rates: Inexpensive
Essentials: No credit cards; cribs
Extras: Meals included; hot tub; ski trails; ice rink; play yard; babysitting (by pre-arrangement); fishing pond

The North Cascades Base Camp is 2.2 miles northwest of of the Mazama Store on Lost River Road. Sue and Dick Roberts have built a wonderful inn in a beautiful setting with a set-up that is great for families with children. They rent out a room with a double bed and four- and six-person rooms with bunk beds, all with shared bath. It's hard to get a reservation here in the winter—it's been discovered by families who love the cross-country skiing in the Methow Valley.

The Roberts have two kids of their own, so the place is geared to children. A huge sandbox converts in winter to a skating rink, and they have plenty of skates for you to borrow. There are also swings and a playhouse, and a swimming hole and trout pond a short walk away. The Base Camp land borders the river, so it's easy to reach, but not so close as to be a worry. Indoors, there are a playroom with plenty of toys, a library, and lots of games and magazines.

All meals are included with a stay at the Base Camp, and they are healthful and tasty. Breakfast and dinner are served, and lunch fixings are put out for you to make your own. The Roberts recommend the Mountain Song Cafe in Marblemount, about 100 miles west on Route 20, as a good place to stop on your way to or from their inn in the summer.

PARENT COMMENTS: *"A perfect place for a family vacation to the almost wilderness; you get a bed, meals and all conveniences for a reasonable price. Kids are welcomed and enjoyed. We had no desire to even get in our car the four days we were there."*
"The Roberts are very familiar with the area and can tell about hikes and expeditions with their children."

SUN MOUNTAIN LODGE
509/996-3133 or 800/572-0493;P.O. Box 1000, Winthrop, 98862
Rates: Expensive
Essentials: Credit cards; cribs
Extras: Restaurant; outdoor pool; hot tub; horseback riding with lessons; TV in the lodge; tennis courts; hiking trails; mountain bike rentals; skiing trails, rentals and lessons; sleigh rides,; ice skating; boat rentals; fishing rentals; river rafting and scenic rafting; pool tables and ping pong; exercise room; organized activities for kids; babysitting (by pre-arrangement)

This beautiful lodge in a magnificent setting is located 12 miles from Winthrop, on the top of Sun Mountain, with a spectacular view of the Methow Valley and surrounding Cascade Range. It offers a variety of accommodations ranging from 50 rooms with a magnificant view located in the lodge, to 28 rooms with refrigerators and fireplaces in the Gardner Building. The lodge has seven fireplaces for informal gatherings and a charming library. A mile down the road from the lodge on Patterson Lake, Sun Mountain has 13 cabins with kitchens and fireplaces. Guests at the cabins are welcome to use all lodge facilities.

The swimming pool, located next to the lodge, has marine fossils in its rock walls, preserved when hot lava spilled from the sea bottom when the Methow Valley was under an ocean.

Activities vary according to the season, and organized programs for kids are available upon request, with a minimum of 24 hours' notice. There are often movies and special family-style dinners available. In summer, there are hiking trails of $^1/_2$ to 2 $^1/_2$ miles; some of these are marked with placards that give interesting nature information. Hayrides are also offered, followed by a picnic or barbecue. In the winter, there are 50 miles of marked cross-country ski trails; 30 of these are groomed.

The main restaurant provides a breathtaking view of the Methow Valley but the food has had mixed reviews in recent years and is quite expensive. A less formal cafeteria-style restaurant provides a more economical, family-oriented option. Another option is to drive into Twisp or Winthrop to eat.

PARENT COMMENTS: *"The setting is spectacular and activities endless. If I could afford to, I'd spend all summer there."*
"The most gorgeous resort in Washington state. It is hard to choose between a summer or winter visit—sleigh rides, ice skating and cross-country skiing versus biking, horseback riding and river rafting. "
"The highlight for our kids was the horseback ride and the cowboy dinner—complete with western music."
"It would be nice to see a special kids' menu in the dining room to cut the cost. The refrigerator in our room also helped keep our food costs down because we bought yogurt and dry cereal in town and had breakfasts in the room."
"The Sun Mountaineer activities were great—nature walks, crafts, games, etc."

THE VIRGINIAN
509-996-2535; PO Box 237, Winthrop, 98862
Rates: Inexpensive to moderate
Essentials: Credit cards; cribs
Extras: Kitchens (in some units); TV; restaurant; hot tub, outdoor pool (seasonal); ski trails, bike trails; volleyball

The Virginian, located on Hwy 20, just east of Winthrop, offers a variety of accommodations: cabins with small kitchens, some eight-plexes with very large rooms, and a row of motel units with smaller rooms. The place is built of logs, which lends it a rustic western feeling. However, the rooms are new and modern. Two grocery stores are located right next door — a good place for kids to get "treats."

The informal and friendly setting at the Virginian makes it an obvious choice for a family. Cross-country ski trails begin behind the hotel and follow the Methow River; others begin across the street. In summer, the outdoor pool gives relief from the heat.

The restaurant at the Virginian is casual and the food is excellent. There is a children's menu for kids under 12 with a choice of chicken, spaghetti or fish served with soup or salad. Prices are reasonable.

PARENT COMMENTS: *"Our family goes to the Winthrop/ Twisp area at least twice a year, and the Virginian is always the children's favorite place to stay."*

WOLDRIDGE RESORT
509/996-2828 or 800/237-2388; Rt 2, Box 655, Winthrop, 98862
Rates: Moderate to expensive
Essentials: Credit cards; cribs
Extras: Kitchens in some units; outdoor pool, Jacuzzi; TV; playground; cross-country ski and biking trails

Located six miles northwest of Winthrop on the Wolf Creek Road, this attractive new resort is well-suited to families. In the hand-crafted log lodges you can choose from a suite or a complete unit, that includes a well-equipped kitchen complete with dishwasher. The 50-acre resort sits right on an extensive cross-country trail system. On the premises there is a public warming hut with a river rock fire pit. Hot beverages and baked goods are served to skiers taking a rest.

PARENT COMMENTS: *"A great addition to the area. Definitely the best place for families vacationing in the Methow. Very attractive and comfortable."*

PLACES TO EAT

DUCK BRAND CANTINA & BAKERY
509/996-2192; Main street, Winthrop

Hours: Breakfast, lunch and dinner
Essentials: Credit cards; highchairs
   The servings are plentiful and the food healthy and delicious at the Duck Brand. The menu ranges from fat burritos to pasta dishes and thick sandwiches, along with delicious fresh baked goods.

   Also recommended: **The Virginian** restaurant described under Places to Stay.

THINGS TO SEE AND DO

CROSS-COUNTRY SKIING. Most cross-country skiers consider the Methow the finest place to ski in Washington, if not the country. Dry snow and miles of trails lure skiers from all over the world. The valley has six areas offering a variety of terrain and challenges for every skiing level: Mazama, Sun Mountain, Winthrop, Twisp, Loup Loup and Rendevous, with the European tradition of mountian skiing from hut to hut. Huts have bunks, a wood stove and a cookstove. They make a cozy place to warm up during the day, as well as a fun overnight stop.
   For trail and hut information call 509/996-2148 or 800/422-3048.

HIKING. It is hard to imagine a better place to hike than the Methow area. You can choose between spectacular alpine trails or lush paths down in the valley. To take an overnight hike without the hassle of heavy packs, consider taking horses with **Early Winters Outfitting and Saddle** (509/996-2659) or **North Cascade Safaris** (509/996-2326) or via llama with **Pasayten Llama Packing** (509/996-2326).
   For specific information about trails and conditions, contact the Winthrop Ranger Station at 509/996-2266, the Early Winters Ranger station at 509/996-2534 or Twisp Ranger Station at 509/997-2131.

MOUNTAIN BIKING is almost as popular as cross-country skiing in this part of the state and that is no surprise—the same extensive system of trails and logging roads that provide so many choice skiing options in the winter turn into biking routes when the snow melts.

RIVER RAFTING on the nearby Methow or farther away on the Columbia is a dandy way to enjoy the natural beauty while having fun. Unless the ride is very tame, rafting isn't recommended for young kids.

Call Osprey River Adventures at 509/997-4116 for details.

CALENDER

MAY: Memorial Day Rodeo
JULY: Winthrop Rhythm and Blues Fest
SEPTEMBER: Mule Days Rodeo

RESOURCES

METHOW VALLEY CENTRAL RESERVATIONS
Provides reservations for the whole valley—from Mazama to Pateros—plus information about river rafting, cross-country skiing and other things to see and do in the region.
509/996-2148 or 800/422-3048

WINTHROP CHAMBER OF COMMERCE
P.O. Box 39, Winthrop, 98862
509/996-2125

WINTHROP RANGER STATION
509/996-2266

OKANOGAN

You are almost guaranteed a sunny vacation in this high, dry part of Washington State. Towns are few and far between—plan to settle down for a week and slow down.

GETTING THERE
Take Highway 2(Wenatchee) or Highway 20 (North Cascades) east to Highway 97 north. At Oroville, follow signs to Sun Cove Resort and Wannacut Lake, which is located 12 miles (on a gravel road) southwest of town.

SUN COVE RESORT
509/476-2223; Rt 2, Box 1294, Oroville, 98844
Rates: Inexpensive
Essentials: Credit cards; cribs
Extras: Kitchens; outdoor pool; boats; horseback riding; playground; laundry
Wannacut Lake is four miles long and has only a handful of houses and Sun Cove Resort along its shores. Ponderosa pines

and sagebrush cover the landscape. The clear, cold mineral water is great for swimming, boating and fishing (bring your own gear). There is no water skiing allowed on the lake. The resort rents small motor boats, paddleboats, and fiberglass canoes and kayaks.

Sun Cove is a funky little place with a variety of accommodations, including some RV and tent sites. There is one long log building divided into ten cabin units. Each sleeps four comfortably and has a fully equipped kitchen. In addition, there are two cottages, Mama Bear and Papa Bear, which sleep groups of six and eight respectively. These are available by the week only, and you have to provide your own bedding and towels.

The place is set up for families. The small pool is heated, and there is a playground. The barn is nearby. Trail rides as well as wagon rides are offered.

There is a small store, but it is best to bring your own food, or buy it in Oroville before heading out to Sun Cove. The tiny restaurant at the resort has the basics—burgers, pizza, etc.

PARENT COMMENTS: *"The only drawbacks were a shortage of hot water and low water pressure at peak hours."*
"The warm weather, beautiful scenery, and lack of TV made for a great family vacation. We explored the lake by boat, swam, read books, and played cards to our hearts' content."

COLUMBIA GORGE

The Columbia River Gorge slices between the mountains and hills of southern Washington and Northern Oregon. It is a gorgeous region, often overlooked by vacationers from outside the Portland area.

GETTING THERE
Take I-84 east from Portland. On the Washington side take Highway 14 from Vancouver.

PLACES TO STAY

LLAMA RANCH BED & BREAKFAST
509/395-2786; 19980 Hwy 141, White Salmon, WA 98672
Rates: Inexpensive
Essentials: Credit cards; cribs
Extras: Breakfast; kitchen in some units; playground; llama, peacocks

This is a comfortable, informal and very child-friendly place to stay in the pretty town of White Salmon, near the Columbia Gorge. To get there from Seattle or Portland, take Interstate 84 out of Portland. At Hood River go north on Highway 141 into Washington to the ranch (four miles south of Trout Lake). A visit in the spring, when the baby llama are born is especially fun.

In the summer there's rafting, horseback riding and hiking nearby. In the winter cross-country skiing is popular.

Accommodations include a room with two queen beds ($65) or a room with a king, a queen sofa bed and a kitchen ($75). The kitchen in the lodge is available for use by all guests.

PARENT COMMENTS: *"This friendly place is well-suited to young children. The llamas and many peacocks are right outside along with a playground and an area to run and play without any cars around."*

SKAMANIA LODGE
800/221-7117; 1131 SW Skamania Lodge Dr, Stevenson, WA 98648
Rates: Expensive
Essentials: Credit cards; cribs
Extras: Restaurant; swimming pool (indoor); tennis; nature trails; golf; horseback riding; mountain biking

Located just 45 minutes from Portland and three hours from Seattle, the Skamania was opened in 1994 by the same people who own Salishan Lodge on the Oregon Coast and Salish Lodge, overlooking Snoqualmie Falls near Seattle. With its gorgeous location overlooking some of the most beautiful sections of the Gorge and first-rate accommodations, it is a marvelous addition to the area. The lodge was designed in the mountain lodge tradition of America's national parks and it is an impressive structure with 195 rooms sitting on 175 acres. Soothing earth tones and first-class service create an atmosphere of woodsy luxury.

PARENT COMMENTS: *"Very deluxe—maybe best as a splurge for the parents. But if you do bring the kids, there is plenty to keep them busy at the resort and in the surrounding area."*

THINGS TO SEE AND DO

COLUMBIA GORGE INTERPRETIVE CENTER
This splendid new attraction opened in May, 1995. The $10.5 million interpretive museum depicts Native American lifestyles,

the fur trading era and the harnessing of geologic forces of the gorge. Children will especially enjoy the full-scale, 38-foot replica of a fish wheel and the diorama of a Native American dipnet fisher. It is located on Rock Creek Drive adjacent to the entrance to Skamania Lodge above Highway 14. One of the highlights is continuous showings of a stunning nine-projector show dramatizing the geologic forces that carved out the Columbia River Gorge.

990 S.W. Rock Creek Drive; 503/427-8211. Admission: $5/ adults, $3 children ages 6-12, under 6 free. Hours: Tues-Thurs and Sun, noon-5 pm; Fri and Sun, noon-6 pm. Call to confirm hours.

See also Hood River and Mt. Hood in Oregon for more information and resources about this area.

Portland chapter by Elizabeth Hartzell DeSimone

PORTLAND

Situated on the Willamette River in Oregon's northern reaches, Portland is the state's largest city. Yet it is built on a human scale, with short city blocks, wide sidewalks and lots of parks and open spaces. Somehow Portland's thriving commercial and cultural sectors don't detract from the relaxed, unpretentious atmosphere. And its heavy dose of civic pride helps keep the streets clean and the residents smiling. People are happy to visit—happier still to live here.

GETTING THERE

From Seattle, drive south on I-5, 175 miles.

Amtrak (800/872-7245) operates six trains a day along the Seattle-Portland corridor. Choose a morning, late morning or evening departure, a morning, afternoon or evening return. The trip takes about four hours. Round-trip adult fares range from $26 on a weekday to $32 on a weekend. Children ages 2 to 15 years ride for half-price. Reservations required.

REFUELING. About halfway to Portland on I-5, just when your backseat passengers can't bear another minute in the car, take advantage of the refueling wonderland of Centralia, Exits 81 and 82. Just two blocks off Exit 82, on the right at the light, **Country Cousin Family Restaurant** serves typical lunch fare well-prepared and quickly. Or turn right at the light and drive a block to **Andre's** (look for the Dutch windmill) for nice pastry, hearty soups and sandwiches and a good selection of fresh salads. Parents may welcome an espresso drink to pump them up for the remainder of the trip, and kids will enjoy perusing the small gift shop, which features novelties from Holland.

A third alternative is the **Winter Kitchen**, two blocks east of Exit 81, a cheerful little green house decorated for Christmas year-round. The menu is short—sandwiches, salads, oyster stew—well-prepared and cheap. Tell the kids that if they behave all the way to Centralia, you'll get them a red (strawberry) or green (lemon-lime) float. (No credit cards, lunch only.)

If you can't stand to stop long enough to sit down in a restaurant, there are several fast-food options (with drive-throughs) nearby. Signs are visible from the freeway.

If you have the time, cruise through Centralia's **Factory Outlet Center** next to the freeway. Several stores here sell deeply discounted children's clothing and shoes. **Toy Liquidator** offers brand-name discontinued items, including a good selection of car games and beach toys, at rock-bottom prices.

ROADSIDE ATTRACTIONS. The **Mount St. Helen's National Monument Visitor Center**, just off I-5 at Castle Rock, has first-rate exhibits, a walk-through volcano mock-up and a dramatic film about the 1980 eruption, as well as views of the crater by telescope. The **Coldwater Ridge Visitors Center**, a stunning new facility 38 miles closer to the mountain on Hwy 504, explores the regeneration of this region through state-of-the-art multimedia exhibits and paved trails. There's an inviting outdoor playground at the Weyerhauser exhibit hall. Stop by on your trip back out to I-5.

See also **Olympia: What to See and Do.** .

PLACES TO STAY

PORTLAND MARRIOTT
503/226-7600, 800/228-9290; 1401 SW Front Ave, Portland, 97201
Rates: Moderate to expensive
Essentials: Credit cards; cribs
Extras: Indoor pool/Jacuzzi, fitness rooms (open 24 hours a day); video games; restaurant; TV & cable movies; pets allowed; refrigerators & babysitting service on request

This large, bustling hotel with conference facilities and a hotspot sports bar is nonetheless a good bet for families. With a prime downtown location across from Waterfront Park and the Willamette River, it's within walking distance of much of what you'll want to see and do. If you are lucky, your room will have a view of the river.

Champions Sports Bar is open to minors for lunch and dinner until 6 pm. A better bet is the restaurant, Fazzio's, where the separate kids' menu comes with an activity booklet.

> **PARENT COMMENTS:** *"Every time we go to Portland we stay here—they often have good weekend deals. We love the nice big pool and the location is excellent."*

RESIDENCE INN BY MARRIOTT
503/288-1400, 800/ 331-3131; 1710 NE Multnomah St, Portland ,97232
Rates: Moderate to expensive
Essentials: Credit cards; cribs
Extras: Full kitchens; complimentary continental breakfast buffet;

wood-burning fireplaces; free grocery shopping service; coin-operated laundry facilities; TV & HBO, board games & books for children; outdoor pool, sport court; pets OK (deposit & fee required); free on-site parking

This eastside all-suite hotel, designed primarily for longer stays, is also ideal for families preferring the facilities of home. Rooms are spacious and comfortable with full-size kitchens, appliances and kitchenware for four. Choose from a studio with a queen-sized bed and hide-a-bed, a one-bedroom unit, and a split-level two-bedroom/two-bath suite. The recreational facilities rival any in town: outdoor pool, scaled-down sport court for basketball, volleyball and badminton, games and books for kids.

There is no restaurant here, but a complimentary breakfast buffet is served daily in the lobby. There are numerous family restaurants and an attractive shopping mall (Lloyd Center, see "Shopping") with an ice rink and cinemas within walking distance. The light-rail line that crosses the river to downtown is just two blocks away.

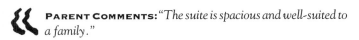 **PARENT COMMENTS:** *"Very comfortable and very family-friendly. The fabulous athletic facilities and breakfast buffet are a big treat for our two middle-schoolers."*

RIVERSIDE INN
503/221-0711, 800/899-0247; 50 SW Morrison,
Portland, 97204
Rates: Moderate
Essentials: Credit cards; cribs
Extras: Cafe; roomy one-bedroom suite; access to local corporate fitness club; free off-street parking; pets OK (fee)

Like the Marriott several blocks to the south, this smaller hotel is well-situated: directly opposite Waterfront Park and the Willamette River and within easy walking distance of most of downtown activities. An added bonus for families is its one suite. Formerly a one-bedroom residential apartment, it has a full kitchen with service for six. Families can also mix and match bedding options by taking advantage of the hotel's many adjoining rooms. The restaurant features a view of the river.

PARENT COMMENTS: *"The suite is spacious and well-suited to a family."*

EMBASSY SUITES
503/644-4000, 800/362-2779; 9000 SW Washington Square

Rd, Tigard, 97223
Rates: Expensive
Essentials: Credit cards; cribs
Extras: Free breakfast & "happy hour" nightly; refrigerators,
microwaves & wet bars; TV; indoor pool, whirlpool & sauna

Located in the suburb of Tigard, 25 minutes southwest of Portland, this attractive 10-story hotel works hard to make families feel welcome. The giant central atrium provides a lovely setting in which to relax. The two-room suites are especially comfortable for families, and the free cafeteria-style all-you-can-eat breakfasts, with fresh pancakes, eggs cooked to order, fruit, cereal, sausage and bacon, are offered from 7:30 to 10:30 am. You can bring the meal to your room, eat in the atrium or poolside while the kids swim. The pool is large and well-suited to kids. The refrigerators, microwaves and wet bars and the grocery/deli nearby are very convenient if you don't want to go out to eat. Utensils and dishes are available upon request.

PARENT COMMENTS: *"The hotel pool so thoroughly captivated our three children it was hard to get them to leave. We liked it that we could sit in the atrium having our free breakfast and watch our daughters go up in the glass elevator and walk to the door of our room! The atrium and the pool area are a very nice place to host visitors."*

"The countryside and nearby wineries are good for biking and/or winetasting."

THE GREENWOOD INN
503/643-7444, 800/289-1300; 10700 SW Allen Blvd,
Beaverton, 97005
Rates: Moderate to expensive
Essentials: Credit cards; cribs
Extras: TV & cable movies; 2 outdoor pools, sauna, Jacuzzi,
weight room; restaurant; free parking & shuttle to area attractions;
free grocery shopping service

Located near the Washington Square shopping mall and cinemas in an inner suburb, the Greenwood Inn is 10 to 15 minutes by car from downtown Portland. An independently managed 20-year-old hotel, it prides itself on its Northwest character, with original artwork, decor and landscaping that typifies the region. Having just completed a $5-million renovation, the Greenwood Inn is looking mighty fine. Families have several rooming options here. Choose from adjoining rooms, a one-room studio with full kitchen, or a two-room apartment with kitchen.

The glass-enclosed atrium setting of The Pavilion Bar & Grill is airy and inviting. Open daily, 6 am to 11 pm, it offers a separate kids' menu with entrees priced under $4. Adults can select from a light bistro menu or a more eclectic array of entrees that showcase fresh Northwest cuisine.

GEORGIAN HOUSE
503/281-2250; 1828 NE Siskiyou, Portland, 97212
Rates: Moderate
Essentials: Credit cards; crib & highchair
Extras: TV/VCR & videos; laundry facilities; common recreational & dining areas; family board games; neighborhood setting, backyard garden; parking in driveway & on street

Innkeeper Willie Ackley loves children. That explains why she's outfitted her inn with all the stuff necessary to make children—and their parents—feel at home. She offers families the large, private basement-level room with its queen-sized bed, queen-sized futon, TV and VCR. She'll share your bath and let you use the washer and dryer, but the kitchen is off-limits.

Situated in a quiet residential neighborhood six blocks from the Lloyd Center mall (see "Shopping") and 14 blocks from a park with playground, the Georgian House has a lovely backyard (featured on the cover of *Better Homes & Gardens*, July 1992) with a deck and gazebo.

PLACES TO EAT

Like any other city in the Northwest, Portland has its share of chain restaurants that successfully cater to families. Look for Fuddruckers, Tony Roma's, Cucina Cucina Italian Cafe, International House of Pancakes, Macheezmo Mouse, Olive Garden and Red Robin, to name a few. The establishments listed below offer a little more Portland personality.

NEWPORT BAY
503/227-3474; 0425 SW Montgomery
Hours: Lunch & dinner, Sunday brunch
Essentials: Credit cards; highchairs

One of seven in the area, this Newport Bay location is the jewel in the crown. A circular restaurant floating on the Willamette River with views of the marina, it occupies a prime bit of real estate. The panorama eclipses the food, but you can't complain about the prices. A separate kids menu features fish & chips, fried shrimp, burgers and chicken tenderloins ($2.29-$2.95). Sunday brunch choices include Belgian waffles and scrambled eggs & bacon ($3.95). Adults have many options among pasta, steak, seafood & salad entrees ($6-$15).

HARBORSIDE RESTAURANT & PILSNER ROOM
503/220-1865; 0309 SW Montgomery
Hours: Lunch & dinner daily
Essentials: Credit cards; highchairs
Part of the McCormick & Schmick empire, this restaurant wins accolades for design. Huge plate-glass windows and tiered seating provide everyone with an excellent view of the Willamette River. This place is quite chic; take the kids as a "treat." The separate child's menu includes a coloring page (crayons are provided) and such choices as cheeseburger and fries, mini-pizza, chicken quesadilla, fish and chips ($3.95 including ice cream sundae). The "grown-up" cuisine emphasizes fresh Northwest seafood ($9.95-$22.50 a la carte).

CHEZ JOSE EAST
503/280-9888; 2200 NE Broadway
Hours: Lunch & dinner Monday-Saturday, dinner only on Sunday
Essentials: Credit cards; highchairs; children 6 years & under eat free from 5-7 pm daily
Of the two area locations, this, the larger, considers families its primary customers. Fidgeting children are diverted with crayons, Etch-a-Sketch and Magnadoodle. Then the meal arrives—wholesome, plentiful Mexican food: cheese quesadillas, bean burritos or chimidogs ($2.50) for the kids; enchiladas, Mexican fish entrees, chili rellenos, hearty soups and salads for the adults. You can't beat the value or the hospitality.

OLD WIVES' TALES
503/238-0470; 1300 E Burnside
Hours: Breakfast, lunch & dinner daily
Essentials: Credit cards; highchairs, play structure
This place is funky—from the menu that stresses healthful, multi-ethnic cuisine (no red meat) to the colorful, sculptural climbing structure that was designed by a local artist. Family tables are adjacent to the playroom, so expect the kids to come and go. On the menu: grilled cheese, pasta, salad bar, and turkey franks; waffles, pancakes and Moroccan oatmeal at breakfast ($1.50-$2.75). On the adult menu: Greek and Mexican specialties, salmon cakes, seafood sandwiches, Tofu Shepherd's Pie,

East Indian soup, salad bar ($4.25-$12.50).

B. MOLOCH/HEATHMAN BAKERY & PUB
503/227-5700; 901 SW Salmon St
Hours: Breakfast, lunch & dinner daily
Essentials: Credit cards; highchairs

This artsy pub, next door to the Widmer Brewery downtown, was originally designed to serve as a commissary for the Heathman Hotel. Its wood-burning ovens still turn out the breads, pastries and smoked salmon served down the street at one of the city's best restaurants. But the Heathman Pub, with its informal, neighborly atmosphere and country-style European comfort food, has developed its own loyal following. This place is very popular. At peak hours expect at least a 15-minute wait.

There are no kids' menus here, but the mix-and-match selections lend themselves to sharing. Everyone orders at the counter, where deli salads, cheeses and desserts are on display. At breakfast choose from omelettes, oatmeal, granola and pancakes. Lunch and dinner offerings include soups, sandwiches, salads and pizzas (conventional and gourmet). Prices: $5-$9.

OLD SPAGHETTI FACTORY
503/222-5375; 0715 SW Bancroft St
Hours: Lunch & dinner daily
Essentials: Credit cards; highchairs

This flagship of a 30-restaurant chain is spacious, seating 450 guests at capacity. If possible, plan your visit to avoid the peak hour crowds. Adjacent to the bar is a video room showing children's movies. Older kids can entertain themselves in the video game room. The dining room features a trademark trolley car, antiques and pasta menu. There are two kids' menus. Served on plastic dinosaur plates, Kiddie Meals (for 2- to 5-year-olds) feature spaghetti with choice of sauce, applesauce, drink, cookie and ice cream or popsicle ($2.95). Junior meals come with spaghetti, salad, drink and ice cream ($3.75). Adults choose from pasta and chicken dishes ($4.25-$7.75).

WHAT TO SEE AND DO

STROLL & BROWSE
Downtown Portland is oriented around two grand public spaces: **Waterfront Park** (see "Parks"), a two-mile greensward along the west side of the river and site of festivals and athletic events throughout the year; and **Pioneer Courthouse Square**, affec-

tionately referred to as the city's "living room." Two maps of walking tours are available locally. *Powell's Walking Map of Downtown Portland*, published by Portland's famous book emporium, is free. Pick it up at Powell's Books (see "Shopping") or at Powell's Travel Store at Pioneer Courthouse Square (SW 6th Ave. & Yamhill, 503/228-1108). Stop by the offices of the Metropolitan Arts Commission (309 SW 6th Ave., Suite 100, 503/823-5111) for a copy of its *Public Art Walking Tour*, which costs $1.

Two highlights for children: the magnificent iron *Portlandia* statue, which leans out over the street from its perch on the Michael Graves-designed Portland building (1120 SW Fifth Ave); and the Ira C. Keller Fountain, a full block of terraces, trees and cascading water (SW 3rd Ave. & Clay St). The Portland/Oregon Visitors Association (26 SW Salmon St at Front Ave; 503/275-9750) can also provide brochures and information.

PIONEER COURTHOUSE SQUARE was erected in 1984 on a central downtown site formerly a parking lot. To fund its construction, more than 63,000 personalized bricks were sold. Look at their names under your feet as you walk through the square. Look also for the Weather Machine in the northwest corner. Every day at noon a two-minute fanfare announces the forecast. With its distances to nine sister cities and other whimsical destinations, the Mile Post (along SW Sixth Ave.) also amuses children. Designed to accommodate formal and informal gatherings, the square serves as a town common. Brown-bagging executives sprawl on its steps for lunch, teens congregate to play hacky-sack, mothers bring their toddlers to romp, and commuters stand in line for the ride home. Flanking the old courthouse, directly opposite the square, are pools decorated with life-sized birds and beasts cast in bronze (SW Yamhill & SW Morrison between Fifth & Sixth Aves.). Kids love to climb on them.

THE SOUTH PARK BLOCKS FROM PORTLAND STATE UNIVERSITY (at College St) to the Performing Arts Center (at Salmon St) feature a shady central island punctuated by statuary, paths and benches.

NORTHWEST 23RD AVE. is a chic neighborhood of boutiques, cafes, antique stores and bakeries. Start at Burnside and continue north. Many of the shops carry fragile crafts and other expensive breakables. But a few welcome children, most notably one of the city's finest toy stores, **Child's Play** (907 NW 23rd Ave.). You can snack at a coffee shop or pick up a salad or deli sandwich and find a sunny spot on somebody's front steps for an impromptu picnic.

SOUTHEAST HAWTHORNE BLVD. is funky and earthy, with its dusty antique shops and tofu and sprouts eateries. Take the kids into **Pastaworks**, where they can watch chefs preparing noodles and drool over the cheeses, savories and desserts. The **Bagdad Theatre & Pub** across the street serves a full menu of multi-ethnic entrees inside its renovated theatre. Minors are welcome at weekend family matinees only.

Call for film titles and times (503/230-0895).

PARKS

TOM MCCALL WATERFRONT PARK, named for the governor credited with helping clean up the state's rivers, was once a freeway. Today this two-mile stretch of riverfront greenery is popular with strollers, joggers, skaters and picnickers. Festival-goers flock here most weekends during the clement months for city-wide celebrations. Don't miss Salmon Springs (at Salmon St.), a fountain where wading is encouraged. Continue your walk south to RiverPlace, which features a small marina, restaurants (see "Where to Eat") and several shops, including a gourmet deli that sells ice cream cones.

WASHINGTON PARK should top the itinerary of every family visiting Portland. It is set in the hills to the west of downtown with a spectacular view out over the city. You can see Mt. Hood on a clear day. This oasis of rolling lawns and winding trails entrances newcomers and natives alike.

ROSE GARDEN CHILDREN'S PARK. This innovative new playground, the first of its kind in the nation, was designed to serve the needs of physically challenged children and their families—as well as the community at large. Located near the Rose Test Garden (see below), the 3 1/2-acre site features a clock tower, water play area, undulating bridges, fanciful ladders and dozens of other stimulating and colorful components, all wheel-chair accessible. Wide paved trails provide a link to the nearby Zoo Train, Children's Amphitheatre and the refurbished Elephant House, which houses picnic tables and restrooms.

INTERNATIONAL ROSE TEST GARDEN. The panorama is best from here. Beginning in early summer, the air is heady with the fragrance of more than 400 varieties of roses—all labeled. On weekends you're likely to see bridal parties posing for their photographers against the stunning backdrop.

400 SW Kingston Ave. Open daily. Free.

METRO WASHINGTON PARK ZOO. In true Portland fashion, this zoo is a small gem. With a whole day and lots of energy you can tour the entire facility. But it may be more fun to pick and choose several favorite habitats (African Rain Forest, Savanna, Antarctica, Alaska Tundra, Cascade Range) or animals (primates, elephants, bears, felines). Given adequate time, you'll be likely to let the kids clamber on the sculptures and somersault on the amphitheatre lawn.

4001 SW Canyon Rd; 503/226-1561. Open daily 10 am-4 pm in winter, 9:30 am-6 pm in summer. Cost: $5.50/adults, $4/seniors, $3.50/youth 3-11 years, free/2 & under. Free admission second Tuesday of month, 3-5 pm. Strollers & wagons for rent.

The Metro Washington Park Zoo has the most successful elephant breeding program of any zoo in the world, with 27 births to its credit. Packy, the "celebrity" pachyderm, has sired seven calves in captivity.

JAPANESE GARDEN. Come here for serenity. Kids love the hide-and-seek trails, fish ponds and cascading streams. Leave the stroller in the car; backpacks work better on the uneven, pebble paths.

611 SW Kingston Ave; 503/223-1321. Open daily 10 am-6 pm in fall & spring, 9 am-8 pm in summer, 10 am-4 pm in winter. Cost: $5/adults, $2.50/seniors & youth, free/under 6 years.

CRYSTAL SPRINGS RHODODENDRON GARDEN. On the eastside of the river near Reed College, this peaceful enclave is a wonderful small park with duck ponds, bridges, winding paths and ample lawns. Come for bird-watching; bring cracked corn (no bread, please) for the waterfowl.

SE 28th Ave north of Woodstock. Open daily until dark. $2 admission in summer.

SAUVIE ISLAND sits in the Columbia River just north of the city. This is the place to come in summer and fall to pick berries, apples and vegetables or to buy fresh produce. Sauvie Island is also a haven for bicyclists and bird-watchers.

In summer you can tour the historic Bybee House (Howell Park Rd; 503/222-1741. Open weekends only, noon-5 pm. $1 donation). Built in 1858 by pioneers who arrived from Missouri via the Oregon Trail, the nine-room Classic Revival dwelling was restored in 1966 by the Oregon Historical Society. Located behind the house and adjacent to the Pioneer Orchard is the

Agricultural Museum. Children are entranced by the horse-drawn equipment and harness and woodworking shops. Many items may be handled. Even when the house is closed to the public, visitors are welcome to explore the grounds and neighboring wetlands.

From Portland drive northwest on Hwy 30 to the Sauvie Island Bridge.

TRYON CREEK STATE PARK is tucked into a southern suburban corner between Lewis & Clark College and Lake Oswego. Heavily wooded, with 14 miles of trails popular among walkers and runners—and bike paths besides—this 640-acre canyon is home to woodpeckers and wildflowers. The paved half-mile Trillium Trail is perfect for the short-legged members of your family. The Nature Center has a bookstore and small exhibit hall.

11321 SW Terwilliger, 1 mile west of Hwy 43; 503/636-4398. Open daily. Free.

MUSEUMS

OREGON MUSEUM OF SCIENCE & INDUSTRY. This museum's sleek new facility has sweeping views of the Willamette River from its eastside location. Inside there's something for everyone: six exhibit halls with lots of hands-on activities, an OMNIMAX theatre, demonstrations, multimedia planetarium shows, laser-light shows, an attractive riverfront cafe, and Discovery Space—an area for exploratory play reserved for children to age 7. Don't miss a tour of the *U.S.S. Blueback*, the 219-foot Navy submarine now permanently docked here.

1945 SE Water Ave; 503/797-OMSI. In winter: Saturday-Wednesday 9:30 am-5:30 pm, Thursday & Friday 9:30 am-9 pm. In summer: Saturday-Wednesday 9:30 am-7 pm, Thursday & Friday 9:30 am-9 pm. Cost: $7/adults, $6/seniors, $4.50/youth 3-17 years. Theatre/planetarium tickets extra.

CHILDREN'S MUSEUM. A Portland institution loved by legions of kids, teachers and parents, this creative play center is in a quiet southwest neighborhood adjacent to a large playground. Everything is tactile and "let's pretend"—from the basement-level Clayshop to the Kid City Thriftway (grocery store) and Bistro (eatery). Omokunle Village, a Nigerian town exhibit, is on permanent display in the annex. Make rubbings, dress as a king and play in the marketplace. Leave the stroller in the car.

3037 SW Second Ave; 503/823-2227. Daily 9 am-5 pm. Cost:

Covering 4,683 acres, Forest Park (which encompasses Washington Park) is the nation's largest wooded city park. Explore the trails through the Hoyt Arboretum or bite off a bit of the 27 1/2-mile Wildwood Trail. It begins at the World Forestry Center near the zoo.

$3.50/person, free/under 1 year.

PORTLAND ART MUSEUM. If you're not in the habit of sharing art with your children, this museum might make a fitting introduction. Founded in 1892, it is the oldest art museum in the Pacific Northwest. The collections are small but sterling: Northwest Coast Native American art, African art from the Cameroons, Asian art, and prints, drawings and photographs by masters—old and young. Especially for families is the museum's series of Sunday open houses, where hands-on crafts, demonstrations and performances serve to introduce disparate cultures and their art to children. Held bimonthly, September-June.

1219 SW Park Ave; 503/226-2811. Tuesday-Saturday 11 am-5 pm, Sunday 1-5 pm, first Thursday of month 11 am-9 pm. Cost: $5/ adults, $3.50/seniors, $2.50/students, free/under 5 years, $10/ families. Free admission first Thursday of month, 4-9 pm.

OREGON HISTORY CENTER. Located across Park Avenue from the Portland Art Museum and operated by the Oregon Historical Society, this is the place to come to learn about the state's rich heritage and its dreams for the future. The dramatic, interactive exhibits are designed with children in mind.

1200 SW Park Ave; 503/222-1741. Tuesday-Saturday 10 am-5 pm. Sunday noon-5 pm. Cost: $4.50/adults; $1.50/seniors, students; free/5 years & under.

END OF THE OREGON TRAIL INTERPRETIVE CENTER. Opened in June 1995 as the second of four Oregon Trail history centers to criss-cross the state, this Oregon City museum resembles a Paul Bunyan encampment. Its three main buildings, shaped like wagons, are topped by 50-foot steel hoops and stretchy fiberglass mesh. Inside, guides are dressed in period clothing, a multimedia dramatization depicts life on the trail, and there are abundant collections of historic artifacts. Outside, the surrounding gardens are planted with heirloom vegetation and the grass-covered amphitheatre hosts an Oregon Trail Pageant each summer.

1726 Washington St, Oregon City; 503/657-9336. Monday-Saturday 9 am-6 pm, Sunday 10 am-5 pm. Cost: $4.50/adults; $2.50/seniors, children 12 years & under.

SHOPPING

SATURDAY MARKET. There's a weekend street fair 10 months of the year in Portland when some 300 craft and food vendors cluster under the west end of the Burnside Bridge to sell their handmade goods. Much of what's available is ethnic in flavor—from Peruvian wall hangings to Chinese lo-mein. Stage entertainment and street performers abound. One warning: Keep tabs on the kids; it's easy to lose sight of them amid the crowds and warren of booths.

Saturdays & Sundays, March-December. Free.

POWELL'S BOOKS. This store is the first destination of visiting book lovers. Occupying a full city block downtown, Powell's displays new and used books side by side on its floor-to-ceiling shelves. The children's literature section overflows with classics and picture books. Tots are welcome to settle in and browse (even the pop-up books are open for inspection). The adjoining Annie Hughes Coffee Shop serves light meals.

1005 W Burnside; 503/228-4651.

HANNA ANDERSSON. A Portland success story, this popular children's clothing catalog company operates two retail stores here. The all-cotton, Swedish-inspired fashions are durable, colorful and comfortable, if pricey. Visit the outlet store in Lake Oswego for bargains on discontinued items.

327 NW 10th Ave; 503/242-0920. 7 Monroe Parkway at Boones Ferry Rd, Lake Oswego; 503/697-1953.

SAFEWAY. To stock up the hotel refrigerator or get supplies for a last-minute picnic, you can't beat this grocery store for location and selection.

SW 10th Ave & Jefferson.

PORTLAND'S ENCLOSED SHOPPING MALLS are clean, attractive and welcoming. Several offer special diversions for children.

Ideally situated in central downtown, **Pioneer Place** has a lovely food court with cascading water fountains. Enter the Saks Fifth Avenue foyer (SW Fifth Ave. & Taylor) and descend on the escalator. There are lots of options here for finnicky eaters: Chinese Cafe, Hot Dog on a Stick, Gyros 'N' Grill, Let's Talk Turkey, Macheezmo Mouse, Mamma Ilardo's and California Crisp (fresh salads & sandwiches), as well as coffee drinks and baked goods for breakfasts and snacks. The only drawback: On weekdays, crowds of businesspeople arrive at lunch hour and it can get very noisy.

On weekends you can ride a vintage trolley across the river from downtown to **Lloyd Center** (NE Multnomah & 11th Ave.). Recently refurbished, this mall features an ice-skating rink and a

Discovery Zone kids' fitness playground (503/288-2900).

Farther north is the **Jantzen Beach Center** (take Jantzen Beach Exit off I-5 north) whose claim-to-fame is one of the nation's last remaining handcarved wooden carousels. Built in 1917, it's found inside the mall near Lamonts. Rides cost 50¢ each.

EXCURSIONS

COLUMBIA GORGE. Though Portland spans the Willamette River, it's the Columbia that gets more attention. And it should. Just 40 miles east of town is some of the state's finest scenery— fir-speckled cliffs and granite outcroppings, bubbling brooks and waterfalls and peaceful pastureland. **Crown Point** and **Multnomah Falls** attract the largest crowds, but there are other nice vistas and winding wooded trails that beckon you to stop.

From Portland take I-84 east. If time allows, follow signs for the Columbia River Scenic Highway (U.S. 30, Exit 17). Opened in 1915, this road passes nine waterfalls and six state parks.

More and more development in and around Cascade Locks on the Columbia River is luring visitors farther east. **Fort Oregon,** a pioneer theme park on Thunder Island, opened in May 1995. Less authentic than entertaining, the village and fort are constructed to resemble similar structures of the 1850s. Activity centers throughout the park feature hands-on pioneer-style crafts: dipping candles, stringing beads, weaving brooms and whittling arrowheads. Visitors are also encouraged to pan for gold, survey the mountainman camp and blacksmith shop and take aim in the shooting gallery.

Thunder Island, Cascade Locks; 503/646-2256. 10 am-7 pm daily. Cost: $4/adults, $2/children 6-16 years, free/children under 6.

For a made-to-order hamburger with all the fixings to go with the spectacular river view, stop at the **Charburger** (503/374-8477) just beyond the Bridge of the Gods. The gift shop sells yummy homebaked cookies for snacktime. Another option is the **East Wind Drive-In** (503/374-8380) just down the street, where a skyscraper of soft-serve ice cream costs about $2.

Cross the **Bridge of the Gods** in Cascade Locks and turn east to reach Stevenson, Washington, home of two new destinations worth a special visit. Opened since 1993, **Skamania Lodge** sits regally on a rolling meadow facing the Columbia. Constructed of heavy timbers with a massive stone fireplace in the lobby and Mission-style furnishings throughout, this place is reminiscent of Mt. Hood's Timberline Lodge (see "Mount Hood" below). Come on a Sunday to indulge in the sumptuous brunch buffet ($16.50/ adults, $9.50/7-12 years, $1 per year/4-6 years, free/children to 3 years; reservations suggested: 800/221-7117, 509/427-7700). Then explore the nature trails and stay for a swim. The fitness center is equipped with lockers, saunas, an indoor swimming pool and whirlpool and an outdoor whirlpool and small wading pool. Towels are provided. *(Daily rate: $6/adult, $4/under 13 years.) Rent mountain bikes to see the countryside ($8/hour); horseback riding is another option.*

Columbia Gorge Interpretive Center, a gem of a museum opened in May 1995, was designed to resemble the sawmills located here earlier in the century. Children are especially intrigued by the basalt cliff adornments, indoor waterfall, replica fishwheel, Corliss steam engine and logging truck. A short slide presentation explains the geologic formation of the gorge. Other exhibits highlight the rivers' resources—salmon, timber, hydro-electric power and chain of ports—and the people who built its communities.

509/427-8211. Open daily 10 am-7 pm in summer, 10 am-5 pm in winter. Cost: $5/adults, $4/seniors & students, free/under 6.

BONNEVILLE DAM. On the way back to Portland, turn in at the Bonneville Dam (503/374-8375). The Visitors Center offers an observation deck, historical displays and an underwater viewing area where you may see migrating salmon. Get your fill of fish at the neighboring fish hatchery.

HOOD RIVER is a sailboarder's mecca. A walk down Oak St. reveals shops hawking every device necessary for outfitting a board and sailor—as well as the requisite souvenirs. The town is quaint, nonetheless, with pretty bungalows, rolling lawns and views of the river.

If the wind is up you can get a front-row seat at sporting entertainment down by the water. Otherwise, take a drive in the countryside, for the Hood River Valley is home to acres and acres of orchards—mostly Anjou and Bartlett pears and Pippin apples. Pick up a copy of the *Fruit Loop Guide to Local Farm Stands* (available at shops and restaurants in town). **River Bend Farm** (2363 Tucker Rd.; 503/386-8766) sells homemade jams from its cozy country store. Kids can feed goats and twin burros and get within spitting distance of llamas.

THE MOUNT HOOD RAILROAD is another way to experience the bucolic splendor of this region. The railroad, built in 1906, climbs steep canyons and rolls through lush orchards on its excursions through the valley. Choose a morning or afternoon trip. Reservations suggested, 503/386-3556. *From Portland take I-84 east, 60 miles. Exit at Hood River—City Center.*

MOUNT HOOD. Native Americans called it Wy-East, and at 11,247 feet, it's the state's tallest peak. Ski lifts run year-round, but even if you don't ski, the trip to the top is rewarding. At the end of the road sits Timberline Lodge (503/231-5400, 800/547-1406). Built during the Depression as a showcase for the talents of local craftsmen and artisans, it is a masterpiece of hewed logs and great stone fireplaces. Stay for the slide show, which highlights the handiwork and graphic themes echoed throughout the hotel. Children with energy to burn after the drive have three lobby areas to explore. There's also a tabletop shuffleboard game, pub and formal dining room.

Perhaps the best meal option for families can be found in Government Camp. Owned and operated by Timberline, **The Brew Pub** (on Hwy. 26; 503/272-3724) serves pizza, hamburgers, salads, sandwiches and chili in an informal chalet setting. *From Portland take I-84 east to Hwy 26, about 55 miles. At Government Camp, watch for signs to Timberline Lodge.*

FORT VANCOUVER was northwest headquarters for the Hudson's Bay Company from 1818 to 1860. Its warehouses stocked supplies for the fur brigades and Indian and settler trade. The stockade and five major outbuildings were reconstructed in 1966 after fires and decay destroyed the original fort. Visit the blacksmith shop, bakery, Indian trade shop, wash house, Chief Factor's residence, kitchen and bastion. For special events, volunteers dressed in period costumes act in living history dramas. *612 E. Reserve St, Vancouver, WA; 360/696-7655, 800/832-2599 (toll-free from Oregon only). Daily 9 am-4 pm in winter, 9 am-5 pm in summer. Cost: $4/familes, $2/adults in summer.*

GETTING AROUND TOWN
Tri-Met buses and MAX light-rail cars offer free travel within a 300-square-block area downtown called the Fareless Square. Fares for longer rides begin at $1 for adults and 75¢ for children 7 to 18 years old; children 6 years and under ride free. A restored vintage trolley makes weekend runs between the Galleria mall (921 SW Morrison) and Lloyd Center mall (NE Multnomah &

llth Ave, see "Shopping") every half-hour. Fee: $1 per person. Information: 503/238-RIDE.

Calendar

May: Cinco de Mayo
June-August: Outdoor concerts at Pioneer Courthouse Square Washington Park Zoo & Oregon Square
June: Rose Festival
July: Fort Vancouver Fourth of July Celebration, Vancouver, WA Waterfront Blues Festival
St. Paul Rodeo
August: Oregon State Fair, The Bite (food festival)
September: Artquake
October: LitEruption, ZooBoo!
November: Meier & Frank Holiday Parade
December: Zoolights Festival, Nutcracker, Parade of Christmas Ships

Resources

Portland/Oregon Visitors Association
26 SW Salmon St, Portland 97204;
503/275-9750

Oregon Tourism Division
800/547-7842

Tri-Met, bus & light-rail transportation information
503/238-RIDE

Portland Women's Crisis Line
503/235-5333

Oregon Poison Center
503/494-8968

Babysitting Services: Auntie Fay Agency, 503/293-6252;
Care Givers Placement Agency Inc., 503/244-6370;
Northwest Nannies Inc, 503/245-5288

Portland Parent. A free, monthly newsmagazine for parents, with a complete calendar of local activities and outings for families, this paper is available at most children's shops and

libraries in the tri-county area.
503/245-8036.

HOOD RIVER

Apple and pear orchards line the roads around this pretty little town on the Columbia River and at 11,245 feet Mt. Hood towers just thirty miles to the south. In recent years the area has attracted the windsurfing crowd—a strong wind in the opposite direction of the river current creates ideal boarding conditions. Families will find plenty else to keep them busy on a weekend getaway to the area—including hiking, fishing, skiing and several interesting local attractions.

GETTING THERE

Take Interstate 84 out of Portland. For a more scenic route, Exit I-84 at Troutdale and take U.S. 30. Follow U.S. 30 or I-84 to Hood River.

ROADSIDE ATTRACTIONS. The 60-mile stretch from Portland to Hood River on I-84 or U.S. 30 has many interesting views and short tours. The two highways parallel the river, but at different elevations. U.S. 30, also called the Columbia River Scenic Highway, is the upper road. The first paved highway in the state, it was built around 1915 to follow the contours of the land. As such it is more scenic than the modern I-84 freeway built at river level.

Between Troutdale and The Dalles on U.S. 30 you will pass **Crown Point State Park**, with the famous Vista House, which provides legendary views up and down the gorge. Six miles east you'll come to the awesome 620-foot **Multnomah Falls**, with a short, steep paved trail to the top of the falls, interpretive displays and a lodge with food and a gift shop.

Driving along I-84 you are following the route of the famed **Oregon Trail.** It is still possible in some places to see the ruts from the thousands of wagon wheels that passed this way. For information about the Oregon National Historic Trail, call 503/378-5012.

PLACES TO STAY

BEST WESTERN HOOD RIVER INN
503/386-2200; 1108 E Marina Rd, Hood River, 97031

Rates: Moderate
Essentials: Credit cards; cribs
Extras: Outdoor pool; TV; small pets OK; kitchenettes

This motel is located right on the Columbia River, has lovely views and is set well away from the highway, so it is nice and quiet. The 64 rooms are clean, modern, comfortable and roomy, and there is a small reading area on each level with books and magazines. Outdoors there is a large grassy area where kids can play, a playground and a heated pool. This is wind-surfing territory, and there is a marina down the road where you can rent equipment.

The two-bedroom units have a Jacuzzi, mini-fridge and microwave.

The motel gift shop has limited picnic supplies, wine and food specialties from Hood River. The restaurant attached to the motel has an area for "formal dining" as well as a cafe for lighter, more casual food. You can eat outdoors, overlooking the Columbia River. Service is fast and children are well tolerated. If you want to leave the motel, an outing to Multnomah Falls will turn up both fast food and a dining room with moderate prices.

PARENT COMMENTS: *"Optimum seasons for visiting are spring, summer and fall. Spring for all the waterfalls and apple blossoms, summer for the good weather, fall for the spectacular leaves and color."*

"There is no fence between the grassy area and the river so younger children will require supervision."

"We visited Hood River for a long weekend in the spring with our boys, four and six. We took the Fruit Blossom Train Trip and hiked to Multnomah Falls. It was a great fun."

WHAT TO SEE AND DO

BONNEVILLE DAM, 44 miles east of Portland on I-84, is the oldest hydroelectric project on the Columbia. It has a visitor center at Exit 40 with displays about dam operations and salmon viewing through underwater windows.

Visitor center hours 10 am-6 pm daily, Memorial Day-Labor Day, 9 am-5 pm other months.

HOOD RIVER COUNTY HISTORICAL MUSEUM displays pioneer artifacts and exhibits on area history.

Port Marina Park; 503/386-3811. Open April-Oct, Wed-Sat 10 am -4 pm, Sun noon-4 pm. Free.

MOUNT HOOD RAILROAD, departing from the Hood River Depot with a stop in Parkdale, provides a 4-hour scenic trip through the Hood River Valley. *Mount Hood Railroad, 110 Railroad Ave, Hood River 97301; 503/386-3556. Cost: $19.95 adults; $11.95 kids.*

M.V. COLUMBIA GORGE is a 599-passenger sternwheeler that plies the Columbia three times daily June through September. You can begin the two-hour trip from Cascade Locks Marine Park, Bonneville Dam or on the Washington side, at Stevenson. *503/223-3928; $11.95/adults; reduced fare for children age 4-12; 3 and under free.*

RESOURCES

HOOD RIVER COUNTRY CHAMBER OF COMMERCE
Port Marina Park, Hood River, 97031
503/386-2000 or 800/366-3530

MT. HOOD

Just 55 miles southwest of Portland, Mt. Hood is a fine year-round outdoor playground. During the winter cross-country and downhill skiing are popular. (At Timberline, downhill skiing is available year-round.) In the summer, hiking trails honeycomb the area.

GETTING THERE
From Portland, take I-84 east. Take Wood Village Exit right to 238th. Follow Burnside and go left to U.S. 26.

PLACES TO STAY

TIMBERLINE LODGE
800/457-1406; in Oregon 503/272-3311; Timberline, 97028
Rates: Moderate to expensive
Essentials: Credit cards; cribs
Extras: Restaurant; outdoor pool, sauna; hiking trails; skiing; TV; babysitting (by pre-arrangement);
Timberline Lodge is one of the great mountain lodges in the west with the characteristic stone fireplaces, heavy timbers and large windows with small panes. This beautiful building was built by the WPA in 1937 and sits 6000 feet up the side of Mt. Hood.

It is a real showplace of arts and crafts, including handmade furniture, fabrics, hand-hooked rugs, mosaics and paintings.

Both the restored and unrestored rooms are quite attractive. In the winter, these rooms need a cozy fire, so it is worth the extra cost to get a room with a fireplace.

Skiing is offered year-round at Timberline, and the lifts are right outside the door. You can rent all your gear here. There are lessons for all age levels; the Skiwee program for kids ages 3-12 is a fully supervised program offered seven days a week. Cross-country skiing is also excellent in this area. The outdoor pool is kept at 86 degrees and is open all year, so you can swim while it snows. Be sure to bring chains for your winter drive up to the lodge.

PARENT COMMENTS: *"The lodge is so beautiful even my kids were impressed. Our teen-agers like to come on New Year's Eve—lifts are open all night long!"*
"Timberline is not a great place for kids under three. They get too cold in the snow, there is no lifeguard at the pool, and once inside, there's little to do save a little ping pong."

THE RESORT AT THE MOUNTAIN
800/547-8054; in Oregon 800/452-4612; 68010 E Fairway Ave, Welches, 97067
Rates: Moderate to expensive
Essentials: Credit cards; cribs
Extras: Kitchens; TV; restaurant; indoor and outdoor pools, sauna, hot tubs; fireplaces (in most condos); tennis courts; bicycle rentals; golf; babysitting (by pre-arrangement); organized activities for kids (summer only)

This resort is located on 400 acres on the western slopes of Mt. Hood and consists of 250 units—motel rooms and one- to five-bedroom condominiums. The condominiums, with private patios, are the best choice for families. Older sections of the facility are very nicely maintained; new sections have modern northwest architecture. Grounds are spacious, the countryside is wooded, and the feeling is one of quiet relaxation. Outdoors, activities center around the golf course (27 holes) and swimming pools. There are bike trails, a five-mile jogging path, and six tennis courts. Ample opportunities for activities such as white water rafting or fly fishing, a large recreation building houses a big pool with a wading pool alongside, as well as saunas, hot tub and a game room.

Condominiums have kitchens, but if you do not want to cook

every meal, there are a dining room and a more relaxed coffee shop, which includes an outdoor eating area, at the resort. Both eating spots have highchairs.

 PARENT COMMENTS: *"It's a country club atmosphere in a beautiful part of Oregon."*
"The indoor pool was fabulous for our young (ages 2 and 5) children."

WHAT TO SEE AND DO

DOWNHILL SKIING. Mt. Hood Meadows (503/337-2222) is the largest ski area on Mt. Hood, with over 60 trails and a vertical drop of 2,777 feet. **Timberline ski area** (503/231-7979), at Timberline Lodge, is less extensive and less expensive than Mt. Hood Meadows. It is a good area for beginners and intermediate skiers. **Mt. Hood Skibowl** (503/272-3206) has a 1500-foot vertical drop with good expert runs but it is not great for intermediate or beginners.

CROSS-COUNTRY SKIING. Mt. Hood is a popular place for cross-country skiing. There are trails of all different stages of difficulty throughout the area. You need a Sno-Park permit to park at the trailheads; most sporting goods stores in Oregon carry them. Ask at the Mt. Hood Information Center or at Timberline Lodge for specific trail information.

HIKING. U. S. Forest Service Guides are on hand at the Timberline Lodge in the summer to lead guided hikes and alpine wildflower walks. "Day Hikes Around Mt. Hood" is an informative, free booklet that provides details on hikes in the area. You can pick one up at the Mt. Hood Information Center, 503/622-4822.

CALENDAR

JULY: Sandy Mountain Festival
AUGUST: Mt. Hood Jazz Festival

RESOURCES

MT. HOOD INFORMATION CENTER
65000 U.S. 26E, Welches, 97067
503/622-4822.
Open daily 8 am-4:30 pm.

WARM SPRINGS

Warm Springs is just a crook in the road in the middle of the high desert, halfway between Mount Hood and Bend on Highway 26. There are two good reasons to stop here: The magnificent **Museum at Warm Springs** and **Kah-Nee-Ta Resort**.

GETTING THERE

From Portland take I-84 to The Dalles. Turn south on Highway 197, then west on Highway 26.

ROADSIDE ATTRACTIONS. See Bend/Sisters:Getting There.

PLACES TO STAY

KAH-NEE-TA RESORT

800-/831-0100 or 503/553-1112; Warm Springs, 97761
Rates: Inexpensive-expensive
Essentials: Credit cards; cribs
Extras: Kitchens in some units; TV; restaurants; outdoor pools; hot mineral baths; sauna; horseback riding; tennis courts; golf; bicycle rentals; hiking trails; fishing rentals; miniature golf; basketball courts; casino

Kah-Nee-Ta is owned and operated by the Confederated Indian Tribes of Warm Springs. It is the centerpiece of a half-million-acre Native American reservation, complete with working ranch and wild horses. The resort has two sections—the Lodge and the Village—and an array of accommodations that will fit any budget. At the low, and fun, end of the accommodation scale are authentic teepees. Also in the Village are one- and two-bedroom cottages, some with kitchens. More elaborate quarters can be found at the Lodge.

Sun shines over 300 days of the year in Warm Springs, and the warmth of the mineral pools makes swimming a year-round activity. A bigger-than-Olympic-size pool is heated by the hot springs, and there are hot mineral baths. Miniature golf and biking, white water rafting and trout fishing in the well-stocked Warm Springs River are some of the many things to do on a visit to Kah-Nee-Ta.

The Juniper Room in the Lodge is a formal dining room with an impressive view. The menu includes buffalo steak and venison. Make reservations early. The informal Appaloosa Room serves breakfast and lunch and offers the option of eating at poolside. In the Village, the River Room is very informal and well suited to families. Food is tolerable: the best part of the meal is feeding the bread scraps to the hungry and aggressive trout from the deck of the restaurant.

> **PARENT COMMENTS:** *"The kids were enthralled by the Native American dances performed regularly at the resort. We enjoyed horseback riding in the desert and lazing in the pool."*
> *"Service was excellent. The only drawback to this resort is the lack of good restaurants, which can be easily resolved by securing a cabin with a kitchen at the Village. Anticipate all your needs in advance as Kah-Nee-Ta is very isolated and the nearest town for supplies or gas is 11 miles away."*

WHAT TO SEE AND DO

THE MUSEUM AT WARM SPRINGS, on Highway 26, is a small but spectacular museum the whole family will enjoy. Built in 1993 by the Confederated Tribes of the Warm Springs Reservation to preserve their local history and culture, the museum houses treasured tribal heirlooms in a magnificent building. The kids may move quickly through the beaded artifacts and woven baskets exhibits, but they'll slow down for a multi-media presentation that allows them to participate in a traditional hoop dance. And they'll enjoy exploring the traditional dwellings (tule mat lodge, wickiup and plankhouse) constructed to show the tribal life of the past.

503/553-3331; 2189 Hwy 26, Warm Springs. Hours: daily 10 am-5 pm except major holidays. Cost: $5/adult, $2.50/child 4-12, under 4 free.

BEND/SISTERS

The central Oregon desert is a recreational haven for active families. The summers are hot and dry and smell of sage and Ponderosa pine—ideal for camping and hiking or just for kicking back at a resort. Winters are cold, with crystal-clear skies and enough snow to satisfy any ski bum.

Bend was founded in 1900 and originally named "Farewell Bend." In 1904, when the town was incorporated, the post office opted for the shorter moniker. For decades, Bend residents were largely ranchers and farmers. Today these "old timers" seem to coexist fairly peacefully with the "new generation" of writers, outdoor enthusiasts and real estate investors who have moved into the area. Even Hollywood has discovered Bend, and covets it as a movie-making location because of its dependable four-season climate and rugged beauty.

As the county seat of Deschutes County, Bend has a decidedly upscale air. At the same time, it doesn't take much imagination to sense the "Old West" in the region. For kids, this area can provide a wonderful introduction to the history, geology and Native American lore of central Oregon.

Sisters is an old west town of stagecoach rides and western storefronts. It is quiet and laid-back, except during the annual June rodeo when 50,000 rodeo fans flood the town.

GETTING THERE

To get to Bend and Sisters, there are two main routes: heading east off I-5 near Salem to Highway 20 or from Portland taking I-84 to Hood River, Highway 35 south to U.S. 26 and then further south to connect with U.S. 97, the main north-south artery through Central Oregon.

The Amtrak train from Seattle-Portland stops 65 miles south of Bend at Chemult station.

The Bend/Redmond Airport (503/382-1687) is about 16 miles north of Bend, off U.S. 97. Horizon (800/547-9308) and United (800/241-6522) fly here from Portland and Seattle.

ROADSIDE ATTRACTIONS. Near Sandy, 24 miles southeast of Portland on Highway 26, are a couple of intriguing stops. **Oral Hull Park**, three miles east of Sandy, provides more than just a chance to get out and run around. Designed especially for the blind, this park offers the Gardens of Enchantment, which have five sections dedicated to the five senses. It's a lovely experience, providing food for thought and family discussion about physical challenges. (*May1- October 1, 503/668-6195*)

Five miles east of Sandy is the **Oregon Candy Farm,** where master candymakers create hand-dipped chocolates, truffles, caramels and other sweets. Kids can watch the whole process and, parents willing, try a sample. (*503/668-5066*)

Forty-two miles southwest of Portland is beautiful **Timberline Lodge**. It makes a nice stop, approximately halfway between Portland and Bend, to view peaks, stretch legs and satisfy hungers. When you can tear yourself away from the mountain view, the lodge itself is a wonder to behold. Built in 1937 in the Oregon tradition, it features massive hand-hewn beams, sculpted metalworks and impressive (and cozy) stone fireplaces.

On Highway 26, two hours southeast of Portland, is the **Mu-**

seum at **Warm Springs,** built in 1993 by the Confederated Tribes of the Warm Springs Reservation to preserve their local history and culture. (See Warm Springs section).

PLACES TO STAY

BLACK BUTTE RANCH
503-595-6211 or 800-452-7455; PO Box 8000, Black Butte Ranch, 97759
Rates: Expensive
Essentials: Credit cards; cribs
Extras: Kitchens; restaurant; outdoor pools (4); saunas; horseback riding; tennis courts; bicycle rentals; canoe rentals; golf; lawn games; hiking trails; babysitting (by pre-arrangement); TV; VCR and video rentals; organized activities for kids.

The setting of this 1800-acre resort is quite spectacular. A large meadow dominates the middle of the ranch and there are snow-capped peaks on the horizon. Black Butte was a family-owned cattle ranch from the late 1800s until 1970 and is still a working cattle operation. In the summer the climate is warm and dry, and in winter you can usually count on snow for skiing at nearby Hoo Doo Bowl or Mt. Bachelor.

The units at Black Butte are individually owned, so furnishings vary, but they are still well-designed and are geared to accommodate families. Several units have a third bedroom that can be included with the rental if needed or closed off, reducing the rate. All units have kitchens. There is a two-night minimum for condominiums and a four-night minimum for private homes in the peak season.

The range of things to do at Black Butte is impressive, for both children and adults. Guests can fly fish, with barbless hooks, and fish must be released. There are 16 tennis courts, two of which are lighted; use of them is free, but reservations are needed. Two golf courses, 16 miles of bike paths, four swimming pools (located at strategic sites to decentralize activity), riding, canoeing, hiking, even white-water rafting can keep a family busy for days in the summer. There is a Recreation Barn, with planned activities for all ages.

The dining room is excellent, but you need reservations for dinner. The setting is stylish and may not be comfortable for families with young children. There are snack shops by the main pool and the golf clubhouses, which are good for lunch. Bend and Sisters also have several good restaurants for families if you want to venture off the ranch.

❝❝ **PARENT COMMENTS:** *"There is so much to do at Black Butte that I can't imagine wanting to leave it, with the possible exception of skiing in the winter or going into the town of Sisters, seven miles away. Sisters is a great-looking town—just what the ideal Western town should look like."*

"This is a well-planned resort in a spectacular setting. We shared a house with friends who have children the ages of our children, which worked well. The ranch is so spread out it might have been hard to get to know other families."

INN OF THE SEVENTH MOUNTAIN
503/382-8711 or 800/452-6810; PO Box 1207, Bend, 97709
Rates: Moderate to expensive
Essentials: Credit cards; cribs
Extras: Restaurants; fireplaces (in some units); kitchens (in some units); TV; rink for ice and roller skating; sauna, hot tubs (3), heated pools (2 outdoor heated), tennis, biking, golf; horseback riding; bicycles; sleigh rides; rafting; organized program for children

Located seven miles west of Bend, this condominium facility offers the closest accommodations to Mt. Bachelor. The location and the wide range of activities offered at the resort make it a popular place for families. When making reservations, ask to be in a building situated close to the resort center and in an apartment so you have a kitchen. There is a rink that is used for ice skating in winter and roller skating the rest of the year; the two swimming pools—one with a long slide—are heated and open year-round.

❝❝ **PARENT COMMENTS:** *"We go off-season when the rates go way down. Our kids love the pool with the water slide and the busy schedule of activities offered by the resort."*

"The staff is very helpful about helping you plan activities for the kids."

LAKE CREEK LODGE
503-595-6331; Star Route, Sisters, 97759
Rates: Moderate to expensive
Essentials: No credit cards
Extras: Breakfast and dinner included in rates during the summer; kitchens; restaurant; outdoor pool; horseback riding; tennis; hiking trails; fishing; playground; organized children's activities; babysitting (by prearrangement)

It is hard to get reservations in July and August at Lake Creek Lodge, since returning guests have first choice and some families have been coming for 20 years. This is a charming place, with pine cottages and houses in a wooded setting overlooking a small lake. Each cottage has a refrigerator and two bedrooms joined by a bathroom; each house has a full kitchen and a living room, some with fireplaces. There is a lodge with shuffleboard, ping pong, pool table and lots of magazines. The rooms in the lodge are too cramped for families.

Outdoors, kids 12 and under can fish in the stocked trout stream—be sure to bring your own poles. The heated outdoor pool and two tennis courts are supplemented by a sport court and lawn games like horseshoes.

Breakfast and dinner are served at the lodge, but not lunch. Food is plain family fare and served buffet style. Children go first and are seated with other kids; adults can bring their own wine. A few highchairs are available.

PARENT COMMENTS: "*A great place to spend your vacation. I read a 1500-page book by the pool, my husband climbed mountains, the six-year-old fished, rode horses and swam. The baby napped and wandered about in a backpack and had an occasional swim.*"

"*This place is lazy, lovely, relaxed. Kids are not only welcome but catered to.*"

"*Just exploring the woods was absolute heaven for our two little boys.*"

THE RIVERHOUSE

800/452-6878 (Oregon), 800/547-3928, 503/389-3111; 3075 N Hwy 97, Bend
Rates: Moderate
Essentials: Credit cards; cribs
Extras: Three restaurants; TV; VCRs, movie rentals; mini-kitchens, kitchens (some units); fireplaces (some units); indoor and outdoor heated pools, saunas, spa, exercise room; jogging trails

To describe this spot as a motel may be accurate, but it seems incomplete. With its great location straddling the Deschutes River, The Riverhouse has a more refined feel than that description suggests. Although it's located on the main drag, it doesn't feel like it; the river provides a calm and beautiful setting. Little ones will enjoy scampering along the large, flat river rocks and watching folks fishing right on the grounds.

The wide variety of units includes luxury suites, river view rooms and rooms with a spa. Consider a living room suite, which offers a common space with Murphy bed and separate bedroom with queen bed. The kitchen suites (two rooms, three queen beds and kitchen) are a bit more pricey, but will save the family some bucks on food. Unless you're calling at the last minute, request a river view room (small additional fee). You might get lucky.

PARENT COMMENTS: *"Be sure to take advantage of the lovely deck overlooking the river. Although it's adjacent to the bar, kids are allowed to sit there and enjoy a kiddie cocktail. There's a delicious complimentary shrimp cocktail with each room.*

ROCK SPRINGS GUEST RANCH
503-382-1957; 64201 Tyler Road, Bend, 97701
Rates: Expensive
Essentials; Credit cards; cribs
Extras: All meals included; horseback riding; babysitting (by prearrangement); organized activities for kids; outdoor pool

Nine miles northwest of Bend, located on 2000 acres adjacent to the Deschutes National Forest and next to a small lake, Rock Springs Ranch is truly a family vacation place. From the end of June until Labor Day, there is a daily children's program for ages 5 to 12 that runs from 9 a.m. to 1 p.m. and from 5 pm to 9 .m Children meet each morning with their own wrangler/counselor to plan their day. If they do not want to participate in the excellent riding program, they can go for a hike, swim, or do arts and crafts. At night, there are hayrides, talent shows, and movies. In the meantime, the parents can ride, swim in the new pool, play tennis, or just soak up the natural beauty of the area. For teens, there are special outings. A free-formed whirlpool includes a fifteen-foot waterfall and there is a sand volleyball court and two stocked ponds for fishing (be sure to bring your own fishing gear).

The 24 knotty-pine cabins are comfortable and well-furnished. They sleep from two to eight people and generally include kitchens and fireplaces. There are 70 horses and nine wranglers. The dining room, open to guests of the ranch only, serves good, basic food. The all-inclusive rate for one week-$1175 for adults, ages 6-16, $975; ages 3-5, $775-includes all meals, snacks, riding, children's program, special events. Special rates are available for babysitters accompanying families.

The rest of the year the ranch is a conference center, except certain three-day holidays when it is open to families.

PARENT COMMENTS: *"The staff makes a big effort to make families feel welcome and it shows. The children's program was excellent."*
"Unlike some ranches, you can go here and not ride and still have a great vacation. I don't ride, but my husband and children do. I was

perfectly content to loaf by the pool."

SUNRIVER LODGE AND RESORT
1-800-547-3922 or 503-393-1246; Sunriver, 97707
Rates: Moderate to expensive
Essentials: Credit cards; cribs
Extras: Kitchens; TV; restaurant; outdoor pools (2), sauna, hot
tub; horseback riding; tennis; bicycle rentals; golf; hiking trails; ski
trails; fishing rentals; boat rentals; playgrounds; babysitting (by
pre-arrangement); organized activities for kids.

Sunriver is a huge (over 3000 acres) resort and residential community located 15 miles south of Bend. It is designed for those who like wilderness and comfort. The natural environment has not been sacrificed and the accommodations are anything but primitive. There are a total of 360 units, including houses, housekeeping suites, and two- and three-bedroom units.

The scenery on this pine and sagebrush studded plateau is spectacular and there is no shortage of activities for all ages. In fact, making a decision as to what to do can be exhausting. Recreation facilities include: the north pool area which has a lap pool for serious swimmers and a large wading pool with lawn for sunning and the south pool area which has a large round pool of uniform depth, a diving area and a separate wading pool; 22 tennis courts (three indoor); stables with a great program for kids beginning with pony rides from age 2 $1/2$ and up; a marina; 25 miles of paved trails and all kinds of bikes to rent, including tandems, bikes with kid trailers, and bikes with kidseats; a Nature Lodge with a staff naturalist where kids can see recovering wildlife and learn about the high desert; an arts and crafts center. There is also a great playground complete with forts and a daycare/playroom facility.

For winter skiing, there are cross-country trails on the resort grounds; and part of Sunriver Mall is frozen into a small skating rink with skate rentals available. Mt. Bachelor is just 18 miles away for downhill skiing. In addition to two dining rooms and a coffee shop in the main lodge, there are a number of restaurants scattered throughout the resort grounds including Chen's, which has grade B Chinese fare (spicy Szechwan items are best) and the popular Hot Peppers, which has a good Mexican menu. For the treat of the day, Goody's is a dazzling old fashioned ice-creamery/candy store with espresso for the adults.

There is a wide range of accommodation choices and price ranges available at Sunriver. The motel-like condo units across the parking lot from the grocery called "The Country Store" are very reasonably priced, have a good central location and are perfectly adequate for the amount of time one spends indoors. The lodge itself is costly and too formal for families with little kids. A good way to cut the cost and get a nice home is to share a house with another family. In the spring or fall, there are special offers that are a real bargain for families. Be sure that the offer includes pool, tennis and hot tub privileges.

PARENT COMMENTS: *"We unfortunately chose the most formal of the lodge eateries—The Meadows at the Lodge—in which to have our restaurant meal. The staff tolerated us but the place didn't have that good old family ambience."*

"Because the resort is strung out, you are dependent on your car for getting around to various activities and one might feel a little isolated. Unlike other vacations, we didn't meet any other families."

"Any hedonist would like Sunriver."

"We came with another family with children close to the ages of our children. It was an ideal arrangement. They even drove with our kids and we drove with theirs and everyone was much better behaved."

PLACES TO EAT

CAFE PARADISO
503/385-5931; 945 NW Bond St
Hours: Breakfast, lunch and dinner
Essentials: No credit cards or highchairs

This is the place to go for your morning eye-opener. This old-style coffee house, located in an historic downtown building, offers a good, strong espresso and a tasty collection of pastry. Stop back later in the day for a light meal or one of their delicious homemade desserts.

CAFE SANTE
503/383-3530; 718 NW Franklin
Hours: Breakfast and lunch daily, dinner Weds-Sat
Essentials: Credit cards; highchairs

Here's your chance to introduce the kids to health food they'll love. Cafe Sante serves creative natural cuisine, concentrating on low-fat and low-cholesterol meals. What's more, they truly cater to children, with a healthy and imaginative kids' menu (including tofu scramble, tofu hotdog and black beans and rice). If your kids won't go for the health foods, you'll find the ubiquitous pancakes, grilled cheese and peanut butter and jelly are also available. Adults choose from a wide range of hearty and heart-healthy selections. Don't be put off by the healthiness of these offerings; there is no sacrifice of good taste.

DESCHUTES BREWERY AND PUBLIC HOUSE
503/382-9242; 1044 NW Bond (at Greenwood)
Hours: Lunch and dinner daily
Essentials: Credit cards; highchairs
   Who'd think of taking the family to a brewery for dinner? You'd be surprised! The small restaurant area is separate from the bar, and children are more than welcome. (Plan to dine fairly early, though, as state law requires children be off premises by 8:30 pm) The quarters are close and the energy is high, so families with toddlers might want to stroll by and see if it looks "do-able."
   The core menu here is standard, but tasty, pub food — sandwiches, soups and salads. But the best bet is the specials board, which features seven specials during the day and seven different ones in the evening and focus on homemade foods. The kids' menu offers some fun variations on the usual themes, such as chicken nuggets shaped like dinosaurs.

FLAVORS/HOWARD'S CATERING
503/382-2848; 235 SW Century Dr
Hours: 8 am-6:30 pm
Essentials: Credit cards; highchairs
   This is a small spot in a rather out-of-the-way location, but it is casual and offers exceptional fare at reasonable prices. There are several tables on the premises, but the take-out gourmet meals offer families the makings for an exquisite picnic. Specific selections vary, but there is always a choice of delicious gourmet sandwiches made to order, fresh salads and a number of tasty hot dishes.

   PARENT COMMENTS: *"This is on one of the roads to Mount Bachelor, so it's a great place to grab a bite or put together a picnic, before heading up the mountain."*

PAPANDREA'S PIZZA
503/549-6081; E Cascade Hwy, Sisters
Hours: Lunch and dinner
Essentials: Credit cards; highchairs
   It's a gorgeous eight-mile drive to the little town of Sisters, where you'll find Papandrea's, one of a chain of pizza spots that are favorites of eastern Oregonians. The ingredients are fresh and the combinations are appealing. Don't expect "fast food," how-

ever; these folks take their time to get it right. While you're waiting, you can window shop the length of the Western-style main street. Or, if your lodging includes a kitchen, try a take-out pizza from the You-Bake line.

WESTSIDE BAKERY AND CAFE
503/382-3426; 1050 NW Galveston
Hours: Breakfast and lunch daily
Essentials: Credit cards; highchairs, boosters
This is just a great place for families. The meals are wholesome and delicious, and the attitude of the servers seems to be, "the more the merrier." Here you will find everything from dad-sized omelettes to kid-sized pigs-in-blanket (and most everything in between). Other favorite breakfast selections include croissant scramble, huevos rancheros and homemade granola. For lunch, the Westside serves sandwiches chock full of meat or cheese on their delicious homemade breads.

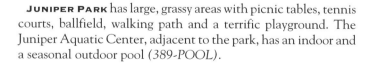 **PARENT COMMENTS:** *"There are four rooms of tables, but this is a very popular place. We suggest bringing books for kids to look at during the inevitable wait for seating."*

WHAT TO SEE AND DO

PARKS
DRAKE PARK winds along the banks of the Deschutes River as it passes through downtown Bend. It's named after A.M. Drake, the city founder, though many people assume it's a reference to the hordes of ducks residing here. Kids will enjoy feeding these feathered friends, but you'll want to wipe everyone's shoes before you get back in the car.

JUNIPER PARK has large, grassy areas with picnic tables, tennis courts, ballfield, walking path and a terrific playground. The Juniper Aquatic Center, adjacent to the park, has an indoor and a seasonal outdoor pool (*389-POOL*).

SMITH ROCK STATE PARK, a 641-acre park 22 miles north of Bend, has taken pains to preserve the rocky spires of the Crooked River Canyon, making it a haven for rock climbers and those who seek majestic viewpoints. For families, a short hike from the main parking area provides a panoramic view of the canyon floor. If the kids are fairly seasoned hikers, take the two-mile developed trail to the top of Misery Ridge; the view is tremendous, and the whole family will enjoy watching climbers scale the vertical rock walls. Wildlife is abundant in the area, including deer, small mammals, birds (watch for birds of prey and their cliffside nests) and geese.

TUMELO STATE PARK. This popular camping area is nestled amid the juniper, Ponderosa pine and sagebrush along the Deschutes River. Most campsites are small and fairly close together, but they are well-maintained. Larger families might look for one of the larger sites, located on a cul-de-sac near the river. There is a pleasant, though dusty, playground area the kids will enjoy. Local fauna, especially ground squirrel and lizards, inspire "hunting" expeditions. For day use, a shady picnic area is located across the highway from the campground. A swimming area is located at the far end of the trail through the campground.

EXCURSIONS

DESCHUTES NATIONAL FOREST. Just six miles south of Bend is the entrance to the third-largest national forest in Oregon, replete with volcanic fascination for imaginative young ones. The **Lava River Cave** (11 miles south) is a mile-long tunnel formed by lava flows. It's cold and damp inside, so be sure everyone has a warm, waterproof jacket and sturdy shoes. Lanterns are available for a small fee. The walk may inspire a hunger; there is picnicking on the grounds, but no drinking water is available.

The nearby **Lava Butte Area** is dominated by 500-foot Lava Butte, a volcanic cinder cone. At the top is an observation/fire lookout and a $1/4$-mile trail that circles the peak. It's worth the small fee to take the shuttle to the top; it departs on the half-hour daily, 10 am-4 pm. Kids with a fascination for things volcanic will want to take a quick look in the Visitor Center at the base of the butte, offering dioramas and other displays.

Three miles south and 11 miles east (FR 9720) is the **Lava Cast Forest Geological Area,** where an easy self-guided nature trail winds through the molds of pine trees engulfed by lava thousands of years ago. Yes, it's a lesson in history and geology, but it's also a nice walk. Choose morning hours during the summer, as there is precious little shade along the way. Some of the molds are large enough for kids to crawl into, so keep a close eye on the younger ones.

NEWBERRY CRATER, 22 miles south and 13 miles east on CR 21, is a popular area for camping and hiking. Families can drive or hike the 7,686 feet up Paulina Peak for a panoramic view of the Oregon desert. There are some interesting examples of obsidian (black glass) lava flows. The Visitor Center is open daily 10 am-4 pm during the summer.

HIGH DESERT MUSEUM. This participatory museum is manageably sized and beautifully conceived; it is a must-do for families. Located six miles south of Bend on Highway 97, the museum offers indoor and outdoor exhibits on history, geology and science.

Don't hurry past the dioramas on the history of the American west; they are fascinating. Also allow plenty of time for the trailside exhibits on forestry settlement. Kids love these real-life exhibits; from time to time, real people demonstrate the huge saws and other logging machinery.

The live animal exhibits house a variety of desert animals living in natural enclosures. Highlights include the raptors, porcupine and otter. Daily presentations provide answers to all those little "whys?"

59800 S Hwy 97; 503/382-4754. Open daily 9 am-5 pm. Cost: $5.50/adult, $2.75/child 5-12, under 5 free.

MOUNT BACHELOR. Just 22 miles west of Bend on the beautiful Cascade Lakes Highway looms Mt. Bachelor, offering year-round entertainment. In winter there's Nordic and Alpine skiing and snowboarding on Bachelor's renowned powder snow. Ten lifts offer skiers 54 downhill runs. Next door is a 60 km system of cross-country trails. Six day lodges serve unexpectedly good food. For a ski report, updated daily, phone 503/382-7888.

After Memorial Day the summit chair lift operates for sightseers. Other services include cafe, picnic sites and mountain bike rentals. For general information about enjoying Mt. Bachelor in any season, phone 800/829-2442.

PILOT BUTTE. If you gaze east from the center of town, you can't miss Pilot Butte, a 511-foot cinder cone surrounded by 101 acres of park land. There's a good road to the top, which offers a magnificent panoramic view of the Cascade Mountains. This is a great first stop to orient visitors to Bend and the surrounding landscape.

Just east of town on Hwy 20. Open daily dawn-dusk. Free.

PINE MOUNTAIN OBSERVATORY. If you have little stargazers along, you may want to visit Pine Mountain Observatory, the University of Oregon's astronomy research facility. It's the only major observatory in the northwestern U.S.; one of its three telescopes is the largest in the Northwest.

Visitors must call first, then may visit on Friday or Saturday evenings (or by appointment) May 1-September 30. *Thirty miles southeast on Hwy 20; 503/382-8331 (after 3 pm). Suggested donation: $2/adult.*

SUNRIVER NATURE CENTER. Most families will appreciate the mission of the Center, "to create and maintain a community in which man and nature can coexist." It's a lofty goal, but the Center is doing its part to see it becomes a reality. In keeping with the philosophy, Sunriver Nature Center offers a relaxed schedule of interpretive programs including an astronomical observatory, self-guided geology trail and a botanical garden. Particularly intriguing to young visitors is the bird rehabilitation program, which cares for sick and injured wildlife and encourages people to recognize how their actions directly affect wildlife. *Located at Sunriver, 15 miles south of Bend; 503/593-4394. Open pending. Cost: $1/adult, $.50/child 12 and under.*

CALENDAR

JUNE: Festival of Cascade Music, Bend
Rodeo, Sisters
JULY: Summer Festival, Bend

RESOURCES

BEND CHAMBER OF COMMERCE/CENTRAL OREGON WELCOME CENTER
63085 N Hwy 97
503/382-3221

DESCHUTES NATIONAL FOREST INFORMATION
503/388-2715

MT. BACHELOR INFORMATION
800/829-2442

OREGON STATE PARKS AND RECREATION DEPARTMENT
503/378-6305

SISTERS CHAMBER OF COMMERCE
125 W Cascade St, Sisters 97759
503/549-0251

ASHLAND

Once a sleepy little cowtown, Ashland has become a busy crossroads for culture and outdoor recreation. The Oregon Shakespeare Festival, established in 1941, now offers a season of 11 plays and this town of 17,000 plays host to 350,000 visitors for a nine-month season. And while it is often the theater that brings visitors here, many other families come to enjoy the beautiful Rogue River area that provides hiking, swimming and rafting opportunities.

GETTING THERE

Ashland is right off I-5, approximately five hours south of Portland and just 30 minutes north of the California border.

REFUELING. For refueling in the larger towns along the interstate, see the Eugene section. Between Eugene and Ashland you'll find a lot of hills and a smattering of small towns. For a sweet treat, try **K and R's Drive Inn**, 20 miles north of Roseburg at the Rice Hill Exit. The Drive Inn,which dishes up mounds of delicious Umpqua ice cream, is a favorite stop for tourists and locals alike (503/849-2570). The **Wolf Creek Tavern**, off Exit 76 at Wolf Creek, offers good, inexpensive fare. It's located in an historic inn, a stagecoach stop in the 1850s, which was purchased and restored by the state (503/866-2474; 100 Railroad Ave).

PLACES TO STAY

ARDEN FOREST INN

503/488-1496; 503/488-1496; 261 West Hersey, 97520
Rates: Moderate
Essentials: Credit cards; cribs

The Arden Forest Inn is one of the few B&B's in Ashland that welcomes children. Located in a quiet neighborhood within easy walking distance of the theaters, the Inn is a turn-of-century farmhouse updated to become a light, airy B&B. On the second floor of the main house there is a suite which has two bedrooms, one with a queen-sized bed and the other with two beds. The other options for families are the adjoining rooms in the carriage house—one with a king-size bed and other with twin beds. Since they have separate entrances, the cottage rooms are more private and parents won't have to worry about their kids thumping about and bothering guests staying below. All rooms have private baths.

PARENT COMMENTS: *"This a wonderful place to stay. Hosts Art and Audrey Sochor are very gracious about accommodating children of all ages. There are no TVs, radios, VCRs—just lots of books and games and chances for stimulating discussion."*

THE ASHLAND HOSTEL
503/482-9217; 150 N Main, 97520
Rates: Inexpensive
Essentials: No credit cards
These dormitory-style rooms are open to all ages and they are the best deal in town if you don't mind sharing a kitchen and common space. A typical room costs about $32 a night. The hostel is located just a few blocks from the Shakespeare Festival theaters.

PARENT COMMENTS: *"It is expensive to take a family to the Shakespeare Festival so we go low-budget on accommodations by either camping or staying at the Ashland Hostel. It is clean and comfortable and the clientele is nice—fellow theater buffs."*

OAK STREET COTTAGES
503/488-3778; 171 Oak St
Rates: Expensive
Essentials: Credit cards; cribs
Extras: Kitchens; fireplaces; jacuzzis; TV; yard with barbecue
This spot offers two- and three-bedroom cottages just one block from the theaters. The cottage that accommodates ten is specially set up for kids—with bunks, highchair and cribs. The location—across the street from lovely Lithia Park and walking distance to theaters—is a plus. We didn't get a chance to send a family to review this place but if you can share the cost with another family it sounds like a good option.

QUALITY INN FLAGSHIP
800/334-2330; 2520 Ashland Avenue, Ashland, 97520
Rates: Moderate
Essentials: Credit cards; cribs
Extras: Continental breakfast; restaurant; refrigerators, fireplaces, TV & VCRs; outdoor pool; microwave and stovetop in the suites; shuttle to theaters; pets OK
Rooms are comfortably furnished and well-kept. The outdoor pool is a nice bonus—it is hot in Ashland in the summer. You are located three miles from the theaters—a shuttle service will get you there.

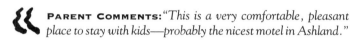

PARENT COMMENTS: *"We were relieved to find a comfortable, affordable motel in Ashland that would take pets and had an outdoor pool. We didn't mind not being right near the theaters because that wasn't our only focus—we spent several days exploring the wonderful Rogue River area."*

WINDMILL'S ASHLAND HILLS INN
800/547-4747 or 503/482-8310; 2525 Ashland St, 97520
Rates: Moderate to expenisve
Essentials: Credit cards; cribs
Extras: Restaurant; refrigerators in suites; TV; outdoor pool,
whirlpool, exercise room; shuttle service; tennis, bikes
The 231 rooms are spacious and comfortably furnished at Ashland Hills Inn. The grounds are attractive and there is a pleasant center courtyard. If you get a one-bedroom suite (opened in early 1995) you will have a refrigerator.

PARENT COMMENTS: *"This is a very comfortable, pleasant place to stay with kids—probably the nicest motel in Ashland."*

HOUSE RENTALS. If you are travelling to Ashland with another family or two, consider renting a home in the area. For information about house rentals, available by the night or the week, as well as helpful advice about B&Bs and motels in the area, call the Ashland Clearinghouse at 503/488-0338.

PLACES TO EAT

CALLAHAN'S
503/482-1299; 7100 Old Hwy 99 S
Essentials: Credit cards; highchairs
Hours: Dinner Tues-Sat, brunch and dinner Sun
This rustic dining room/lounge, under the same management since 1947, is set among the beautiful Siskiyou Mountains six miles south of Ashland. It's what you might call a "nicer" family restaurant: kids are more than welcome, but you'll hope they're on reasonably good behavior. The specialty is Italian cuisine, but there are a number of other choices as well (try one of their seafood specials). Spaghetti comes as a side dish with any entree.

Now for the best news: all dinners (except steaks) are half-price for children 12 and under. If Italian doesn't appeal, kids may choose hamburgers, sandwiches, poultry or seafood. Courses are generally well-timed here, but there are color books and crayons just in case.

OMAR'S FRESH FISH AND STEAKS
503/482-1281; 1380 Siskiyou Blvd
Hours: Lunch and dinner daily
Essentials: Credit cards; highchairs

At first glance, this may seem a strange recommendation in a town where intimate Continental restaurants abound. But Omar's offers a lot that families can't get at those intimate little spots — such as food their kids will eat. There is no children's menu, but kids may order smaller portions of any of the meals. Known for steak and seafood, Omar's has a menu that's extensive enough to provide for the preferences of younger palates.

WHAT TO SEE AND DO

LITHIA PARK. Ashland's lovely central park runs for 100 acres along Ashland Creek, providing picnic areas, playgrounds, nature trails and a Japanese Garden along its length. Located just behind the beautiful Elizabethan Theater is a small pond known for its beauty and for its swans. The park plays host to the annual "Feast of the Tribe of Will," a celebration heralding the beginning of the summer theater season in June.

JACKSONVILLE. A town born in the Gold Rush of 1851, Jacksonville provides an opportunity for families to step backward in time. Pioneer-era buildings have been beautifully preserved — more than 80 have historical markers. Take a self-guided tour of the historic downtown area; maps are available at the Rogue River Valley Railway Depot (503/899-8118; Oregon and C streets).

Of particular interest are: the **Beekman Bank** (1863), the second bank built in Oregon, and the **Beekman House** (1875). A **Children's Museum**, housed in the historic county jail, portrays the life of Native Americans and pioneers 1850-1930. Many of the artifacts here may be handled (503/773-6536; 5th and D streets).

Jacksonville is located 14 miles northwest of Ashland on Hwy 99.

MOUNT ASHLAND. Just 18 miles south of town is a full service ski area, operating November through April. With a 1,150-foot vertical drop and four chair lifts, Mount Ashland Ski Area offers 23 separate runs for all classes of skiers and snowboarders. For cross-country skiers there are 100 miles of trails.

A lodge with cafe and bar is located at the summit.

Located 18 miles south of Ashland; 503/482-2897.

OREGON SHAKESPEARE FESTIVAL. Among the oldest and largest regional theater companies in the U.S., the Oregon Shakespeare Festival presents an ambitious program mid-February through October. The Festival is an excellent place to go with a school-age child. The season includes eleven plays, four by Shakespeare and seven by classic or contemporary playwrights, presented on an authentic outdoor Elizabethan stage and in two superb indoor theatres. A word to those who remember the good old days of last-minute "rush" tickets: these days, audience attendance routinely exceeds 90%, making "rush" tickets very hard to come by.

Families will enjoy taking the **Backstage Tour**, a behind-the-scenes look at the Festival. It includes admission to the exhibit center, a small museum featuring costumes (some are available for dress-up), props and other paraphernalia associated with past productions.

Backstage Tours begin at 10 am daily, and reservations are required. Cost: $8/adult, $6/child ages 5-17.

Parents of very young children face a challenge when including the Festival in vacation plans: children under five are not admitted to the theaters or related events. However, theater and hotel staff can usually assist in locating reliable babysitting services. To determine which plays are appropriate for older children, read descriptions carefully. The box office can provide guidance regarding appropriateness of certain productions for children.

503/482-4331; PO Box 158; box office (15 S Pioneer St) open Tues-Sun, mid-Feb-Oct. Cost: $17.50-$26.50/adult, children ages 5-17 receive a 25% discount.

PACIFIC NORTHWEST MUSEUM OF NATURAL HISTORY. A recent arrival on the Ashland scene, this museum of natural history offers multi-sensory exhibitions, interactive video adventures, hands-on experiments and live animal shows celebrating the diverse ecosystems of the Pacific Northwest. There's something here for everyone.

503/488-1084 or 800/637-8581; 1500 Main St . Open Apr-Oct 9 am-5 pm; Nov-Mar 10 am-4 pm. Admission: $6/adult, $4.50/child 5-15, children under 5 free.

CALENDAR

MID-FEBRUARY-OCTOBER: Oregon Shakespeare Festival
JUNE: Feast of the Tribe of Will

RESOURCES

ASHLAND CHAMBER OF COMMERCE
110 E Main, PO Box 1360, 97520
503/482-3486

EUGENE

As anyone who's raising a family here will attest, Eugene is a wonderful place to be with children. It's small enough to feel safe and manageable, yet large enough to offer plenty of entertainment opportunities. And for outdoor activity, it simply can't be beat—whether you stay close and enjoy the excellent city parks and riverside areas, or venture farther out. To the west is the unsurpassable coastline (see "Oregon Coast"); to the east, beautiful drives upriver and into the mountains (see "Excursions").

Eugene is situated where the Willamette and McKenzie rivers meet amid forests, farmland and mountains. It is the second largest city in Oregon, and home of the University of Oregon. Eugene's role as a college town lends it an air of sophistication, but at the same time it is an earthy, "counter-culture" kind of place.

The town was named after pioneer Eugene Skinner, whose wife was the first white woman in the area. Incorporated in 1862, Eugene still has a lively pioneer atmosphere, but it's also a great place for kids to get a taste of more recent history. Refreshingly, the 1970s are still alive and well here (yes, your kids will likely spot some real "hippies").

Eugene suffered greatly during the decline of the forest industry in Oregon in the late seventies and eighties. Real estate values crashed, and many people were forced by circumstances to leave the area. But due in part to the constancy of the University, Eugene has made a slow, steady recovery. Today, the city has a population of 113,000 and has managed to attract new industry to fill the gap left by logging.

The central Willamette Valley area has a lot to offer vacationing families, particularly in terms of outdoor activity. Rivers, parks and ocean are all easily accessible. If the rains fall, there are plenty of indoor activities to interest young minds and stave off cabin fever.

GETTING THERE
Eugene is located right on I-5, 108 miles south of Portland. Plan

on 2¹/₂ hours on the road, including a short rest stop.

REFUELING. This stretch of I-5 is fairly monotonous, so you might plan a meal break in Salem (approximately midway). At any rate, you'll want to be armed with a "goodie bag" and ideas for car games.

ROADSIDE ATTRACTIONS. Salem, the state capital, is worth a stopover. The **Capitol Building**, built in 1938, is topped by the statue "The Oregon Pioneer," recently regilded by the children of the state. The interior has historic murals and exhibits. There are extensive grounds where little ones can run the wiggles out before climbing back into the car. (Take State Capitol Exit and follow signs; 503/378-4423)

MISSION MILL VILLAGE is a five-acre park highlighting the history of the area. Exhibits and tours are available, or picnic with the ducks by the mill stream. (1313 Mill Street SE; 503/585-7012. Take Exit 253 west and follow signs. Open Tues-Sat, 10 am-4:30 pm; Sundays, June-Sept, 11 am-4:30 pm.)

For a lovely nature experience, visit **Silver Falls State Park,** 26 miles east of Salem. The largest of Oregon's state parks, Silver Falls encompasses more than 8,000 acres of dense forest and 10 spectacular waterfalls. (20024 Silver Falls Hwy SE, Sublimity; 503/873-8681. Take exit to Hwy 22 and follow signs to park.)

PLACES TO STAY

HILTON HOTEL
503/342-2000; 66 E Sixth (at Oak)
Rates: Moderate to expensive
Essentials: Credit cards; cribs
Extras: Restaurant, cafe; TV; refrigerators (suites); indoor pool, whirlpool, exercise room

The biggest selling point of the Hilton is its great location, downtown adjacent to the Hult Performing Center and a short walk from the Fifth Street Market and Eugene Saturday Market. Rooms are nicely appointed but on the small side. So, if budget allows, opt for one of the six suites; each has a separate bedroom and a refrigerator.

The restaurant here is quite good, and affords the best view in town (short of hiking the butte, of course). Children are welcome, but it's a "best behavior" kind of place. For a more relaxed atmosphere, the cafe on the lobby level serves three meals a day, plus special buffets and salad bar. The children's' menu offers standard choices and the placemats come with crayons.

VALLEY RIVER INN
800/543-8266; 1000 Valley River Way
Rates: Moderate to expensive
Essentials: Credit cards; cribs
Extras: Restaurant; pool, sauna, whirlpool; bike/walking trail
If peace and quiet are more important to you than convenience, this is a good choice. (Nothing is really inconvenient in Eugene; the Inn is only a five-minute car ride from downtown and University areas.) Located near a large regional mall of the same name, the Inn sits right on the Willamette River. A paved bike path passes in front of the inn and continues along the river for several miles through two area parks.

The rooms are spacious, and many overlook the river or face onto grassy courtyards. If you're visiting in the spring or summer, the large outdoor swimming pool and hot tub will be huge hits with the kids.

PARENT COMMENTS: *"We love the easy access to the river and parks. We rented bikes from the inn and took the river path to the campus, Alton Baker and Skinner's Butte. There are stops along the way where older kids can wade safely."*

PLACES TO EAT

NAPOLI RESTAURANT AND BAKERY
503/485-4552; 686 E 13th (13th and Hilyard)
Hours: Breakfast, lunch and dinner Mon-Sat
Essentials: Credit cards; highchairs
This is a "nicer" restaurant, but perfectly comfortable with kids of any age. Black-and-white checked floor and marble tables may look daunting, but take a closer look—the tabletops are easy-wipe "faux marble" and the floor is none the worse for a spill or two.

Though it's located only a few blocks from campus, you can shut your eyes and believe you're in an upscale cafe in Italy. Best of all, Napoli serves food that's equally convincing. There is a nice selection of Italian appetizers and lighter fare such as soups and salads. But the fresh pastas are the strong suit here, and you may choose from a tasty array. The servers bend over backward to accommodate families, taking special requests from fussy eaters and happily splitting orders. If you've got the room, check out the dessert tray.

Our parent reviewer reported their order was a little slow in coming, but they were served focaccia as a starter and that helped settle down the kids.

GLENWOOD CAFE
503/687-8201; 2588 Willamette St
Hours: Breakfast, lunch and dinner daily
Essentials: Credit cards; highchairs
If you're looking for creative Northwest cuisine, this isn't your stop. But Glenwood Cafe is the old standby for well-prepared, standard fare at a very reasonable price. Breakfast is especially popular here, and they serve it all day (until 5 pm). The extensive menu provides all the choice you can imagine, and then some: eggs any style, pancakes, French toast, organic granola and fruit. At lunch and dinner you'll find a selection of burritos, sandwiches, salads and soups, as well as (we are, after all, in Eugene) tofu dishes. There is a standard kids' menu, and plenty of crayons and paper.

JAMIE'S GREAT HAMBURGERS
24th and Hilyard St
Hours: Lunch and dinner
The whole family will get a kick out of Jamie's. This colorful version of a Fifties soda fountain features an antique red Vespa, jukebox and pinball machine, not to mention great burgers. There are 12 varieties of burger here, as well as other assorted sandwiches; all are served in old-fashioned burger baskets amid mounds of French fries. To complete your return to a decade past, splurge on a thick shake or traditional ice cream soda (one is enough to satisfy two kids).

THE ORIGINAL PANCAKE HOUSE
503/343-7523; 782 E Broadway
Hours: Breakfast, lunch and dinner daily
Essentials: Credit cards; highchairs
This Eugene institution is still one of the best breakfast spots in town. Though frequented by a cadre of "old timers," the atmosphere is great for families. The extensive list of pancakes is an experience in itself (the apple and German pancakes are specialties of the house, but be forewarned that they take 20 minutes to prepare). For kids, the Pancake House offers junior plates of popular dishes such as "pigs in a blanket" and dollar pancakes. For that rare little one who doesn't much like pancakes, try the crisp waffles, cooked or cold cereals.

THINGS TO SEE AND DO

STROLL & BROWSE

FIFTH STREET PUBLIC MARKET. Located by the train tracks and a few blocks from beautiful Skinner's Butte Park (see Parks), the Public Market includes a variety of intriguing shops built around a three-story courtyard. Plan on spending some time perusing the quality array of local arts and crafts. When hunger strikes, you're in luck; there are fourteen cafes and restaurants in this complex, offering a great selection of ethnic foods and healthy versions of kid favorites (check out the hot dog stand). Be sure to pick up a freshly-baked baguette at the **Metropol**, which enjoys a deserved reputation as one of the finest bakeries on the West Coast.

While mom and dad sip an espresso next to the fountain, the kids will enjoy riding the "bubble" elevator; it only climbs three levels, but it's a fun ride and there's a nice view from the top. There are occasionally special events for kids, such as the petting zoo and play day.

503/484-0383; 296 E 5th (corner of 5th and High St). Open daily, 10 am-6 pm, Oct-May; Mon-Sat, 10-7, and Sun, 10-6, June-Sept. Free.

SATURDAY MARKET. Saturday Market is a local tradition and a great place to get a true "taste" of Eugene. The oldest weekly open-air crafts fair in the U.S. (since 1969), it occupies four square blocks among the tall trees and fountains of downtown. Stroll and admire the fine collection of local crafts while munching a falafel or sipping a fresh-squeezed lemonade. Or sit a spell while you eat, and enjoy the local entertainment. You might want to make sure your little ones make a "pit stop" before going to the Market; the only restrooms are Sani-cans that can be unpleasant in hot weather. Free car and bicycle parking is available.

503/686-8885; downtown Eugene at 8th and Pearl. Saturdays, 10 am-5 pm ("rain or shine"). Free.

PARKS

ALTON BAKER COUNTY PARK. This is a beautifully tended urban park, located adjacent to the river. The small man-made lake is a favorite; kids love to explore the island at its center and feed the resident ducks. There are acres of grass to run the wiggles out. From here, the Willamette River bike trail heads east to the University or west to Valley River Mall.

MOUNT PISGAH ARBORETUM affords a good opportunity to feel you're out in the wild without travelling far from the city center. The arboretum encompasses 118 acres of wooded hillsides and more than five miles of wide, all-season trails. The Visitor Center features a "touch-me" nature exhibit, natural history displays and trail guides.

To get there, head east on 30th Ave past Lane Community College. Cross over I-5 and jog left one block to Seavey Loop Rd. Follow Seavey Loop until it dead-ends and follow signs to parking area. 503/747-3817. Open daily dawn-dusk. Free.

SKINNER'S BUTTE PARK. This graceful little park is on the Willamette River near downtown Eugene. A bike/stroll path winds through the park, hugging the river bank. At the west end of the park are the beautiful **Owen Memorial Rose Gardens**, at their peak May through July. There is a nice play area and a few scattered picnic tables.

SPENCER'S BUTTE PARK. Those who do nothing else in Eugene will want to hike one of the two relatively easy trails up 2,065-foot Spencer's Butte, the highest point in the area. Along the way, enjoy wildlife sightings and sneak peeks at the surrounding terrain; at the top you're rewarded with an incredible bird's-eye view of surrounding urban and pastoral areas.

The Butte is surrounded by acres of coniferous forest through which threads the South Hills Ridgeline Trail.

EXCURSIONS

DORRIS RANCH is a 250-acre farm which operates as a non-profit organization, giving families an opportunity to experience early Oregon history first hand. Year-round walking tours, led by experienced guides, emphasize early farming, trapping and Native American activities. Purchased by the local Park and Recreation District in 1972, the farm has recently expanded to include new interpretive and living history exhibits.

Don't worry if your kids aren't big history buffs—this place has a way of making history "come alive" for the greatest skeptics. And then there are the acres of land to enjoy: meticulous orchards, lush forests, pastures and wetlands. Tours last approximately 1½ hour and follow a flat, two-mile trail.

Located on S 2nd St in Springfield (across the river from Eugene); 503/726-4335 or 503/726-2748. To get there, take Franklin Blvd east across the river. Follow Main St east , then turn right on S 2nd to the ranch.

HULT CENTER FOR THE PERFORMING ARTS. This world class concert facility, noted for its architectural and acoustical design, is home to a number of local arts organizations, including Eugene Symphony, Eugene Opera, Oregon Bach Festival, Eugene Festival of Musical Theatre, Eugene Ballet Company and Oregon Mozart Players. In addition, it features national acts, Broadway musicals and children's theatre.

Guided one-hour tours of the concert center are offered free, Thursdays and Saturdays at 1 pm.

503/342-5746 (recorded message), 503/687-5000 (tickets), 503/687-5087 (tour information); Sixth and Willamette Sts. Lobby and ticket office open Mon-Fri, 11 am-5:30 pm, Sat noon-4 pm.

LANE COUNTY ICE is a state-of-the-art skating facility with a regulation-size floor. Ask about Cheap Skate Night and Family Night.

503/687-3615; 796 W 13th (at the Lane County Fairgrounds). Admission: $4.25/adult, $3.25/student, $2.25/skate rental

UNIVERSITY OF OREGON. One of the prettiest campuses on the West Coast, the U of O was selected as the setting for the movie *Animal House* because it reminded producers of a small East-coast college. It's a fun place to stroll amid grassy quads, old-growth oaks and intriguing sculptures (kids love to be photographed with the "Pioneer Mother," located on the grass in front of the graceful University Library). Near here are two University museums older kids will enjoy—the Museum of Art and the Museum of Natural History (see "Museums"). Guided tours of the campus depart from the information desk in Oregon Hall Monday-Friday at 10 am and 2 pm. Free. (503/346-3201)

A fun afternoon may be had on bikes; tour the campus, then cross Franklin Boulevard and intercept the bike path that follows the river. From here you can ride several miles, making stops at Skinner's Butte or Alton Baker parks (see Parks).

MUSEUMS

UNIVERSITY OF OREGON MUSEUM OF ART leans toward Asian and contemporary American art and photography. There are frequently changing exhibits, though, so call or stop in to see what's current.

1430 Johnson Ln (near the Library); 503/346-3027. Open Weds-Sun, noon-5 pm. Admission by donation.

UNIVERSITY OF OREGON MUSEUM OF NATURAL HISTORY

focuses on the archeology and natural science of the Pacific Northwest. It does a particularly good job with its travelling exhibits, which show the anthropology of various cultures throughout the world.

1680 E15th Ave; 503/346-3024. Open Weds-Sun, noon-5 pm. Admission: $1, additional fee for special exhibits.

WILLAMETTE SCIENCE AND TECHNOLOGY CENTER (WISTEC). This small museum is a good rainy-day excursion for families. It offers interactive displays that change every eight to ten weeks and an impressive planetarium.

2300 Leo Harris Parkway (near Autzen Stadium), 503/687-3619 or 503/484-9027. Open Weds-Sun, noon-6 pm. Admission: $3/ adults $2/child 4-16, under 4 free.

CALENDAR

JUNE/JULY: Oregon Bach Festival
JULY: Oregon Country Fair
TUESDAYS, JULY/AUGUST: Concerts in the Parks
JULY/AUGUST: Eugene Festival of Musical Theatre
AUGUST: Lane County Fair
SEPTEMBER: Oregon Festival of American Music
Eugene Celebration

RESOURCES

CONVENTION AND VISITORS ASSOCIATION OF LANE COUNTY
305 W 7th, Eugene, 97401
503/484-5307

EUGENE WEEKLY
Free newspaper features a calendar of local arts, events and entertainment.
1251 Lincoln, Eugene, 97401
503/484-0519

OREGON COAST

The Oregon Coast is one of the Pacific Northwest's most scenic and interesting places to go with children. The wind-battered shoreline is magnificent, with miles of sandy beaches, rocky outcroppings, sand dunes and sea stacks. There is something special to see around each bend—capes and observation points, lighthouses, little museums, tidal pools, wildlife, tiny beach towns and quirky little shops. Vacation spots are as diverse as the 360-mile coastline, from grassy dunes to redwood groves, first-class resorts to funky cabins right next to the beach.

A word of warning: On weekends in the spring and all summer long, accommodations along the coast fill up fast. Make your reservations early.

GETTING THERE

From the Seattle area, take I-5 south. The fastest route to the north coast leaves I-5 at Longview-Kelso, takes Highway 433 across the Columbia River bridge at Longview, and connects with Highway 30 to Astoria and U.S. 101. Travel time from Seattle to Cannon Beach is about 4 $^1/_2$ to 5 hours.

An alternate route is I-5 to Portland, then Highway 26 to Cannon Beach. If you are headed to the central or southern coast, there are several clearly designated routes from I-5 west to the coast.

Once you reach the coast, Highway 101 hugs the coastline the entire length of the state. Allow plenty of time for your journey—Highway 101 is an excellent two-lane highway but at almost every curve a magnificent vista, a trail leading off the highway, a quaint town or an interesting attraction beckons you to make a stop.

ROADSIDE ATTRACTIONS. For ideas on interesting stops and places to eat if you travel south from Seattle, see the Olympia and Portland sections.

If you take Highway 30 from Longview to the coast, you'll find many interesting attractions in Astoria. For Roadside Attractions further south on the coast, see What to See and Do at the individual town listed below.

REFUELING. See Olympia: Places to Eat and Portland: Refueling and Places to Eat.

RESOURCES

BEST HIKES FOR CHILDREN IN CENTRAL AND WESTERN OREGON by Bonnie Henderson. Published by The Mountaineers, 1992. Includes several hikes along the coast.

LIGHTHOUSE BROCHURE. Describes all the lighthouses on the

coast, including ones open to the public.
Oregon Parks and Recreation; 800/452-5687

OREGON COAST is an outstanding guide published bi-monthly
by Oregon Coast Magazine. The maps, in-depth stories and
carefully detailed descriptions of the attractions along the
coast are very helpful. Available by subscription for $16.95 per
year, but also offered free at many hotels along the coast.
Oregon Coast Magazine, PO Box 18000. Florence, Oregon
97439-0130.

THE OREGON COAST ASSOCIATION has plenty of detailed
information about the coastline in Oregon. For $3 to cover
postage and handling, they'll send you their "Coast Travel
Pack" which includes a guide, events calendar, brochures,
maps and tidebooks.
 PO Box 670, Oregon Coast, OR, 97365. Phone toll-free 800-
98-COAST

OREGON'S SOUTH COAST IN A NUTSHELL TOURMAP AND
OREGON'S NORTH COAST IN A NUTSHELL TOURMAP are
travel guides and road maps combined. Featuring recreational
opportunities, restaurants, lodging, and camping information,
these colorful maps are easy to read and even include ratings
(the Golden Acorn Awards are the most highly recommended
places). Notes include whether or not a place is recommended
for kids, costs and useful travel tips. Plus you get an excellent
map! $5.95 each. Available at many hotels and stores on the
coast, but we recommend you get the Tourmap before you
leave home. To order the Nutshell Tour Maps, send $8 ($5.95
plus $2.05 shipping and handling) to PO Box 230998, Tigard,
OR 97281-0998.

OREGON'S COAST: A GUIDE TO BEST FAMILY ATTRACTIONS
FROM ASTORIA TO BROOKINGS by David and Carolyn Gabbe.
Published by Johnston Associates International. This informative 192-page book offers interesting historical background
and useful details on the many events and attractions of
interest to families along the coast.

ASTORIA

This little town near the mouth of the Columbia River in the
northwest corner of Oregon is a pleasant mix of working fishing

docks and restored Victorian mansions. While not located on the ocean, the beach is within ten minutes driving time and there are enough activities right in town to keep a family entertained for a weekend.

PLACES TO STAY

RED LION INN

800/547-8010; 400 Industry St, Astoria, 97103
Rates: Moderate
Essentials: Credit cards; cribs
Extras: Restaurants; pets OK

If you brought the family hound along, this comfortable hotel is a good choice. There are 124 units but only one has two-bedrooms, so book early if your clan is large.

The location, right at river's edge, on Highway 101 one mile west of the junction of Highway 30 and 101, gives guests a good view of the Columbia River.

PARENT COMMENTS: *"We enjoyed standing on our balcony and watching the river activity."*
"The hotel restaurant had good seafood and pasta dishes."

ROSEBRIAR HOTEL

503/325-7427; 800/487-0224; 636 14th St, Astoria, 97103
Rates: Moderate to expensive
Essentials: Credit cards; cribs
Extras: Full breakfast and afternoon tea; TV

Built in 1902 as a home for banker Frank Patton, this lovely hotel on a hill overlooking town has retained the charm of its roots, although now there are phones, TVs and baths in all the rooms.

The ground-floor suite could work for a small family—it has a queen-sized bed plus a sofa bed in a sitting room. If you don't mind your kids in your sleeping area, the new Carriage House, across the courtyard from the Inn, has a kitchen, sitting and sleeping area all in one large room.

PARENT COMMENTS: *"Every last detail has been taken care of at this elegant inn to make sure you have a relaxed and pleasant visit. I came for a weekend getaway with my two daughters (ages 6 and 9). We explored Fort Stevens Park all day and returned in time for afternoon tea sitting by the fire in the parlor."*
"Divine breakfasts!"

PLACES TO EAT

THE SHIP INN
503/325-0033; on the waterfront at the foot of 2nd St
Hours: Lunch, dinner daily
Four-star halibut fish and chips plus a great view of boat activity
on the Columbia.

WHAT TO SEE AND DO

THE COLUMBIA RIVER MARITIME MUSEUM on the main street
in Astoria is an outstanding maritime museum well worth a visit.
Visitors can climb aboard the lightship Columbia River, peer
through a submarine conning tower with a view of the Columbia
River, see the actual bridge of a ship and whaling exhibits and
photos of shipwrecks. When in port, the Coast Guard ship
Resolute is moored outside at the 17th street pier and open for
tours.
*503-325-2323, 1793 Marine Dr, Astoria. Hours: 9:30 am to 5 pm
daily from April to October; closed Mondays, October through
March. Admission $5 for adult, $2 for children.*

THE ASTORIA COLUMN. To get a panoramic view of the town
(and an aerobic workout) climb the 166 steps to the top of this
125-foot column. Decorated with friezes depicting the history of
the area.
503/325-6311. On Coxcomb Hill Road. Open 8 am to dusk. Free.

FORT CLATSOP NATIONAL MEMORIAL, six miles south of
Astoria off Highway 101, is a replica of the log fort where Lewis
and Clark wintered in 1805-1806. During the summer, employees dress in authentic period costumes. They demonstrate some
of the frontier skills necessary to survive the winter and show how
dugout canoes were made, fires were started by hand, hides
tanned and maps and clothing made.
*503/861-2471; Daily 8 am-5 pm through mid-June; until 6 pm,
June 15 to September. Free.*

FORT STEVENS STATE PARK, to the west on U.S. 101, is at the
mouth of the Columbia River. It is Oregon's largest state park.
Within the 4,000 acres there are numerous biking and hiking
trails as well as boating, fishing, two large picnic areas and
swimming at Coffenbury Lake.
The Union Army built Fort Stevens during the Civil War to

keep Confederate frigates from entering the Columbia. Although that threat never materialized, the Fort was fired on in 1942 by a Japanese submarine thereby becoming the only U.S. fort to be fired on since the War of 1812. At the park there are old artillery installations and an Interpretive Center displaying weapons, maps and other relics. At low tide, you can see the hull of the British schooner *Peter Iredale*, shipwrecked in 1906.

503/861-2000. Interpretive Center open daily 10 am-6 pm in the summer, 8 am-5 pm the rest of the year. Free.

CALENDAR

MAY: Maritime Week

RESOURCES

ASTORIA CHAMBER OF COMMERCE
111 W. Marine Dr, PO Box 176, Astoria, 97103
503/325-6311

SEASIDE

Oregon's largest and oldest ocean resort is the first town you will come to on Highway 101 after leaving Astoria. Seaside is at the western end of the Lewis and Clark Trail, and apparently many modern-day travelers also consider it the end of the trail—the town is crammed with hotels, game arcades, fast food restaurants, cotton candy and throngs of vacationers looking for good times. You may also be tempted to stop, especially if you have made the long trip from Seattle, but several of our parent reviewers gave Seaside thumbs down due to overdevelopment and urged parents to drive on to more scenic and restful spots farther down the coast.

However, one of our reviewers loved the carnival atmosphere of this lively town. We have included their recommendations under Seaside: Places to Stay and What to See and Do.

GETTING THERE
Seaside is about 12 miles south of Astoria on Highway 101.

PLACES TO STAY

SHILO OCEANFRONT RESORT
503/738-9571, 503/737-9571 or 800/222-2244; 30 N Prom, Seaside, 97138

Rates: Expensive
Essentials: Credit cards; cribs
Extras: Restaurants; kitchens in some units; TV; indoor pool,
whirlpool

A string of places to stay crowds the two-mile promenade along the beach front in Seaside. There is so little space between the different hotels and motels that you can't see the ocean on the other side. But if you have opted to stay in Seaside, you have decided that crowds and a "Coney Island" atmosphere will suit your family, and you probably won't mind choosing your place to stay on this strip.

Our parent reviewer stayed at the five-story Shilo Inn along "hotel row" and found it very satisfactory. The rooms are spacious and clean. The indoor pool is exceptionally nice—it overlooks the ocean—and the common areas large and comfortable.

PARENT COMMENTS: *"We loved both the Shilo and the town of Seaside. The nearby Arcade wowed our kids—bumper cars, video games, cotton candy, etc. Most of the time we cooked our own meals but there were many family-friendly restaurants to choose from in town. One afternoon we drove down to Cannon Beach to browse and eat."*

"Just don't picture a cozy beach cabin on a lonely beach or you will be sorely disappointed."

WHAT TO SEE AND DO

MILLION DOLLAR WALK. Chances are your kids will zero in on this half-mile stretch from Roosevelt Drive to the beach that is "Broadway" on the map. Good luck getting past the bumper cars, miniature golf, skee-ball, video games, pinball, caramel corn, carousel, cotton candy and saltwater taffy—parents might as well dole out the quarters and resign themselves to some fun people-watching.

MONKEY BUSINESS BOATS rents kayaks, paddle boats and rowboats to explore the Necanicum River that runs through Seaside but the small bumper boats attract the most business. The one-person boats are powered by two-horsepower motors—and the idea is to smack head-on into each other with enough impact to get everybody soaked. Small children can ride in "buddy boats" which are designed to hold an adult and a child.
503/738-8209; Quatat Marine Park, between First and Ave A. Daily 12-8 summer only.

WHEELED FUN, whether on a bicycle, tricycle, quadricycle or skates, is popular in Seaside. The following shops rent all shapes and sizes of wheeled self-propelled vehicles. Note: The three-wheeled "fun cycles" that are designed to be ridden on the beach are loads of fun for all ages. They sit low to the ground and are so easy to pedal that even a pre-two-wheeler, four-year-old can hop on and take off while mom and dad get a good work-out struggling to keep up.

Manzanita Fun Merchants, *(503/738-3703; 200 Ave A and South Columbia. Open daily 9-8 summer, 9-6 winter).* Rental equipment includes traditional bicycles, jogging strollers, three-wheeled "fun cycles" and complimentary trailers to carry toddlers that can be attached to bicycles or "fun-cycles."

Prom Bike Shops, *(503/738-8251; 622 12th).* Bicycles, three-wheeled cycles, training bikes, tandems, all terrain bikes, skateboards, scooters and skates. Plus child carriers and bicycle trailers.

Seaside Surrey Rental, *(503/738-0242; 332 S).* Columbia. Daily 10-7. Everything from 18-speed mountain bikes to 4-wheel carriages called "surreys." These quadricycles come with either two pedals or four and enable families to ride together. The four-pedal model allows eight passengers (four peddlers).

THE LEWIS AND CLARK HISTORICAL PAGEANT takes place in Seaside in July and August. Actors re-enact the hazardous journey of Lewis and Clark, the famous explorers sent west in 1805 by President Thomas Jefferson. The lively historical drama takes place outdoors along the banks of Neawanna Creek. Children will enjoy the colorful costumes and scenery while they learn an easy history lesson.

800/444-6740 or 503/738-5869. Location Broadway Park. Performances throughout July and August, 8 pm on Thursday, Friday and Saturday, with 2 pm matinees on Sunday and Monday. Cost: $7.50 adults; $3 ages 6-16.

RESOURCES

SEASIDE CHAMBER OF COMMERCE
7 N Roosevelt, PO Box 7, Seaside, 97138
800/444-6740 or 503/738-6391

CANNON BEACH/TOLOVANA BEACH

Seven miles down the coast from Seaside is the picturesque town of Cannon Beach. While Seaside had been allowed to grow apparently unrestricted, Cannon Beach is a testimony to careful planning. With a fabulous seven-mile beach marked by hulking 235-foot-high Haystack Rock, white-washed cottages and Hemlock, the main street full of interesting shops and good restaurants, Cannon Beach is often described as a less fancy version of Carmel, California. It is a fine place to come if you want to mix the fun of the beach with the diversions of an interesting town.

Tolovana Park, just south of Cannon Beach, is a much smaller town, within easy driving distance of the activities and restaurants in Cannon Beach.

Both the Puffin Kite Festival (503/436-2623), on the last weekend in April, and Sandcastle Day (503/436-2623), on a Sunday in late May, are wonderful events that are ideally suited to kids. Competition at the Kite Festival includes the highest kite, the ugliest kite, kite relay races and quickest reeling in. Sandcastle Day is a world-renowned event with over 1000 participants producing unbelievably imaginative sand sculptures to the delight of over 20,000 spectators. Kids are encouraged to join in the fun in both events.

PLACES TO STAY

BEST WESTERN SURFSAND
503-436-2274; 1080 Ecola Court, PO Box 219, Cannon Beach, 97110
Rates: Moderate to expensive
Essentials: Credit cards; cribs
Extras: Kitchens; TV; indoor pool, hot tub; fireplaces (in some units); pets OK

This large, 174-unit motel is right on the ocean, has good service and is located just a few blocks from the center of town. Wood is left at your door, as is the morning paper. It's hard to get reservations, particularly in the summer.

Access to the beach is excellent—you can see your children digging in the sand while you have a cup of coffee on your balcony. The beach is wide and good for kite flying and playing in the tidepools at Haystack Rock, located just to the south of Surfsand. The indoor swimming pool is never very crowded. On Saturday nights in the summer there are wiener roasts around a beach fire.

If you do get a unit with a kitchen, shop in Seaside—Cannon Beach has limited grocery shopping facilities. If you want to go into Cannon Beach proper, you can walk down along the beach and then cut into town to shop.

PARENT COMMENTS: "*It's fun for little kids to feed the seagulls leftovers on the balcony.*"

"*Surfsand is wonderful anytime - the ocean is so close. We love this place.*"

HALLMARK RESORT

1-800-345-5676 or 503-436-1566; 1400 S. Hemlock, Cannon Beach, 97110
Rates: Moderate to expensive
Essentials: Credit cards; cribs
Extras: Kitchens; TV; indoor pool;, sauna, hot tub; fireplaces (in most units); pets OK

This attractive, cedar-shake resort sits on a bluff just opposite Haystack Rock. Units come in all different sizes, with various sleeping configurations. Typical accommodations for four would be a living room with fireplace, lanai, and pull-down Murphy bed, kitchen, bathroom, and separate bedroom with twins or queen.

Beach access is via a wooden staircase that takes you down the bluff. The beach is lovely and wide, and the tidepools at Haystack Rock replete with starfish and sea anemones—right in front of the resort. Firewood is provided each room, and the morning paper is delivered every day.

The pool facilities are exceptionally nice. In addition to the swimming pool, there is a separate wading pool for little people, two large hot tubs, one warmer than the other, a sauna and exercise room.

 PARENT COMMENTS: "*The wall bed in the living room is such a good idea. We housed the kids in the bedroom, and then were able to enjoy the ocean and fireplace from the living room after they'd gone to bed. It was also great having two TVs.*"

"*The long stairs to the beach might be a nuisance with very young children.*"

"*In my opinion, this is the nicest place to stay with kids on the northern Oregon coast. The panoramic vista of the ocean, beach and Haystack Rock is magnificent (splurge and get an oceanfront room). The indoor pool facilities were as nice as I've seen at a hotel and Cannon Beach is a great little town to explore.*"

"*Lovely but too upscale for a beach vacation.*"

"*One night we brought take-out meals from Dooger's, the restaurant across the road, back to our room because we were tired of eating out with our one-year-old. It worked well—we ate on our balcony enjoying the magnificent sunset while our toddler fed the seagulls.*"

THE WAVES

503/436-2205; P.O. Box 3, Cannon Beach 97110
Rates: Expensive
Essentials: Credit cards; cribs
Extras: Kitchens (in some units); fireplaces (in some units); TV;
oceanfront spa.

The four clusters of beautifully-designed buildings that comprise this new upscale resort offer a variety of accommodations that are suitable for families. Considering the high cost ($165 one-bedroom), families may be disappointed there isn't an indoor pool, but what you do get is a new, beautifully furnished unit in a wonderful location—next to the beach and just one block from the center of town.

PARENT COMMENTS: *"The craftsmen-style buildings are lovely; the units are tastefully furnished with every convenience. The beach was about ten feet away. It was pricey but worth it for a couple days."*

THE SEA SPRITE

503-436-2266; Tolovana Park, 97145
Rates: Moderate
Essentials: Credit cards; cribs
Extras: Kitchens (with highchairs); woodstoves, free wood;
laundry; TV

The Sea Sprite is a lovely quiet spot right on the beach, a ten-minute walk south of Haystack Rock. It is located on a dead-end street, so there is no traffic noise and kids can wander about the grounds safely. Decor is comfortable and homey, complete with rocking chairs and fireplaces. All units are supplied with firewood, and kitchens are fully-equipped. Of the six available units, two are for two people, two will accommodate up to five people, one up to six, and the last, a separate two-bedroom cottage, will hold up to eight people. There are picnic tables and flower gardens on the grounds. Parents in charge of sand control will appreciate the free use of motel beach towels and blankets and the washer and dryer on premises.

Because of the small size of the Sea Sprite, it's a good idea to make reservations in plenty of time, especially for the summer.

PARENT COMMENTS: *"It is very hard to find a funky but clean and comfortable little place right on the beach that welcomes children. The Sea Sprite is perfect—quiet and away from it all but an easy walk or drive into the charming diversions of Cannon Beach."*

TOLOVANA INN
503/436-2211; Tolovana Park, 97145
Rates: Moderate to expensive
Essentials: Credit cards; cribs
Extras: Kitchens; indoor pool; small playground; game room; pets OK

These condominium-type units were built in the late 60's and early 70's. Decor is functional but not especially attractive. Each unit except those on the ground floor has a lanai, fireplace and view (as usual, the better the view the higher the price.) Staff supplies a new log for the fireplace and a morning paper every day.

Kitchens are well-equipped. The two-bedroom units have two TVs which is convenient for a large group.

The Tolovana Inn is a good choice if you want to be next to the beach, near Cannon Beach and have an indoor pool, but don't want to spend as much as the Surfsand and Hallmark would cost.

PARENT COMMENTS: *"We highly recommend the Tolovana Inn. We visited with our 6-month-old baby and twin 3-year-old boys. We were relieved it was not too fancy—we didn't have to worry about the kids damaging the place (green shag rug is very forgiving). Less pretentious than the fancier places in Cannon Beach."*

"We rented "fun cycles" in Cannon Beach and rode on the beach. All of us—kids ages 14, 10 and 8 months—had a ball. The baby fell asleep in the trailer right away—she got a nap while we had fun."

A NOTE ABOUT LODGING IN CANNON BEACH:

Accommodations in Cannon Beach on the ocean front are expensive. Most of the hotels and motels also rent houses or units in town that are several blocks away from the ocean. Ask the Surfsand, the Hallmark and The Waves for information about their less expensive options. The Chamber of Commerce also will be helpful in telling you about various possibilities.

Finally, **Cannon Beach Rental Homes** (503/436-2021) has over ten houses available to rent to families. While not necessarily a cost saver, staying in a private home is a nice option if you are a mid- to large-sized group. A one-week minimum stay is required in July and August (weekly rent ranges from $875 to $2240 at high season).

PLACES TO EAT

DOOGER'S SEAFOOD AND GRILL
503/436-2225; 1371 S Hemlock, Cannon Beach
Also at 505 Broadway, Seaside

Hours: Breakfast, lunch and dinner
Essentials: Credit cards; highchairs
Dooger's is famous for good seafood and when you look at the menu you'll know why. There's a wide selection of fish and shellfish—including calamari, halibut, sea scallops, rock shrimp, salmon, petrole sole and, on occasion, razor clams. You choose the preparation—lightly coated and fried, sautéed, Cajun style or poached. If you don't want seafood, you can get a good sandwich, vegie or regular burger, fettucini, steak and so on. Prices are moderate and except the occasional wait to be seated, service is quick. There is also a good kids' menu. Breakfasts include some interesting variations well-suited to a beach town—fresh oysters and eggs ($7.95) and Hangtown Fry, a concoction of eggs, oysters, bacon, onions and bay shrimp ($8.50).

KNOODLZ
503/436-0123; 171 Sunset Blvd, Cannon Beach
Hours: 11:30 am-8 pm
Their menu calls it "Global Dining for the Next Millennium" but we're slightly worried this imaginative place won't last through the slow winter season. The location, at the south end of town on the road that takes travelers back up to Highway 101, makes it easy to overlook. That's a shame because the food is a refreshing break from the typical vacation fare. Menu items include noodle dishes prepared with vegies, tofu, turkey, beef or seafood ($5) in six styles ranging from Malaysian to Vietnamese. There's also C.B. Soba—fresh noodles with vegies, prawns and scallops ($9), Indonesian Satay, ethnic beans and rice and a fruit and vegetable juice bar that serves a mean smoothie.
Best of all you'll dine on good karma at Noodlz—not only is food prepared low-fat and no MSG but at Knoodlz all associates are "true managers" i.e. sharing in the profits and deciding how to run the business.
Eat in, take out or get your meal delivered to your hotel—by bicycle, of course.

MIDTOWN CAFE
503/436-1016; 1235 S. Hemlock, Cannon Beach
Hours: Breakfast & lunch, Weds-Sat; Sun breakfast only
Essentials: No credit cards; highchairs available
You might feel a bit cramped for space but kids will likely love this hole-in-the-wall seven blocks south of the center of town. Decor is random—wind-ups toys and ceramic figurines. Food is healthy (burritos, tofu egg scrambles, smoothies, etc), servings

generous. Don't go in January—it's closed.

MO'S RESTAURANT
503/436-1111; Tolovana Park, 97145
Hours: Lunch and dinner daily
Essentials: Credit cards; highchairs
　　More than a place to eat, Mo's is an institution that has become part of the experience of visiting the Oregon coast. Food reviews are mixed—some folks say the seafood is mediocre, others swear the clam chowder and oyster stew are among the best served anywhere. For kids there's the standard fare, including fish and chips, burgers, hotdogs and grilled cheese. All the Mo's Restaurants are busy, noisy places that work well for families.

WHAT TO SEE AND DO

ECOLA STATE PARK. A short, pretty drive through a canopied forest brings you to the parking area overlooking Crescent Beach. Here there are a number of picnic areas, but be sure to prepare for the ubiquitous coastal breezes. The beach itself, a short trek down the bluff, is better protected from the wind. The walk down to the beach can be difficult in parts, such as navigating large driftwood logs and stones, so little ones should be carried or closely supervised. It's a two-mile drive or hike from the parking lot to Indian Beach, an equally beautiful (and often less crowded) spot.
Off US 101 just north of town.

THE COASTER THEATER offers year-round live entertainment for a family audience in a rustic theater on N Hemlock, the main street in Cannon Beach. It is considered one of the finest community theaters in the Northwest. Productions includes plays, musicals, comedy and dance performances.
503/436-1242; 108 N Hemlock. Prices and schedules vary, call for details.

CYCLING. You may not have thought of riding a bike on the beach before, but on the wide beach at Cannon Beach it is a popular activity. With no traffic and no hills, beach cycling is ideal for young riders. The three-wheeled "fun cycles" are loads of fun for all ages. They sit low to the ground and are so easy to pedal that even a child who hasn't learned to ride a two-wheeler can join the fun.
Manzanita Fun Merchants. *(503/436-1880; 1140 S. Hemlock.*

Daily 9-8 summers, weekends 9-6 winter). Traditional bikes, three-wheeled "fun cycles" and complimentary trailers for carrying toddlers that hook to the bikes and "fun cycles."

Mike's Bike Shop. *(503/436-1266; 248 N. Spruce. Open 10-6 daily).* Offering three-wheel beach bikes, mountain bikes and single speed beach cruisers for rent. Trailers for youngsters also available.

THE HAYSTACK PROGRAM, run by Portland State University, has offered residents and visitors to Cannon Beach enrichment courses in music, art, writing, theater arts and the environment for nearly a quarter-century. Classes run anywhere from one day to two weeks and while their parents are learning, kids ages three to twelve can enjoy special classes of their own.

503/725-4081 or 800/547-8887 outside Oregon. Runs in July and August, call for details.

HAYSTACK ROCK. This monster monolith—235 feet high—fascinates young and old alike. Looming just off-shore, at the south end of Cannon Beach, at low-tide the pools at the base of Haystack teem with intertidal creatures. At low-tide on summer weekends, look for volunteers in the Haystack Rock Interpretive Program offering on-site lessons about the tidepools to anyone who cares to listen.

HORSEBACK RIDING on the beach or through coastal forest is available at **Sea Ranch Stables,** located at the north end of Cannon Beach. Horses are available to suit all ages and all skill levels on guided rides. Reservations advised.

503/436-1268. Daily 9-5, May-September.

KITEFLYING on an ocean beach is perfect for a child's first experience with a kite. No trees, no wires, steady winds. **Catch the Wind,** the kite shop with eight locations on the coast (Seaside, Cannon Beach, Lincoln City, Rockaway Beach, Depoe Bay, Agate Beach, Newport and Florence) will dazzle you with their selection of windsocks and kites of every size and shape.

NEAKAHNIE MOUNTAIN. The short (two-mile) but steep trail that climbs Neakahnie leads to a magnificent mountain top view of the sea from 1,800 feet. On the way, depending on the season, you may cross meadows of vividly colored wildflowers, or spot some of the abundant wildlife. Due to steepness, recommended for hikers five and up.

Beach Safety:
Never turn your back on the surf. Never play in the ocean alone. Do not use inflatables. Stay in water no more than knee-to-waist deep.

Off Highway 101, 8 miles south of Cannon Beach. Look for a sign just before Oswald West viewpoint.

Kiteflying Tip: To avoid a kite fly, fly, flying away— unwind the string, fasten the end of the string to the spool and rewind.

CALENDAR

APRIL: Puffin Kite Festival
MAY: Sandcastle Day

RESOURCES

BEACH BABIES & KIDS STUFF. If you left home without an essential piece of baby equipment, don't worry about it. This delightful store rents baby equipment to visiting parents. Everything you can imagine is available, including cribs, beach play yards, jogging strollers, frame backpacks, potty seats, rocking chairs, high chairs, baby swings, car seats and much much more. They will deliver and pick-up equipment. Don't we wish every town had this service?
The store also carries an exceptionally good assortment of beach hats and beach toys, along with the usual cute kids clothing.
503/436-1033 or 800/305-1033; 171 Sunset Blvd, Cannon Beach, 97110

CANNON BEACH CHAMBER OF COMMERCE
2nd and Spruce, PO Box 64, Cannon Beach, 97110
503/436-2623. Open daily 9-5.

TILLAMOOK

Tillamook is on Highway 101 at the point it moves away from the coast for a short stretch. This is dairy country. Most travelers just drive through on their way to the ocean so we don't include places to stay. However, there are several attractions that are worth checking out if you vacation in a nearby coastal town.

WHAT TO SEE AND DO

BETWEEN TILLAMOOK AND LINCOLN CITY U.S. 101 moves away from the ocean into the forest. By taking a 35-mile loop road to the coast, you can drive one of the most beautiful stretches of road in the Northwest and visit scenic **Capes Meares,** which is home to the famous Octopus Tree, a gigantic twisted Sitka Spruce.

OREGON COASTLINE EXPRESS. Take a 44-mile round trip ride along the coastline between Tillamook and Wheeler, with stops along the way at Garibaldi and Rockaway and a scenic run past dairy farms, quaint towns and rugged coastline. Barview Jetty County Park offers views of the often turbulent entrance to Tillamook Bay, the largest bay on the Oregon Coast.

A shorter ride, the Caboose Express, takes passengers in rebuilt cabooses along a three-mile stretch past sawmills, pasture and to the blimp hangars (see below).

503/842-2768; Southern Pacific Depot, E 3rd St, Tillamook

TILLAMOOK CHEESE FACTORY, two miles north of the town of Tillamook, is a very popular tourist attraction but if you decide to pass it up you won't miss much. The self-guided tour is not very informative and the tiny samples will only make the kids hungrier.

503/842-4481; on U.S. 101. Daily 8 am - 8 pm.

TILLAMOOK NAVAL AIR STATION MUSEUM AND BLIMP HANGARS. Even if you don't want to pay the $5 admission fee ($2.50 for kids), to look at vintage aircraft from World War II, take the five-minute drive off of Highway 101 to show the kids the huge building that houses the museum. It is a former blimp hangar and the largest wooden building in the world.

503/842-1130; two miles south of town, east of U.S. 101. Summer, 10 am-6 pm daily; from 9 am to 4 pm the rest of the year.

TILLAMOOK COUNTY PIONEER MUSEUM. Located in the old county courthouse, built in 1905, this wonderful museum offers three-floors of interesting exhibits. In the basement, be sure to show the kids the Tillamook-to-Yamhill stagecoach and back in the corner, the jail. The second-floor natural-history exhibit is remarkable.

503/842-4553; 22106 Second St (northbound on Highway 101 at Second). Daily 8:30 am-5 pm, Sunday noon-5 pm. Closed Mon, Oct -April.

LINCOLN CITY

Lincoln City is a very popular resort town that until 25 years ago was five little towns. With seven miles of sandy beach, three-mile long Devil's Lake and the Siletz River, there are plenty of ways to have fun. Resident sea lions are sometimes visible at the mouth of the Siletz River.

PLACES TO STAY

HIDEAWAY MOTEL

503/994-8874; 810 SW 10th, Lincoln City, 97367
Rates: Moderate
Essentials: Credit cards; cribs
Extras: Fireplaces (in some units); TV; Pets OK

This pleasant little motel sits on a bluff west of the busiest section of Lincoln City. A trail leads to the beach. Nearby there is a lake and park. The six units are just what you hope for at a reasonably-priced motel at the beach—clean, comfortable but not fancy. All have a lovely view of the ocean.

The largest unit has two-bedrooms, a knotty-pine-paneled living room, a dining area near a bay window and a fully-furnished kitchen.

PARENT COMMENTS: *"We love the Lincoln City area and this is our favorite place to stay. Very clean and pleasant but not too fancy."*

PLACES TO EAT

OTIS CAFE

503/994-2813; Hwy 18 at Otis Junction
Hours: Breakfast and lunch daily, dinner Fri-Sun
Essentials: Credit cards; highchairs

Otis is two miles off Highway 101 near Lincoln City. The Otis Cafe is a real blast from the past. An old-fashioned diner in size and decor, the cafe is best known for its generous breakfasts, which include a bear-shaped pancake for kids. At lunch and dinner you'll enjoy surprisingly complex soups, juicy burgers (there's a three-ounce version for little ones) and a variety of country-style specials such as chicken-fried steak. Be sure to have some of the delicious brown bread (and some to go, it'll be ages before you get a loaf this good again). The fresh berry shakes and pies are to die for.

Space is at a premium at the cafe, but the place is so delightfully informal that even an active toddler won't ruffle any feathers.

ROAD'S END DORY COVE

503/994-5180; 5819 N Logan Rd, Lincoln City
Hours: Lunch and dinner daily
Essentials: Credit cards; highchairs

There's almost always a line here, but get your name on the list, then walk the beach at the state park next door. Dory Cove is a good place to satisfy diverse tastes: the seafood and chowder are satisfying, the 20 kinds of burgers the answer to a child's dream. Fresh pie a la mode, the dessert of choice, will suit most everyone's taste. The restaurant is small and generally crowded, creating an ambiance befitting the Coast experience. But it may not work well for families with active toddlers.

What to See and Do

Boating at Devil's Lake provides fun diversion from the ocean beach. It is a good-sized freshwater lake located just east of Lincoln City. At **Blue Heron Landing** canoes, bumper boats, paddle boats, aqua bikes, motor boats and any other vessels that float are available to rent.
503/994-4708; 4006 W Devil's Lake Road

Kiteflying is made easy thanks to **Catch the Wind**, the famous kite shop with eight locations on the Oregon coast. You find every size, shape and color kite and windsox imaginable and the staff is eager to suggest which kite will be best for you and give flying tips. The International Fall Kite Festival, held the last weekend in September, attracts kite flyers from all over the world and includes such breathtaking events as kite fights, team-kite choreography, and a lighted night kite fly.
Catch the Wind, 503/996-9500; 266 SE Highway 101. For information about the International Fall Kite Festival call 800/452-2151 or 503/994-3070.

Resources

Lincoln City Chamber of Commerce
3939 NW Hwy 101, PO Box 787, Lincoln City, 97367
800/452-2151 or 503/994-3070

Gleneden
Gleneden is a quiet, upscale coast town put on the map by Salishan Lodge, the major resort nearby.

Places to Stay

Salishan Lodge
800/452-2300 or 503/764-3600

Essentials: Credit cards; cribs
Extras: Restaurants; golf; tennis, indoor pool, whirlpool, sauna,
fitness center; video game arcade; library; playground; nature
trails; childcare; private beach; pets OK

One of Oregon's largest and oldest resorts, Salishan continues
to attract not only conventions but families who want to relax
and recreate on its beautifully landscaped grounds. But don't
expect a beachfront resort or you will be disappointed—the
Salishan private beach is a half-mile away.

Covering over a thousand acres (including a 750-acre forest),
and located on a beautiful stretch of the coast, it is an easy place
to forget the rest of the world for a few days. Kids can play in their
own game room and a good playground, as well as play tennis,
swim in the pool and walk the trails through the woods.

The units are large and comfortably furnished, with brick
fireplaces, balconies and carports.

PARENT COMMENTS: *"Be sure to specify where you want
your room—the resort is very spread out. We were near the golf
course which for a family of non-golfers was unfortunate."*

DEPOE BAY

The harbor at Depoe Bay is the world's smallest. There is a U.S.
Coast Guard base and commercial and charter fishing boats also
take advantage of the sheltered, deep harbor. Located on one of
the most beautiful stretches of the coast, the area has five state
parks with forests, creeks, places for whale watching and magnificent tide pools. Not surprisingly, this picturesque town fills up
fast during July and August.

PLACES TO STAY

INN AT OTTER CREST
503-765-2111; Otter Rock, 97369
Rates: Expensive
Essentials: Credit cards; cribs
Extras: Kitchens; TV; fireplaces, outdoor pool, sauna, hot tub,
miniature golf; playground; game room; laundromat; tennis
(indoor and outdoor); babysitting (by pre-arrangement); organized
activities for children (summer only)

The Inn is 17 miles south of Lincoln City on Highway 101. To
get there take the Otter Crest Scenic Loop off 101. Set in 100
acres of a beautifully landscaped park, this is a place to relax and

soak up the magnificent scenery. On arrival you park your car and are driven to the lodge so the accommodations are surrounded by quiet greenery, not roads. A tram takes you up and down a steep slope to the pool, restaurant and rooms.

The suites are comfortable and include kitchens, fireplaces, and cable TV. There are four tennis courts, an outdoor heated pool, basketball and volleyball. During the summer there are organized activities for children such as nature walks and arts and crafts. Nearby there are lake and stream, golf course and deep-sea fishing and crabbing in the ocean.

As of spring 1995 the restaurant at the Inn was temporarily closed.

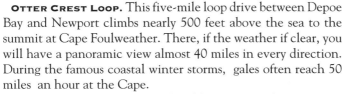 **PARENT COMMENTS:** *"The calm, quiet surroundings were very relaxing. Our children loved riding the tram back and forth and the pool was great."*

"This is a beautiful but expensive way to enjoy the Oregon coast. We had a good time, but decided we prefer the funkier, on-the-beach kind of place when we travel with the kids."

"It was foggy during much of our visit and we felt too far away from the ocean. The organized activities for kids were a nice feature but overall we think Otter Crest is better suited to conventions than family vacations."

WHAT TO SEE AND DO

ALDER BEACH II is a glass blowers' studio where viewers can watch the wondrous process of molten glass being transformed into vases, bowls, paperweights and goblets.
503/996-2483; On Immomen Rd, Gleneden Beach. Daily 9-5.

OTTER CREST LOOP. This five-mile loop drive between Depoe Bay and Newport climbs nearly 500 feet above the sea to the summit at Cape Foulweather. There, if the weather if clear, you will have a panoramic view almost 40 miles in every direction. During the famous coastal winter storms, gales often reach 50 miles an hour at the Cape.

Warning: The road, part of the old Oregon Highway, is very windy and comes close enough to precipitous drops to give the kids a thrill but some drivers may find the drive too harrowing.

THE UNITED STATES COAST GUARD STATION plays an important role in insuring the safety of ocean swimmers and boaters. If you are lucky, when you tour the station you will see Coast Guard personnel practicing their rescue drills. *Located on east side of harbor, Depoe Bay. Hours: Mon-Sat, 4-8 pm, Sun 1-8 pm.*

WHALE WATCHING. Every year, mid-December to February, California gray whales can be spotted off the Oregon and Washington coast migrating from the Arctic south to the warmer waters of Baja. From March to June, whale watchers will see the whales returning to the Arctic for the summer.

About the third week in March, volunteers sit at sites from Astoria to Brookings, spotting whales and answering questions for curious fellow whale watchers. Look for signs that say "Whale Watching Spoken Here." Be sure to bring binoculars and waterproof clothing—it is easy to get drenched by pounding surf. The best time to see the whales is between December and May.

Depoe Bay has one of the best gray whale viewing points on the Oregon coast. Good lookouts are at the Depoe Bay State Park and the Observatory Lookout.

If you want to experience the unforgettable thrill of a close-up view of these massive creatures, there are many companies offering whale watching cruises in both Depoe Bay and Newport. Most run hourly trips when whale sightings are occurring. Ask the host at your lodging or the local Chamber of Commerce to recommend a cruise.

CALENDAR

SEPTEMBER: Indian Salmon Bake

RESOURCES

DEPOE BAY CHAMBER OF COMMERCE
663 SE Hwy 101, PO Box 21, Depoe Bay, 97341
503/765-2889

NEWPORT

Two hours from Portland and situated on beautiful Yaquina Bay, with wide beaches in both directions, Newport is the most popular resort town on the coast. Don't make this busy sprawl your destination if you are looking for a quiet coastal retreat, but several attractions—especially the Oregon Coast Aquarium—are too good to miss. If you stay anywhere in the region, be sure to visit Newport at least once.

GETTING THERE

Once you spot the ocean, it is hard not to let the kids get out of the car for a quick romp. A parent reviewer headed to Newport with a five-year-old and a two-year-old described the following beach stop:

"We stopped at Sand Beach, 15 miles southwest of Tillamook. It is an excellent beach—long and sandy with several sand mountains that people hike up and slide down. Atop the mountain (hill, really) are trails with spectacular views out to the ocean. There are also rocky tide pool with caves. (Don't get caught when the tide comes in!)"

PLACES TO STAY

EMBARCADERO RESORT
503/265-8521; 1000 SE Bay Blvd, Newport, 97365
Rates: Moderate
Essentials: Credit cards; cribs
Extras: Kitchens (in most units); restaurant; indoor pool, hot tub, sauna; boat, crab ring, fishing pole and clam shovel rentals

This is a quiet, comfortable resort. Both hotel rooms and condominium rentals are available. Every room has a private patio with a view of Yaquina Bay and the ocean beyond. The one- and two-bedroom suites have a comfortable living room and dining area, fireplace and fully equipped kitchen.

A wide boardwalk takes you around the end of the Bay past moored boats (available for rent and fishing trips), a small grocery and souvenir shop and the resort's seafood restaurant. Most units are available with kitchens.

PARENT COMMENTS: *"We stayed in a very comfortable, modern, cheerful condo with nautical decorations. It was nice being able to stroll around Yaquina Bay (about 1-1 1/2 miles) to the "Bay Front Area"—touristy but fun with quaint shops and eateries."*
"Our kids enjoyed watching the steady stream of boat traffic from our patio."
"Don't miss the Oregon Coast Aquarium!"

PLACES TO EAT

MO'S RESTAURANT
503/265-2979; 622 SW Bay Blvd, Newport
Hours: Lunch and dinner daily
Essentials: Credit cards; highchairs

More than a place to eat, Mo's is an institution that has become part of the experience of visiting the Oregon coast. This Newport restaurant, located in Old Town, was the first in the chain, which now includes others in Florence, Otter Rock, Lincoln City and Tolovana. The fish and salads are just good; the clam chowder and oyster stew are outstanding. For kids there's the standard fare, including fish and chips, burgers, hotdogs and grilled cheese. All the Mo's Restaurants are busy, noisy places that work well for families. If you arrive extra-hungry, start with a couple orders of the cheese bread. It won't win any health-food contests, but it's a buttery favorite with kids."

WHALE'S TALE
503/265-8660; 452 SW Bay Blvd, Newport
Hours: Breakfast, lunch and dinner daily
Essentials: Credit cards; highchairs
You can count on "the Whale" for an informal, upbeat atmosphere and a thoroughly satisfying meal. Large, fluffy omelettes are breakfast favorites; kids will enjoy the poppyseed pancakes, french toast (breads are homemade on the premises) or homemade granola. Lunch and dinner feature thick, tasty soups, fresh pastas (including a lasagna from heaven) and creative seafood specials. The children's menu offers the requisite hamburger and grilled cheese, but also a tasty fish sandwich and — here's a winner — a peanut butter and banana sandwich. There's no fat-fried food, and no smoking. Also located in Old Town.

WHAT TO SEE AND DO

ELECTRIC BEACH. If you've had enough of the natural wonders and want to plug the kids into some arcade fun, head over to this family entertainment complex that includes a miniature golf course with electrical obstacles, pool and foosball tables and, of course, a video arcade. The snack bar and soda fountain will refuel the kids as needed.
503/265-2200; 424 South Coast Hwy. Daily 10 am-10 pm (summer), 10 am-8 pm (winter).

HATFIELD MARINE SCIENCE CENTER, located south of Newport across the Yaquina Bay Bridge, is a coastal research facility of Oregon State University. It has a small but excellent collection of exhibits including underwater viewing chambers in a natural aquarium and a touch tank that includes a friendly octopus.

503/867-0226; 2030 Marine Science Dr. Open daily 10 am-6 pm in summer, 10 am-4 pm the rest of the year. Donations.

OLD TOWN BY YAQUINA BAY is a good place to take a stroll. Big shellfish steamers are operating right on the sidewalk, and there's a dock from which you can watch the fishing boats bring in and dump their catches.

OREGON COAST AQUARIUM is an outstanding collection of indoor and outdoor marine exhibits. The four acres of outdoor exhibits include an aviary, an underwater cave with an octopus and a rocky pool with sea lions and seals and a big jellyfish tank, outdoor seal and otter caves. This is a must-see on your visit to the coast.

503/867-3123; 2820 SE Ferry Slip Road. Daily 9 am-6 pm, mid-March to mid-Oct; 10 am-4:30 pm, rest of year. Admission $7.75/ adult, $5.50/ youth 13-18, $3.30/child 4-12.

WHALE WATCHING. See Depoe Bay.

KITEFLYING. If you like kites stop at the headquarters of **Catch the Wind Kite Shop** on Hwy 101 north of Newport. They have numerous outlets along the Oregon coast and here you will see some of their more spectacular designs.

YAQUINA BAY LIGHTHOUSE, in Yaquina Bay State Park, was built in 1871. It is open for tours, providing parents a rare opportunity to show their kids a fascinating part of coastal history.

503/867-7451. Daily 11 am-5 pm, June 1-Labor Day; Sat-Sun, noon-4 pm the rest of the year. Donations.

THE WAX WORKS, UNDERSEA GARDENS AND RIPLEY'S BE-LIEVE IT OR NOT are also in Newport. Our parent reviewers reported they are "overpriced tourist attractions not worth the price of admission."

CALENDAR

JULY: Lincoln County Fair and Rodeo

RESOURCES

NEWPORT CHAMBER OF COMMERCE

555 SW Coast Hwy, Newport, 97365
503/265-8801 or 800/824-8486

WALDPORT

This sleepy little fishing town, situated on the Alsea River estuary, calls itself the "Salmon Fishing Capital of the World." There's also an abundance of Dungeness crabs and clams in the Alsea Bay.

PLACES TO STAY

CAPE COD COTTAGES

503/563-2106; 4150 SW Pacific Coast Hwy, Waldport, 97394
Rates: Moderate
Essentials: Credit cards; cribs
Extras: Kitchens; fireplaces, free wood

Kids are more than welcome in these home-style cottages, which sit on a low bank above the beach 2 ½ miles south of Waldport on 300 feet of ocean frontage. Each tidy one- or two-bedroom unit has a fireplace, well-equipped kitchen, deck and picture window overlooking the ocean; some have adjoining garages.

PARENT COMMENTS: *"We love this quiet little town—away from the tourist hustle and bustle of Newport. The kids can frolic on the beach while we sit on our deck and read."*

EDGEWATER COTTAGES

503-563-2240; 8400 Hwy 101, Waldport, 97394
Rates: Inexpensive to moderate
Essentials: Credit cards; cribs
Essentials: Kitchens;TV; Pets OK; Babysitting; by pre-arrangement

This is a lodging on the central Oregon coast that books up early, especially in the summer and all holidays. Comprised of a four-plex, a duplex and several individual cabins, Edgewater is situated on a wonderful expanse of beach. Though it's close to the highway, the focus is definitely towards the beach. Cabins are comfortable, with fireplaces and decent beds, fully stocked kitchens and cable TV.

There's an area of lawn for Frisbee or soccer, and beach access via stairs. An old tree stump on the beach is perfect for playing ship or fort.

Lots of vendors in the harbor at Newport, 15 miles north, sell fresh, live crab—a delicious treat that you can cook in your Edgewater kitchen.

> **PARENT COMMENTS:** *"Edgewater Cottages is a great spot and satisfied all of us, ages 8 months to 10 years and up."*
> *"This is a comfortable place with easy access to a great beach. We like to go to* **Fudge** *in Waldport for a sweet treat."*

WHAT TO SEE AND DO

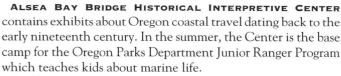

ALSEA BAY BRIDGE HISTORICAL INTERPRETIVE CENTER contains exhibits about Oregon coastal travel dating back to the early nineteenth century. In the summer, the Center is the base camp for the Oregon Parks Department Junior Ranger Program which teaches kids about marine life.

503/563-2002; south end of Alsea Bay Bridge. Daily 9 am-6 pm summer, 9 am-4 pm the rest of the year

HIKING. Just seven miles from the ocean, the nine-square mile **Drift Creek Wilderness** area, part of the Siuslaw National Forest, is a magnificent place to explore. Talk to the Waldport Ranger Station at 503/563-3211 for information about the three trails through the area.

RESOURCES

WALDPORT CHAMBER OF COMMERCE
Highway 101, south end of Alsea Bay Bridge, PO Box 669, Waldport, OR 97394
503/563-2133

YACHATS

This quiet seaside town on the Yachats River is the favorite of several of our parent reviewers drawn by the combination of breathtaking natural beauty and good restaurants and lodging far from the crowds.

PLACES TO STAY

FIRESIDE MOTEL
503/547-3636, 800/336-3573; 1881 Hwy 101 N, Yachats, 97498
Rates: Inexpensive

Essentials: Credit cards; cribs
Extras: TV, VCR (some units); convenience refrigerators;
fireplaces (some units); whirlpools (some units); pets OK
This is a no-frills spot, but it offers amenities for families. The 43-unit motel is set well back from the highway, partially secluded by landscaping. Request a unit with a deck overlooking the ocean, as these provide extra space and privacy. The Fireside maintains a lovely walking trail along the beach, where families may picnic, enjoy beach fires or, in late summer, harvest berries.

PARENT COMMENTS: *"The folks who run the place have kids of their own, and really made us feel comfortable. They also knew good places to take kids in the area."*

SHAMROCK LODGETTES
503/547-3312; 105 Hwy 101 S, Yachats
Rates: Moderate
Essentials: Credit cards; cribs
Extras: TV, free movies; kitchens (some units); fireplaces, free wood; sauna, hot tub, exercise room; pets OK
The Shamrock is beautifully set at the southern end of town, where the Yachats River meets the ocean. Modern motel units and cottages are available and both offer lovely ocean and/or river views. The motel units are nicely appointed, each with fireplace and deck.

But the rustic cottages, with adjoining carports, offer an ambiance more befitting a visit to the coast. They are situated to afford privacy, have separate bedrooms and well-equipped kitchens. The grounds are nicely landscaped and maintained. A large indoor hot tub, sauna and exercise room are centrally located.

PARENT COMMENTS: *"My husband and I felt comfortable letting our kids go back and forth to the beach without much supervision. The owners seemed genuinely pleased to have them around."*
"Sometimes it's the little things that count. We appreciated the newspaper dropped at our doorstep each morning."

PLACES TO EAT

LA SERRE RESTAURANT
503/547-3420; 160 W 2nd, Yachats
Hours: Dinner daily, breakfast Sun, July-Sept Winter hours vary
Essentials: Credit cards; highchairs

"La Serre" means "the greenhouse" and this light, airy restaurant lives up to the name. This is a safe bet for fresh seafood prepared with imagination and for specialty Italian fare (including a particularly tasty cioppino). The chef is health-conscious in all offerings, and willing to prepare special dishes for vegetarians. But the best trick in their book is the "children's corner" menu: a "baby distraction plate" of crackers, fresh fruit and cookie and a choice of catch-of-the-day or pasta meal for kids under 12.

WHAT TO SEE AND DO

CAPE PERPETUA. One of our parent reviewers called Cape Perpetua, three miles south of Yachats, "my favorite stop on the Oregon Coast." Stop in first at the Visitor's Center. You needn't be a geologist to find yourself fascinated with "Discovery at the Edge," a 15-minute film describing the natural forces that formed the coastline. You can also get assistance with hiking trails; there are some easy ones that kids can enjoy.

Then drive or hike up the 800-foot cape to the highest point on the Oregon Coast. From the top there's a dramatic view of the jutting coastline to the south. From the viewpoint, a short, easy trail affords ocean views south and north, takes a circular route through a gorgeous coastal woodland and arrives back at the parking lot.

Down below again, stop at nearby **Devil's Churn** and take the short walk down to the rocky observation point. It's especially magnificent on a stormy day. Several hiking trails begin here, and the tidepools are spectacular at low tide.

Three miles south of Yachats on Highway 101. 503/547-3289. Visitor Center open daily, 9 am-5 pm, Memorial Day-Labor Day.

RESOURCES

YACHATS CHAMBER OF COMMERCE
441 Hwy 101, PO Box 174, Yachats, 97498
503/547-3530

FLORENCE

Dunes, dunes, dunes are what lure most families to the Florence area. From here and south for 50 miles the rugged northern coastline is replaced by rolling sand dunes, some of them 600 feet high. And if you can pull the kids out of the sand, strolling through charming Old Town is fun.

PLACES TO STAY

DRIFTWOOD SHORES
503-997-8263; 88416 First Ave, Florence, 97439
Rates: Moderate to expensive
Essentials: Credit cards; cribs
Extras: Kitchens; TV; restaurant; indoor pool, sauna, hot tub

This oceanfront resort motel on the south central coast, located four miles north of Florence and west of US. 101 along Heceta Beach Rd, is exceptional because it is right on the beach. It has 136 units, of which 25 are three-bedroom units and 21 are two-bedroom units. Most have kitchens, lots have fireplaces (and firewood), and some suites come with two bathrooms. It's comfortable and clean, but not fancy. Decks overlook the beach, which is lovely and long. In rainy weather or when the beach is cold, it's nice to be able to fall back on the indoor swimming facilities. There's a laundromat on the premises to dry wet bathing suits.

The restaurant at Driftwood Shores has moderate prices and satisfactory food and a spectacular view. They've got highchairs and the service is good.

PARENT COMMENTS: *"This was a relaxing place with just enough diversion to keep everyone from getting tired of the beach. We did spend hours and hours on the long stretches of sandy, driftwood-strewn beach and loved it."*
"The staff was friendly and accommodating. It was wonderful to be able to walk out the door onto the beach."

PLACES TO EAT

BLUE HEN CAFE
503/997-3907; 1675 Hwy 101 N, Florence
Hours: Breakfast, lunch and dinner
Essentials: Credit cards; highchairs

Delicious fried chicken with mashed potatoes, homemade pies, and pasta and burgers for the non-chicken eaters. The Hen offers cheerful service, generous servings and reasonable prices.

WINDWARD INN
503/997-8243; one mile north of Florence on Hwy 101
Hours: Lunch, breakfast, dinner
Essentials: Credit cards; highchairs

The selection of fresh seafood is outstanding at this attractive restaurant, as well as the homemade desserts. There is a gift shop in the restaurant and a new courtyard.

WHAT TO SEE AND DO

THE SEA LION CAVES are 11 miles north of Florence. This is the only year-round home for wild sea lions on the mainland, and the honking, rollicking, slippery sea lions are an amusing sight. The sea lions are not held captive here; they are wild and choose this giant sea grotto as their home. Visitors descend in an elevator to a 1,500-foot-long cavern full of barking and roaring sea lions.

Open from 8 am to dusk daily, July-August; 9 am-dusk, rest of year. Admission $6 for adults, $4 ages 6 to 15.

THE OREGON DUNES NATIONAL RECREATION AREA, operated by the U.S. Forest Service, encompasses a 40-mile stretch of sand dunes with sand hills hundreds of feet high. Here visitors are treated to some of the most scenic stretches of coastline in the world. Before setting the kids loose to romp and roll in this giant playground, stop at the Dune Recreation Area Headquarters on Highway 101 just south of the Umpqua Bridge in Reedsport. You'll learn about the dunes, including which areas have the least amount of dune buggy traffic, and find out about summer programs.

503/271-3611. Open daily in summer, Mon-Fri the rest of the year.

SANDLAND ADVENTURES, one mile south of Florence on Highway 101, features dune buggy rides to the top of the South Jetty Dunes near the Siuslaw River. Four-wheelers are also available. If you are under 16 you must be accompanied by an adult. Drivers under 18 are not permitted on four-wheelers.

There's also a go-kart track and bumper boats here.

503/997-8087; Sandland open 9 am-7:30 pm daily, June 1 to Labor Day; 9 am-5 pm rest of year. Rental fee $30-$35. Dune buggy guided tours also available for $15-$25.

SEAHORSE STAGECOACH transports riders back to the mode of coast travel most common in the early part of this century— along the beach. Riders climb in the 16-passenger coach (heated during the winter with an on-board wood stove) and are whisked away by three Percheron draft horses. The trip along the packed, wet sand lasts about an hour.

503/999-0319. Sea coaches rides by reservation only. Cost: $5/ adults; $3 under 14.

THE SOUTH SLOUGH SANCTUARY at Coos Bay is an interesting diversion from the coast scenery and getting there is a beautiful drive. The sanctuary protects over 4,400 acres of estuaries and flats.

503/888-4448. Turn off Cape Arago Hwy onto Seven Devils Rd. and travel four miles to the new visitors center and headquarters for information about the hiking trails and the ecology of the area. Open daily 8:30 am-4:30 pm during the summer, Mon-Fri the rest of the year. Free.

RESOURCES

FLORENCE CHAMBER OF COMMERCE
270 Hwy 101, PO Box 26000, Florence, 997439
503/997-3128

GOLD BEACH

The area's main attraction is the Rogue, a designated wild and scenic river. Most visitors come to fish, jet boat and raft the river but Gold Beach also provides access to the beautiful hiking trails of the Kalmiopsis Wilderness and Siskiyou National Forest.

PLACES TO STAY

TU TU TUN LODGE
503/247-6664; 96550 North Bank Rogue, Gold Beach, 97444
Rates: Expensive
Essentials: Credit cards; cribs
Extras: Dining room; outdoor lap pool; 4-hole pitch-and-putt course; pond; pets OK except July and August

Tu Tu Tun Lodge is not an ocean resort. It sits on the Rogue River, seven miles from the coastal town of Gold Beach. Two houses, the Garden House, with three bedrooms and the new River House with two-bedrooms are ideal for families but the less expensive River View rooms with two queen beds, a soaking tub and a patio are also very nice. The suites are more spacious and deluxe.

Three meals a day are available in the dining room by reservation only. Before dinner there is a "get-together" with all the guests. Appetizers and drinks are served. Kids are welcomed and given soft drinks. The meals are excellent but expensive. If kids don't care for the adult menu, the staff will gladly cook up your child's favorite fare.

PARENT COMMENTS: *"There is nothing negative to say about the Lodge. The owners greet you by name, make sure the children feel at home by providing games, letting them play on the Par-3 golf course, etc. The "cocktail hour" every night before dinner includes kids and it is a great way to meet other guests."*

WHAT TO SEE AND DO

HIKING. For information about trails into the Kalmiopsis Wilderness or the Siskiyou National Forest, contact the Gold Beach Ranger District, 1225 Ellensburg, Gold Beach 97444, 503/247-6651.

JET BOAT TRIPS are an unforgettable experience that will thrill all ages. Guides relate the area's rich natural history and point out the abundant wildlife as you are whisked 64 to 104 miles up the Rogue.

Rogue River Reservations, (503)247-6504 or 800/525-2161 is a central booking agency for jet boat and river rafting trips on the Rogue.

THE ROGUE-PACIFIC INTERPRETIVE CENTER offers educational and recreational activities highlighting the rich natural environment. Programs for the entire family include tidepooling expeditions, clam digging, exploring early gold mines and studying forest wildlife.

503/247-6023; 510 Colvin St, Gold Beach.

RESOURCES

GOLD BEACH CHAMBER OF COMMERCE
510 S Ellensburg, PO Box 55, Gold Beach, 97444
800/525-2334 or 503/247-7526

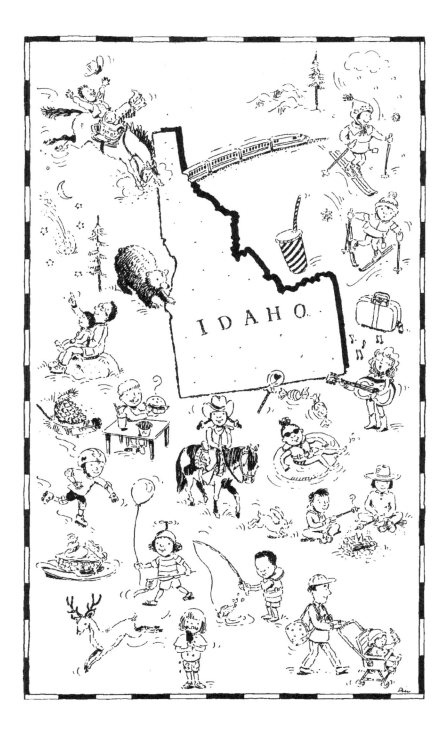

IDAHO

COEUR D'ALENE

Flanked by two outstanding skiing mountains and on the shores of one of the most beautiful freshwater lakes in the country, it's no surprise that Coeur d'Alene is such a popular resort town. The top-rated Coeur d'Alene Resort on the Lake is the center of the action, both for summer and winter recreation.

GETTING THERE

Coeur d'Alene, Idaho, is just 33 miles east of Spokane on I-90. It is about 306 miles from Seattle, 396 miles from Portland. Many visitors from Seattle, Portland and beyond fly into Spokane and drive to the resort.

ROADSIDE ATTRACTIONS. While the drive from Spokane to Coeur d'Alene is quite short, a stop in Post Falls, Idaho, 24 miles east of Spokane, offers several interesting attractions. Begin by taking Exit 2 off I-90 and visiting the Factory Outlet Mall. Several children's clothing stores and a toy store are of particular interest to families.

In Post Falls there's Treaty Rock, on which petroglyphs and pictographs describe the purchase of land from the Coeur d'Alene Indians over 100 years ago (Exit 5 from I-90; turn right on Spokane S., then right on 4th Ave). Nearby at Falls Park on the Spokane River, there are picnic tables, a sandy beach, and a restroom, along with a good view of the waterfall created by Post Falls Dam.

See also Spokane for ideas on interesting stops along the way.

REFUELING. See Spokane for ideas about places to eat along the way.

PLACES TO STAY

COEUR D'ALENE RESORT
208/765-4000 or 800/826-2390; 2nd and Front St, Coeur d'Alene, 83814-1088
Rates: Expensive
Essentials: Credit cards; cribs
Extras: Restaurants (4); indoor and outdoor pools, sauna; bowling; racquetball; indoor and outdoor golf, TV; childcare; organized activities for kids; ski packages; shuttle to ski areas; cross-country skiing

There are two schools of thought about this huge (over 300

rooms) resort that spreads along the shores of the lake. One opinion holds that it is a monstrous testimony to overdevelopment that has overpowered a pretty little town and destroyed its beautiful natural surroundings. The other view is that it is a grand resort that is a fabulous place to take a vacation. Rated the top resort in the world in 1990 by Conde Nast, it is recommended by many as the place to go for a true resort experience: plenty of amenities, indoor and outdoor activities, shopping nearby. At least one thing is certain: with the exceptionally good assortment of activities offered in summer and winter, both by the resort and the surrounding community, a family with a variety of ages and interests should find something here to suit everybody.

In the summer there is so much to do right at the resort, it is easy to stay put. However, should you want to go horseback riding, river rafting, jet skiing, mountain biking, hiking or skating, the hotel will gladly make arrangements for you.

In the winter, Coeur d'Alene offers a good deal for skiing families. Their stay-and-ski-free package allows kids ages 17 and under to ski free at both Silver Mountain and Schweitzer, stay free (in their parents' room), ride free on the ski shuttle to the mountains and eat a free continental breakfast.

Kids are also given special treatment in the Very Important Kids (V.I.K.) program, with half- or full-day activities for ages four to 14. The program is available every day from March to November and weekends during the winter. Activities in the summer program include hikes, arts and crafts, scavenger hunts, bowling, swimming, sandcastle building and water games. In the winter, in addition to the indoor activities, kids may cross-country or downhill ski, skate and play in the snow. Meals are also included. Cost is $18 for four hours for the first child and $15 for additional children and for a full (7-hour) day the cost is $30 for the first child and $25 for each additional child. Reservations 24 hours in advance are required.

All four restaurants at the resort have highchairs and all but the fanciest—Beverly's—have a children's menu. The Tito Macaroni works well for families—delicious pizza and fresh homemade pasta are served in a fun setting (there's a full-sized pickup truck in the middle of the restaurant).

Note: Like many large resorts, off-season discounts and package deals offer significant savings at Coeur d'Alene. If you are considering a visit, inquire carefully about the price options available.

 **PARENT COMMENTS:** *"Gorgeous, very clean and comfortable. The stay-and-ski-free package for kids is a great deal!"*

"The holiday season is the best time to visit—sleigh rides, festive decorations, beautiful scenery, great ski packages."

"We stopped for two days on our way to Montana in July. We had a very relaxing stay. Service was excellent."

"Tito's was the perfect place for us to eat with a 2-year-old, 6-year-old and 15-year-old. You can watch the pizza being made—good entertainment for hungry kids."

HOUSEBOAT RENTALS are available on Lake Coeur d'Alene through Northwest Travel and Recreation. Rates vary from a $550 four-day mid-week package to $1,390 for a full week on the biggest boats during the peak summer season.

509/535-6422; PO Box 2586, Spokane, WA, 99220

PLACES TO EAT

HUDSON'S HAMBURGERS

208/664-5444; 207 Sherman Ave
Hours: Lunch and dinner (until 6 pm)

As anybody who likes a good burger knows—there's all the difference between the fast-food version and the real thing. At Hudson's the patties are made up fresh while you wait and that is just the start of the careful attention given to producing a juicy, fabulous burger. They also make great pies. Customers sit at bar stools at a counter—no highchairs available.

THIRD STREET CANTINA

208/664-0581; 201 N 3rd
Hours: Lunch and dinner
Essentials: Credit cards; highchairs

This cheery Mexican restaurant is just one mile from the Coeur d'Alene Resort. The atmosphere is lively and fun and the food good—interesting and quite spicy as opposed to bland American-style.

WHAT TO SEE AND DO

BOATING. During the summer canoes, kayaks and paddle boats are available for rent at North Shore Rentals at Independence Point at City Park.

North Shore Rentals: 208/664-1175

GONDOLA RIDE. Don't miss the chance to take the world's longest gondola ride at Silver Mountain. It takes just 19 minutes to travel the 3.1-mile span from the city of Kellogg to the Silver Mountain Ski area. Even if you don't ski, in the winter you can ride to the top to enjoy the view and a meal in a variety of restaurants. In the summer, numerous hikes begin from the top of the chair (trail maps available at the gondola terminal.) *208/783-1111. Silver Mountain is just off Interstate 90 at Kellogg. To reach the gondola base, take the Bunker Hill Exit 49.*

HIKING. The area around Coeur d'Alene is laced with good hiking trails. Ask at the Coeur d'Alene Visitors Center or the Fernan Ranger District (208/765-7381) for advice about trails in the Idaho Panhandle National Forest.

See also Sandpoint/Schweitzer: What to See and Do

For a fun walk right in town, take the two-mile loop **Tubs Hill Nature Preserve Trail**. You'll get a great view of the lake and the hillside. The trail is steep and rocky in some places so wear comfortable shoes. You can get a Tubs Hill Nature Trail brochure at the Chamber of Commerce.

Trail begins and ends at the south end of the parking lot of Front St (between Third and Fourth St) in Coeur d'Alene.

Mineral Ridge Trail is another good walk for young hikers. The 3.3 mile trail has 22 numbered stations identifying natural features of Mineral Ridge. The trail climbs 735 feet to an elevation of 2,874 feet, providing an excellent view of the lake and nearby mountains.

Take Exit 22 off I-90 (just east of Coeur d'Alene), then go south on I-97 to Beauty Bay Recreational Area.

LAKE CRUISES are offered by the Resort at Coeur d'Alene several times a day. The departure dock is west of the resort at Independence Point. On the 90-minute cruise you'll see the famous floating 14th hole of the resort's golf course

Cruises depart May thru October several times daily. $9.75 (adults); $5.75 (10 and under). Also dinner and Sunday brunch cruises.

NORTH IDAHO HISTORY EXCURSION. Head east on I-90 and experience some of north Idaho's colorful history.

Thirty-nine miles east of Coeur d'Alene take Exit 39 to see **Old Mission State Park.** Self-guided tours and nature trails are available on the 19 acres. Be sure to show the youngsters the **Mission of the Sacred Heart.** It is Idaho's oldest building, built completely without nails by the Coeur d'Alene Indians in the mid-1800s.. The visitor center at the park does a good job telling the colorful tale of early inland Northwest history.

208/682-3814. Open daily June-Aug, 8 am-6 pm; Sept-May, 9 am-5 pm. No admission, $2 parking.

Near Exit 43, you've entered the **Silver Valley**, (also known as "Coeur d'Alene Mining District,") the world's richest silver mining area. The environmental devastation caused by years of mining is very visible on this stretch of the highway.

The town of **Kellogg**, off Exit 49, is home to the Silver Mountain ski area with the country's longest gondola ride (open year-round, see Gondola Ride above for details). Also in Kellogg is the Memorial to the Sunshine Miners, which commemorates the 1972 Sunshine Mine fire that took the lives of 91 miners.

Another mining town, Wallace, is off Exit 61 and features some interesting museums, including the **Wallace District Mining Museum** (509 Bank St; 208/753-7151) and the **Northern Pacific Department Railroad Museum** (219 Sixth St, 208/786-4141). Both are open year-round.

Next to the mining museum you can buy tickets for the **Sierra Silver Mine Tour**, an hour-long tour into a real silver mine. Tourists are taken in the mine by vehicle. On a walk of about 1,000 feet you will see mining equipment and methods used to mine the silver ore. Kids under four aren't allowed on the tour due to the loud noise of the machinery.

208/752-5151; Tours every 20 min, 9 am to 4 pm daily during summer. Adults $7; $6 for ages 4-16. Family pass: $26 for two adults and two or more kids. For a brochure write to PO Box 712, Wallace, Idaho 83873

About 26 miles up the road from Wallace (north on Highway 456), visit Murray—North Idaho's "living ghost town". (The population has dropped from 15,000 to 60). Try your hand at panning for gold at the **Bedroom Gold Mine Bar** (208/682-4394). Cost is $5 to pan all day or they will cut you a deal if you want to try your luck for a shorter time. .

PARKS. City Park, just west of the Resort has boat rentals, a big sandy beach and a swimming area. A walking/biking/skating/ wheelchair pathway along the lake's shore connects this park with the four other lakefront city parks.

SILVERWOOD THEME PARK. See Spokane: Excursions.

SKIING CROSS-COUNTRY. When the city is snow-covered, there are trails nearby (including at the resort) for skiing. Up near Sandpoint, Farragut State Park has numerous cross-country trails as does Round Lake Park and Schweitzer Mountain. Ask at the resort for details.

SKIING DOWNHILL. Silver Mountain and Schweitzer both offer excellent skiing and good programs for kids. If you are staying in Coeur d'Alene, Silver Mountain will likely be where you spend most of your time skiing, just because the hour drive to Schweitzer is a bother.

Silver Mountain offers a good mix of runs, 60% at the beginner and intermediate levels. Kids will enjoy the ride on the "world's longest gondola." Skiing and snowboarding lessons are available for all ages; there's also childcare for ages two to six that includes snow play and skiing ($20/half-day; $30/all-day).

208/783-1111

WILD WATERS WATERSLIDE THEME PARK. If the kids have had enough of the lake but still need to be cooled off, take them to slip and slide for a few hours.

208/667-6491; Intersection of I-90 and Hwy 95. Open 11 am to 7 pm, weather permiitting during summer months. Cost: $12/Adult, $7/children under 12 $. After 4 pm everyone pays $7.

CALENDAR

JULY-AUGUST: Art on the Green
DECEMBER: Coeur d'Alene Christmas, at the Resort

RESOURCES

BABY YOUR BABY HOTLINE
1-800-926-2588

FERNAN RANGER DISTRICT
2502 E. Sherman Ave, Coeur d'Alene 83816
208/765-7381

GREATER COEUR D'ALENE VISITORS CENTER
202 Sherman Ave, PO Box 850, Coeur d'Alene 83816
800/232-4968 or 208/664-0587

TUNE IN TO CHANNEL 13 on cable TV for the "What to Do Channel" highlighting local activities and attractions

SKI CONDITIONS
Schweitzer Mountain Resort 208/263-9555

Silver Mountain, 208/783-1111

SANDPOINT/SCHWEITZER

On the shores of beautiful Lake Pend Oreille and a mere 20-minute drive from world-renowned Schweitzer Mountain Resort, Sandpoint, Idaho is a delightful little town to visit any time of the year. Unlike the more developed Coeur d'Alene, where the resort has taken over a considerable part of the shoreline, in Sandpoint a quarter mile of sandy beach is city park.

There's plenty of outdoor activity year-round in the Sandpoint area—from ice skating, ice fishing, skiing, snowshoeing, sledding and sleigh rides in the winter to fishing, biking, hiking, camping, swimming, boating, water skiing and rollerblading in the summer. Although there are accommodations at the mountain, many skiing families prefer to stay in this pleasant town and make the quick 9-mile drive to the slopes.

GETTING THERE

Sandpoint is reached from Spokane by traveling I-90 east to I-95 (at Coeur d'Alene) then traveling north one hour. It is about a 90 minute drive. Many visitors from Seattle, Portland and beyond fly into Spokane and drive to the ski resort.

Amtrak service is also available to Sandpoint, but the train arrives from the west at 3 in the morning.

ROADSIDE ATTRACTIONS. On I-95 the sight of Silverwood Theme Park will beckon to the kids, but this is not a "quick stop," so save it for a full day trip. (see Spokane: Excursions).

Instead, if you need a road stop turn east off Highway 95 onto State Highway 54 ("Idaho's shortest state highway') and continue to **Farragut Sate Park**. There you will find a museum that tells about Farragut' s earlier days, including World War II when it was the second largest Naval Training center. Located at the southern tip of Lake Pend Oreille, the park has a protected swimming area, sandy beach, hiking and biking trails. In the winter, cross-country skiing, sledding and showshoeing are popular.

208/683-2425 for information. There is a $2/day charge per vehicle .

PLACES TO STAY

LAKESIDE INN

800/543-8126 or 208/263-3717; 106 Bridge St, Sandpoint, 83864

Rates: Inexpensive to moderate
Essentials: Credit cards; cribs
Extras: Free continental breakfast; kitchenettes; Jacuzzi (indoor and outdoor),TV; pets OK

The Lakeside sits right next to the large city park on the lake and rooms are comfortable and clean. Some units have a stove and refrigerator. Ask for a room with a view. Kids under 12 stay free.

 PARENT COMMENTS: *"The nicest motel in Sandpoint with a good location next to the city park."*

MONARCH WEST LODGE
208/263-1222 or 800/543-8193; Hwy 95 N, PO Box 3171, Sandpoint, 83864

Rates: Inexpensive
Essentials: Credit cards; cribs
Extras: Continental breakfast, three hot tubs, sauna, shuttle service available

The Monarch West is just one mile north of Sandpoint by the Schweitzer Mountain turn-off. The free continental breakfasts include rolls, juice, fruit, bagels and cream cheese, etc. The friendly staff go out of their way to make families feel welcome.

 PARENT COMMENTS: *"A comfortable place. The staff was very helpful and nice to our kids."*

QUALITY INN SANDPOINT
800/635-2534 or 208/263-2111; 807 N 5th Ave (I-95)

Rates: Inexpensive to moderate
Essentials: Credit cards; cribs
Extras: Indoor pool, Jacuzzi, restaurant; TV; pets OK

This is the only motel in town that has an indoor pool. Kids under 17 stay free. Conveniently located on I-95 at the north end of town, accommodations are clean and comfortable.

PARENT COMMENTS: *"In the summer, with the refreshing lake swimming nearby, the indoor pool might not be very important but after a day on the ski slopes, the pool was a nice place for the kids to spend the evening."*

GREEN GABLES LODGE

208/265-0257 or 800/831-8810
Rates: Moderate to expensive
Essentials: Credit cards; highchairs
Extras: Efficiency kitchens in some units; restaurant; outdoor pool
(as of August 1995), Jacuzzi (two, outdoors); TV; laundry
facilities
   Green Gables Lodge is the heart of the $100 million expansion
currently taking place at Schweitzer. The native stone and white
pine, four-story hotel offers lovely views of Lake Pend Oreille and
the surrounding mountains. The efficiency kitchens available in
some suites have a small refrigerator, microwave ovens, toasters,
and coffee makers. No utensils or dishes are provided.
   Schweitzer Mountain Resort works hard to attract families.
Daycare is available for infants and toddlers. Kinder Kamp, for
three- to six-year olds, keeps kids busy with art projects, games
and a ski lesson in the resort's Enchanted Forest (ski area for kids
only). Mogul Mice, a full-day ski program caters to kids ages five
to eleven.

PARENT COMMENTS: *"We liked staying right at the mountain*
at this fabulous ski area. The program for our kids—ages four
and eight—was excellent."

PLACES TO EAT

THE CUPBOARD
208/263-9012; 116 N Second Ave
   Locals tell us the food is wholesome, delicious and creatively
prepared at this popular spot with a Greek twist. Quick service
and kid-friendly, too!

THE FLOATING RESTAURANT
208/264-5311; Hope, Idaho
Hours: Lunch, dinner, Sunday brunch
Essentials: Credit cards; highchairs
   This charming restaurant sits on Lake Pend Oreille in the tiny
town of Hope, just outside Sandpoint. In the summer there's
outdoor dining next to the water. Dishes include Penn Cove
mussels, fresh seafood, pasta and excellent salads. Our parent
reviewer called The Floating Restaurant the "best place to eat in
the area."

SECOND AVENUE PIZZA
208/263-9321; 215 S Second

Our parent reviewer described the pizza as "the best they have ever eaten—anywhere."

WHAT TO SEE AND DO

STROLLING AND BROWSING through Sandpoint doesn't take long—it is a small town. But there's plenty to see on its few main blocks—including art galleries and antique shops. Kids in your car looking for souvenirs or a beading project for the ride home should check out the **Little Bear Trading Company** (324 N First Ave). This little shop claims to have the largest supply of beads and bead supplies in the Northwest!

At the **Cedar St. Bridge Public Market**, a shopping mall built on the bridge over Sand Creek, there are little shops selling games, books, Native American artwork, clothing, ice cream and candy.

If you want to walk outside town to get a look at the magnificent surroundings, stroll the mile-long **Pedestrian Long Bridge** located just south of the city limits. It spans Lake Pend Oreille and offers great views of the lake and the Selkirk Mountains.

THE ARTS AND CRAFTS FAIR, usually the second weekend in August, features 100 booths of works by artists and crafts people from throughout the western states and Canada. Held on the lawn at City Beach, there's also live music and food booths provided by the best restaurants in town. *Call 208/263-6139, Pend Oreille Arts Council, for more information.*

FESTIVAL AT SANDPOINT is a three-week music fest in late July and August with national acts performing country, blues, rock, symphony and big band concerts. Call 208/263-6858 for performance schedules.

SKIING. Schweitzer Mountain Resort, about nine miles (a 20-minute drive) above Sandpoint, recently completed the first stage of its $100 million-plus expansion. It is is a full-service resort with on-mountain lodging (see Green Gables Lodge above). With 2,350 skiable acres, two magnificent bowls with 2,400 feet of vertical drop and 300-plus inches average snow, it offers some of the finest skiing in the West. And with the wide range of runs—20% beginner, 50% intermediate, 25% advanced, 5% expert, a family with a variety of skiing skills should be happy. Childcare is available at the slopes, as well as ski instruction for all ages. A free regular shuttle service links the

condominiums at Schweitzer, ski facilities and the town of Sandpoint.
800/831-8810

HIKING AND BIKING. There is a massive ridge at Schweitzer called the Great Divide. It splits the ski area into two alpine basins—the North and South bowls. In the summer one can hike along the Great Divide by taking the Great Escape chair lift to the top of Schweitzer Peak. The 1,500 foot rise in elevation has breathtaking lake and mountain views. The two-mile-long trail on the ridge top affords sweeping views of Lake Pend Oreille and the Panhandle Although the trail is two miles and all downhill, allow three hours and bring along water. Trail maps are available free at the shops at the resort.

Mountain biking along the 8 kilometers of forest roads on the northwest end of the Schweitzer village is also popular. The more advanced riders take their bikes up the Great Escape lift and ride the Kamikaze Trail down. Rental bikes available at the resort.

Great Escape Chair lift, adults $7; 18 and under $5; Family (up to four) $20.

SKATING. Depending on the weather, there may be a city-maintained ice skating area at City Beach near the boat ramps. Another outdoor skating area is at Round Lake State park (10 miles south, take I-95 south; at Dufort Road, turn right and continue for 2 miles).

Skate rentals are available at The Outdoor Experience in Sandpoint, 208/263-6028.

CALENDAR

AUGUST: Arts and Crafts Fair
Festival at Sandpoint
JANUARY: Winter Carnival

RESOURCES

SANDPOINT CHAMBER OF COMMERCE
800/800-2106

SANDPOINT CENTRAL RESERVATIONS SERVICE
800/876-8921
Free service that arranges accommodations, shuttle service from Coeur d'Alene airports and Amtrak, and ski packages.

SCHWEITZER MOUNTAIN RESORT
800/831-8810

PRIEST LAKE

It is a long drive from Seattle to the lakes and forests of the Idaho panhandle (six to eight hours depending on stops), but that does not diminish the enthusiasm families have for this corner of the Pacific Northwest. From the Fourth of July until Labor Day it offers the optimum conditions for a summer vacation. Weather is hot and sunny. Priest Lake is a large, deep, clear, body of water noted for its fine sandy beaches and many miles of surrounding Forest Service hiking trails. In the winter cross-country skiing, snowshoeing and snowmobiling are popular. Upper Priest Lake can be reached only by boat or hiking. It is very remote and has no cabins and resorts.

GETTING THERE
Take Interstate 90 to Spokane. From Spokane follow Highway 2 to Newport and Priest River. Turn north on Highway 57 at Priest River to Nordman and Priest Lake.

ROADSIDE ATTRACTIONS. See Snoqualmie Pass, Cle Elum and Spokane for interesting stops along the way.

PLACES TO STAY

ELKINS RESORT
208/443-2432; PO Box 40, Route 1, Nordman, 83848
Rates: Moderate
Essentials: Credit cards; cribs
Extras: Restaurant; kitchens; boat rentals; cross-country ski rentals
At Elkins Resort, you stay in rustic log cabins on a bluff overlooking Priest Lake. Cabins have kitchens and baths and are situated for privacy. Elkins is an old-fashioned resort (it's been around for more than 30 years) that caters mainly to families. The chances are good that your children will find others to pal around with.

The beach at the resort is nice and sandy. Access to the beach is via trails from the bluff (about 100 feet). Swimming, canoeing, huckleberry picking and hiking are typical warm-weather activities. Elkins is in the mountains, and weather can be variable, with occasional exciting thunder showers and rainbows.

There is a small store with groceries and gift items. The restaurant at the lodge will come in handy if you don't want to cook all your meals in the cabin kitchen. Prices are moderate, food good and children are well tolerated.

PARENT COMMENTS: *"The lake is COLD until after July 1."* *"We generally "hit the beach" on nice days to canoe, swim and read, or we hiked if the weather is cloudy. Our kids were ages eight and ten. This resort is best for families with children above age 5. Younger kids would need to be watched constantly at the lake —no lifeguard— and might not enjoy the hiking."* *"There is the lake and hiking and that's about it. Our sons spent most of their time trying to learn to sailboard and waterski and we took two long hikes during the week we were at Elkins. It was an ideal vacation for us except next year we will make it two weeks."*

HILL'S RESORT
208/443-2551; PO 162A, Route 5, Priest Lake, 83856
Rates: Moderate
Essentials: Credit cards; cribs
Extras: Kitchens, restaurant, tennis courts; fishing rentals; boat rentals; babysitting (by pre-arrangement); pets OK

There are about 50 units of various sizes and with various arrangements at Hill's ranging from one-bedroom housekeeping units that sleep two to three-bedroom cabins that sleep 10, but the best deal for families is the less-expensive housekeeping cabins. They don't have fireplaces or views, but you don't really need these, as all cabins let you see a little of the lake and are close to the water. The beach has numerous places to have a fire.

Hill's a family-oriented and family-run resort. Most guests have been coming back for years and kids typically outnumber adults. It is an easy place to make friends.

Unless you come for cross-country skiing in the winter, July and August are the best months to visit. Days are long and Priest Lake has had a chance to warm up a little. It's a good lake for water sports and the beach is huge, sandy and picturesque. On Monday nights, there are movies on the beach, on Thursdays family barbecue.

There is a dining room at Hill's which is quite nice; if you take children, go early. They do have booster seats and high chairs. There is no children's menu, but they have hamburgers and chicken and are willing to split an order. Another option is to go 20 miles north to Elkins Resort, where the eating situation is similar but cozier, and where there's a children's menu.

WHAT TO SEE AND DO

HUCKLEBERRY picking is one of the distinctive treats of summer vacationing in this part of the country. These berries are scare in markets and it is lots of fun for the family to pick them, eat them heartily and take large quantities home to freeze. The local ranger station will tell you where the picking is good.

PRIEST LAKE MUSEUM AND VISITORS CENTER. The purpose of the Museum/Visitors Center is to dispense information about recreational opportunities within the National Forest and to exhibit interpretive historical displays about Priest Lake's past. It is housed in a log cabin that was built by the Civilian Conservation Corps (CCC) for the Forest Service in 1935. The cabin is a prime example of hand-crafted oil-treated tamarack log construction. Inside are two rooms equipped as they might have been in the 1930s.

208/443-2676. To get there drive 32 miles north from Priest River on Highway 57. Turn right at Luby Bay Road. Turn left on Lakeshore Road. Proceed 1/4 mile. Open 10 am-4 pm in the summer.

Free.

RESOURCES

PRIEST LAKE CHAMBER OF COMMERCE
PO Box 174, Coolin, Idaho 83821-0174
208/292-6233

PRIEST LAKE RANGER DISTRICT
Rt 5, Box 207, Priest River, Idaho 83856
208/443-2512
Contact for information about hiking and camping in the Priest Lake area.

VANCOUVER

With its unique blend of cosmopolitan excitement and relaxed style, Vancouver is a veritable gold mine for vacationing families. As Canada's gateway to the Pacific Rim, it has a rich ethnic mixture. The Asian-American district is the second largest in the western hemisphere (next to San Francisco's), and there are substantial Greek, Italian, Japanese and Indian populations as well.

Flanked by mountains and waterways, and blessed with a temperate climate, Vancouver is a city of natural beauty and charm. For families from the U.S., Vancouver combines the excitement of travel to a foreign country with the convenience of a familiar culture and language. It is a friendly city, easy to navigate and with enough going on to guarantee no dull moments.

A word about money: You may want to obtain Canadian currency at a bank before you arrive. While most shops and restaurants in Vancouver will accept U.S. currency, the exchange rate will be lower than at a bank. It is also a good idea to change Canadian money into U.S. before your return. In the U.S. stores generally do not accept Canadian currency.

A federal Goods and Services Tax (GST) is applied to most accommodations, services and products in Canada. Tourists are eligible for a rebate of the GST they pay while visiting the country. The easiest way to apply for rebate is to pick up a GST reporting form as you pass through the border station. Be sure to keep all your receipts, and to file the report within one year of your visit.

GETTING THERE

Vancouver is 150 miles north of Seattle, a straight shot on I-5 (via the Blaine-Douglas border crossing). Driving time is approximately three hours but will be affected by traffic at the border station. It is not unusual to have a 30-90 minute wait, especially on weekends and holidays.

In May 1995 **Amtrak** began running train service from Seattle to Vancouver for the first time in 14 years. The train makes one round trip daily, with stops at Edmonds, Everett, Mount Vernon-Burlington and Bellingham. The train departs Seattle's King Street station at 7:15 am and arrives at Vancouver's Pacific Central station at 11:50 am. Returning, it departs Vancouver at 6 pm and arrives in Seattle at 10:35 pm. (Travel time may get shorter—check exact arrival times when you make your reservation). Round-trip fare is $46 Friday-Sunday, $42 Monday-

Thursday; children ages 2-15 are half price. The train is the Talgo, a very comfortable, Spanish-made train with nice, wide windows.

The train arrives at the Pacific Central station on the southeast edge of downtown Vancouver, a half-block west of Science World. The easiest way to get to downtown is to take a cab ride, costing about $8-$10 (Canadian). Or, for a more exciting (and cheaper) ride, take the SkyTrain. Its Main Street Station is just 100 yards west of the train station. (See SkyTrain below for more details).

800/USA-RAIL

ROADSIDE ATTRACTIONS. For interesting road stops on the U.S. side of the border, see the Bellingham and La Conner sections.

Also consider visiting the **Newton Wave Pool** on your way to or from Vancouver. The pool, located on the outskirts of Vancouver, has a graduated floor so non-swimmers can enjoy a splash. Two large water slides add a fun option for older kids. Periodically, three-foot waves are generated and the whole family will enjoy riding them. Parents who need a break can lounge in beach chairs under heat lamps! Refreshments are available and suits, towels and equipment may be rented.

604/594-SURF; 13730-72nd Ave, Vancouver. Going north from the border, take Hwy 99, then Exit 99A and go north on King George Hwy. Turn right at 72nd Ave.

REFUELING. There are plenty of places to refuel along the way, but for the greatest selection, stop in **Bellingham,** the last major city before you reach the border. (See the Bellingham section for suggested eateries.) Or pack a cooler of favorite picnic items and enjoy them at the **Peace Arch** (at the Blaine-Douglas border crossing).

GETTING AROUND TOWN. Vancouver has an exceptionally good public transportation system that will get you around town while providing a fun ride.

THE SKYTRAIN is an automated, light-rail train that travels on an elevated track except in the downtown core when it goes underground. The four downtown stations are Stadium, Granville, Burrard and Waterfront. From these stations the train goes to Main Street station which is right next to the train station and Science World.

Trains run about every five minutes. Fare for Main Street to any of the downtown stations is $1.50/adult; $.75/child 2-15.

THE SEABUS is a passenger-only ferry that shuttles people back and forth across Burrard Inlet, between downtown Vancouver and North Vancouver. It is a fun ride that offers a great view of the city's major harbor.

It leaves from the Waterfront Station, the SkyTrain terminus, every 15 minutes. The crossing takes 12 minutes. The fare is $1.50 for adults, $.75 for kids. Return in 90-minutes and you only need one fare.

CITY BUSES aren't as exciting as the a train or boat, but they will get you where you need to go most of the time.

Basic fare is $1.50. By picking up a copy of the pamphlet 'Discover Vancouver in Transit," you'll find out how to get to Vancouver's major sights by bus, SkyTrain or SeaBus. It is available at the Tourist Information Centre at 200 Burrard St and in some hotels. Or you can call B.C. Transit Information at 604/521-0400.

Fares are the same on the buses, SeaBus and SkyTrain and you can transfer between the systems.

PLACES TO STAY

COAST PLAZA
604/688-7711 or 800/663-9494; 1733 Comox St,V6G 1P6
Rates: Expensive
Essentials: Credit cards; cribs
Extras: Restaurant; TV; kitchens (some units); indoor pool,
whirlpool, sauna; babysitting by pre-arrangement; pets okay

This hotel, originally an apartment building, offers rooms that are large and comfortable for families. Each of the 300 guest rooms and suites has a balcony and a view of the city, mountains or bay. You can't beat this location with nearby Stanley Park and the beach at English Bay. Most downtown destinations are only minutes away by car, but also easily accessible on foot.

In addition to the pool and sauna, guests enjoy privileges at the squash and racquetball courts next door (Club Cardio). The hotel can provide box lunches for picnics, jogging maps and playing cards.

PARENT COMMENTS: *"Even in the rain, we enjoy a stay at the Coast Plaza because the accommodations are self-contained and central to the downtown area."*
"The rooms are so large, it's possible to bring along a teen-aged babysitter."

FOUR SEASONS HOTEL

604/689-9333 or 800/332-3442; 791 West Georgia St, V6C2T4
Rates: Expensive
Essentials: Credit cards; cribs
Extras: Restaurants; swimming pool, exercise equipment, saunas, whirlpools; laundry; TV; pets OK

The Four Seasons is well-known for dedication to good service. For parents traveling with their children, there are countless "little things" that the staff will offer your family that will add up to a very satisfying hotel experience.

As in other Four Seasons, children receive a toy, a fluffy, little bathrobe just like their parents' to use during their stay and a cookies and milk snack. If you are traveling with an infant, whatever special needs you may have will graciously be provided—including strollers, playpens and baby toys.

The lovely pool is designed so that it is both indoors and out. Exercise machines in the pool area let you enjoy the fresh air while working out and there is a large sundeck for sunbathing.

The Four Seasons is centrally located in the heart of downtown and the staff is very helpful about suggesting attractions and activities of interest to families.

PARENT COMMENTS: *"Two years after our visit, my eight-year-old daughter still talks about the robe and fresh cookies delivered to our room unannounced soon after we arrived."*

"It has become a family tradition. Every year during the holiday season dad takes his two daughters for a fabulous two-night stay at the Four Seasons. The hotel is beautifully decorated for the holidays. We use our Entertainment coupon for a 50% discount on the room price. My only regret is that on my last visit I used valet parking at the hotel. The parking bill was painfully high. Next time I'll look for a better parking deal."

"The large swimming pool is half-inside and half-outside. Our kids loved it. "

THE GREENBRIAR APARTMENTS

604/683-4558; 1393 Robson St, V6E 1C6
Rates: Inexpensive
Essentials: Credit cards; hide-a-beds, cribs
Extras: TV; kitchens

This is a good choice if you don't care about being fancy, want the option of cooking your own meals, and appreciate a central location. Rooms are large, and feature bedroom, living room with hide-a-bed, and kitchenette. There is free underground parking (a real plus in downtown Vancouver).

The heart of downtown is a half-mile walk away; Stanley Park is five minutes by bus or car. Robson Street is an attraction in itself, with ethnic restaurants, bakeries, corner groceries and intriguing shops within easy walking distance.

> **PARENT COMMENTS:** *"This is a good value, but it's just a place to stay—comfortable and clean, but slightly tacky."*
> *"Good location, but significantly funky."*

PACIFIC PALISADES
604/688-0461; 1277 Robson St, V6E 1C4
Rates: Expensive
Essentials: Credit cards, cribs
Extras: Restaurant; TV; small refrigerators, microwaves; pool, sauna, whirlpool; exercise room

A Shangri-la International hotel, Pacific Palisades offers a luxurious stay at a great location. Formerly an apartment building, the hotel has some of the most spacious rooms in the city. All rooms have a view of the water or the mountains.

The indoor recreation area is a real plus for families. The large pool, whirlpool and exercise room are located in a separate building. The staff is friendly and thoroughly accommodating.

> **PARENT COMMENTS:** *"The concierge was friendly and very helpful. She researched activities for kids and sent a packet of information to our room."*
> *"We spent a three-day weekend just playing in the pool and strolling on Robson Street. We found a number of great restaurants within easy walking distance."*

SYLVIA HOTEL
604/681-9321; 1154 Gilford St, V6G 2P6
Rates: Inexpensive
Essentials: Credit cards; cribs
Extras: Kitchens; pets OK

For over 20 years, visitors to Vancouver who prefer to spend their vacation money on good food and entertainment rather than lodging have taken advantage of the low rates at the Sylvia. The brick, ivy-covered building was originally one of the nicest apartment buildings in town. Now a bit shabby, it still offers reasonable rooms, a friendly staff and a sterling location. Across the street from English Bay and 2 1/2 blocks from Stanley Park, this spot is convenient for families who prefer not to spend too much time in the hotel room..

PARENT COMMENTS: *"It's a nice walk along English Bay to the playground in Stanley Park. And nearby Denman Street has a nice choice of restaurants and coffee shops."*
"The newer rooms are less shabby but lack the "charm" of the older rooms."
"We stay here when we are going on to ski at Whistler. An economic choice before we spend big bucks skiing."

PLACES TO EAT

BUD'S
604/683-0661; 1007 Denman
Hours: Lunch and dinner daily
Essentials: Credit cards; highchairs
  For traditional, English-style fish and chips, you simply can't beat Bud's. The atmosphere is traditional, too: a rather dark, crowded room full of booths and tables. But if you don't mind the occasional spot of grease, it's a relaxed place to take kids. Located just three blocks from English Bay, there's the option of picking up a meal to go and walking down to the waterfront.

ISADORA'S
604/681-8816;285-4998; 1540 Old Bridge St
Hours: Breakfast, lunch, dinner daily, brunch Sat-Sun
Essentials: Credit cards; highchairs
  Isadora's is a landmark Vancouver restaurant, made to order for families. For starters, it's located adjacent to the popular water play area at Granville Island Market. It also offers a small, indoor play area the kids can enjoy until food is served. The children's menu has several fun choices, such as clown-faced pizza. The adult menu includes several tasty vegetarian meals.

THE PINK PEARL
604/253-4316; 1132 E Hastings St
Hours: Dimsum daily 9 am-3 pm; dinner daily 5 pm-10 pm (11 pm Fri, Sat)
Essentials: Credit cards; highchairs
  Vancouver is famous for its Asian restaurants, and this is one of the best. The Cantonese chefs have built their reputation on fresh seafood dishes. There are live tanks, and servers bring live seafood orders to the table for approval.
  Though there's no kids' menu, The Pink Pearl offers plenty of

Cantonese favorites. The more adventurous will find some unusual treats, as well. Dare to experiment!

The restaurant is essentially one large room, so it can be quite noisy. Families with talkative little ones will feel right at home. Take your own crayons and paper, or visit the seafood tanks for live entertainment.

THE RED ONION

604/263-0833; 2028 W 41st Ave
Hours: Breakfast, lunch, dinner daily
Essentials: Credit cards; highchairs

If it's hamburgers, hotdogs and fries the family craves, look no farther than The Red Onion. The french fries are served with a deliciously simple, lightly spiced sauce. If you're interested in lighter fare, they have it here, too, including quiche, homemade soups and veggie sandwiches. At breakfast, lovely pastries are prepared on premises.

With its relaxed atmosphere, The Red Onion is a comfortable place to take the kids. Bring along some books, though, as the food preparation can take time. In fact, the menu provides a disclaimer: "We blushingly apologize," it reads, "if your meal seems slow to cook. . ." It's worth the wait.

SOPHIE'S COSMIC CAFE

604/732-6810; 2095 W 4th Ave
Hours: Breakfast, lunch, dinner daily; brunch Sat-Sun
Essentials: Credit cards; highchairs

At Sophie's, a fantastically funky spot in the Kitsilano neighborhood, it's tough to decide which is better—the food or the decor. It's a visual cornucopia of kitsch, its walls dripping with paraphernalia. From the rack of antlers that supports a dozen whimsical hats to the BeeGees lunchbox (and don't forget the billiards table with the red lobster crawling out of the corner pocket), this spot will entertain children of all ages. Check out the booth railings made of original Coke bottles. There's also a toy box available, for anyone who tires of looking at the walls.

As if the incredible decor weren't enough, the food at Sophie's is fantastic. There is no kids' menu, but then none is needed—the nine-page menu dares any child to walk out hungry. And don't plan on "cleaning your plate," as the helpings are enormous. Choose from falafels, soups, salads or deli sandwiches. Try the juicy hamburger with a thick, cappuccino milkshake. Or opt for one of Sophie's lively breakfasts, served all day. For those with iron wills, there's even a "lighter side" section in the menu.

PARENT COMMENTS: *"There's almost always a line at Sophie's, and another wait for your food to be served. Hang in there — you'll be glad you did."*

WHAT TO SEE AND DO

It is well-nigh impossible to be bored in Vancouver. You will find a variety of indoor and outdoor activities, both strenuous and casual. The Vancouver community seems to genuinely cares about kids, and designs programs and spaces to suit their needs.

STROLL & BROWSE

There are scores of interesting neighborhoods and shopping areas in this cosmopolitan city.

A stroll through Gastown is sure to lend historical perspective to your Vancouver visit. A village was founded here in 1876, but burned to the ground 10 years later. As the city grew up around it, Gastown began an economic decline and was in danger of being torn down until the community rallied support in 1971. Now fully renewed, Gastown is a maze of cobblestone courtyards, Victorian architecture, shops and sidewalk cafes. Kids will enjoy seeing the steam-powered clock which plays tunes on the quarter-hour (at Cambie and Water streets).

West of downtown on Burrard Inlet, along Powell, Water, Alexander, Carrell and Cordova Streets.

GRANVILLE ISLAND, tucked away beneath the Granville Bridge, was once an industrial site. The old warehouses have been remodeled to house artists' studios, shops, theaters, restaurants and a huge European-style open market. This waterfront development offers lots of options for browsing. Grab a snack at the market and stroll along the dock, watching the boat traffic, feeding the pigeons or enjoying live entertainment. Poke around the shops and art galleries. When the young ones have had enough shopping, they'll love a stop at the water park. Or stop in at the Kids Only Market, a whole warehouse full of kids' clothes and toy shops.

Enter Granville Island off W 2nd or W 4th from Granville Bridge or Burrard Bridge.

ROBSON STREET. If you have window-shopping and people-watching in mind, be sure to stroll Robson Street. You'll find a fascinating collection of upscale clothing stores, novelty shops and restaurants. For a mid-jaunt treat, stop by **Yogurty's** (1194 Robson) for made-to-order frozen yogurt, or get the kids a fancy caramel apple at **Rocky Mountain Chocolates** (1017 Robson). Parents who crave a bit of the bean will find two **Starbucks Coffee** shops nearby (1099 and 1100 Robson).

Walk west on Robson from Burrard Street.

PARKS

QUEEN ELIZABETH PARK. The beautiful grounds at Queen Elizabeth Park, the city's first civic arboretum, are simply a joy to walk. Paths wind among acres of native and exotic plant life, sunken gardens and waterfalls. Worth a visit is the fabulous triodetic **Bloedel Floral Conservatory**, a lush, tropical greenhouse offering collections of 500 species of plants from jungle to desert environments. Kids will love the pools of colorful Koi fish and flocks of tropical birds.

Enter the park at 33rd and Cambie St Bloedel Floral Conservatory Hours: summer: daily 10 am-9 pm, winter: daily 10 am-5 pm

STANLEY PARK. Surely one of the most beautiful urban parks in the world, 1000-acre Stanley Park offers outdoor recreation and indoor entertainment. The whole family will enjoy hiking or biking the 5^1/$_2$-mile "seawall promenade" around the periphery of the park. You'll find glorious scenery and, for the kids, a fire engine playground. If the weather's warm, pack your swimsuits and stop by the Variety Kids Water Park, which features slides, water cannons and a full-body blow drier. If the little ones need incentive on the walk, suggest they watch for the controversial sculpture, Girl in Wetsuit, a takeoff on Copenhagen's mermaid (hint: this one's wearing scuba gear).

Also of special interest to kids is the 1^1/$_2$-mile walk around **Lost Lagoon**, where the family will likely spot Canada geese, trumpeter swans, raccoon, skunks and box turtles. (These animals are more friendly than they should be, so be sure your kids don't sneak them any food).

Within the park you'll find the **Vancouver Public Aquarium, Stanley Park Zoo** (see "Animals, Animals") and a wonderful **miniature train ride**.

To get there, follow Georgia Street west through downtown to the park entrance.

VANDUSEN BOTANICAL GARDENS. OK, so gardens are not on every kid's "top ten" list. But these gardens are special, featuring plants from all over the world which blend perfectly with some spectacular indigenous plants. Any time of year, you'll find blooms and shrubs galore, set amid dramatic rockeries and waterways. There's even a special garden for kids. Let them run off their excess energy, then stop in at Sprinklers Restaurant to revitalize.

37th and Oak St; 604/878-9274. Open daily 10 am-dusk. Cost: $2.50/adult, $1.25/youth, 6 & under free, or $5/family.

VANIER PARK. Whether they're fascinated by the sea or the stars (or both), kids will find plenty of interest in Vanier Park. The **Vancouver Maritime Museum and St. Roch National Historic Site** offer travelling nautical exhibits and historic sailing vessels. A tour of the Arctic patrol ship RCMP St. Roch will take young imaginations back to an era when sailing ships faced, and not always overcame, the perils of ice, fog and blizzards.

1905 Ogden Ave; 604/737-2212 (museum); 604/666-3201 (historic site) Winter: Tues-Sun, 10 am-5 pm; summer: Daily 10 am-6 pm. Cost: $5/adult; $2.50/child.

Also at this site is the **H.R. MacMillan Planetarium**, which offers a wide range of astronomy programs for families. Some of the shows are pretty seriously scientific and better for older children or those with a strong leaning toward astronomy. But there are plenty of light, whimsical offerings as well.

1100 Chestnut St; 604/738-7827. Programs Tues-Sun at 3, 7:30 & 9 pm, additional shows weekends and holidays. Cost: $5.50/adult, $3.75/child.

ANIMALS, ANIMALS

STANLEY PARK AQUARIUM What kid doesn't delight in viewing aquatic animals? At Stanley Park you'll find a wide range of fish and mammals in an exceptional setting. Best known for its killer whale show, the Aquarium is also home to two stunning Beluga whales, fast becoming the "darlings" of Vancouver. You'll watch harbor seals and sea otters cavort and discover aquatic wildlife from all over the world, including octopus, sharks and reptiles. If you've promised the kids a souvenir of Vancouver, the Aquarium gift shop has an especially nice selection.

Located at Stanley Park; 604/682-1118. Hours: daily 10 am-5 pm. Cost: $9.50/adult, $8.25/student, $6.25/child 5-12, 4 & under free or $27/family.

STANLEY PARK ZOO. This is a small, rather undistinguished zoo. But admission is free, and it can be fun for a stroll. The monkeys are usually the hit of the trip. Next door is the petting zoo, where kids can "get a feel" of llamas and a variety of farm animals.

Located at Stanley Park. 604/ 681-1141. Hours: daily 11 am-4 pm. Cost: Zoo is free; petting zoo, $2/person.

VANCOUVER GAME FARM is a fun spot for viewing animals. Families will marvel at the giraffe, elephants, lions, tigers and rhinos that roam the 120 acres of farmland. Young children will get a kick out of the petting zoo, and everyone will enjoy the train ride that skirts the perimeter.

604/856-6825; 5048 264th St, Aldergrove. Open daily 8 am-dusk. Cost: $9 adults, $7 children, children under 4 free.

THE GREAT OUTDOORS

HIKING. For city "hiking," you won't find anything grander than the seawall promenade at Stanley Park (see "Parks"). Along the waterfront of West Vancouver is the West Van Seawall Walkway. The **Baden Powell Trail** in North Vancouver is a lovely hike for families who prefer to escape the city. Access the trail at Mt. Seymour Provincial Park (take the Second Narrows Bridge from downtown and follow signs to the park). Two miles into the park you'll see trail signs.

BURNABY LAKE REGIONAL PARK offers nature trails of various lengths, so families can put together the hike that's right for them. The focus of this park is on nature education, and kids will enjoy visiting the nature house and climbing the viewing tower. From the nature house, loop trails take off to the east and west; some are accessible to strollers.

This area is a wildlife sanctuary, so bring the binoculars. Children enjoy searching the marshes for wildlife, including osprey, grebe, muskrat and turtles.

For information about any of the regional parks, phone the Greater Vancouver Regional District, 604/432-6350, and ask for the "systems brochure."

For those who want to get really serious about hiking B.C., recommended reading includes David Macaree's *109 Walks in B.C.'s Lower Mainland.*

SKIING. Vancouver is a gateway to paradise for skiers, offering three local resorts within one-half hour of the city: **Grouse Mountain, Cypress Bowl** and **Mount Seymour.** Each ski area has its own 24-hour snowphone: Grouse Mountain (604/986-

6262); Cypress Bowl (604/926-6007); Mount Seymour (604/986-2261).

If you're up to a longer trip, the outstanding Whistler Mountain Ski Resort is just 75 miles north (see the "Whistler" chapter).

SWIMMING. Two excellent indoor swimming pools feature Olympic size pools and, ever popular with families, whirlpools and toddlers pools. Call the **Vancouver Aquatic Centre** (604/665-3424) or the **University of B.C. Aquatic Centre** (604/822-4521) for more information.

For outdoor swimming or beach-bumming, the options are many. Stanley Park has its Second and Third Beaches, which are handy for a quick mid-day dunk. Along English Bay (west of downtown) you'll find English Bay Beach and Sunset Beach, excellent for swimming, walking or sunning. Lovely beaches are also accessible from Northwest Marine Drive, near the University of B.C. Kitsilano Beach, a local favorite, boasts an outdoor saltwater pool, concession stands and plenty of parking. It is located just off Cornwall Avenue at the southern end of Burrard Bridge.

MUSEUMS

SCIENCE WORLD This hands-on, high-tech museum is sure to please the science buffs in your family. Science World offers exhibits that make sense out of the everyday world. Kids can create a cyclone, blow square bubbles or discover the science behind today's popular music. There's a search gallery where the youngest visitors will enjoy crawling though a beaver lodge or walking inside a hollow tree. Also located here is one of the world's largest IMAX theatres, with a 28-speaker sound system.

1455 Quebec St/(604)268-6363. Hours: Mon-Fri 10 am-6 pm, Sat & Sun 10 am-6 pm. Cost: $7/adult, $4.50/child (IMAX is extra).

UNIVERSITY OF B.C. MUSEUM OF ANTHROPOLOGY. Older kids and those with a penchant for Native American lore will appreciate this marvelous collection of Northwest Coast First Nations art, including huge totem poles, feast dishes, war canoes and carved works in silver, gold, stone and wood. And it's all housed in an award-winning building, located on the Point Grey cliffs.

(604)822-3825; 6393 NW Marine Dr (on the UBC campus) Hours: Tues-Sun 11 am-5 pm (9 pm Tues). Cost: $5/adult, $2.50/student, 6 and under free or $12/family; free to all on Tues.

EXCURSIONS

NORTH VANCOUVER. The area north of Burrard Inlet, known as North Vancouver, is definitely worth exploring. Getting there can be half the fun, too, on the city's **SeaBus** (604/261-5100). SeaBus is actually two ferries that shuttle passengers between North Vancouver (at the foot of Lonsdale Avenue) and the Skytrain station at the foot of Granville Street downtown. Boats leave every 15 minutes, and fares are the same as city buses. It's a fun, inexpensive and scenic ride.

The SeaBus terminal is at the foot of Burrard St, near Gastown.

At **Grouse Mountain** you can take the Super Skyride to the summit, where you can stroll, eat and enjoy panoramic views. The indoor Theatre in the Sky offers a short multi-media presentation about Vancouver. In the winter there's great skiing and snowboarding, sleigh rides and special kids' programs.

604/984-0661; 6400 Nancy Greene Way. Hours: Daily 9 am-10 pm. Cost: Adult $14.50; youth $9.95, child $5.95, 5 and under free.

On your way to the mountain you'll pass through Capilano Canyon Park, featuring the **Capilano Suspension Bridge**. The 450-foot span bridge sways 230 feet above the rushing Capilano River; most kids are invigorated by the crossing, but some adults feel a bit queasy. Also fun for kids are the rainforest trail, forested nature park, trout ponds, totem poles and trading post.

604/985-7474; 3735 Capilano Road. Free.

PLAYLAND AMUSEMENT PARK. Families will find just the "thrills and chills" they seek at this quintessential amusement park. Recently upgraded, the park offers a choice of 35 rides, including Canada's largest wooden roller coaster. When you've had your fill of thrills, there's more: take in one of the musical revues, visit the petting zoo, play miniature golf or check out the arcades. Daily admission covers unlimited entertainment.

604/255-5161; On Hastings at Cassier St Hours vary. Cost: $15.95 ($12.95 in advance at 7-Eleven stores)

CALENDAR

MAY: Children's Festival
JUNE: Folkfest
JULY: Vancouver Sea Festival

RESOURCES

B.C. TRANSIT

Information about the Bus, Skytrain and SeaBus
604/261-5100

GREATER VANCOUVER REGIONAL DISTRICT
Information about Regional Parks
604/432-6350

TOURISM VANCOUVER
604/683-2000; 200 Burrard St B6C 3L6

The Vancouver Book is a free 63-page visitors' guide provided
by Tourism Vancouver. It lists lodging, attractions, tours, etc.
Phone 604/683-2000; allow at least two weeks for delivery.

Vancouver Parent Newsmagazine
Monthly publication available free in bookstores, libraries,
restaurants.

SALT SPRING ISLAND

A group of nearly 200 tiny islands that lie between southern
Vancouver Island and the mainland, the Gulf Islands are an
enchanting mix of serenity, beauty and recreation. Salt Spring,
only 20 miles long and eight miles wide, is the largest and most
populated. With inland lakes and rocky coast, quaint little towns
and a temperate climate, the island is an idyllic place for a family
vacation.

GETTING THERE
The B.C. Ferries operates three ferries to Salt Spring. One
departs from Tswawwassen near Vancouver, another departs
Crofton, near Duncan on Vancouver Island; the third leaves
from Schwartz Bay, 32 kilometers from Victoria. Call B.C.
Ferries (604/537-2311) for the schedule. Reservations are rec-
ommended on the Tswawwassen route (must be pre-paid).
Daily transportation is also offered by two airlines, with flights
between Ganges Harbor and Vancouver harbor and Vancouver.
Hanna Air Salt Spring (604/537-9359 or 800/665-2FLY) based
in Ganges and Harbour Air (8//665-0212) in Vancouver offer
float plane service.
One of our parent reviewers described their journey to Salt
Spring as follows:
"From Seattle we drove I-5 north and exited to Anacortes (Exit

230). We took Highway 20 west and followed signs to the ferry terminal. The ferry goes to Sidney, B.C. We then drove to Schwartz Bay (about four miles) to take the ferry to Salt Spring Island. The signs to the BC ferries/Gulf Islands are well-marked.

We left at 5:15 am from our Queen Anne home to catch the ferry from Anacortes (it is about a 90-minute ride to the ferry dock but the boat fills up during the summer months). We arrived in Sidney B.C. about 11 AM. After going through customs at Sidney we got to the BC Schwartz Bay terminal at 11:35 am and made the 11:45 am ferry. We arrived at our destination about 1 pm, tired but happy!"

Our other reviewers drove to Tswawwassen outside Vancouver, B.C. and from there took the two-hour ferry ride to Salt Spring. When you make your reservations ask your hosts at the resort where you will be staying for the route they recommend from your home town.

PLACES TO STAY

GREEN ACRES RESORT
604/537-2585; 241 Lang Rd., Ganges, VOS 1EO
Rates: Moderate
Essentials: Credit cards; crib
Extras: Kitchens; playground; TV; rowboats, canoes, paddleboats; woodstoves; barbecues

Green Acres is a family-oriented resort located on seven acres of south-facing waterfront on the lovely shores of St. Mary Lake. Each cottage has its own private deck facing the lake. One and two-bedroom units are available, each with a modern, fully equipped kitchen. Most cottages also have cozy, new woodstoves.

Parents will appreciate the new outdoor play area, the safe and sandy beach and the dock with complimentary boats. In the summer the lake is warm enough for swimming. Furnishings are comfortable and very clean, but not too fancy so you can relax with your kid.

During the off-season the resort is popular for fishing—the lake is stocked with small-mouth bass, cutthroat, steelhead and rainbow trout. During July and August Green Acres is always booked solid with families.

PARENT COMMENTS: *"The mood of Salt Spring is relaxed and rural. Despite some rain, the weekends we have spent at Green Acres have been very enjoyable and memorable. Kids are warmly welcomed."*

"Though it takes a while to get to Salt Spring from Seattle, it is a lovely place and well worth the trip. Make reservations on the B.C. ferry so you don't have to worry about getting on."

SALTY SPRINGS RESORT

604/537-4111; 1460 North Beach Rd, V8K1J4
Rates: Expensive
Essentials: Credit cards; playpens
Extras: Kitchens; mineral baths in each room; fireplaces; games/ puzzles, mountain bikes, boats, coin washer/dryer; clamming gear, crab traps

At Salty Springs Seaside Mineral Bath Resort, the very attractive chalets with skylights and large windows take full advantage of the view of the ocean. Each chalet has a two-person whirlpool bath which uses the soothing natural mineral waters found at the north end of Salt Spring that are the source of the island's name. Kitchens are small but well-equipped. There are bikes available for no charge (bring your own helmets) as well as rowboats.

The rocky beach is across the street and down a path. (Our parent reviewers didn't consider this a problem but they were traveling with a ten-year-old.) Although there are no cribs available, the resort does have playpens that can be used as beds. In the game room there is a ping pong table plus toys, board games and puzzles.

There is no TV here and no telephone in the chalets. It is the kind of place where the outside world gets forgotten for a few days.

PARENT COMMENTS: *"This is good place for families that like to fish, kayak and just relax in a gorgeous setting."*
Our bath was huge and had 70 airjets. No arguments about getting our son to take his bath!"
"The town of Ganges is crowded and touristy. (We had to drive around to find a parking spot.) We recommend staying out of town where it's beautiful and coming into town just for supplies."
"We were disappointed there weren't any bike paths. Everyone bikes on the main road which can be very hilly, full of heavy traffic and lots of curves. However we did find some quiet side roads."
"There's a movie theater in a church auditorium. 'Forrest Gump' was playing. Get there early—it fills up fast!"

WHAT TO SEE AND DO

BIKING is quite popular on Salt Spring but the roads are hilly, traffic is quite heavy and shoulders are narrow to non-existent so it is not a good place for children to bike.

GANGES. Most of the Salt Spring Island residents live in or near Ganges, a pretty little town that reflects both the lively artist community and the agricultural roots of the island. All summer long Gange hosts ArtCraft, a sale of the work of more than 200 artists and artisans who are residents of the Gulf Islands. On weekends, artists demonstrate their skills.

Every Saturday during the summer, the Farmer's Market in Ganges offers a colorful display of the abundant produce grown in the farms on Salt Spring.

HIKERS. Many of the hikes on Salt Spring lead to awesome views over the southern Gulf Islands, Vancouver Island and points beyond. Be sure to bring a camera and binoculars. Some of the hikes may be too steep or dangerous for young hikers; ask locals for advice about "child-safe" trails. For a good overview of the island's trails, pick up a free copy of *Salt Spring Outdoors*, a detailed map showing public island trails, available at the Visitors Center and many hotels.

HORSES. A fun way to enjoy the beauty of Salt Spring is to view it from horseback. ***Salt Spring Guided Rides*** operates on the slopes of Mount Maxwell, where riders have access to 700 acres of land. Caroline Hickman has been offering guided tours for more than ten years for groups of two to eight people. *Call 604/537-5761.*

KAYAK PADDLERS are likely to see birds, sea lions, mink, otters and other marine life that can easily be overlooked if you're standing on the shore. Most kids will be thrilled to sit close to the water in a two-person kayak (with mom or dad typically doing most of the paddling).

Salt Spring Kayaking, 604/653-4222. Sea Otter Kayaking, 604/537-5678

MT. MAXWELL PROVINCIAL PARK. Open all year, this park offers spectacular views of south Salt Spring, Vancouver Island and the other Gulf Islands from Baynes Peak. You can follow the road signs to the park but our parent reviewers recommended a map (available at hotels and major tourist spots). They had this to say about their visit to the park:

"The road is gravel and it is steep and bumpy. It took us about 35 minutes to get from the town of Ganges to the park entrance.

You are rewarded at the top with an amazing view. You can see for miles. A sign says 'Young children must be accompanied. Steep drop-offs!' and they are right! The area is not suitable for strollers but we saw some toddlers doing fine with adult assistance. There is a day-use area with benches and picnic tables. Our 10-year-old loved this view and so did we."

CALENDAR

JULY: Salt Spring Festival of the Arts

RESOURCES

B.C. FERRIES
604/537-2311

TRAVEL INFOCENTER
121 Lower Ganges Rd, Box 111, Ganges, B.C. VOS 1EO
604/537-5252

VICTORIA

This lovely town has a well-deserved reputation as the city of cricket in the park, double-decker buses and exquisite flower gardens—an image that attracts thousands of tourists who visit each year and enjoy a spot of properly-served tea. But in fact, not all of Victoria is fragile and quaint. When your children see the magnificent Parliament Building magically lit at night or step into one of the breathtakingly realistic dioramas at the Royal British Columbia Museum, you'll see why Victoria is a fine place to take a vacation with kids.

An added reason for making Victoria a destination for a family getaway is that the town is accessible by boat from Seattle, so parents can avoid the hassle of driving. It is an ideal place to take a child for a special "time alone" with a parent.

Keep in mind, however, that Victoria, like many tourist towns, is much more crowded and expensive in the summer than any other time of year. On a mid-winter visit you can often get excellent discounts at the more expensive hotels (be sure to make clear you are shopping for the best rate) and enjoy a quieter, less-crowded city.

However, despite its many charms, it is possible to overstay in the "City of Gardens." If you are traveling with the kids, Victoria is best as a one- or two-night getaway. Set sail for home before boredom sets in and you become susceptible to the numerous and costly tourist traps.

GETTING THERE

Unlike many of our vacation destinations, getting there is half the fun when you are traveling to Victoria. There are several ways to go:

The passenger-only *Victoria Clipper*, a jet-propelled catamaran, makes its round trip between Seattle and Victoria three or four times daily, depending on the season. Get there early to get seats by the windows and to get a seat with a table. Once the boat gets out on the open sea, boredom often sets in; bring along games and books to help pass the time on the 2 $\frac{1}{2}$-hour trip.

There is food service at your seat on the boat. A typical breakfast is yogurt, bagel and cream cheese and juice ($4.25) and for the dinner meal home you might choose between a salmon dinner or a croissant sandwich ($6.25). Better yet, bring your own picnic.

206/448-5000, 604/382-8100 or 800/888-2535. Round-trip fare: $89/adult, half-price ages 1-11. During off-season rates are reduced.

The Victoria Line provides car and passenger service on the *Royal Victorian* from Seattle to Victoria from mid-May to September. It departs from Pier 48 once a day at 1 pm, arriving Victoria at 5:30 pm. The ship departs from Victoria at 7:30 am and arrives back in Seattle at noon. Reservations are suggested for cars only.

206/625-1880. One way fare: $42/car and driver, $19.10/adult passenger, half-price fare ages 5-11, under 5 free.

A Washington state ferry runs from Anacortes (85 miles north of Seattle) to Sydney, near Victoria. It is a beautiful, three-hour ride through the San Juans. Ferries depart from Anacortes twice a day during summer months at 8 am and 2 pm. Arrive at least one hour in advance of your departure time. Reservations are allowed on the ferry from mid-June through mid-September. You may make your reservation beginning May 1.

206/464-6400 or 604/381-1551. One-way fare: $35.65/car and driver, $6.90/adult passenger, half-price fare ($3.45)/ages 5-11, under 5 free.

Port Angeles-Victoria ferry service is available on the *Coho*, operated by Black Ball ferry. The trip takes about 1 $\frac{1}{2}$ hours. Car and passenger service is provided. Reservations are not available.

206/622-2222. One way fare: $26/car and driver, $6.50 adult passenger, $3.25 ages 5-11, under 5 free.

The **B.C. ferry** departs from Tswawwassen near Vancouver and travels to Schwartz Bay near Sydney, about 32 kilometers from Victoria.
604/386-3431.

Seaplanes offer a breathtakingly scenic and quick (approximately one hour) flight from Seattle to Victoria. **Kenmore Air** departs both Lake Union and Kenmore at the north end of Lake Washington in Seattle for Inner Harbour in Victoria year round. *800/826-1890. Round-trip fare: $135/adults,$86.50/children*

A number of the hotels offer transportation and hotel special "package deals." Ask your travel agent about what's available.

PLACES TO STAY

THE BOWERY GUEST HOUSE
604/383-8079; 310 Huntington Place, VBV 2N5
Rates: Moderate
Essentials: Credit cards; cribs
Extras: Complimentary breakfast; kitchen; TV; free passes to the Royal Museum; babysitting available

This is an attractive and comfortable B&B where the gracious hostess goes out of her way to make parents and children feel welcome. The upstairs suite has a kitchen, living room, master bedroom (with sofa and chairs), guest bedroom, and loft (with two single beds). The decor is white wicker furniture—charming but not fragile. Paddington Bear is lent to the children for their stay and there are a resident cat and dog. The delicious breakfast includes homemade muffins, bagels and cream cheese, cereal, fresh fruit, juice, coffee and teas.

The Bowery has an excellent location for families. It is within easy walking distance of downtown and Beacon Hill Park is nearby with duck ponds, a petting zoo (in summer) and a good playground.

PARENT COMMENTS: *"The three-year-old slept in the loft, grandma got the extra bedroom, the baby was in the porta-crib in the living room and mom and dad got privacy on a family vacation!"*
"Our daughter was thrilled to find Paddington bear, complete with sou'wester and boots, waiting in our room for her (on loan). In his paws, he held a brochure about the Beacon Hill Park petting zoo."
"What a delight—a B&B that likes kids! The hostess was just right—helpful and gracious but not hovering. Our stay at the Bowery with two kids was relaxing and economical. We will definitely go back."

"Owner Beverly Dresen should have substituted for Julie Andrews as Mary Poppins."

LAUREL POINT INN
604/386-8271 or 800/663-7667
Rates: Expensive
Essentials: Credit cards; cribs
Extras: Complimentary breakfast (except July and August); restaurants, TV; indoor pool; refrigerators (some units); microwaves (some units)

You will likely notice this brick zigzag building as you enter Inner Harbour. Built in 1979, it does not have the "old English" charm of many of Victoria's accommodations. What it does offer is modern, spacious furnishings, great views of the busy harbor, a good restaurant that serves three meals a day and a lovely swimming pool overlooking a reflecting pond. There's also a path between the hotel and the water that leads to the Parliament Building, the Royal B.C. Museum and downtown—a pleasant, five-minute walk.

PARENT COMMENTS: *"We got a good discount on our room rate when we visited in February. The staff was exceptionally helpful and warm. We all enjoyed watching the harbor boat and seaplane traffic out our window."*

OAK BAY BEACH HOTEL
604/598-4556 or 800/668-7758; 1175 Beach Drive, V8S 2N2
Rates: Moderate to expensive
Essentials: Credit cards; cribs
Extras: Restaurant; TV; fishing rentals; babysitting available

Sitting majestically by the sea in the elegant Oak Bay district outside Victoria, the Oak Bay Beach Hotel offers guests a retreat into British civility and charm. It is not a place to bring rowdy youngsters, but is suitable if you are planning a special getaway with older children who would be impressed by landscaped gardens and "high" tea.

Only ten minutes from Victoria, the Oak Bay is less than a mile from a beautiful public beach and if you bring your bikes you can explore the neighborhood with its mansions and lovely gardens.

The dining room is formal and expensive—not recommended for young children. Afternoon tea is served daily in the grand lobby or on the verandah overlooking the sea and gardens if the weather is warm. Half a mile from the hotel is the Oak Bay Marina Restaurant, with moderate prices and excellent food.

❝❝ **PARENT COMMENTS:** *'We expected to spend more time in Victoria but our kids just wanted to hang out at the beach near the hotel."*
"The hotel is truly grand and fine for civilized kids".
"I stayed at the Oak Bay on a getaway with my daughter. It was interesting to get out of Victoria. We loved riding bikes through the gorgeous neighborhood where the hotel is located."

SWANS HOTEL

604/361-3310; 604/361-3310 or 800/668-7926; 506 Pandora Ave, Victoria, V8W 1K8
Rates: Expensive
Essentials: Credit cards; cribs
Extras: Kitchens; TV
These 29, attractively furnished suites near the Johnson Street Bridge are well-suited to families. Each split-level unit has a fully-equipped kitchen, separate dining and living room.

There's an up-scale pub, a popular cafe and a brewery (with daily tours) on this recently renovated property. The Swans is within easy walking distance of the heart of downtown.

❝❝ **PARENT COMMENTS:** *"We were traveling with three young kids and the separate bedrooms and spacious living room/dining room were wonderful. The kitchens were also convenient —we saved money and headaches by eating breakfast and lunch in our suite."*
"Ouch! The crib provided by the hotel cost $15 a night. Since we were already paying dearly, that hurt. But the Swans is a very attractive, small hotel in a convenient location."

ROYAL SCOT MOTOR INN

604-388-5463; 425 Quebec St, V8V1W7
Rates: Moderate
Essentials: Credit cards; cribs
Extras: Kitchens; TV; restaurant; indoor pool; sauna; hot tub; game room; coin-operated laundry; babysitting (by pre-arrangement)
To get you in the right mood for a stay in Victoria, all of the employees at the Royal Scot wear beautiful kilts. The Inn itself is comfortable if not fancy and the landscaped grounds are quiet. Most of the 150 units include kitchens and living rooms. The luxury suites have one or two bedrooms, a living room with sofa bed, and a fully-equipped kitchen and dining room.

The indoor pool, shower area and hot tub are not large but they are clean and well-maintained. There are coin-operated washers and dryers for wet suits and other laundry. Older kids will like the game room.

In addition to the good value, the Royal Scot offers an excellent location for a stay in Victoria. Located just south of Inner Harbour, at the hub of the city, everything that this wonderful city has to offer is within easy walking distance.

PARENT COMMENTS: *"Service was wonderful, right down to our beds being turned down while we were at dinner with mints on our pillows and our daughter's stuffed animals all tucked in."*
"We have visited Victoria several times with our three kids—mainly to visit the fabulous B.C. Museum. The Royal Scot works very well for us."
"We found it to be an excellent value. Having a kitchen was great for breakfast and, one night when we couldn't stand to take the group out to dinner again, we had Chinese food delivered."
"After a busy morning of sightseeing we were all rejuvenated by a long visit to the Crystal Gardens. The parents brought a newspaper to sit and read and the kids delighted in trying to figure out if the beautiful birds amidst the greenery were real or not (they're real)."

SHAMROCK MOTEL
604/385-8768; 675 Superior St, Victoria, V8V 1V1
Rates: Moderate
Essentials: Credit cards; crib
Extras: TV; kitchens; small pets OK
The Shamrock is a 15-unit, three-story motel located right across the street from Beacon Hill Park. The units are clean and have a living room with a sleep sofa, kitchen and bedroom and a balcony. The kitchens are well-equipped. The proprietors are very friendly and helpful.

PARENT COMMENTS: *"We visited with our 2 1/2-year old and 3-month old. The location was wonderful. We liked sitting out on the balcony and looking across to the lovely park. We would highly recommend the Shamrock for families."*

NORTH OF VICTORIA
BLACKBERRY INN B&B
604/748-4665; RR1, Box 29, Cowichan Bay, VOC 1N0
Rates: Inexpensive
Essentials: No credit cards; crib
Extras: Full breakfast; private bath
Beyond Victoria, Vancouver Island extends more than 280 miles northward. Visitors come to hike, fish, sail, enjoy the

spectacular scenery and most recently, tour the many wineries. The coveted brown and tan Cowichan sweater, knitted of unbleached wool by the women of the Cowichan tribe, is available in this region and can be purchased for less than you would pay in Victoria. At Duncan, just before you reach Cowichan Bay, the British Columbia Forest Museum features an authentic logging camp and a steam train ride.

The quiet fishing village of Cowichan Bay, located about 40 miles north of Victoria, is one of the many small towns scattered along Trans-Canada 1, the only north-south highway running along the rugged coast. The owners of the Blackberry Inn have two children (ages five and seven) plus two cats. For $45 a night (U.S. dollars) a family of four can stay in a room with a queen-sized bed and two twin beds and enjoy a complimentary full breakfast—often waffles. Guests are in a separate wing of the house so there is privacy.

We didn't have a chance to send a Parent Reviewer to check out Blackberry Inn but we include it anyway because it offeres an excellent bargain in an interesting location. The hostess Vivian Sager, emphasizes she caters to families. If you decide to check it out, please use one of the review forms at the back of the book to let us know about your visit.

PLACES TO EAT

BLETHERING PLACE
604/598-1413; 2250 Oak Bay
Hours: Breakfast, lunch, dinner, tea daily
Essentials: Credit cards; highchairs

If you want to treat the kids to an authentic English tea while visiting Victoria, Blethering Place is a good choice. You'll enjoy excellent scones, jams, Devonshire cream and tea for $7.95—a good price in this town. And the atmosphere is appropriately civil and leisurely.

The hearty English meals (sandwiches, meat pies), served three times a day, are also very good—if a bit heavy. Well-prepared English food suits many children—plain and simple without fancy sauces.

CECCONIA'S PIZZERIA AND TRATTORIA
604/592-0454; 3201 Shelburne, across from Hillside Mall
Hours: Lunch, dinner daily
Essentials: Credit cards; highchairs

Cecconia's is a noisy relaxed place that is ideal for families. The outstanding wood-oven pizza and marvelous freshly made pasta make this place deservedly popular with the locals.

EATON PAVILION (1150 Douglas St) is a large indoor shopping mall that has a variety of "fast food" restaurants on its top floor. You'll find pizza, teriyaki, sandwiches and other fare that is popular with kids.

SIAM
604/383-9911; 1314 Government St
Hours: Lunch daily except Sun, dinner daily
Essentials: Credit cards; highchairs
The Thai food you will find at this restaurant in the heart of the downtown shopping area is as good as you will find anywhere. Most kids will love the Phad Thai noodles as long as you order them prepared not spicy. Everyone will likely find a favorite on the excellent 54-item menu.

WHAT TO SEE AND DO

One of this compact city's greatest charms is that you can see most of it on foot. If you arrive by boat or plane from Seattle , or the Black Ball ferry from Port Angeles, you will dock in the Inner Harbour, right in the hub of downtown. Three of the most famous landmarks—the Empress Hotel, the Parliament Buildings and the Royal British Columbia Museum, as well as the downtown shopping district are all within easy walking distance. Most of the other interesting attractions lie within a few blocks.

Note: Many of the popular attractions extend their hours during the summer season. Call for up-to-date information on schedules and rates.

Pick up a self-guided walking tour map at the **Visitor's Bureau** at 812 Wharf Street, across from the Empress. Sitting regally over the harbor, the grand Empress Hotel has since 1908 welcomed visitors arriving by sea since 1908. Recent extensive ($45 million) renovations have improved accommodations but we still recommend that you stroll through the elegant lobby and perhaps splurge on afternoon tea in the Palm Court (very expensive), but stay overnight elsewhere.

GOVERNMENT STREET, just north of the Empress, is packed with shops that will delight kids who like to look at trinkets, glass figurines, Indian dolls and beadwork and other assorted wonders. This is the place to spend the souvenir money; plan on at least an hour of browsing. Grown-up shoppers might enjoy the English tweeds, fine china, the famous Cowichan sweaters, Scottish tartans, teas and candies.

THE MASSIVE PARLIAMENT BUILDINGS, across the street from the Empress Hotel, have lively guided tours daily during the summer, weekdays only the rest of the year. The free half-hour tours are offered all day. The Legislative Assembly, with all its pomp and circumstance, can be observed when in session, offering a view of the magnificently costumed sergeant-at-arms bearing a gold mace and the Speaker sitting on a gilded throne. Tours are conducted in six languages during the summer; three languages during the rest of the year.

Don't miss seeing the Parliament buildings at night, outlined by more than 3,000 tiny lights.

604/387-3046; 501 Belleville Ave. On the Inner Harbour. Open weekdays 8:30 am-5 pm; weekends and holidays 9 am-5 pm.

THE ROYAL BRITISH COLUMBIA MUSEUM, across the street from the Inner Harbour, will captivate even a child who doesn't like museums. It displays the province's rich natural history and native heritage and is considered by many to be the finest museum in Canada. Your admission ticket is good for two days, so consider visiting for a couple hours each day rather than one long visit that wears out the kids.

Of special interest to children are the highly realistic, life-size dioramas—complete with authentic sounds and smells. Visitors walk through a rain forest and along a seashore, sit in a Kwakiutl Indian longhouse and hear the sound of the village, stroll down a Victorian cobblestone street, complete with wood smoke and the smell of baking gingerbread, and stand in the captain's quarters of the *HMS Discovery*. The only exhibit that got less than rave reviews from our parent reviewers is the underwater simulation—part of which is very dark and claustrophobic Two families (one with a five-year-old, the other with a seven-year-old) mentioned that they had to bolt through the emergency exits with a panicked child. Those children who lasted through the exhibit were reportedly confused and bored.

While you are there, check out the Museum shop. The collection of science, nature and Native American books for children is one of the best you will ever find.

604/387-3014; 675 Belleville St. On the Inner Harbour. Admission $5.35/adult, $2.14/child 6-18 years, under 5 free. Tickets good for two days. Annual family pass $12. Open daily 10 am-5:30 pm.

BEACON HILL PARK is a lush and elegant 184-acre park with a gorgeous view of the Strait of Juan de Fuca, playgrounds, several little lakes, a petting farm (in the summer), a ceremonial longhouse, totem pole collection and numerous places for a picnic. Ponds and flower gardens are scattered about the manicured lawns. If you come on a Sunday afternoon in the summer you will probably be able to watch a cricket match.

A short walk from downtown along Douglas Street or take Bus #5.

THE CRYSTAL GARDEN is located in an elegant turn-of-the-century building that originally housed a grand indoor swimming pool. It has been converted into a tropical garden, complete with live flamingos, macaws and the smallest monkeys in the world. One parent reviewer put the Crystal Garden in the category of an expensive tourist trap not worth visiting, with "tiny cages that are cruel for the animals". One reviewer said it was "a great place to visit when it is raining in Victoria—a restful retreat from the outside hustle-and-bustle that she enjoyed and that entertained her five- and seven-year-old for a good two hours".

604/381-1213; 713 Douglas Street. Behind the Empress Hotel. Cost: $6.50 for adult, $4 ages 6-16, under 6 free.

MINIATURE WORLD, located inside the Empress Hotel, will enchant a child interested in dollhouses and miniatures—anyone else will be bored to tears and annoyed they've walked into a tourist trap. One parent reviewer said her nine-year-old daughter voted the Miniature Museum her "second favorite part of the trip" (B.C. Museum was first).

Exhibits include a Fantasy land with scenes from Gulliver's Travels, Santa's Workshop and more, miniature soldiers in mock battle (providing quick history lessons), a miniature railway and dozens of exquisite dollhouses with proper period furnishings.

604/385-9731; 721 Government Street (inside Empress Hotel). Hours: 8:30 am - 9 pm summer, 9 am-5 pm rest of year. Cost: $6.75/ adult, $4.75 ages 5-11, under 5 free.

THE ROYAL WAX MUSEUM is another one of the attractions near the Harbor that will put a dent in your wallet, but most kids will find it fascinating if a bit spooky. If mom or dad are in the professorial mood, the highly realistic depictions of historic figures offer a good opportunity for a quick history lesson. Children under seven will likely be bored and possibly frightened. One of our parent reviewers reported going to the Wax

Museum in a spontaneous act of desperation on a rainy after-noon. She said her eight-year-old son remembers it as the highlight of his trip to Victoria.

Warning: One section of the museum, the Chamber of Horrors, is not a "Disney-style" exhibit meant to give a little frightening fun. It features graphic depictions of barbarian torture methods you might not want your child to see. It is clearly marked and can be easily avoided.

604/388-4461; at Inner Harbour. Hours: 9 am-9 pm daily. Cost: $7/adult; $3 ages 6-12.

SOME ATTRACTIONS TO AVOID:

The **Craigdaroch Castle, Anne Hathaway's Thatched Cottage** and the **Butchart Gardens** are popular attractions well worth seeing but best left for a trip without the children. Entrance fees are steep and few children care to see historical homes or formal gardens, no matter how exquisite they may be.

The Pacific Undersea Gardens and the **Classic Car Museum** are tourist attractions located at the side of the harbor that are overpriced and not recommended.

Sealand of the Pacific, a four-mile drive from downtown, is a "mediocre" aquarium in the opinion of several of our parent reviewers. We suggest you save your money for the far superior Seattle or Vancouver aquariums.

CALENDAR

MAY: Victoria Day
JULY: Victoria International Music Festival
DECEMBER: First Night (New Year's Eve)

RESOURCES

TOURISM INFORMATION CENTRE

812 Wharf Street, Victoria V8W 1T3 (at Inner Harbour)
604/382-2127

WHISTLER

Located 75 miles north of Vancouver in the Coastal Mountain Range of British Columbia, Whistler/Blackcomb is a world-class resort that lies between the two greatest vertical rise mountains in North America. In all seasons, parents vacationing with their children will find much to like about Whistler/Blackcomb.

In the summer, the outstanding inter-connecting trail system that runs through the valley is popular for in-line skating, hiking, mountain biking, and skateboarding. Horseback riding and golfing, plus swimming and boating in the five surrounding lakes will also keep everybody busy.

In the winter, most people come for the skiing. In 1995, for the third year in a row, *Snow Country* magazine called Whistler the number one ski resort in North America. The rating is based on vertical drop, terrain, lifts, slopeside lodging and other amenities. With more express lifts (12) than any resort in the world, Whistler and Blackcomb combined offer almost 7,000 acres of skiable terrain.

In the winter, bitter cold is rare on these mountains, which is an advantage—especially for young skiers. However, the same conditions that make harsh conditions unlikely, occasionally bring rain and fog to the lower slopes. The summer climate is warm and dry.

The resort consists of several communities. The two largest and most developed are Blackcomb and Whistler. The village of Whistler sits at the base of the two mountains. Accommodations are right in the Village, within easy walking distance of the stores, restaurants and lifts. Cars are parked in an underground parking garage so there is no traffic. If you can afford it, staying in Whistler Village is optimum for families.

The Blackcomb base also is developed with a village and extensive condominiums and houses in the "Benchland" area. It is ritzier than the Whistler Village with the five-star, swank Chateau Whistler Hotel at its center.

Other communities in the area include North Village and Whistler Creek. North Village (a five minutes walk from Whistler Village) has recently become more developed. With a parking lot in the middle of the village and the largest grocery store in the area, it is not as charming as Whistler or Blackcomb, but accommodations here are more affordable. Whistler Creek is an area that is older and also less expensive than the Village. It is right off Highway 99 as you enter the area. Located on the backside of Whistler, it has a lift with access to the ski area.

Whistler is a fine place to vacation with kids but the cost may appear prohibitive. The strong U.S. dollar does help improve the rates for American visitors. Keep in mind also that rates vary greatly depending on the time of year. Unfortunately, the most expensive winter rates coincide with the school holidays. If you are willing to take the kids out of school, you can save substantially. Package deals on lifts, lodging and breakfast are another way to reduce your costs—check your local papers or ask your travel agent. With free bus service to the Village from throughout the area, it is also possible to get a good deal by staying in accommodations outside the Village. Finally, many of the condominiums at Whistler/Blackcomb are eager to have families stay at their facility at rock-bottom rates in exchange for considering a time-share purchase. The Whistler Information at 604/932-2394 can help you find the best rate.

Note: Many lodgings require a three-night stay. You will need to make reservations early, particularly during the "high season." However, be aware that the cancellation policy at most hotels and condos at Whistler/Blackcomb is strict. If you cancel within 30 days of your scheduled arrival you will often be charged the cost of one night of lodging.

One of the most convenient features of the Whistler Resort is the **Whistler Activity and Information Centre**, located at the front of the Whistler Convention Center. It provides complete information about activities, events, restaurants, accommodations and transportation and will make arrangements and reservations for you. If you want some help planning your trip, give them a call at 604/932-2394.

GETTING THERE

Whistler is 75 miles north of Vancouver. From Seattle, the drive of about 225 miles takes five to six hours. One of our parent reviewers described their route as follows:

"We departed from Issaquah and headed north on Hwy 405 to Interstate 5. At Blaine we exited and took the truck crossing over the border. We headed east on Highway 1 to Horseshoe Bay, then north on Route 99 to Whistler. It took us six hours to reach Whistler, including stops for meals and several roadside attractions, and five $^1/_2$-hours to get home."

The drive up Highway 99 from Vancouver to Whistler is on a winding two-lane road aptly named Sea to Sky. (If you have carsick prone passengers take precautions.) The vistas are spectacular along Howe Sound, with breathtaking views of green fjords and mountain peaks. The once treacherous road has been straightened in recent years but it is still a demanding drive on a curvy mountain highway.

A more relaxing alternative is to drive to Vancouver and catch the train from Vancouver to Whistler or take the train from Seattle to Vancouver, spend the night in Vancouver and catch the train to the ski resort. It is a beautiful 2 $^1/_2$-hour train ride from

North Vancouver along the coastline through Porteau Cove and Britannia to Squamish before turning inland between snowy mountain peaks en route to Whistler. There is a large parking lot at the Vancouver train station where cars can be parked free while you are at Whistler. The train departs daily with one morning departure from North Vancouver and one evening departure from Whistler.

B.C. Rail 604/631-3500. Rates: $13/adult one way; $7 child /one way

ROADSIDE ATTRACTIONS. The **Peace Arch Park** at Blaine is a pleasant place to stop for a picnic in good weather. At **Horseshoe Bay** there are numerous shops, restaurants and a nice park. **Provincial Park** at Porteau Cove, just before Britannia beach, is a good place to picnic and enjoy gorgeous views.

If you are driving to Whistler during the summer consider stopping at the **B.C. Museum of Mining** in Britannia Beach for an underground tour of a copper mine. Our parent reviewers had favorable reports on the tour, which includes a train ride into the mountain, live demonstrations of mining equipment and a tour of Britannia Village.

604/688-8735; 45 minutes before Whistler at Britannia Beach. Open mid-May to mid-Oct, Wed-Sun in May, June and Sept, daily in July and August. Cost:$8.50/adult, $6/child, under 5 free. Family rate $30.

At **Murrin Provincial Park**, just past Britannia Beach, there's swimming in the lake, fishing and nice spots to picnic. Farther on at **Shannon Falls,** just before Squamish, there is a short trail to a waterfall and a viewpoint with picnic tables, along with old logging and mining artifacts that kids like to climb on. At **Squamish** there is a **McDonalds,** with an indoor play area.

PLACES TO STAY

CRYSTAL LODGE (formerly Nancy Greene Lodge)
604/932-2221 or 800/667-3363; PO Box 280, Whistler, V0N 1B0
Rates: Moderate to expensive
Essentials: Credit cards; cribs
Extras: Restaurants; TV; outdoor pool, hot tub, indoor Jacuzzi, steam room; kitchenettes in some units; fireplaces in some units; laundry facilities

Crystal Lodge is a very clean, attractive five-story hotel with an ideal location in Whistler Village. Guests may choose from standard, deluxe, studio and studio loft-type accommodations.

Kitchenettes and fireplaces are available in some units. Rooms are spacious and comfortable.

The hotel overlooks the Village Square so noise might be a problem in some rooms. The accommodations with balconies overlooking the swimming pool and the mountain valley are quieter and offer better views.

There are two restaurants in the lodge. Irori is a Japanese restaurant not well-suited to young children. Wainwright's is highly recommended as a family restaurant (see review in Places to Eat below). The large, outdoor (year-round) pool and hot tub are located on the side of the lodge.

As with all accommodations as Whistler, rates at the Crystal Lodge vary considerably depending on the time of year and the length of your stay. Ask about five- or seven-day packages that include lifts, lodging and breakfast.

 PARENT COMMENTS: *"This is an attractive, friendly place that is in a great location right in the heart of the Village."*

DELTA WHISTLER RESORT
604/932-1982 or 800/877-1133; 4050 Whistler Way, Whistler V0N 1B0
Rates: Expensive
Essentials: Credit cards; cribs
Extras: Kitchens (in some units); fireplaces (in some units); outdoor pool; tennis (indoor); golf; exercise room; TV; restaurant; laundry facilities; pets OK

The Delta Whistler (formerly the Delta Mountain Inn) is one of the largest (300 rooms) and oldest hotels in the Village. The location is outstanding—about 50 yards from the ski lifts.

At the Delta the units best suited for families have a loft with a queen bed and a full bath and sauna and downstairs a sunken living room, two single beds, a queen sofa bed, kitchen, fireplace and another full bath with a Jacuzzi. The pool is outdoors with a large hot tub both indoors and out. Dome-covered tennis courts are available year-round.

There are two restaurants. The Whistler Garden serves Chinese food and Evergreen is a fun, hip eatery with a toy box and a children's menu. Kids under age six eat free.

 PARENT COMMENTS: *"We like to eat at Peter's Underground, about one block away. It has inexpensive, good food that includes some great Greek specialties."*
"The Delta is very comfortable and convenient. It was handy to be so

close to the ski lifts and to have two good restaurants right in the hotel. After skiing all day we enjoyed having everything—food, swimming, tennis—right at our hotel. The Evergreen is a good restaurant for both kids and parents."

SHOESTRING LUNCH
604/932-3338; 7124 Nancy Greene Drive, Whistler, V0C 1B0
Essentials: Credit cards; no cribs
Extras:TV; common kitchen; shuttle service

The Shoestring is a good option for families on a tight budget. It is similar to a youth hostel, although rooms are private (all have TVs) with private baths. It is very clean, but sparsely furnished. During the ski season it offers some of the cheapest accommodations in Whistler. (A four-bunk room is $17 per person in the summer, $25 per person at the high season.) Families are welcome at the Shoestring. There is a fully equipped kitchen for the use of guests. It is a good place to get to know other parents and kids.

Free shuttle service to the ski area is provided in the morning and afternoon. In the evening there is shuttle service to Whistler Village.

PARENT COMMENTS: *"Thanks to the Shoestring we could afford to ski Whistler. The staff was very friendly—meeting other families from all over the world was part of the fun."*
"Noise could be a problem. The Shoestring has a popular nightclub and is located right off the highway. Ask for a quiet room."

TIMBERLINE LODGE
604/664-5633 or 800/633-5474; 4122 Village Green, Whistler, V0N 1B0
Rates: Moderate to expensive
Essentials: Credit cards; cribs
Extras: Complimentary breakfast; refrigerators; outdoor pool, hot tub, indoor sauna

The Timberline is a casual, comfortable lodge with a good location at the backside of the Village. There is less noise and activity in this part of the Village and you have an easy walk to the lifts. An enormous stone fireplace in the lobby is a cozy place to congregate after a day on the slopes. Be careful to request a room that is not near the popular nightclub located in the Lodge.

The furnishings in the rooms are "elegant rustic"—lots of attractive woodwork with beds made of rough-hewn frames. The loft-style accommodations are convenient for families—adults can relax in the sitting room while the children sleep upstairs.

PARENT COMMENTS: *"The loft-style room worked well when we stayed at Timberline with our kids—ages four and eight. For families with younger children the stairway to the loft might be a safety concern."*

"In 1994 we paid $200 (Canadian) per night for a unit with a queen bed in the loft and a sofa bed downstairs. The same room during low season (fall and spring) costs $80."

"The complimentary breakfast helped reduce costs and it was very convenient with our two young children. When we visited, discount coupons for the Lodge were available with Budget Car Rental. Watch out for the cancellation policy—full payment is due (by credit card) within 30 days and there is no refund with cancellation except due to illness."

CONDOMINIUM RENTALS are an excellent option for families visiting Whistler. For information about location and rates, call 604/932-2394.

PLACES TO EAT

LA FIESTA
604/938-2040; At the Chateau Whistler Resort
Hours: Dinner daily.
Essentials: Credit cards; highchairs
The sizzling hot fajitas prepared right at your table get the most attention at this colorful Spanish Mediterranean restaurant in the Chateau Whistler Resort in Blackcomb, but they are only one of the many outstanding entrees, including fresh snapper and a sensational paella brimming with prawns, mussels, chicken, chorizo and more. If you have worked up a good appetite on the slopes, start out with a few of the inspired tapas and find room for a touch of mango sorbet. Prices are reasonable and there is a good children's menu.

PETER'S UNDERGROUND
604/932-4811; Located downstairs at the Whistler Conference Centre
Hours: Breakfast, lunch, dinner daily
Essentials: Credit cards; highchairs
Kids love watching the model train that runs around the top of the room at this casual, cafeteria-style restaurant with an American and Greek menu. Ribs are popular with meat lovers and

vegetarians like the fabulous spinach pie. There is also a good selection of salads. Peter's was most often mentioned by our parent reviewers as the best place to eat at Whistler with kids—thanks to outstanding food that was a hit with both grown-ups and youngsters and good service. Free delivery.

WAINWRIGHTS
604/932-2221; located in the Crystal Lodge
Hours: Breakfast, lunch, dinner
Essentials: Credit cards; highchairs

The relaxed atmosphere, with just a touch of class and well-prepared food, makes Wainwrights a popular choice for families. They describe their menu as "Canadian Heritage." Adult entrees include well-prepared steaks, chicken and seafood selections. Our parent reviewers had high praise for the filet of sole with shrimp sauce. Reservations recommended.

The $6.95 children's menu includes the usual hot dogs, hamburgers and grilled cheese sandwiches plus a drink and ice cream. Crayons are provided.

WHAT TO SEE AND DO

WHISTLER ACTIVITY AND INFORMATION CENTRE provides excellent information about activities and events available in the Whistler/Blackcomb area including ski rentals and lessons. They will make arrangements and reservations for you or direct you to the right place. Stop by at the front of the Whistler Convention Centre, or call 604/932-2394.

BOATING. Kayaks, sailboards, canoes and Laser sailboats can be rented at both Lakeside and Wayside parks on Alta Lake.

CROSS-COUNTRY SKIING. More than 22 kilometers (13.5 miles) of track-set cross-country trails wind through the scenic Lost Lake and Chateau Whistler Gold Club trails. There are also public trails along the valley floor that are good for beginners and free of charge. The trails at Lost Lake are lit for night skiing. Note: Often there is not enough snow at the Whistler base for cross-country skiing.

There are several shops in the area renting equipment for adults but our parent reviewer found only one shop—Sports West—renting skis and boots for children. The smallest boot size is a "one," which would fit about a seven- or eight-year old. Parents planning to cross-country ski with their kids should check snow conditions before leaving home and bring their own equipment for the youngsters.

Information available at Whistler Activity Centre, 604/932-2394. The cost at Lost Lake is $6 for adults, $3.50 for youths and under age 12 free. The area is open 9 am-4 pm daily, 4-11 pm nights. Night skiing is free.

DAYCARE is not available for non-skiing kids at Whistler but it is offered at the Kids Kamp at Blackcomb from 8:30 am to 4 pm for ages 18 months to three years. The facility is modern, clean and bright and a maximum of ten kids per group is allowed. Cost is $50 a day, including lunch. There is also a "Pepsi Kids Night Out" on Wednesday and Saturday nights. Kids ages six to 16 may be dropped off from 5:30 to 8:45 pm. The program includes dinner and entertainment and cost is $23 per child.

DOWNHILL SKIING. More than 6,900 acres of skiable terrain and over 5,200 feet of vertical drop on two magnificent side-by-side mountains, have earned Whistler/Blackcomb a reputation as a world-class ski area.

The area has offered excellent skiing ever since it opened in the late 1960's and continues to improve each year. At Blackcomb in 1994, a new eight-person gondola and connecting high speed quad were added which link Whistler Village to the Glacier Express and transports skiers more than one mile high. At Whistler, a new high-speed quad opens more than 1,200 acres and four bowls. Between the two areas, there are more high speed lifts (12) than anyplace in the world.

There is access to both ski areas from Whistler Village. The Gondola takes you up into the Whistler ski area. Also from the Village, the Fitzsimmons chair transports skiers from Whistler Village into the Blackcomb ski area. You can purchase ski tickets for both resorts at the Whistler base area, although skiing both areas in one day would be a challenge. Depending on the amount of snow, you can sometimes ski back to Whistler Village from both ski areas.

All our parent reviewers raved about skiing at Whistler. One mother had this to report:

"Whistler was a great place for kids to ski. There are plenty of groomed runs and many areas designated "Family Only" where skiing speed is well-controlled. The middle of the mountain around the Olympic Station area is best for beginners and there are lots of great intermediate runs off the Green chairs."

"We liked getting a delicious breakfast at the top of the Whistler

Express Gondola at "Pika's". It got us going in the morning and we beat the crowds by riding up the gondola early ."

"Whistler and Blackcomb are both large mountains. You would want to make sure kids know their way around before letting them ski alone! Also at both areas, it is so spread out that it is difficult to check in with kids at day care or ski school."

Lift ticket rates: Whistler $42/adult, $33/youth, $18 child, under age 6 free. Blackcomb $44/adult, $36 youth, $19 child, under 6 free. Dual mountain 3-day tickets: $132/adult, $117/youth, $63/child, under 6 free.

DOWNHILL SKI LESSONS are available at both resorts. The Ski Skamp program at Whistler (604/932-3434) is open to ages 2 to 12. One-half day to 10-day rates are offered. Our parent reviewer reported the following about the instruction program at Ski Skamp: "A one-day lesson for a four-year-old in the winter of 1994 cost $38 plus $5 extra for lunch. Drop-off was at 8:30 am and pick-up at 3 pm. Kids were transported up the Gondola to the "Ski Skamp" area. It has easy terrain and a big tent area for lunch and rest periods. Ski rentals with the Ski Skamp program are $10 a day and include a helmet. (Helmets on kids skiing at Whistler are very popular).The lessons worked well for our daughter. Other families we spoke to were very happy with the program."

Blackcomb Resort offers their own Kid Kamp Program. There is a large Kids Kamp building at the base. Lessons are right out the door, so there is less transportation for the kids than at Ski Skamp, but often snow conditions are not as good at the lower elevations. The Kids Kamp program is available for ages 2 to 12. Rates for day lessons are similar to the Ski Stamp program.

INDOOR HEALTH CLUB. If you have the energy after a day of skiing or if you are having a rainy day, consider an afternoon or evening of recreation at the Mountain Spa and Tennis Club at the Delta Inn. The indoor tennis courts, pool, exercise room and hot tubs that are free to hotel guests are also available for a fee to other visitors. This is a very busy place at the end of the ski day. Same day reservations only for tennis.

604/932-1982;Delta Mountain Inn. Hours: 7 am-10 pm. Cost:$12/person, $20/family.

GONDOLA AND CHAIR LIFT RIDES. In the winter, even if you don't ski, a ride in Whistler Mountain's fully enclosed gondola or on one of the Blackcomb express quad chairs is a thrilling ride and offers spectacular views of the surrounding mountains and valleys.

You can ride the Whistler Express Gondola weekends from early June to mid-October. There are restaurants (Pika's and Roundhouse) at the top and frequently you'll find outdoor entertainment. Scenic hiking routes and guided tours are also available.

604/932-3434. Cost: $15 at either Whistler or Blackcomb— discount tickets often available.

ICE SKATING. The new indoor skating rink Meadow Park Arena is about 10 minutes from Whistler Village. Operated by Whistler Parks and Recreation, the rink has nifty push-bar devices that kids can use while learning to skate.

604/938-PARK. Open to public skating most days, noon-3 pm and some evenings. Cost: $3.50/Adult, $1.50 ages 5-12, under 4 free. Skate rentals additional $2.25.

SLEIGH RIDES through the open fields will thrill the kids. Musical entertainment, a campfire and food are part of the fun. Departures are from the Chateau Whistler and the Delta Whistler.

Whistler Outdoor Experience Co. 604/932-3389

THE RAINBOW MOVIE THEATRE shows first-run movies at the Whistler Convention Centre.

SNOWSHOEING. If you can walk you can learn to snowshoe in minutes. Both kids and parents will enjoy the chance to trek tranquil forest trails, far from the crowds. Guiding, instruction and rentals are available through Canadian Snowshoeing Service. There's about 1 1/2 -hour of travel time to the starting point of their guided snowshoes hikes.

604/932-7877. Cost:$29-$58 plus $5 for snowshoe rental.

SWIMMING BEACHES are found at Lost Lake Park, Wayside Park and Alta Lake. Lost Lake is the warmest and smallest lake.

THE WATERPARK in the Meadow Park Area, north of the Village provides free fun on a hot summer day. Run by the Whistler Parks and Recreation Department, the park pipes river water down slides and into wading pools and waterspouts.

604/688-8735. Free.

WHISTLER WONDERLAND. an amusement arcade located on

the bottom level of the Whistler Conference Centre has apres-ski fun for all ages with air hockey, nine-hole golf, video games and pool tables.

Whistler Conference Centre. Open noon to midnight, daily.

CALENDAR

FEBRUARY: Winter Carnival
MAY: Lillooet Lake Rodeo
JUNE: Children's Art Festival
JULY: International Fest
AUGUST: Whistler Classical Music Festival
OCTOBER: Oktoberfest
DECEMBER: Christmas at Whistler

RESOURCES

HIGHWAY REPORT
604/938-4997

WHISTLER SNOW AND INFORMATION LINE
604/932-4191

WHISTLER ACTIVITY AND INFORMATION CENTRE
Whistler Resort Assoc., 4010 Whistler Way, Whistler B.C. VON 1B4
604/932-2394 or 1-800-WHISTLER
Provides helpful information about activities, festivals, events, restaurants, accommodation and transportation. Located at the Whistler Convention Centre in Whistler Village. Before you make your reservations, ask for the 'Whistler Vacation Planner."

LAKE OKANAGAN

From Osoyoos on the Canada-U.S. border north to the Okanagan Valley is British Columbia's semi-arid desert, situated between the rugged Coast Mountains to the west and the Rockies to the east. Its numerous lakes, plentiful sunshine, lakefront resorts and beaches make the area an ideal place to vacation with kids.

Called the "Lane of Beaches and Peaches", the Okanagan Valley is arid, but irrigation makes it a rich fruit-producing area.

In summer, stands, loaded with fresh local fruits, cheeses and wines dot the roads and there are plenty of U-Pick orchards. Look for cherries in late June, apricots and peaches in July and August, apples and pears in August and September and plums and grapes in September and October.

In the winter, there is excellent skiing in the Okanagan at Silver Star, Last Mountain, Big White and Apex.

Lining 70-mile long Lake Okanagan are the resort towns of Penticton, Summerland, Kelowna and Vernon. Some say the legendary monster Ogopogo lives in Okanagan Lake near the city of Summerland, although Kelowans say it is closer to them, and the folks in Vernon also claim ownership. The creature's name is a palindrome because it supposedly looks the same from either end. See a statue of the serpent at Kelowna.

GETTING THERE

There are two popular routes to Lake Okanagan. The first is on either I-90 or U.S. 2 to Wenatchee. Near Wenatchee, take U.S. 97 north to the border station at Oroville.

The second route takes you east through British Columbia on Highway 97C. Travel on I-5 to Bellingham and cross into Canada at Sumas, get on Hwy 1 east to Coquihala (Trans Canda Highway 5), a $10 toll-road. At Merit take 97C north to Okanagan Lake. The Trans-Canada Highway 5 is a toll-road ($10) but it is very scenic and 65 mph most of the way.

Note: Fill up the gas tank before going into B.C.—gas is more expensive in Canada.

PLACES TO STAY

LAKE OKANAGAN RESORT

604/769-3511 or 800/663-3273; 2751 Westside Rd, Kelowna, V1Y 8B2
Rates: Moderate to expensive
Essentials: Credit cards; cribs
Extras: Kitchens; restaurants; three swimming pools (outdoor), two hot tubs (indoor and outdoor), sauna; TV; boating, water-skiing, tennis (seven courts); horseback riding; golf, laundry facilities

Once you reach Lake Okanagan Resort you'll want to settle down for a comfortable and memorable vacation. This 300-acre spread is everything a family resort should be. Now open year-round, the grounds are beautiful and accommodations comfortable, though not fancy. You can choose between large condominiums or Swiss-style chalets—all have kitchens and most have fireplaces. The rooms in the inns are too small for families. The resort is on a steep hillside, so units are sometimes a good climb from activities but a resort shuttle makes the trip easy.

The fancy, "dress-up" restaurant is not for kids but there is a very good family restaurant. There is an excellent horseback riding program. Children under 12 must have a riding lesson before they can take a trail ride.

In the game room crafts and movies are offered on rainy days (which are rare).

PARENT COMMENTS: *"The horseback riding program was very safe and well-supervised. The trail ride was the best we have ever seen for kids."*

"This place was above our budget but a good value. We had breakfast and lunch in our room and ate at the family restaurant at night, which was very tasty and reasonable."

"There is plenty to keep everybody busy. Our kids enjoyed keeping a lookout for Ogopogo, the local 'Lochness' monster."

PONDEROSA POINT RESORT
604/497-5354; PO Box 106, Kaleden, V0H 1K0
Rates: Moderate
Essentials: No credit cards; cribs
Extras: Kitchens; tennis (lit at night); boats; playground; children's events

Cozy log cabins and A-frames sit under tall pines on the shores of Skaha Lake, a few miles south of Penticton. Cabins have one, two, or three bedrooms and are immaculately kept and comfortable. Campfires, games and other activities are organized for the kids.

PARENT COMMENTS: *"We worried about the one-week minimum but we should have stayed two weeks. It took about four days for us to really start to relax and settle into this wonderful family resort."*

"Our kids quickly met other kids. Ponderosa Point is a very safe, clean and beautiful place."

SANDY BEACH LODGE
604/495-5765; Box 8, Naramata, V0H 1N0
Rates: Moderate
Essentials: Credit cards; playpen
Extras: Outdoor pool; rental boats; tennis; kitchens in duplexes

If you are searching for the perfect "cabin-on-the-lake" family resort, you have found your spot. The only drawback to this idyllic place on the shores of Lake Okanagan, is that so many families come back every year you will have trouble getting reservations. A wide lawn gently slopes to a sandy beach on a quiet cove. The nine new duplexes all have decks and barbecues (Ask for one next to the beach). If the kids get bored with swimming and the beach they can play in the small swimming pool, rent a rowboat or play some tennis. Open only during the summer.

PARENT COMMENTS: *"The Canadian Okanagan is relatively unknown to Seattle families but it is a fabulous place to vacation. Hot weather, great swimming, fun resort-town amusements. The sandy beach is ideal if you just want to kick back and relax. When the kids got restless, we ventured into Kelowna to the waterslides."*

HOUSEBOATING on 70-mile Lake Okanagan is an interesting vacation for the family willing to spend several days together in close quarters. (We haven't found any parent reviewers). No previous boating experience is necessary and yes, it is easy to go ashore to explore. Most houseboats will sleep at least six and are fully outfitted, including microwaves and waterslides. This style of vacation is also popular on Shuswap Lake at the northern end of the Okanagan Valley.

Houseboating on Lake Okanagan, call 604/769-4411. Houseboating on Shuswap Lake, call 604/836-2505.

PLACES TO EAT

TALOS GREEK RESTAURANT
604/763-1656; 1570 Water St, Kelowna
Hours: Lunch, Thurs-Fri, dinner daily
Essentials: Credit cards; highchairs

Delicious Greek cuisine is served in a simple, pleasant setting. The souvlaki sandwich—with lamb or beef—is outstanding, as are the prawn dishes.

WHAT TO SEE AND DO

BUTTERFLY WORLD, located just off Highway 97 in Kelowna, has more than 100 species of free-flying exotic butterflies living in a climate-controlled tropical jungle sanctuary, including butterflies with six- to seven-inch wing spans. A Plexiglas observation hive for honeybees will also likely fascinate the kids. *604/769-4406. Mid-March to Thanksgiving.*

FLINTSTONE BEDROCK CITY has paddle boats, rides on the Bedrock Express, an 18-hole mini-golf course and other amusements.
604/763-2780; intersection of Hwy 97 and McCurdy Road.

KELOWNA CITY PARK. With 32 acres of recreational space including a long sandy beach, playground, lawn bowling, tennis courts, paddle and sail boats rentals and a children's waterpark (complete with giant body heater/dryers), this is the largest park in the city of Kelowna. There is good swimming for kids, with a very gradual slope into deep water.
Downtown Kelowna

AT OLD MAC DONALD FARM, 10 miles south of Kelowna, kids can climb on the "Ladybug Train," feed the animals at the Petting Zoo, enjoy small waterslides, a fishing pond and take a pony ride. Fun for younger children.
604/768-5167; Eight km south of Kelowna off Highway 97

SKIING at the numerous ski areas in the Okanagan is an excellent option for families who want to take a ski vacation but don't want to spend the higher prices at the more glamour resorts such as Whistler. Silver Star, with many runs suited to novices and intermediate skiers and a full-blown ski village with restaurants, ski shops, hotels and condos, is especially suitable when winter vacationing with kids. Many resorts at Okanagan Lake also have good ski packages.
Silver Star 604/542-0224.

WATERSLIDES. Wild 'N Wet Waterslide Park, high above Okanagan Lake, is the largest water entertainment park in the valley. It features two thrilling twister slides, two kamikaze slides, the famous river raging ride, two intermediate and three children's slide, plus hot tubs.
Wild Waters, next door to Flintstones on Highway 97, is a smaller waterslide park with several slides, a kiddies water playground , three hot tubs plus ping pong and volleyball.
Wild 'N West 604/768-7600; Wild Waters 604/765-2344

WINERY TOURS. Twenty-two of British Columbia's 25 wineries are found in the Okanagan Valley and many are just a short, scenic drive from Kelowna. The following wineries offer tours: *Calona Wines 604/762-9144; Cedar Creek Estate Winery 604/764-8866; Gray Monk Estate Winery 604/767-2525; Missions Hill 604/768-7611; Summerhill Estate Winery 604/764-8000; St Hubertus Wineyard 604/764-7888.*

CALENDAR

APRIL: Kiwania Music Festival
JULY: Westside Daze in Kelowna
OCTOBER: Okanagan Wine Festival

RESOURCES

KELOWNA VISITOR AND CONVENTION CENTER
604/861-1515

GOING PLACES NOTES

We are interested in your comments on using this guide. Did we give you the information you needed? Did you have a terrific experience at one of the places we suggested? Or a disaster? Also, tell us about any places you felt were left out. Give us the details!

_____

_____

_____

_____

_____

_____

_____

_____

_____

_____

_____

_____

_____

_____

_____

_____

_____

_____

_____

Your name _____

Address _____

City/State/Zip _____

Phone (   )_____

Mail to: Northwest Parent Publishing, Inc.
            2107 Elliott Ave, Suite 303, Seattle WA 98121